AND HERE'S THE
Kicker

CONVERSATIONS WITH
21 TOP HUMOR WRITERS
ABOUT THEIR CRAFT

By Mike Sacks

ISBN-13: 978-1-63064-011-8

"This is it." — Chris Elliott as Skylark,
the Chris Elliott Impersonator,
Late Night with David Letterman, May 21, 1987

Table of Contents

Foreword by
Adam McKay

There are a few ways that you, the reader, have come to this book. Either you hope to someday write comedy professionally and want to see how the "masters" do it, or you are a comedy fan and want to read some funny stories from funny people. Or you are friends with someone interviewed within, or maybe you even hate someone within and want to see if they come off as much like an asshole in print as they do in real life. Or you work for the F.B.I. or C.I.A. and are forced to scan books for potentially inciting or dangerous content. Then there are those of you who are trapped in a flood or hurricane and the only book that is within reach is this one. So, you read this book not so much for its content but for its affirmation that human interaction is possible even as the water rises and your faith erodes. Lastly, there are probably one or two people out there who are mentally ill or under the influence of methamphetamine and are using this book as a bible to decipher the signs of the impending end-time—or "Ragnarök," as it's referred to in Norse mythology.

Only you, and you alone, know which of these paths have led you to hold this book at this very exact moment. And yet, no matter the reason, I encourage you to take a deep breath to give thanks for the knowledge you are about to receive.

Each of the writers interviewed here has devoted his or her life to making people laugh or smile. Some call these people "comedy writers" or "humorists" or, within the business itself, "guffaw generators." My twin and I call them "chaba honloos." In general, and in the United States in particular, comedy writers are not usually met with a great deal of legitimate literary respect. They are admired for making a living on their wits, or even praised for their earning power, but unless a writer's work appears on the pages of *The New Yorker*—which, in fairness, a few of the individuals within have—or drifts into the realm of "satire," accolades are rare and celebrity almost nonexistent.

Why is this, you ask? The answer might be that this genre of writing needs to provoke a bodily response: a laugh. As we all know, the body and all of its emissions (fluids, sounds, gases, the occasional kidney stone) have never officially made the domain of "high art." They exist on the periphery. And yet, interesting and subversive voices have always come from that murky area far beyond the world of "high-end" literary circles. Case in point: George Meyer, Bob Odenkirk, and Buck Henry are dirtbags by *Paris Review* standards. But I would argue that *The Simpsons, Mr. Show,* and *To Die For* are all works that understand our culture and its narcissistic obsession with fame, greed, and other weighty matters better than—or as well as—anything written by Martin Amis or Jonathan Franzen.

(Note: In order to make that last statement I am depending heavily on the fact that Mr. Amis and Mr. Franzen will never be within five miles of this book. If by some freakish chance either of you is reading these words, I am terribly sorry. You are literary titans. I made that previous and ridiculous claim because I'm writing for the riffraff, and I hope to see you both at Elaine's on Tuesday! Good cheer, chums!)

So, if you're reading this book to find out "how they do it," you've come to the right place. There are five or six pie charts, three or four formulas, and one dance mat that will show you precisely where to place your feet and hands. More important, look at this book as an invitation to see some great writers finally put on a three-piece suit and load up a cigarette case and then try their damndest to provoke a bodily response. Again, hopefully a laugh—and not bloody urine to signify a kidney stone.

Adam McKay is a writer and director of movies such as *Anchorman, Talladega Nights,* and *Step Brothers.* He was head writer of *Saturday Night Live* from 1996 to 1999, and a founding member of the improv- and sketch-comedy group Upright Citizens Brigade. He started the website Funny or Die with Will Ferrell and Chris Henchy, and is a regular contributor to *The Huffington Post.*

Author Introduction

E. B. White once wrote—and perhaps you already know where I'm going with this—that "humor can be dissected, as a frog can, but the thing dies in the process." There's no denying that this quote is accurate and pithy and memorable and must be included within every book that has anything to do with humor, even in the most tenuous of ways. And maybe for good reason: the sentiment is easy to agree with. Yes, if dissected, the frog will certainly die. That's pretty obvious, even to someone who nearly flunked biology in tenth grade, chemistry in eleventh, and, for some strange reason, earth sciences in college.

But is that our only choice? Can we not take the frog out of its cage and play with it for a spell? Watch it hop, watch it leap from table to table, watch it enjoy a freedom that may not last long but long enough to be enjoyable and interesting to both us and the frog?

Like all questions involving metaphors, there may not be one correct answer—or any answer—but for the sake of this introduction, let me provide one: Why not? What harm can it do? As long as the frog is treated gently, as long as it is cared for in a respectful manner and then placed ever so carefully back into its cage after the allotted time (or, if you're really kind, released), what was the harm to you—or the frog?

This book contains conversations with 21 top humor writers. If you're wondering what constitutes a "top" humor writer, I would say an impressive résumé, deep respect from peers within the industry, and a willingness to sit still for five to fifteen hours over a period of two to three days—usually on the phone, or in front of the computer, or in the back of a coffee shop—to answer question after question, in greater and greater detail, from a total stranger. And always for no payment. (Please keep in mind that if you cannot find your favorite writer[s] in this book, perhaps he or she had "better things to be doing," such as "spending time with family" or "earning a living." Those are actual excuses that I was given, and, I have to admit, pretty good ones.)

If you are a student who wants to write humor as a career, or if you're a humor writer who wants to improve your standing within the industry, or if you're a reader who's interested in a bizarre, secretive occupation at which few will ever succeed and those lucky enough to do so tend to go slightly mad (or, at the very least, become horribly depressed), this book might be for you.

I use the word "might" because, to be perfectly honest, I really don't know to whom this book will appeal. I have no special degree in humor, but I do know what I like, and I hope you will like it, too. I did not write this book for academic tenure; I wrote it because I wanted a (relatively) reasonable excuse to talk at length to my favorite humor writers. But let's admit it: If you find the subject matter not entirely to your liking or taste, I'll just assume this introduction is not going to convince you otherwise, regardless.

I have no great words of wisdom to impart about today's state of humor—I'll let the experts do that for me, in their own, more succinct words. I only ask (plead, really) that you be extra careful with our new friend, the metaphorical frog. Observe the little fella, enjoy his company, even tickle him if you must, but please (please!) do not kill or dissect him—if only so we'll never have to hear about the poor bastard's fate again.

Gently ... there we go ... careful, now ... nice ...

—Mike Sacks

For Kate and Little D.

Buck Henry

Buck Henry seemed destined for a life in show business from an early age. At just sixteen, he was performing as one of the sons in the touring production of the mega-hit *Life with Father* (1947). A few years later, stationed in Germany and maintaining helicopters and aircraft, he found time to write, direct, and star in a cheerful (if somewhat unorthodox) musical review called *Beyond the Moon*, in which two GIs are accidentally rocketed to a distant planet, where they find a race of "weird but gorgeous women."

The sixties were, by all accounts, a golden era for Henry. In 1965, he and Mel Brooks co-created the Emmy Award–winning sitcom *Get Smart*, which ran until 1970. Though fans and critics adored its obvious spoofing of the James Bond spy genre, *Get Smart* was also a satire of government incompetence (and possible menace), a topic Henry revisited in his Oscar-nominated adaptation of Joseph Heller's *Catch-22* (1970). But, arguably, Henry's biggest cultural impact was the screenplay for *The Graduate* (1967), the Mike Nichols–directed comedy about alienation, plastics, and MILFs, which would soon come to define the baby-boomer generation.

In the seventies, Henry continued to create or co-create original TV shows, such as the little-seen but well-remembered 1975 Robin Hood parody *When Things Were Rotten*, and, in 1977, the science-fiction spoof *Quark*, starring Richard Benjamin as the outer-space garbage collector Captain Adam Quark. Henry also wrote hugely popular feature films, such as the Barbra Streisand vehicles *The Owl and the Pussycat* (1970) and *What's Up, Doc?* (1972). But it was *Saturday Night Live* that turned Henry into a household name. During the late-night sketch show's first five years (1975–1980), Henry hosted a remarkable ten times, becoming (along with Steve Martin) a de facto cast member. He's probably best remembered for playing Uncle Roy, the middle-aged pedophile babysitter who invited two young girls, played by Laraine Newman and Gilda Radner, to find his "buried treasure."

Henry's later comedy was never as dangerous, but for every misstep or creative flop during the eighties—*First Family*, *Protocol*—he would come up with something to remind his fans that he still had a few fresh tricks to offer, whether it was writing the celebrity satire *To Die For* (1995) or doing a hilarious parody of himself—all too eager to sacrifice his own masterpiece *The Graduate* for sequel material—in Robert Altman's *The Player* (1992). And then came his biggest coup: in August 2007, Henry, in his eighth decade, was hired by Comedy Central's *The Daily Show* as its "Senior Historical Perspectivist." His first segment was introduced as "The Henry Stops Here," and when host Jon Stewart questioned the title, Henry informed him, "Well, Jon, it's because my name is Henry, and I'm stopping right here. It's just common sense."

"Beyond the Moon," the musical review you wrote while in the military, doesn't sound like your typical USO production.

It was a romantic comedy in which two lame GI's were accidentally rocketed to a distant planet, where they found a race of weird but gorgeous women.

We toured around Germany and England, playing military bases. Many of the audiences rioted when they saw our cute dancing—and singing—girls. Our first date was at a supply center in Dachau. We played on the stage inside the actual concentration camp.

It was, uh, different.

It doesn't sound *too* different from *The Day the Clown Cried*, Jerry Lewis's never-released movie about the Holocaust.

I ran into Jerry while shooting in the middle of Tunisia, in the early eighties, for a movie called *Protocol*. He was preparing to make a movie called *The Defective Detective*, which, I believe, never got made.

Jerry played golf every day in the 114-degree heat, and it was reported that his monograms were on his underwear and socks and, possibly, some body parts. He had brought with him two steamer trunks: one was filled with his monogrammed clothing, the other with bottles of Coca-Cola—from America, thus assuring cleanliness and proper taste.

Speaking of proper taste ... In I *Goldstein: My Screwed Up Life* **(the autobiography of Al Goldstein, the former editor of Screw magazine), there's a passage about you visiting a San Francisco striptease club in 1981, where Goldstein had sex onstage with five women. True?**

All true. I've been in various seedy and unacceptable places for many years with Al Goldstein, although we stopped communicating a few years ago.

You've mentioned in the past that you have a voyeur nature. Is this an example?

I think all writers should have a voyeur nature. You have to look and listen. That's why some writers might run out of material; they're not looking, they're not listening.

How do you achieve this? Where do you look and when do you listen?

I think the problem is that, if you live in California—and especially if you live in Hollywood—you aren't connected to what the rest of the world thinks of as real life. Your observations are based on what you see on television and not what is going on in reality.

Feeding from the same trough.

Yes, right. If you ride in limos for too long, you tend to forget what cabs, buses, and subways are like. You lose contact. I think it's important to stay in contact with the outside world.

How early did you begin writing?

Early. The first piece I wrote was in elementary school, and it was an O. Henry–type of story with an appropriate twist.

What was the twist?

I don't remember. But a few years later, when I was twelve or thirteen, I was actually accused of plagiarism for another piece I wrote. This was in a military school, the Harvard School for Boys, in California. I wrote a story that had a paragraph that was metaphorical; I compared a piece of machinery to a caged beast. I'm sure it would be completely humiliating to read today, but I was thrilled with the metaphor at the time. That is, until a couple of teachers in the school started going through magazines and books, searching for this metaphor. I was living at the school, and the teachers looked through all the reading material I might have seen or read.

It was very much like the idiot senator and his staff years later, during the hearings for Justice Clarence Thomas. You know, going through every book until they finally found a pubic-hair reference and then raising the offending paper above their heads with a "Eureka!" shriek.

Did your teachers ever find that metaphor and successfully prove the plagiarism charge?

No, they didn't.

This doesn't necessarily sound like an environment conducive to creativity.

There were maybe one or two teachers who were helpful and good, but for the most part this was a military school, and I was a kid. There wasn't a lot of need for the student body to be doing creative writing.

You had a dichotomous childhood—military on one hand, Hollywood and show business on the other.

That's true. My mother was an actress who had left Portland, Oregon, to make it in Hollywood. She acted in a lot of silent movies, but when she got married and simultaneously pregnant, she quit show business.

My father was a general in the Air Force, and a stockbroker and a political conservative, but one of his closest friends was Humphrey Bogart. Go figure.

Did you always gravitate toward comedy rather than other genres? Did it always come easily to you?

Yes, but I'm actually more a fan of other genres than I am of comedy. I rarely go to comedies. I just don't find comedy as interesting as the forms that I don't do myself. It's harder to make me laugh than it is to make me cry.

You once said that comedy covers a lot of faults.
It is defensive in nature. With comedy, you deflect danger. You cover up emotion. You engage your enemy without getting your face smashed in.

Comedy is also harder to write. Things are either funny or they're not. If you were writing, say, a story about Jesus getting married and having children, you can go for a long period of time faking it before you have to do anything even pretending to be meaningful. You can't fake it with comedy.

How did you first get involved in show business? What was your first professional writing job?
My first job was with an improvisational theater group called The Premise in New York City. I had been involved with writing and acting at Dartmouth, and this seemed like a natural thing for me to do. Improv came easily to me, and it didn't seem like a special art form in and of itself. Not everyone was capable of doing it, though. It's sort of like sight-reading. Some actors can do it, and some can't. And that in no way suggests whether you have real talent or not.

That job really led to everything else. After The Premise, I got a job writing for *The Steve Allen Show* in the early sixties.

What was it like writing for Steve Allen?
He was one of the most interesting comedians working. He was great with language, and he was really more contemporary than anyone else. He also had a good eye for talent. Those who first appeared on that one short-lived show included me, the Smothers Brothers, and Tim Conway. Steve was also one of the first hosts to have Lenny Bruce on his show.

Steve was genial and funny, and he had a lot of interests, including jazz piano. He wrote a lot of songs, which still bring in money. People only remember "This Could Be the Start of Something Big," but he wrote literally thousands of others.

He was very influential with talk-show hosts that came after him. I know that David Letterman was a big fan.

Not just with hosts, but with comedy writers.

Why do you think that was?

It was the type of humor that he performed. There were never any sitcom-type jokes written for Steve, ever. We mostly wrote parodies and satires of politicians and political events, and also pop-culture situations. This was really different from the show that I worked on after Steve Allen, which was *The Garry Moore Show.*

Garry Moore is a talent one doesn't hear about much anymore. Who was he?

He was an actor and a comedian. He had a huge following in the forties and fifties among normal people. There was nothing hip or contemporary or modern or pretentious in any way about him. He was just the nicest, most straightforward guy. Very square.

As opposed to *The Steve Allen Show,* Garry's show was very conventional. He did a lot of strict parodies and that sort of thing. Garry had a segment on his show called "That Wonderful Year," and it was just an excuse for him to sing a song and do a sketch with the best comedians in the country. One week it would be George Gobel; the next week, someone else. And I would write a parody of a movie or a play or maybe a political event.

How did you come to be so proficient with parodies?

I think that it was built-in from having written for my college humor magazine, *The Dartmouth Jack-O-Lantern.*

Do you prefer one form to the other? You're better known for satire than parody.

One is a child of the other. Satire is usually more political, parody is usually more cultural. But on *The Garry Moore Show,* parody was what was called for. You know, if you have to write a skit based on a famous movie, you're not going to write a satire.

With Steve Allen, we did all sorts of different things. Steve was really ahead of his time. He was responsible for a lot of bits and ideas that ran for years and years and that late-night shows still do. All of the "man in the street" bits originated with Steve. Also, Steve fooled around with language. I don't think anyone else was doing that at the time: puns, plays on words, strange captions.

He was a smart man. When we rehearsed the show, we never used real punch lines. We substituted nonsense words for the punch lines. Just dummy text, like "Hutsut rawlston on the rillaw." Nonsense stuff.

Why?

So that the band wouldn't know what the punch lines were. It was important to Steve that the band laugh during the show; it meant more to him. We used to call this the "hot laugh," and it was when the band would laugh at a joke they had never heard before. Sometimes you would hear this very strange laugh on the air, because it would be unbalanced on the band side, particularly if the joke was very hip and the audience didn't quite get it.

I tried to get a hot laugh years later when I was acting in Robert Altman's *The Player.* The joke was that I was pitching a sequel to *The Graduate.*

The pitch was that Ben and Elaine were living in a big, old spooky house with Mrs. Robinson, who had suffered a stroke. You said it would be "dark and weird and funny and with a stroke."

Well, I tried to withhold that joke until the end, but of course I couldn't. There were eight takes, but once the first take was over, everyone knew what the joke was.

By the way, a film executive approached me in the lobby immediately after the screening of *The Player* and said, "You've made a big joke out of it, but I think we could seriously talk about the possibility of a sequel for *The Graduate.*" I then quit listening.

Did you see the potential right away in the 1963 Charles Webb book *The Graduate* when you were asked to write the screenplay?

Yes, but I don't think I read the book until Mike Nichols gave it to me. Once I did, my feeling was, This is going to make a very good movie. There were strong characters and a good story.

The book is dialogue-heavy. Did that make the process of translating it to the screen easier for you?

Sure. The more there is to steal, the easier the job—although, in some cases, it isn't. In fact, sometimes it's just the opposite, because you can't figure out what to get rid of.

I was going to ask if you had any idea whether *The Graduate* would become such a phenomenon, but does anyone ever really know?

Oh, absolutely not. You never really know.

With *The Graduate*, nobody expected that what happened was going to happen. I mean, I thought the movie was going to be a hit, but I didn't know it was going to be that kind of hit.

How about specific lines and jokes? As a screenwriter, do you ever really know if a line or joke will break through?

I can usually tell if a joke will work, but I can't predict if a joke or a line will become iconic.

Such as the famous "plastics" line?

Right. I had no idea what would happen with that line. I just thought that the line was good as a passing moment. Everything about that scene appealed to me, and the "plastics" line was only a part of it.

The line was not in the book. What made you want to write it into the movie?

I had a professor of philosophy at Dartmouth, and he would rail against the "plastic world." I always remembered that phrase. The party scene needed something, just a little something, and "plastics" seemed to be the right word to use. I could have used "mohair" or another word, and if the actors had done it right, it still would have received a laugh.

But "plastics" was just perfect. It captured something in that scene that another word never could have.

Everyone's been through it. Me especially. Every guy in my generation who went to college and had ambivalent relationships with his parents. Every guy who stood around talking with his parents' friends, who were perfectly nice but who were people you'd have *paid* to not have to stand around with.... Well, we've all been through that. Everybody in the middle class, anyway.

What was the audience's reaction at the first screening of *The Graduate*? Did you know right away that you had a hit on your hands?

Actually, I had been out of the country for a few months when it opened, so I didn't see it until it had been running for a while. In those days, as you probably don't recall, movies ran in theaters for months as opposed to weeks.

When I returned to New York, the movie was still running at a theater on 57th Street. And it was still packed. There were kids sitting on the steps of the balcony. And the audience knew all of the lines, which really appalled me.

Why?

It doesn't help your experience, particularly if you've written the movie, or even if you haven't written the movie, to be sitting in the theater and hearing this sort of giggle and chatter preceding the "plastics" line. I heard throughout the theater, "Plastics, plastics, plastics, plastics, plastics, plastics."

I knew where that sort of thing was coming from. It was out of a love for the movie, and I could appreciate that, so I guess I was equally thrilled and mortified.

I found a copy of the original script and noticed that the beginning of the movie was different from what eventually ended up on the screen.

That's right. The original beginning was going to show a graduation scene that Mike Nichols and I had talked about. It was a terrific idea. Dustin [Hoffman] gives a valedictory speech at his graduation ceremony, but it's a windy day. As he's reading the speech, which mostly concerned "What was the point of all of these years at college?" his papers keep blowing away. Dustin's character becomes more and more frantic, and he's unable to improvise a new speech.

Mike and I cribbed this idea from an incident that actually happened at President Kennedy's 1961 inauguration, when Robert Frost gave a poetic benediction. It's an incredible piece of American cultural history. Frost, who was quite old at the time, was standing at the podium, about to read one of his poems, and it was a freezing day in Washington, and the sun was in his eyes and he was unable to read the poem he had written for the occasion. And a few men, including L.B.J., moved to the podium to help Frost. Jesus Christ, I'm going to cry just thinking about it. It was an image that I never forgot, and I thought it would be fitting for the movie.

Why didn't that scene make the final cut?

I think we saved the scene for the end of the shoot, for technical reasons, at which point Mike said, "Well, wait a minute. We've got a whole film here. What do we need to go with that for?"

I'll sometimes start a movie with a scene that's a teeny, teeny capsule version of the movie's sensibility. And this was an example. The movie was about a bright kid who is incapable of dealing with the niceties of social behavior. The elements are against him, and he's going to have to struggle. And that graduation scene captured that essence.

But the movie's sensibility was also captured with the second scene that ended up in the movie, when Dustin is traveling along on the airport's moving sidewalk. It became just as good, if not better, than the graduation scene.

Is that a lesson for screenwriters—that you can sometimes achieve just as much through simplicity?

You bet it is. Absolutely. Less is more; it just works for everything. In the end, who needed that more elaborate scene?

I was struck by how detailed the stage directions were in the shooting script for *The Graduate* and how a lot of these descriptions ended up on the screen just as you imagined them. Here's one example:

"Ben walks quickly into Elaine's room, crosses to the bed and puts the purse down. As he starts to turn back, he looks up at Elaine's portrait. There is a movement reflected in the glass of the portrait. He turns quickly. Mrs. Robinson, naked, is shutting the door to the bedroom behind her."

Directors encourage you to not write anything that has to do with the camera's movement, and I usually try not to do that; it's really up to the director to shoot the way they see fit. With Nichols, though, we were on the same wavelength. There were quite a few descriptions in the *Graduate* script where I was amazed at how closely they resembled what was shot for the movie.

Which other scenes, in particular, made the successful transition from the page to the screen?

Just after Benjamin tells Elaine about the affair with her mother. In the script, I put in a description of how the camera should focus on Mrs. Robinson as she watches Benjamin walk away. And Nichols made it look exactly as I had written it.

Now, there really is a big jump from putting a description on a page to putting it on film, but Mike was able to do it to the point where I later thought, Ah, yes. That's my exact vision up on the screen.

As a writer, this made me feel very good, whether it was true or not.

Mike and I just had an understanding. We came from the same time and place; we had the same cultural references. But later on, I sometimes didn't have quite the same relationship with directors or actors. Words and phrases were misinterpreted or sometimes completely misunderstood. I was encouraged by a couple of producers to overexplain everything in the scripts. They wanted me to insert those terrible adverbs and phrases, like "succinctly," or "with a smile," or "meaningfully, but not pretentiously." I sometimes had to put in all that junk description, because very often studio readers couldn't get a sense of the dialogue without them. I hate those signposts. I'd rather leave it to the actors' imaginations.

One of the descriptions not in your *Graduate* script was Benjamin's and Elaine's facial expressions as they sat in the back of the bus just

having escaped from the church. The only description you wrote was: "They are breathing heavily."

The expressions on both Dustin's and Katharine Ross's faces were not planned, at least to my knowledge. Mike simply let the camera focus on these two people, who were a little lost and a little confused about what had just happened.

Over the years, those expressions have been interpreted as being very meaningful.

They are meaningful, but not in the sense of "Now we can predict what their next ten years are going to be like." But it is meaningful in the sense of "This is very much like life." Movies in Hollywood usually end with two characters, hand in hand, saying, "We're okay. Let's go home. Everything's swell."

In the case of *The Graduate*, these two characters had just busted up a wedding, they're on the lam, they don't have any money. Where the hell are they going to go? They've made a huge leap into an unknown future, and that's what the ending becomes.

I actually wrote a couple of lines of dialogue that we never shot. Something like "Well, what do we do now?" And the other responds: "I don't know." But we didn't need it. Dustin gives that funny little laugh and a handclap, and then both he and Elaine look at all these dopey-looking people on the bus. It's sort of like life. I think it's a terrific end moment. It's the happiest ending I ever wrote.

Are you as happy with *Catch-22* as you are with *The Graduate*?

I love the way that the film looks, and I think Alan Arkin, who played Yossarian, gave a great performance. But it was very difficult. It doesn't have the same tone as the book; it has its own interesting kind of tone, which is surrealistic. The book isn't about surrealism. The book is a black comedy of another kind, but it was hard to figure out how to translate that.

We wanted the movie to be like a dream, and we wanted to have a lot of dreamlike segues. Actually, I always thought of the movie as a fever. Yossarian's fever.

Do comedies work well within that surreal and dreamlike format?

I think it's possible to pull off a comedy that's dreamlike, but it's not easy. I wanted to find a style equivalent to the book, and I thought that was what the book did so brilliantly, which was to take the reader—almost from midsentence—from one place to another. I tried to find interesting ways to do that on film. Most of the scenes worked; a few didn't. The few that didn't, though, were harmful to the rest of the movie.

Which scenes do you think didn't work?

One in particular. It's the scene in which Yossarian takes the place of the soldier who's dying in a hospital bed. The dying soldier's family comes in, and they have this weird pretense that Yossarian is their son. I think it's one of the most powerful sequences I've ever seen in my life. It makes me cry. But when we screened *Catch-22*, the reaction to this moment was shocking. The first two audiences, back-to-back, laughed during it. And that completely destroyed what I thought we had intended.

Why do you think they laughed?

They lost their emotional bearings. Or we lost it for them, and that's always bothered me.

The Sopranos, or even a movie like Brazil, has dream sequences that are just as feverish as Catch-22. Were seventies audiences not yet ready for something like that?

With something like *The Sopranos*, the dream sequences are clearly out of the context of a real waking life. And all of Terry Gilliam's films are surrealistic; you know the whole thing is a dream. In *Catch-22*, it may have been too jarring.

In retrospect, what would you have done differently?

I don't know what I would have done. I probably would have tried to make it all more accessible. Also, I know I screwed up where the actual plot is concerned. I had read the book ten times, but the audience hadn't. Maybe I knew the book too well. I knew which character was running away from which character; I knew which character stabbed which character. The audience might not have known that, but they really should have known or else the point is gone.

It's one of the most beautiful comedies I think I've ever seen. It's gorgeous to look at.

It is great to look at. David Watkin was the cinematographer, and I love the Watkin look. He also did *Chariots of Fire* and *Out of Africa*. It's very beautiful and very moving in its own way. But maybe it was moving in the wrong way for a comedy. I don't think you can do laugh-out-loud comedy that is beautifully backlit.

That's an interesting point—early comedies aren't necessarily beautiful.

Not at all. No one gives a shit. If you look at those early films, such as Laurel and Hardy or Chaplin movies, you can see shadows where there shouldn't be shadows. God knows what the light sources were. The comedies looked terrible. But at least you could make out facial expressions—you can't when a scene is lit from behind. And that's true in films up into the late fifties, actually.

Did Joseph Heller ever comment on the movie?

He did. He was very nice about it. He apparently had written a different version of *Catch-22* at some point, and he said that our movie was similar to that earlier version. I didn't believe him when he said that, but I think he meant it in the best possible way. I once heard him on a radio show in L.A., and the host tried to bait him into insulting the movie. He wouldn't do it; he wouldn't fall for it.

Did your years in military school, and later in the army, prove helpful when you wrote the screenplay to *Catch-22*?

Oh, absolutely. I knew what the military felt like, what it sounded like. Some war films get it right, and some don't. Some writers who were never in the military could capture that by osmosis, I suppose. It depends on how you, as a writer, process things.

A lot of films are made by filmmakers who know nothing except other films. All the great filmmakers from the past knew something about real life.

Do you think that filmmakers today don't know enough about life?

Maybe not. It used to be that writers wanted to experience the world and write the Great American Novel, but that stopped a long time ago. Then they wanted to write for Carson or Letterman. And that lasted about fifteen years, until they thought, No, wait a minute—the real money is in sitcoms or hour-long shows.

By the way, there are a lot of writers nowadays doing something that I find really interesting.

Which is what?

They write for other writers. They write for the owners, and the owner finishes the script. There's a whole bunch of these shows now.

What do you mean by "the owner"?

Well, I mean ... take [screenwriter and producer] Aaron Sorkin. Sorkin writes all those scripts, but there are other writers writing for him. It's like writing for a soap opera—you write for him and he's got the skill and the ingenuity to sit down and put together all that material into a finished product. At least that's the way I understand it. But I think that's great, actually. I think it's a great way to go. It's like the old studio system in a way. I would do a TV series if I had four or six clever people writing ideas, stories, and outlines.

That's something you'd like to do—create a TV series?

I would, I would. I wouldn't mind doing it in that context, because I can't think up stories. I'm not that prolific when it comes to writing plot.

Actually, we used to do something like this for *Get Smart*. Leonard Stern, a writer and an executive producer for the show, was brilliant at plot, and he would just feed me the plot, and I would write the dialogue. I can write dialogue forever. There were three teams of writers coming up with stories, and I'd add jokes—or maybe just add a beginning or an end. It was very easy for me.

Is it true that ABC turned down *Get Smart*—**which eventually ran on NBC and CBS, from 1965 to 1970—because they considered it un-American?**

Yes. Well, that was their excuse, anyway. I mean, in the pilot, here was this dopey hero. And here was this woman who the hero didn't even know was a woman until she took off her cap and let her hair down. And the show also featured a cowardly dog.

All of this is un-American?

Who knows. There was a joke in the pilot about rubber garbage. Maxwell Smart solves a mystery, because he realizes that the garbage is made out of rubber. Oh, it was complicated. Anyway, the executives thought that people shouldn't be eating dinner and be faced with rubber garbage. They thought it was creepy and smarmy.

Mel Brooks was the co-creator of that show. What was it like to work with him? Did you feel that it was a good pairing?

It was, but we took much too long on the script. It took forever to write the pilot, something like four or five months.

Why?

Because we were lazy, and we fucked off a lot and played pool. And we're both no good at plot.

How did you eventually bang it out?

We just beat it to death until it was there. We knew that we had the ending, and we had the beginning, and we had some in-between pieces. So we just hammered it out, eventually.

Get Smart was a good experience. I enjoyed writing for that show. But after two years, I didn't enjoy it any more. So I left.

Do you have any regrets about specific jokes from any of your movies or TV shows? Jokes that you believe have not held up well?

I loved *What's Up, Doc?* I think everything came together so beautifully in that movie. It rattles along, and it has a great mechanism. I think the chase scenes are great. But I think there was one joke in the last scene that didn't work. I wrote a joke that was a parody of the famous line in Erich Segal's *Love Story*—"Love means never having to say you're sorry." I had a character say that line, and another character respond with, "That's the dumbest thing I ever heard." The joke was okay for about ten minutes, but I should have been able to find something that would have had an impact ten, twenty years later.

I'd like to talk about one of your movies, *To Die For*, which still has a strong impact all these years later. The deep hunger for fame and celebrity has only grown more intense since the movie was released in 1995. As one of the characters says, "You're not anybody in America unless you're on TV."

That's an American disease. And it's only become truer now than it was when the movie came out. God almighty, the reality shows alone! You know, it's that mentality of, "Get me on the show, humiliate me, beat me with a stick!" I can give a show like that five minutes, and then that's it. I find it completely revolting.

You've said that to accurately reflect the characters' lack of intelligence in *To Die For*, you took great care in writing carefully structured grammatical errors.

That's true. That sort of thing drives me crazy. Nobody can speak proper English anymore. The kids in that movie, and even Nicole Kidman's character, say lines or words that are purposely wrong.

Most of the characters in that movie aren't very bright, but I'm very fond of them. You can't write characters and not be fond of them, I think.

Were you fond of Nicole Kidman's character, Suzanne? She was a murderer.

Oh, totally. I'm crazy about her. Victims are interesting to me, but even more interesting are the victimizers. Don't we all love the girls who do bad things, who break guys out of jail?

Well, I married one.

Has she got a sister?

Switching gears now to *Saturday Night Live*. You hosted the show ten times, starting in its first season, 1975 to 1976. You were forty-four when the show first aired and quite a bit older than the cast at the time. What do you think Lorne Michaels saw in you?

I think Lorne was a big fan of *The Graduate*, and he couldn't get Mike Nichols. That may be a little bit unfair, I suppose, but I was an actor. And I was a performer. I had done loads and loads of variety shows. And it was different in the early years. The hosts for the show were people you wouldn't think of as being hosts. They weren't just actors plugging famous movies. They were people like Desi Arnaz or Broderick Crawford, from *All the King's Men* [1949]. They were peculiar hosts, almost punch lines.

What did you think of the show when you were asked to host? Were you a fan?

I hadn't even seen the show when Lorne asked me to come on and host. A little later, I went to a party in downtown L.A., and a lot of people were there, but everything came to a dead stop when it came on. I watched the show and thought, Geez, it's really interesting, whatever it is. There were parts that reminded me of the TV show [hosted by British journalist and comedian David Frost] *That Was the Week That Was*, which I had written for in the mid-sixties and which had similar elements. Both shows were live, and I love the live aspect of television. When it's live, you can actually make mistakes but you still have to keep going. It's theater, and it's real.

What was your opinion of the younger writers on *SNL*, such as Michael O'Donoghue, who came from that slash-and-burn sensibility of *National Lampoon*?

I liked O'Donoghue immediately. It took me a couple shows to figure out who was writing what, but on my first show, Lorne told me that O'Donoghue had written a sketch about *Citizen Kane*. Lorne said, "Do you think you'd be interested in being in it?" I said, "God yes. Where else could you ever do something like that? Let's do it."

What was the sketch about?

It was a little odd. It wasn't filled with laughs in the old-fashioned sense, but it was so original and I was so amused by the shaggy-dog punch line that I just had to do it. The joke was that Kane wasn't looking for Rosebud after all; he was simply trying to get a roast-beef sandwich.

At the next show, Lorne said to me, "I want you to see something O'Donoghue does, and I want to see if it interests you." O'Donoghue came into the office, and he did this routine about being an impressionist. He did an imitation, which was no imitation whatsoever, of talk-show host Mike Douglas shoving six-inch steel spikes into his eyes and screaming in pain. It was pure Dada. I laughed so hard I fell on the floor.

But, you know, I don't think that joke ever quite lived up to how funny it was that first time in Lorne's office.

In the early years of *SNL*, there seemed to be a lot of jokes done strictly for the writers' amusement—if the audience didn't understand them, it didn't seem to matter.

Listen, I have some friends who could *never* figure out O'Donoghue's stuff. In fact, I have a literal-minded friend who is a well-known name in the business, and extremely talented and intelligent, but he could never understand the concept of O'Donoghue playing this impressionist. He would say, "He doesn't sound *anything* like the guy! He's not doing Mike Douglas. Why would Mike Douglas put his eyes out?"

You were responsible for one element of *SNL* that is either lauded or criticized: the repeating of characters week after week.

I did suggest repeating certain characters, which didn't seem to me exactly revolutionary, since every comedy I've ever been involved with, including movies, depends on repetition of a kind. I know Lorne has given me credit for saying that he should do certain characters over and over, but if I hadn't, then someone else would have—it was so obvious. Why not do the samurai character in different situations over and over again? The repetition is funny in and of itself.

John Belushi's samurai character had been done before I got there; I think it was "Samurai Hotel." When I came on the show, I said, "Let's do

'Samurai Delicatessen' or something like that." And then came "Samurai Tailor" and "Samurai Stockbroker" and "Samurai Optometrist," and on and on.

What was it like to work so closely with John Belushi? There's been a lot written about his "genius." Do you think he was a genius?

I thought of him as being very, very funny, but he was not the only one there that I thought this about. They were all highly original minds. All of them had a wealth of characters they could do, and they were wonderful to work with. In particular, Dan Aykroyd and Chevy Chase were two of the funniest humans I have ever known.

I don't know what it was about John that made him so good. I think partly it was because he was such a shambles to look at, but he was also so disciplined with physical comedy. It was a great contrast and enjoyable to watch.

What do you think made Gilda Radner so good? You not only worked with her on *SNL* but also directed her in the 1980 movie *First Family*.

No matter what Gilda did, she never lost any adorability; there were no hard edges to her work. But it wasn't as if she was working off sentiment. There's a difference between sentiment and affection. She had affection for all of those characters she played, and it showed. But she also had a sadness to her. I would find her crying from time to time—during shows and after shows. I'm not sure why, really. When she was happy, she was wildly happy, but she had her down times.

It's amazing to look back at those early shows and see how young the cast was. The comedy was so smart, even when it was broad, and yet the cast was mostly in their twenties or early thirties.

When you've been in improvisational theater, you get used to capturing the characteristics of people who are really out there in the world. And if you're up onstage every night for a year, or two years, or three years, with the audience yelling suggestions at you like "Do Chekhov, but do it with Chinese characters," you get used to an immediate commitment to lunatic ideas. You gain a confidence. Most of the *SNL* cast members came from that background.

You played one of the more bizarre and lecherous characters on the show, Uncle Roy, the middle-aged pedophile babysitter. I wonder how many guest hosts today would ever play such a role.

He wasn't the only creepy character I played. I played Charles Lindbergh crossing the Atlantic and jerking off to a pornographic magazine. I welcomed the weirdness of that sketch and others.

I don't think you could do a sketch like "Uncle Roy" these days. I think one of the reasons why it worked was because the two little-girl characters, played by Gilda and Laraine, love their Uncle Roy in the nicest possible way. The games they play are great fun to them. Also, the sketch was written by two women, Anne Beatts and Rosie Shuster, which helped get it on the air. Anne and Rosie were better at convincing the show's censor than two male writers would have been.

We only did a few of those Uncle Roy sketches. In one of them, the parents came back home and said something like, "Oh, Uncle Roy, you're like nobody else. You're so great!" I looked at the camera and said, "Oh, that's not true. I bet there's an Uncle Roy in *every* family." I thought, This is going to be interesting. I wonder if kids across America will turn to their parents and say, "You know, Dad, your brother Jack is *just like* Uncle Roy."

Watching those early shows, it seems there was a real sense of camaraderie between you and the cast.

Oh, absolutely. I've talked about this before, but in one of the samurai sketches, John hit me in the forehead with a samurai sword. He put a real gash in it, and I needed a bandage. And by the end of the show, when the cast members were saying good-bye, all of them had bandages on their heads. I mean, to have the freedom and imagination to do that, it was just great. Obviously, the show has to be live and spontaneous and funny, and all of those elements were incorporated into that event.

Why were you only on *SNL* the first five seasons?

Because on the last show of the fifth season, I said good-bye for myself and good-bye for the cast. We turned off the lights and left. The next year a new cast was brought onto the show, and I never returned.

You've said that luck plays a big part in any creative career. Do you think it played a part in your career?

Oh, sure. Timing is everything.

In what sense?

Timing is when a movie comes out. Timing is what the country's political disposition is when a movie is released. It's what people are thinking about—what they want to see.

You really can't control that as a writer. But if you're talented, it'll all work out in the end. I mean, not all the talented writers will make it, of course. In spite of what's said, there is a great writer out there whose work no one has discovered, and there is a great painter out there whose work nobody has seen or will see. But, for the most part, if you're talented, I think somebody will find you.

Any last words?

In this life? "These were my last words."

In this interview? "No."

Famous Last Words
(of Advice)

Judd Apatow, writer, producer, and director

Advice is tricky when it comes to comedy, because people are either funny or they are not. If someone is funny, there are many ways to get better. Most everything I know, I learned from Garry Shandling. Whenever we got stuck, he always said, "What is the truth here? What would someone actually do?" He pushed his writers to go deeper to the core.

Once he told us, *"The Larry Sanders Show* is about people who love each other but show business gets in the way." There is a way to apply that concept to any story. What are the obstacles to love, to connection? There is always comedy in that area. I encourage all writers to read Andre Dubus, Raymond Chandler, Raymond Carver, James Agee, Frederick Exley and F. Scott Fitzgerald. They are a few of the authors who observe with so much wit, compassion, and depth that it constantly reminds me how I should look at my characters and stories if I want to do good work.

It also helps to take a few beatings in the hallways of your high school or go through some sort of childhood trauma.

Good luck!

Stephen Merchant

It's not often a writer is praised for the words he *didn't* write. But Stephen Merchant has proven that silence—usually anathema to humor—can be a comedy art form in itself. Nowhere was this more apparent than in *The Office,* the BBC sitcom that Merchant co-created with longtime writing partner Ricky Gervais.

A faux documentary about the employees of a London-area paper-supply merchant called Wernham Hogg, the world of this office was as naturalistic as it was realistic: no punch lines, no laugh track, no contrived plots neatly wrapped up within thirty minutes. Merchant and Gervais didn't want conventional funny—they wanted funny that seemed as if it were ripped from the real world. And the real world, as we all know, is most often uncomfortable, awkward, mortifying.

The show's funniest moments—which, not coincidentally, were also the most painful—were usually marked by their wordlessness. One could fill novels with what was left unspoken. Tim Canterbury (Martin Freeman), the sales rep with a crush on the engaged receptionist, Dawn Tinsley (Lucy Davis), relayed comic sonnets with only a furrowed brow or a mournful stare at the woman he loved but could never have. Wernham Hogg's general manager, David Brent, was a man-child whose ambitions were grossly larger than his talents. Invariably, he would utter something foolish—or unfunny. After a pregnant pause, one could see the flash of panic in Brent's eyes, the nervous twitch of his nose as he sought to put a positive spin on his own stupidity. Every silence was an emotional gulf that the most carefully chosen words could not begin to bridge.

Two seasons of six episodes each (as is the British standard), a two-part Christmas special, and countless awards and critical raves later, Merchant and Gervais ended *The Office*. But a few years later (July 2005 in the U.K. and September 2005 in the U.S.), they returned with their next show, *Extras*, which focused on a semi-talented, little-employed actor named Andy Millman (Gervais), striving for his big break in the movie industry.

As with *The Office*, *Extras* continued to explore some of Merchant and Gervais's favorite themes: failed ambition, meritless self-regard, the unrelenting desperation of everyday life. This time, Merchant stepped in front of the camera with a major recurring role, but not as the hero. Rather, he became Darren Lamb, an incompetent talent agent who is not nearly as successful as he wishes to be; a man with huge dreams who is forced to earn extra cash as an employee at the Carphone Warehouse.

Another lost soul, yearning to become someone—anyone.

Tell me how *The Office began.*

I first met Ricky in 1997 at this radio station where we both worked in London called Xfm. Ricky would perform his obnoxious office character as a sort of party piece—really only for me, because it didn't have a name yet. I don't think he did it for anyone else. It was just something he did to amuse the two of us in the office as we worked. It was kind of an observation of the types of people we had both worked with in the past.

Then I left Xfm and joined the BBC. While there, I was asked to make a training film. I said to Ricky, "Listen, we should film that character of yours." We shot a short film in documentary style, because that was the quickest way to do it. We didn't have to worry about lighting and all those technical matters. It was just necessity; we only had one day to shoot it. We shot it fast with only one cameraman.

When we edited the tape, I was just knocked out by Ricky's performance, especially for someone who had never acted before and who had no intention of doing anything like that. His performance seemed amazingly rare and rich.

So that tape started getting passed around the BBC and the other TV channels, and buzz started to build. We shot an official pilot for BBC in 2001, but it never actually aired.

How did that pilot differ from the final version that we're all familiar with?

It all just felt a bit too prompted, and it didn't seem like it had a documentary feel. In a documentary, there's no real narrative. Usually in a documentary, a narrative is just created unofficially. That's what we wanted to get back to. We wanted audiences to completely accept this world as being a real office and a real environment.

We kind of panicked. We thought, We've blown this, and now we're done. But luckily, the pilot was never broadcast. So we went back to the drawing board and tried to eliminate those transparent elements of storytelling.

I can't imagine *The Office* being done in any other format but documentary.

In retrospect, no. The show just wasn't funny if we were approaching it as a sitcom. It's only amusing if you think of it as a real place being filmed by a documentary crew. The documentary seemed so vital at that point, because it seemed like all the jokes were dependent on the way that the character David Brent wanted to portray himself versus the way he was being portrayed by the documentary crew.

Another thing we did was to remove the voice-over track with documentary-style narration. This helped, because in the end it meant there wasn't an explicit editorial voice. This allowed David Brent to just dig his own grave.

It sounds as if you had the luxury of not being bothered by executives. You could spend the necessary time discovering what did or did not work for the show's best interests.

It's sort of a constant source of amazement that we didn't get interference from executives. It felt at the time that we were battling for everything, but I think that was because we were new to the whole thing and we had no experience with the horror stories that other people would tell us later.

In retrospect, it was a fairly easy ride. I think the BBC felt that we were acting sensibly, we weren't being silly and we weren't being egomaniacs.

We reassured them in that respect—that there was very little that could go wrong. We were very low-budget. They didn't have to pay big star fees.

They had nothing to lose.

Exactly. The show went on the air in the middle of the summer, which is not a big TV time. Really, it kind of snuck out, and there was not a huge kind of fanfare, and not many people really got with it.

Weirdly, the day after the first episode aired, I heard two women talking on the train. One of them said, "Hey, did you see that documentary last night about an office? It was hilarious. There's this crazy boss who runs the place, and he's hysterical." The other woman said, "That wasn't a documentary. That was a sitcom." And then the first woman said, "Oh. Then it wasn't very funny."

I thought, That's strange—you just said you laughed. I think it took people a while to acclimate to it. And eventually they did. People tuned into it, and off it went.

I wonder if it's easier to pull off a new show like _The Office_ in Britain, as opposed to America. It seems that British TV comedy writers are allowed to take more chances than your typical American sitcom writer.

Rob Long, an American writer who wrote for _Cheers_ and who wrote the book _Conversations With My Agent_ [Dutton Adult, 1997], once said that America is kind of like a factory machine—your product goes in one end, and if it comes out as you intended it's only by sheer good fortune and luck.

I have to say that it is a little bit different in England. I think generally, particularly on channels like BBC Two, which is slightly more fringy and more akin to the cable networks in America, you are given enough freedom to do what you want as a writer. At the very least, they give you enough rope to hang yourself.

What kind of audience were you hoping for at first? Were you ever going for the masses?

There's nothing wrong with a huge audience. But in reaching for that huge audience, you could possibly compromise your material or maybe try to second-guess what an audience wants. We genuinely thought that *The Office* was funny and that it was truthful, and maybe there would be a million and a half like-minded people who thought it was the funniest thing they'd ever seen. And if that happened, then we'd think, Oh, well, we had fun and that was good. And that would be that.

So when the success started to snowball, it just seemed very bizarre. It became like Godzilla, and it rampaged off through the world.

When you consider some of the great comedians, such as Charlie Chaplin or Woody Allen or the Marx Brothers, they all went through a lengthy process in developing their comic personas, either onstage or elsewhere. Even the animated Homer Simpson character took some time to fully develop. But the David Brent character seemed to emerge fully formed from the beginning—an amazing feat.

In a weird way, Ricky's lack of formal training and his lack of ambition are why that character is so strong. He doesn't have any of the pretensions or the tricks that a lot of actors have. Ricky just approaches acting from what seems the most real. What would this character say? How would he act? It's almost as though Ricky had been storing all this up for years—just taking in observations by osmosis while he was working in offices, and it just seeped into him. He seemed to know exactly how this character would think about everything, and that was remarkable.

But actually, the David Brent character did evolve slightly from when he was first created. The original was a little bit more vindictive and spiteful than the one he would ultimately become. In the pilot, the character is a little bit malicious. In one scene, he turned on Dawn, the receptionist. She made a comment about his drinking, and he launches into her. That was something we eventually toned down. We wanted people to fall in love with David Brent in a strange way and to realize he's not such a terrible person. He's just mixed-up, and he's trying too hard.

Hollywood always talks about "likability." But the David Brent character is not likable in the traditional Hollywood sense.

I've never really understood that idea of likability. When the executives did the preview tests on the American version, audiences were given a knob to turn. "Do you like this character? Do you dislike this character?" The problem with doing something like this is that audiences aren't supposed to really like Brent at first. I mean, of course you're going to turn the knobs to the DISLIKE section! If you give someone a knob, they'll turn it. But is that representative of how you watch TV? Or anything? It's crazy. If you go to a movie, say a new Jack Nicholson film, do you always like Jack Nicholson? Well, no. Sometimes he's a villain. He kills people. Should you then cut him out of the movie? Everyone knows and understands that he's part of the dramatic dynamic.

When we first showed *The Office* to test audiences in Britain, we received one of the lowest scores ever—the only show that beat ours was one that featured women's lawn bowling. That's why you can't judge these focus groups. It's madness, because you need time for characters to crawl under your skin and for worlds to sink into your subconscious and get into your blood. I think that's what the best sitcoms are about, such as *Cheers, Seinfeld, Roseanne*—they're about creating an environment in which you want to return and poke around for another half-hour.

I think that especially holds true for comedy. Two-dimensional characters aren't necessarily as funny as fully-formed characters, who may not be as endearing at first glance.

It really frustrates me. I always think of some of my favorite movie comedies, such as [1982's] *The King of Comedy*. The Rupert Pupkin character is in so many ways unlikable, and yet he remains completely endearing and compelling to watch. That movie will never be a popular mainstream film, but for the kind of movie it tried to be, it succeeded magnificently.

Was *The King of Comedy* an influence on *The Office*?

Without a doubt. Both Ricky and I wanted dead time for *The Office*, and we didn't want to have too many laughs. *The King of Comedy* is a good example of that. It has weird, jarring tones. We liked those tones. Any episode of *The Office* could potentially end on a sorrowful note, or it could end on a melancholic one. It was just what it was. It didn't have to have the sitcom beats.

Besides *The King of Comedy,* what were your other influences?

Ricky and I have taken mood and ideas from a lot of different things. A big influence for us, particularly for the [two-episode] *Office* Christmas Special, was [the 1995 movie] *The Bridges of Madison County,* which a lot of people dismiss as being melodramatic. But for those who've seen it, it's a wonderfully made, very slow-burning, very low-key romance. The film has a wonderful ending, in which Meryl Streep's character is trying to decide between her husband and Clint Eastwood, and her hand remains on the door handle inside her car. Does she get out and run to Clint? Or does she stay? It's beautifully bittersweet and wonderfully made.

There is a scene in *The Godfather* that we both love. It's where Al Pacino fires the gun in the Italian restaurant, and you can hear the train nearby, clattering, getting louder and louder. We tried to re-create that in one episode, in which Tim is photocopying and staring at Dawn. The copy machine gets louder as the camera closes in on his face.

We had a lot of influences. We also both loved Billy Wilder's *The Apartment* [1960].

For the combination of comedy and romance?

I was always very keen on romance in movies and on television, and I wanted to insert that aspect into *The Office.* Ricky was a little bit hesitant initially. Would it work? Would it be done badly? Would it be overly sentimental? The saving grace for him was that because we were so rigid with this documentary style, it created this brilliant, inherent drama where these two people—Tim and Dawn, these star-crossed lovers—could not express their emotions. It was like a Victorian drama, where social conventions don't allow people to declare their love for each other; if a gentleman's hand just touches a lady's glove, there is a sort of electricity in the air. Everything signifies so much more.

The documentary structure gives you such tight parameters that it makes you, as a writer, work even harder to find ways around those restrictions.

Can you give me an example?

Initially, the flirtatious dialogues between Tim and Dawn felt a bit creepy to us. There's something about writing flirtatious dialogue that is very difficult; unless you're very good at it, it can be slightly sickly. So we told Lucy Davis and Martin Freeman, the actors who played Dawn and Tim, just to improvise, but we never asked them to flirt. We told them just to have a conversation, because the characters were friends. If you show flirting in this documentary-style format, the very fact that you're showing it implies that it has some kind of significance. Nothing gets shown in this format by chance—everything is clearly pre-meditated. Suddenly, these things take on significance, providing you've loaded them with a certain meaning beforehand. Everything counts and is magnified. The payoff is big.

I think my favorite moment of the whole series is when Tim unhooks his mic and talks to Dawn behind the closed doors of the meeting room in the final episode of Season Two. We can still see both Tim and Dawn through the glass, but we can't hear them. Ricky and I were so thrilled by that, because it felt like it was the perfect fusion of the documentary form and the type of dramatic storytelling we wanted. You couldn't do that in any other television show, because it would just feel kind of mannered; a little like the end of *Lost in Translation*. And nothing we could have written would have been half as powerful as what the viewers imagined those two characters said.

Did you know from the beginning of the series that you wanted Tim and Dawn's relationship to end happily?

I used to get a little frustrated whenever the show was accused of being cynical and trading on the more unpleasant side of human behavior. I always did want the show to have a happy ending.

The scenes that really thrill me throughout the series are the ones in which Tim and Gareth are kind of getting on with each other—as opposed to fighting—when they put aside their squabbles, and one tries to hug or kiss the other. You're reminded that they're not going to kill each other. They wouldn't socialize outside of work, but there is a sort of unspoken warmth there. I always felt there was so much warmth in many of the show's relationships.

For me, a happy ending is never a cop-out. I think the viewer is kind of hardwired to want romance and a nice ending. It's such a fundamental human thing. As a viewer, you want that sense of good fortune. People do find love in real life. What's wrong with that?

Viewers never seem to tire of a happy ending, as long as it holds true to the story. Even when they see the ending coming, it's still very satisfying.

It almost hits a pleasure center in the brain, like a good melody. When you listen to a song, you don't say, "I can't believe it! Another song with a chorus and a verse and then the chorus again! What a cliché!" No, you think, That's a great song. It's very primal.

But it's really the job of the writer to pull off that sleight of hand. It's like a magic trick. Look *this* way, not *that* way. When we introduced the box of paints, the gift that Tim gives to Dawn, we were really worried that viewers would see the ending coming. We thought they would be able to figure it out. But if you do it correctly, people won't look for how it's done. And maybe they don't even *want* to know how it's done. They want, and need, that surprise.

A lot of viewers weren't expecting that ending, when Dawn leaves her boyfriend, Lee, for Tim. I know it took me by surprise.

At the end of the series, Brent says that the most important things in life are to find a job you like, to make a difference, and to find someone you love. Well, to both Ricky and me, those are the three important things in life. It doesn't get more precise than that. Especially if you come from a fairly comfortable, white, middle-class background, in which you don't have the anxieties and the worries that others might have. We can't relate to a life growing up in a brothel, so our concerns are making the little corner of our world as comfortable as we can.

What was your specific office experience?

I graduated from the University of Warwick in 1996 and then signed up with a temp agency. They assigned me to an office job here and there, and I did maybe three or four different ones before I came to London. All of them were exactly the same. I saw all of the little power plays and the office politics and the hierarchies that go on in these places, such as the boss that goes with workers to training day but then refuses to join in, because he feels it's beneath him. It was extraordinary. It doesn't matter whether you're in the Mafia or working at NASA or in a paper factory, it's all the same. In the end, you still have the same squabbles over who stole your chair, who took your stapler, that type of thing.

Ricky also worked in an office for ten or twelve years. So we could both draw on real life. And, actually, it does now feel frustrating that we're unable to go back to that position and to experience the more everyday aspects of the work life. I try to cling to any moment where I'm forced into a position with people with whom I normally wouldn't socialize. I enjoy getting into that mind-set, that different point of view, as opposed to the rarefied world of the TV writer.

What is it you miss about the office environment? The camaraderie? The sense of belonging to a group?

No, I don't really miss that. I just miss the sense of the unpredictable. You can't make up that life. You have to have lived it. I had a temp job once where a woman had a nervous twitch that made her arm jut out at a right angle. I was next to her, stuffing envelopes on my first day, and her arm involuntarily jutted out. It almost hit me in the head. I didn't realize what it was, and when I asked someone, they told me it was this condition she couldn't help. So this meant that for the rest of the day I had to time my movements so that I would avoid her elbow. I didn't want to be impolite and say, "I'm sorry, but could you move a little farther away? You have a little weird nervous twitch, and I don't want to get hit."

Who could even make something like that up?

How did you write the scripts for *The Office?* The dialogue is so natural. Did you and Ricky improvise it between yourselves?

Pretty much, yes. Initially, we started off trying to improvise, and then we typed the dialogue, but that was a very slow way of working. Ultimately, we bought a Dictaphone tape recorder. We would improvise into it and sort of refine the dialogue a little, and then we would edit it down later so that it could be typed up. It just seemed the only way to create that ebb and flow of real dialogue, where people stop and start and they don't use proper grammar. Speech patterns are very different from what you would get if you were to just write dialogue.

We started by discussing the type of people we had met in our office jobs. We would tell anecdotes, and pictures would form. We had never worked [written] together before, so for four months or so we just sat around talking about things we liked, as well as things we didn't want to see on television. By the end of that process, we felt as if we had this common language.

We actually spent a great deal of time deciding on the characters' names.

Why?

It made it much easier for us to create their backstories. The name David Brent came to Ricky in an epiphany. What we loved about that name was that it was so utterly bland. There is nothing about that name that is evocative or emotive in any way. It's almost like the name James Bond. It's a completely neutral name for a character who has to remain sort of shadowy. It's a nowhere name. It's white noise.

How about the names for the other characters?

Ricky was on public transport one day, and he phoned me up and said, "I've got the name for the rat—Chris Finch. I just heard a guy saying to another guy, 'I spoke to Chris Finch last night.'" And, again, it just seemed exactly right. There is something about the word "Finch" that's got this slightly hard consonant at the end, but it also sounds like a tweety little bird.

The name "Gareth" here in Britain has a very specific association with a particular kind of social group, and it tends to be the working class but with slight pretensions. It's also slightly outdated, probably mid-seventies, early eighties. The name just said a lot to us about Gareth's parentage— subconsciously, without ever being explicit.

As for Dawn, I'm not sure if you have that name in the States, but in this country, it's a bit simpering and a bit wet in its own way. It seemed kind of perfect for the character. I think it has associations, perhaps with a certain class yearning to reach a higher class. It's quite southern England. It says a lot about Dawn's parents and where they come from, and suggests that she's trying to escape the associations of that name. In some weird way, her aspirations for a better life are sort of drawn up in her name. She's constantly reminded about it.

How much of the show was written beforehand versus improvised by the actors on the set?

A large percentage of the show was written. Very little actor improvisation made its way into the show. We would allow the actors to change the rhythms if it didn't quite work for them. We wouldn't really allow them to change the jokes or the structure, but we did allow them to say their own words, or paraphrase here and there.

It has to be a major compliment to you that a lot of critics speculated that the show was improvised.

It's really a testimony to the actors' ability to deliver the dialogue. The actors were extraordinary. But I think the problem with the improvised approach is that sometimes there's a slight jarring of tone that can happen, because actors have slightly different approaches. It's also difficult to improvise emotional beats and moments of dead time. If you're improvising, you've got an inclination to fill the silence with something. Whereas so much of what we did on that show was about silence. We would literally script "Extended Pause" or "Agonizing Silence." That was very important to us.

The characters were never funnier than they would have been in real life. On many sitcoms, each character—whether a teenager or an old woman—crack the same jokes that a professional writer might.

It's funny you say that, because in the original pilot that was one of the problems. The character of Tim would do little bits of stand-up-type material. He would also do a lot more banter with the temp guy. It was like a comedy act. And it just stood out like a sore thumb. It was painful for us to watch. It quickly occurred to us that no one ever talks like this in real life. It just didn't feel right. It felt creaky, and it was the one sour, phony note in the show. You can have a Norm character on *Cheers,* but not in real life. No one can come up with that many brilliant one-liners. So we changed that.

I assume you never contemplated having a laugh track?

That was always a no-no. It just seemed so bizarre to have one. I mean—why?

It seems that most British comedies, especially from the sixties and seventies, not only have a laugh track but a very aggressive one. The audiences almost seemed angry.

I'm actually not down on the idea of the laugh track. I sometimes think that the words "laugh track" are used snobbishly—the implication being that it's been pasted on afterward, which is very rarely the case. I think shows are mostly shot in front of a live audience, and maybe the laughs are massaged a little bit in the editing room. I think there's a lot to be said for a good studio show. I think *Friends* is a masterful example of the rhythms of the laughter, where you almost forget that there is laughter. It somehow feeds into the goodwill and high spirits of the show. For example, in *Seinfeld*, it's really fun to hear Kramer get a round of applause for doing a trick with a cigarette. I quite liked those circus moments, but it's got to be what's right for the show.

M*A*S*H was shown with a laugh track in the States, and it never ceases to amaze me. In England, it was shown without it, and it remains on my Top 10 list of all-time great shows. But I've since watched repeats where the laugh track is included, and I hate the program. I think it's appalling. I think Hawkeye is a snide, sniveling wiseass. It's a completely different show. With the laughter, that character sounds like he's playing to the gallery. It makes him hateful. Without it, he becomes this lone voice in an insane world.

When I interviewed Larry Gelbart, one of the creators of the TV show *M*A*S*H,* he told me he hated the laugh track, too. Yet *M*A*S*H* ended more than two decades ago, and TV audiences *still* seem so comfortable with the laugh track.

I suppose it's similar to listeners telling a radio station they want to hear more Cher or Phil Collins. In a majority of cases that's all they know, because edgier music isn't being played. There's something comforting about hearing the same songs over and over, just as it's comforting to hear a laugh track. Watching television can be a lonely experience. That's what TV viewers are used to hearing, and that's what they want.

But I think with the advent of the DVD and home cinema, viewers are now increasingly used to watching comedy without an audience, and they don't find silence as uncomfortable.

As well as being the co-writer of *The Office,* you were also the co-director, with Ricky Gervais. You've said in an interview that when it comes to comedy, the only thing a director should do is point and shoot. Comedy should never be too beautiful; it becomes a distraction. Buck Henry told me the same thing.

I don't know if you've ever seen the [1983 British] TV show *The Black Adder,* but the first series was a flop. They used to shoot Rowan Atkinson on a horse two hundred yards away, against a silhouette, and that's not funny. It might look good, and it might look real, but it's not funny. But as soon as they put the camera on Rowan's face, it became funny. It all fell into place.

That was something we went into *The Office* knowing. We knew that viewers weren't going to watch the show on a big screen with the best sound. They were going to watch it out of the corner of their eye on a television in their homes. We didn't want viewers to have to struggle for any of the visual information.

And yet the show does contain many details that the viewer can be rewarded with on multiple viewings.

When *The Office* went on the air, DVD sales [in the U.K.] were just skyrocketing and everyone was buying a DVD player. This really excited me, because it meant that you could make television for repeated viewing, which opens up a whole new dimension.

Did you write with that in mind?

Absolutely. Ricky and I wanted to make a show that we could put on our shelves. In years to come, we could pull the show down and re-watch it and notice new details. Characters are doing things in the background; things are going on all the time. I love that you don't have to get everything on the first viewing.

The Simpsons does it famously with all these weird little gags thrown in. I think that's a real luxury, because it also means that the creators were thinking beyond the immediate television audience. They were thinking that even if this show was not a hit, it would still eventually find the right people who would enjoy it—it would still have an afterlife. We were hoping that our show would, too.

Let's talk about *Extras*. The pressure for both you and Ricky must have been great. Did you have any worries that audiences wouldn't accept the show after the great success of *The Office?*

I think we knew that it was impossible to create a show that would have the same impact and would perhaps be as perfectly formed. We just knew that. It's very difficult to make that happen, and we knew that this was going to be a transition show—from *The Office* to the rest of our lives and careers. This new show was going to be a gateway; afterwards we could maybe explore other avenues.

With that in mind, we thought, What have we *not* done? We'd like to keep the elements that amuse us and entertain us and that the audience would be familiar with, but also perhaps not give ourselves the burden of trying to create a show that's iconic.

So we tried to give ourselves a bit of a break and write something that was a bit more frothy. Certainly a little less emotionally wrought. We made *Extras* a lot broader, just to tap into that side of ourselves that we didn't really explore with *The Office*. It was very much a conscious decision to move on from *The Office,* but not so far that people would freak out.

The anxiety we had after *The Office* was not whether we could write another funny one, but whether people would watch it on our terms, as opposed to those set by themselves. The audience's expectation was very high.

If I sit down to watch someone's new project, I always try to be as open-minded as I can. It seems to me that they're writing something from wherever they are at that point in their mind-set. So you're not necessarily going to get *Annie Hall* again; you might get *Interiors*. I was hoping that people would take to *Extras*, but there's no way you can police it, you know? Some people were going to like it, some people weren't. And some people were going to fall by the wayside.

The Andy Millman character that Ricky plays in *Extras* is just as needy as the David Brent character, but his neediness seems to come from a different, almost darker place. Brent wants to be liked, whereas Millman wants to be renowned. But for what purpose, really?

That was the thing we wanted to carry on from *The Office*: this feeling of thwarted ambition and people craving some kind of escape from their world, but never really quite knowing what that escape is. David Brent wanted adoration from the viewers of the documentary, as well as from his office staff. But that was obviously just some desperate attempt to fill a void in his life.

Andy Millman, on the other hand, had those same trappings, but we tried to curse him a little bit more than David Brent. Some viewers have said that Andy Millman is contradictory—sometimes he's Brent-like in his haplessness and other times he's supremely self-aware. To us, that's not a contradiction. There are many people who have those two sides. There are moments when you're blinded by your own ambitions or failings or whatever else. To us, Andy Millman seemed like a perfectly legitimate character.

In the second season, Millman had the success he craved—he became the star of his own sitcom—but it was compromised. He chose success rather than credibility, and that in itself brought its own kind of anxieties and discomforts.

Another difference between the shows is that the characters in *The Office* are people who do not go after their dreams. In *Extras,* it becomes sadder. Characters reach for their dreams and fail.

That's particularly terrifying to me. You know, I watch these reality shows where contestants audition to be singers, like on *American Idol.* And some of these people are in their forties. They'll say, "I thought I'd give it just one last shot." It's apparent that they've waited this long because they've been fearful that they might receive rejection. It's no different than failing to ask someone out on a date.

It really is fascinating, and I often think that if I had not had the good fortune I've had, if I had not met Ricky when I did, if we hadn't shot that first project together, well, there but for the grace of God ...

Talent seems almost secondary now. These contestants on reality shows seem to feel that all you really need is the courage to go up onstage and give it a shot.

Yes, absolutely. It's enough to just wish to be famous, without the need for talent. It's almost as if fame is some sort of shortcut out of whatever hole you've put yourself in.

Also, the contestants on these programs never seem to act like they would in real life. They base their actions not on reality but on how other people have acted on other reality shows. They give the audience what they want to see, rather than act in a truthful manner. It's very strange.

It's such a rich area to explore. The whole culture is preoccupied with it. It seems like a perfectly relative subject for comedy today, almost as much as class was in the England of the seventies.

Was your not having to stay within the documentary format with *Extras* liberating for you as a writer and director?

We looked forward to throwing off the restrictive shackles the documentary imposed on us, but we found that with the first season of *Extras* we were kind of caught a little bit between the two elements. We wanted to use the freedom of traditional storytelling; we were also still a little bit in love with the documentary-realism thing. Maybe *Extras* fell between two stools, I'm not sure.

I remember reading an interview with Larry David after he made the first season of *Curb Your Enthusiasm*. He said that he used that silly circus-style music throughout the show to lighten the mood after a particularly anxious moment, just to remind people that they should be taking it all in a certain spirit. We never did that with *Extras*.

Audiences understood what was going on in *The Office*, because it was in a documentary form. With *Extras*, it was more of a traditional narrative. To some viewers, it might have seemed more odd. Perhaps more sour or depressing. Certainly darker. Maybe the audience didn't get the relief with this format that they got with documentary. There was no editorial voice, and it made some viewers less relaxed.

Do you regret not using music in *Extras*? That you didn't give the audience a wink, of sorts? To say, "This is okay. It's all right to laugh."

Not really. I think we kind of liked that the audience was not entirely sure how they should feel. You can lurch from moments of agony to moments of silliness and slapstick. I just love the fact that those elements can jar against one another. It makes for quite an unusual viewing experience. So many of my favorite comedies are on that brink.

When you look at Laurel and Hardy, it doesn't take too much to tip them into a world of incredible darkness and tragedy and blackness and existential doom. They are always walking that fine line. They are often homeless or living through the Depression.

There are moments in *The Office* that are very explicitly Laurel and Hardy. There's a scene when Gareth stands behind David Brent and starts massaging him, just lightly massaging him. Ricky kind of stares at the camera, and Gareth continues to give him his neck massage. It goes on too long, and Ricky very consciously slumps down into the chair while staring at the camera in that way Hardy did. Which is to say, "I know this is absurd, but have you got a better suggestion? A better idea of what we should do at this moment? Because I haven't."

I think Oliver Hardy might be the greatest comic performer of all time. Everyone always talks about Stan Laurel as being a comic genius, but I think Oliver Hardy's creation of his persona is amazing. The character is a completely believable creation. He's utterly believable, and he has a sort of sophistication to that persona that you don't really see anywhere else. The way that he buzzes a doorbell with that little flourish of his hand, the way he orders a beer by sort of miming it in the air and then blowing off the imaginary foam. There's a sort of pomposity to that and a self-anointed grandeur that just don't befit his kind of idiocy and his standing in society.

Are you also a fan of Abbott and Costello? You can see elements of them in *Extras* and *The Office,* specifically with the way Tim and Gareth speak to each other.

Yes. I really love that cross talk. There's something lovely about listening to that rhythm. There was a scene in *Extras* where my character is trying to figure out the time difference between Los Angeles and London, and he can't get his head around it being eight hours ahead or behind. That's pure Abbott and Costello.

But the problem for me with Abbott and Costello is that there's not quite the same warmth between them that exists between Laurel and Hardy. There's not that same richness.

The character of Abbott could be quite cruel to Costello.

Almost too cruel. Unrealistically cruel. Whereas with Laurel and Hardy, you get the feeling that they really loved each other.

Are there any topics off-limits to you as a writer for television?

I don't think there are any topics that should be off-limits, no. Ricky and I did an episode of *Extras* that dealt with and featured an actor with Down syndrome. We understandably received a letter from a Down-syndrome organization saying, "Some of our members have complained; they felt uncomfortable." Ricky and I had to write what we considered to be a fairly strong defense of the show. For us, we did not feel we were laughing at the subject. We felt we were using the subject to elicit laughter of a different type—that gap between how you *should* behave and how you *do* behave in certain situations.

You know, Ricky and I never sit down and think about what subjects we are going—or are not going—to tackle. We just do what feels right. Audiences see certain topics, and their immediate reaction is anxiety. You can't talk about *this*, you can't joke about *that*. Our feeling is that the more we accept people who may be different, the more we should be able to joke about our own discomfort. If I have friends who are disabled, I can make jokes about their disability, just like they can make jokes about my height or Ricky being overweight. Of course, if you're meeting someone in the street for the first time, you don't start making those cracks, because it's inappropriate. But to us it's that fascinating stew of discomfort and ignorance that becomes a great recipe for laughter. We're not laughing at the disabled; we're laughing at people's discomfort with disability.

Look at a subject as terrible as rape. I can't think of anything funny about rape, and I certainly wouldn't feel comfortable laughing about it. But I could imagine a situation in which a man is uncomfortable around a woman who has been raped and his discomfort might come through in the way he speaks about the subject. It's not joking about a topic; it comes down to your treatment of taboo subjects. If you arrive from a position of ignorance or hate or racism, you're probably going to approach it from the wrong point of view. That's why I think there's a very big difference between exploring a taboo and making a joke about one.

Andy Millman is slightly homophobic—just a little bit strange around gay people. But that's the point of the character. It's interesting that audiences feel uncomfortable with that. It's almost as if all characters now have to be black-and-white. Good and bad. And that all heroes have to be noble and honorable. But that's not what real life is all about.

I was talking earlier about not necessarily going for a large audience. And that's because we want our shows to be aimed at a sort of reasoning, smart, intelligent audience that can steer its way through ambiguities.

Does it frustrate you when you see comedies aimed at intelligent audiences fail, at least in a commercial sense?

Arrested Development is one good example. I thought, What's going on? I couldn't understand why people weren't laughing. I didn't understand why they didn't find this funny. How was this *not* funny? It was so clearly funny to me. I've never quite understood the idea that people have different senses of humor.

On the other hand, I suppose there's always that danger that we as comedy fans are writing comedy for other comedy fans. Whereas the average viewer—and I don't mean this in a disparaging way—but the average viewer doesn't sit around thinking about how jokes work. It's just not something that's important to them. They just want the joke to be funny. So you can't be too clever. You can't assume reference points and sophistication that are not there.

I think this is something I've probably learned as I've gone on. I probably started off being a touch snobbish. I wouldn't want to write jokes that I thought were too easy or cheap. Now I've come to feel that it's just sometimes fun to have silliness.

For instance, take the famous scene of David Brent dancing in Season Two of *The Office*. That scene has become absolutely huge. There were articles in newspapers about how to perform that dance. There were videos of that dance, photos of that dance; it was probably the most repeated clip from the show. But we were really worried about it. We were thinking about cutting that scene, because it was too broad, too zany. And now it's the thing people most associate with the show, which is probably the least typical element of the program. Sometimes you can get too up your own ass, for lack of a better phrase.

And, actually, that's one of the things I like about the American version of *The Office*. It feels a little less constrained than ours. It doesn't obey these scrupulous rules of realism in quite the same way. It indulges itself a little bit more. I love that about it, and it really makes me laugh.

Do you think there are any crucial differences between American and English humor?

People constantly say there are differences, especially in Britain. There's a snobbery sometimes with Brits. They say that Americans don't understand irony, which is just a self-aggrandizing way of saying, "Look how we Brits are so much more clever and smarter."

To me, that's completely misinformed. All the best American humor is steeped in irony. But then there's this inverse snobbery that says that Brits can't do the brilliance of American comedy. And that's just nonsense.

One of the differences, I suppose, is that there's a freedom found in most American humor—they're not ashamed to use slang and vernacular. There's an easier rhythm to American humor. It has almost a jazz quality to it. Whereas in England, there's a need to display one's intelligence. The language can be a little bit airy-fairy, a bit long-winded, deliberately showing off. Compare that attitude with a joke by Woody Allen where he says, "My aunt looked like something you'd buy in a live-bait store."

Now, we don't have live-bait stores in England, and we wouldn't use the term "live bait." It would never be called that. It would never have that succinctness, because we'd want to be sort of grand. We'd have an official-sounding name for it. It's the same way you say "drugstore." It's so blunt. It's a store that sells drugs. In England, we have "pharmacists" and "chemists." It lacks the everyday poetry. That's really what I love.

I suppose another difference would be that American sitcoms tend to have more episodes per season than British sitcoms. Is that an advantage or a disadvantage as a writer?

I think it's an advantage, because as a viewer I want certain shows, like *Fawlty Towers*, to go on and on. One of the things I like about American shows is that they are able to run long enough to create a story arc. *Roseanne*, a show that I really enjoyed, went through so many stages and brought in so many characters that by the end there was a history created. The show created a past that the viewer witnessed and experienced. It created a layered viewing experience.

You mentioned earlier that you considered *Extras* a gateway to the rest of your career. What do you consider it a gateway to?

Both Ricky and I now feel that we've done the awkward silences and the agonizingly uncomfortable moments to death. *Extras* will probably be the last time that we do that sort of thing, because you can only take that so far—you know, when you let a gag crash and fall and burn.

As for the future, I'm excited about doing a darker sort of TV drama. I just love *The Sopranos* and *The Wire*. I just find them utterly mesmerizing. Movies have let me down as of late. They just don't seem to have the richness, the novelistic depth, and the ambition of these TV shows. So many people try to make a film after they have had some success on TV, and then they get their fingers burned. Ricky and I would love to try something on the scope of *The Sopranos*.

Truthfully, I found the office life you depicted in *The Office*, and the show-business industry in *Extras*, just as terrifying as the Mob world in Jersey.

We're not suggesting that our next show would have to have gangsters or policemen as characters, but we like that format because it can be what it wants to be. *The Sopranos* is hysterically funny at times. People take it on its own terms. It loosely falls within the gangster genre, but if you were the average viewer and you watched it expecting a cop show, you wouldn't get it. It demands quite a lot from the viewer.

Those demands usually make for the best television.

Absolutely. And to do something with that scope, that scale, that ambition, well, that would be really exciting. It would be a challenge. So why not then?

Writing Comedy for Live Storytelling

An interview with Adam Wade, 18-time StorySLAM winner and two-time GrandSLAM champion at The Moth

I write for my pieces to be read aloud. Not to sound like Billy Joel circa 1986, but the difference between writing a story for the page and writing a story to be read out loud is a matter of trust. When you perform live, the audience will feed on the truth and on the story being real. When it comes from the heart, the impact is more forceful.

In writing for the page, perhaps I have a little more leeway. I may have room to be less truthful and more creative and exaggerated with the material. The reader is reading in private instead of staring at me on a stage, wondering if I'm full of crap.

When I'm onstage, there is little room for lies and exaggeration. I don't want to stray far from how things occurred, and how those thing effected me at the time. I want to keep it as real as I can. Audiences are smart and can figure out a fraud pretty fast. They're not going to root for someone like that. I often talk to other writers who are going to perform a story, and they tell me they need to "punch up" stories. I can understand the need to do this—you're writing comedy. But oftentimes, if there are too many jokes, you may lose the earnest and vulnerable moments you need to move a story further. Once, after a show at a NYC comedy club, the booker told me that I "needed to punch it up" and to "add something about Viagra" to the story. It was a pivotal moment for me. I didn't do it. And when I look back, I'm glad I didn't. A joke like that would have killed the authenticity of the story, everything I was working for. I guess it's just finding that right balance between heart and humor, or just committing to one or the other.

It's very important to know that failing in front of an audience is okay. After you finally do perform well in front of an audience, there's a confidence that begins to grow. It's such a satisfying feeling. The performance improves; everything changes. But I really do think you need the experience of failure.

I once told a story on stage and I did so without notes. I was well prepared and the performance went great. A week later, I got lazy. I brought up a cheat sheet and looked down a few times. It was the same type of crowd as it was the previous week, but it was a lackluster performance—a complete 180. Something was missing. I wasn't able to fully be myself.

Later that night, I was at a bar with a writer friend of mine who had seen both performances. I expressed confusion, and she said something like, "You need to stay connected to the audience. They're with you the whole way, throughout the story. When you tell your stories, it's like you're reliving them, moment to moment. That's how the first performance was. But tonight, it was different. You were unsure of where you were going sometimes. Every time you looked at your notes, you ruined the moment of 'We are all in this with you.' You lost the audience a bit, and that kept happening over and over again.'"

It was great advice. From then on I stopped using notes on stage. I know what the story is and where I am in that story—I need a clear beginning, middle, and ending. As long as I know where I'm going, I have confidence to tell the story.

In teaching storytelling, I notice that some students get nervous about going on stage without notes. You can see the scared look in their eyes. I try to comfort them by saying two things. It's your story, and only you know it. And two, it doesn't have to be perfect. Just have fun up there. There's no pressure. Just try to do things in a natural way; don't make it look and feel too theatrical.

It can take a long time to write these stories. I'll initially just have an idea, a singular moment. That's how it starts, and it stays with me, days, weeks, months and even years. I tend to nurture these moments and they sort of just develop. I'm taking a walk and thinking about it. Then it's just trying to find the beginning, the middle and the end. It's easier said than done, and I will continue honing it, thinking about what works, trying to attach smaller singular moments to it. Sort of like a jigsaw puzzle of moments; it's up to you to put it together. It continues to evolve even after I perform it a few times. Audience reactions tend to help out a lot. That's why I think it's so close to stand-up in that way. You get immediate notes from the looks on the faces, the reactions to lines and expressions. Some stories I will continue to tell for years; others are put out to pasture at least for a little while.

You need to work hard, all the time. On a night when you connect with an audience and everything is working, you need to—in your heart and mind—cherish it and feel good about it. Maybe hit a Blimpie's for a sandwich before you go home. Treat yourself. You need to experience the ups and downs as a performer, so when you're up, you appreciate it, and when you're down, you know you have the potential to do better. The most important thing is the need to be true to yourself. And it's okay to fail— and fail miserably. It's okay to feel miserable on that long train ride home after a performance as you try to figure out what went wrong. You need those nights to appreciate the feelings you have when you do really well.

There's something very intimate about having someone just get up in front of you on a stage and tell a story without notes. More so than seeing someone read from a book. Or perform stand-up. This might be a bad comparison, but it reminds me of a Neil Young show I saw a few years ago. He did one set and it was just him with his acoustic guitar in front of an audience It was so pure, so heartfelt and beautiful. Then he did a second set with his band and it was heavy, electric, loud. Both sets were great, but the solo acoustic was more vulnerable—it was more raw with emotion.

Harold Ramis

Harold Ramis is not interested in dumbing down his movies for the masses. He recalled to *Believer* magazine that he's baffled when audience members tell him, "When I go to the movies, I don't want to think." When he hears such a thing, he says to himself, Why wouldn't you want to think? What does that mean? Why not just shoot yourself in the fucking head?

Curious logic coming from a man who made his career writing and directing some of the best escapist movie comedies of his generation. From *National Lampoon's Animal House* (1978) and *Caddyshack* (1980) to *Stripes* (1981) and *Ghostbusters* (1984), Ramis perfected a comedy genre with a deceptively simplistic formula: lovable characters, who are considered losers, rebel against the establishment and save the day with their goofball high jinks.

While Ramis's satire may be glaringly mainstream on the surface, it becomes decidedly more subversive and complex when you read between the lines. *The New Yorker* summed it up best: "What Elvis did for rock and Eminem did for rap, Harold Ramis did for attitude: he mass-marketed the sixties to the seventies and eighties. He took his generation's anger and curiosity and laziness and woolly idealism and gave it a hyper-articulate voice."

Born in Chicago in 1944, Ramis didn't set out to become the counterculture's most famous comedy auteur. His first dream was to become an actor. In 1969, Ramis joined the Second City troupe in Chicago, where he performed sketch comedy and improv with such future superstars (and collaborators) as John Belushi, Bill Murray, and John Candy. In 1974, he moved to New York to write and perform on *The National Lampoon Radio Hour* as well as the Off-Broadway sketch revue *The National Lampoon Show.* But while his peers went on to fame and fortune on TV shows like *Saturday Night Live,* Ramis was mostly passed over and ignored.

But he didn't give up his comedy ambitions. If he wasn't destined for a career in front of the camera, he would go *behind* it, crafting the words and directing the movies that would transform his friends into stars. (Occasionally, in movies such as *Ghostbusters* and *Stripes,* he'd even give himself a role.)

Nothing delights Ramis like taking an unflinching look at his own emotional frailties. While he never actually explored that in his early comedies, by the 1990s he had stopped turning to adolescent humor and frat-boy antics for inspiration and had begun to create comedy that better expressed his own thoughts and fears. Perhaps his greatest achievement is *Groundhog Day* (1993), the story of TV weatherman Phil Connors (Bill Murray), condemned to repeat the same day, over and over, in the western Pennsylvania town of Punxsutawney. It's a perfect mix of comedy and philosophy; a morality fable with better gags; a film that can be appreciated for its humor alone, or become fodder for intense debates about religion, rebirth, personal intro-spection, and whether the parallels to Nietzsche were intentional. It should be no surprise that, as *The New York Times* pointed out in a 2003 article, "[S]ince its debut a decade ago, the film has become a curious favorite of religious leaders of many faiths, who all see in 'Groundhog Day' a reflection of their own spiritual messages." It should also not come as a surprise that followers of just about every religious discipline—Catholics, Jews, Buddhists, Jesuits, and even atheists—have all assumed that *Groundhog Day* was an endorsement of their spiritual ideals.

To his credit, Ramis hasn't told any of them they're wrong. Then again, he hasn't said they're right either.

You have very political roots: you're the only writer I'm interviewing for this book who was president of his Hebrew school.

Oh, I'll bet others were, too. They're just afraid to admit it.

What platform did you run on?

I don't remember any kind of an election or anything. I was just a very responsible young fellow, and I felt that being good was the direct path to Heaven.

You've said that irony is more available in Chicago than anywhere else. Why?

I kind of equate it with this experience of always feeling that you're slightly on the outside of the mainstream. Growing up in what was called "the Second City," you always felt like you were on the outside looking in. New York and L.A. were the real centers of culture in America, and we were kind of a sideshow. There's always more comedy in being alienated than in fitting in. It's the alternative comedy posture. It's what Rodney Dangerfield created with his "I get no respect" routine. The other end of the spectrum isn't so funny: "I get so much respect." No one will laugh at how great things are for somebody.

I once analyzed all this. Woody Allen was the great comic genius of my early career, and there was a tendency to measure everything against that standard, that kind of posture. He was always writing about losers and schlemiels and schlubs, but I was never interested in losers. I was more intrigued by the alternative comedy posture. The characters I enjoyed creating were the dropouts and the rebels. They voluntarily opted out of the mainstream. It wasn't because they couldn't join it. It was because it wasn't worth doing. Or there was some serious hypocrisy going on. Or it wasn't cool.

Speaking of which, there's a story about Ned Tanen, the president of Universal, which put out *Animal House*. When he was first shown the film, he was upset with the alternative-comedy stance you took with the Delta House characters.

Right. He was confused, because he thought the main characters should be the good guys, and why would the good guys act like that? He thought they were losers. But anyone who grew up when I did and was in college when I was in college had kind of embraced the rebel. It was a 1960s idea. Counterculture was the new mainstream, and it took the studios a while to catch on to that, I think.

From what I've read, you had an interesting job after you graduated from Washington University, in St. Louis, in 1966.

I worked in a mental institution in St. Louis, which prepared me well for when I went out to Hollywood to work with actors. People laugh when I say that, but it was actually very good training. And not just with actors; it was good training for just living in the world. It's knowing how to deal with people who might be reacting in a way that's connected to anxiety or grief or fear or rage. As a director, you're dealing with that constantly with actors. But if I were a businessman, I'd probably be applying those same principles to that line of work.

How long did you work at the mental institution?

I worked in the psych ward for about seven months, and then I moved back to Chicago and I began to substitute-teach at a public elementary school—kindergarten through sixth grade. While I was teaching, I did some freelance writing for the *Chicago Daily News*, and I took a few of these pieces to show to *Playboy*. They happened to be looking to fill an entry-level editorial staff job, which was joke editor, and they hired me.

You must have had quite a peek into this country's sexual underbelly with some of those unsolicited joke submissions. What were they like?

I had a wall of postcards behind my desk that I was going to one day collate, analyze, and categorize, and then do the definitive treatise on the American Joke. It was amazing how many of these jokes were written in pencil on three-ring notebook paper, or came from people who were incarcerated. It was also amazing how many of them dealt with farmers and farm animals.

At the time—it was the late 1960s—the *Playboy* editors wanted to modernize the jokes a bit, to make them more counterculture. A big part of my job was changing "the farmer" into "a swinging advertising executive."

Did you start to recognize categories of jokes—basic types and groupings?

I would say in the first month, I already knew 95 percent of the jokes in current circulation in America. I could not hear a joke I didn't know.

I could anticipate the punch lines, because most jokes are like any other joke. In fact, the way I did the job was to spend an hour each morning just slitting open the mail and lining the jokes up before me. Then I would read punch lines, one every second. If I knew the joke, I'd throw the card away. I practically recognized them all. But as soon as I'd see one I didn't recognize, I wouldn't even finish reading it—I'd set it aside to savor it later, just because it was new. Not because it was necessarily good, just different.

What percentage of these *Playboy*-joke contributors actually wrote their own jokes?

Most didn't. There were some submissions from people who considered themselves professional joke writers. The jokes would usually arrive on indexed cards that had a serial number on the side, like "C35." The next card would be "C36." The one after that, "C37." They'd just grab a section of their joke file and send it.

How did you not lose your mind with a job like that?

It was just cool being at *Playboy*.

But wasn't the magazine already sort of behind the times by the late sixties?

You know, it's funny—I worked there right at the cusp of its success. The circulation was at its peak. The clubs and casinos were around in all the major cities. Hefner was still in Chicago. The mansion was every guy's wet dream. I was working there in 1968 when the riots happened at the Democratic Convention in Chicago. Hefner started the Playboy Foundation, because he recognized that there was a big seismic shift in American culture. The top brass held a couple of meetings and invited me. There were two of us who had long hair. We were invited as ambassadors of the new counterculture to advise the executives on a couple of corporate decisions. One of the agendas was to bring the Playboy Clubs into the mainstream, because the clubs were not attracting young people. But it never panned out. Even the executives could see the handwriting on the wall, at least as far as the clubs went. The young people just weren't filing in.

How did you then go from *Playboy* to working for *National Lampoon?*

I never worked for the print version of *National Lampoon,* only their road show, as a performer. What happened was that I had told my editor at *Playboy* that I wanted to be an actor, and he knew the director at Second City in Chicago. I auditioned for the spot and got it. I worked there for a few years, and then I took a year off in the early seventies and went to live in Greece. And I remember that Joe Flaherty, whom I later worked with at *SCTV,* wrote me a letter. He said that Second City had just hired a little Albanian guy to replace me. That would have been John Belushi.

John was eventually drafted by *National Lampoon* to star in their stage production of *Lemmings* [1973], which was a parody of the Woodstock music festival. After John did *Lemmings,* he stayed on and put together another stage production, called *The National Lampoon Show* [1975]. He came back to Chicago, and he went to all of the Second City people that he knew, including Bill Murray and Gilda Radner, and asked them to join the show.

Did you write for the show or just perform?

Both. We put the show together like we would a Second City show. We developed material in improv rehearsal, and that became the show. You just kept working the pieces until you had them set, and then you would take them out and try them in front of an audience.

Lemmings really worked. It had a unity to it and a very specific point of view. But *The National Lampoon Show* was hard-edged and really offensive. I always felt that the show brought out the worst in the audience, and I was not comfortable doing it. I don't think it was our best work. It had no real shape. It was just a bad sketch show.

How did you feel about the *National Lampoon* sensibility? Were you a fan of the slash-and-burn style the magazine was famous for?

I was a fan of the magazine. I thought some of the material was great, in particular Michael O'Donoghue's *Encyclopedia of Humor* [1973] and Doug Kenney's *1964 High School Yearbook* [1974]. Those guys were good. The humor was very literate and interesting. In a magazine format, they were able to do things that I thought were very creative stylistically. But that was the problem with the show. The magazine didn't translate to the stage. We tried to write a lot of material that was outrageous for its own sake. But the *Lampoon* material I really enjoyed was the more subtle work.

John Belushi left to do *Saturday Night Live* in 1975. Were you ever asked to join that show?

Lorne Michaels offered me a job after the first year, but I was already writing and performing on *SCTV.* Lorne didn't offer me a guarantee to perform on *SNL*—only to write. But I was happily doing both at *SCTV.* And in a way, and this sounds odd to say, I didn't like *Saturday Night Live* that much.

Really? Why?

The people I knew on the show, I'd seen them all do better work. I also thought the writing was a little weak and gratuitous in a lot of ways. I thought the notion of just repeating scenes over and over, week after week, was not a good thing. It could have just been me preserving my outsider posture, but it felt like Lorne took something that was underground and made it mainstream.

A lot of comedy writers prefer *SCTV* to *Saturday Night Live.* I wonder if *SCTV* will be remembered more fondly than *SNL* in the long run?

People say that, but it never turned into dollars for anybody. Lorne Michaels is filthy rich and successful. And Andrew Alexander, the creator of *SCTV,* well ... you know.

I'm not talking money so much as the show being an influence.

There were really bright people on both shows. But *SCTV* was allowed to be much more obscure. We didn't have to worry about sponsors and networks. We were not mainstream. Even when NBC bought *SCTV,* in 1981, it didn't seem like the executives imposed their will on the show.

One of the great elements of *SCTV* is that it took place in its own little universe. And it had that show within a show. It must have been wonderful to have that format to write for.

You know, that format was a direct reaction to *SNL.* Since *SNL* had already launched, we thought, How do we go up against that? They had all the money in the world. They had a network. They had major sponsorship.

They had a good time slot. So we said, "We might as well just be the poor cousin. Why not embrace our obscurity—become the underdogs."

We became a low-budget station out of some tiny town in North America. So that was a good conceit, and that kind of worked.

Besides Belushi and Chevy Chase and later Bill Murray, another *Lampoon-*er **who made the leap to** *Saturday Night Live* **was writer Michael O'Donoghue. Did you ever work with him?**

He wasn't involved with the stage show that I was in, but I did know him, and I did like him. I actually talked to him in the early stages of *Animal House* about co-writing the script with me, but he didn't think college was his thing. Years later, there was talk of him co-writing the screenplay to the [John Kennedy Toole written] book, *A Confederacy of Dunces*, which I was going to direct. I thought Michael would have a great take on that. If anyone could have pulled it off, Michael could have. But that *Confederacy* story has defeated every writer who's ever tried it over the years.

Why do you think that is? The project is notorious in Hollywood. The book is almost cursed for never having successfully made the transition to the screen.

My final analysis of it is that *Confederacy* violated one of the basic by-laws of movie comedy, which the producer [*Ghost World* and *Pulp Fiction*] Michael Shamberg articulated. He said, "Comedy works two ways. Either you have a normal person in an extraordinary situation or an extraordinary person in a normal situation." And *Confederacy* was about an extraordinary person in a series of extraordinary situations.

So there was nothing to bounce off of?

Right. There was no kind of contextual edge to it. It was one weird person after another, which creates the overall effect of whimsy. And whimsy is not really powerful. You need some sort of center.

In each of your movies, there's a center. You in *Ghostbusters,* **the Chris Makepeace character in** *Meatballs,* **Warren Oates in** *Stripes.*

You need the formality and the rules and the rigid social system. For example, the Ted Knight character in *Caddyshack* represented the country-club values. The movie wouldn't have worked as well without that character.

As far as *Confederacy*, the only way to have successfully made that movie would have been to have the main character Ignatius Reilly work as an air-traffic controller or some such job. Just to put him in a really straight, normal situation and let this guy's sensibility bounce off the walls.

Did you ever work with Michael O'Donoghue after that, and before he died of a cerebral hemorrhage in 1994?

No. We would just meet occasionally. He was not a terrifying presence for me. I actually had an affection for him.

Was that terrifying presence an act?

Michael was a lot of posture. I don't want to say "poseur." That's a little too strong. But he had an image that he had cultivated. In his New York apartment, he had a fur pelt on the floor. And, of course, it didn't take long to recognize it as the skin of a collie.

Where does one buy a collie pelt?

I'm not sure. It's hard to come by these days. It was hard to come by then. Michael's stance was a theater of cruelty. It was like the Brando character in *The Wild One*. "What are you rebelling against?" And the answer was, "What do you got?" Anything you cherished or held safe, Michael would go after. That was the soul of the *Lampoon* style. It was every sick joke you ever heard, whether it was Nazism, death itself, or religion. If it was something you cherished or held safe, Michael would attack it with an axe. Not to mention a sword and a sledgehammer.

How was Doug Kenney—your co-writer on *Animal House*—different? His humor seemed to be more nostalgic and a bit gentler than Michael O'Donoghue's.

Doug was a really loving person, and that expressed itself in his humor, even though it could also turn really acidic.

How did you end up co-writing *Animal House* with Doug and with Chris Miller, another *Lampoon* writer?

I was first hired to write a treatment for a movie project to take place at a college. The plan was to use some of the material from our *Lampoon* stage show, and I tried to use the best material from that show, along with some other stories. My title was *Freshman Year*, and it was about a guy pledging a fraternity that his older brother and his father and uncles had also been in. But, in the end, he chooses not to rush, because the fraternity traditions were kind of odious. They were about privilege and class status and racism and that sort of thing. That was the arc of the treatment that I wrote, but it didn't feel very *Lampoon*-ish.

I could see that the *Lampoon* wasn't really excited about it, but I knew they still sort of trusted me to some extent. So I said, "Well, maybe I should work with a *Lampoon* editor." They said, "Yeah, yeah, that's good."

I got together with Doug, whom I really liked and with whom I shared a sensibility. We went off and we first wrote a high-school movie sort of based on his *1964 High School Yearbook*. We shaped that script into something pretty funny, but we were told that college was a better setting for a *Lampoon* movie. We brought another *Lampoon* writer, Chris Miller, on board, and that proved to be great. The whole project was a nice collaboration in every sense. It took about three months, working eight hours a day or so.

I've heard that many of the scenes from *Animal House* were based on real-life events.

It was probably worse in real life, believe me. All three of us were involved in situations that ended with cars being wrecked and girls being abandoned and people leaving all sorts of bodily substances all over the place. There were all forms of abuse, both physical and psychological. That movie came from a very real experience of college life in the early 1960s.

I wasn't as bad as some of the others, though. I had a whole different kind of persona. I was legendary for having a kind of slacker mentality:

falling asleep on the sofa watching TV in the fraternity house, with a note pinned to my chest: "Wake Me at Noon."

That you placed on yourself?

Yes, of course.

Like a deaf mute from the 19th century.

I'd hate for my kids to read this, but I never went to class. I was famous for never going to class and still doing well in school.

Were you pleased with the result of *Animal House?*

I have to say, as broad as my movies can be, certain elements in *Animal House* struck me as broader than they needed to be. When I saw *Animal House*, my initial reaction was that we, the writers, didn't intend for it to be quite that broad, especially in the way the villains were portrayed. I thought the portrayal of Dean Wormer was over the top. And the mayor too. I like my villains a little more textured. But I thought John Landis did a very good job of nailing the look of it. It's also very well-paced.

Do you remember any specific jokes and scenes that you wrote?

I wrote a good portion of the "Germans bombed Pearl Harbor" speech that Belushi gave. And the speech that Tim Matheson gave before the disciplinary council that went something like: "You can't hold a fraternity responsible for the behavior of a few individuals. If you indict us, shouldn't we blame the whole fraternity system?"

Also, the scene that took place in the Dexter Lake Club with Otis Day & the Nights. The "Do you mind if we dance with your dates?" scene. That was taken from a real-life experience.

What happened?

There was a club on Delmar Boulevard in St. Louis, a blues club called the Blue Note. There was a very good B. B. King–style guitar player called Benny Sharp, who used to perform there. His band was called Benny Sharp & the Sharpees. We used to go there all the time. But, actually, there was also a different club on that boulevard that was similar. We had some girls with us one night at this other club, and a guy came over and asked if he could dance with our dates. We said, "Sure, no problem. Go right ahead! Dance with our dates!"

It didn't end badly. But it wasn't long after that that racial politics in America soured to a point where kids like us were no longer going to blues clubs.

I wonder if you could even include a scene like that in a comedy these days.

Maybe not. But I think that scene was honest—not offensive. I'm always more offended by dishonesty and hypocrisy than by an honest portrayal of the real world.

There was an infamous article written about Doug Kenney in the October 1981 issue of *Esquire*. It implied that Doug was so unhappy with the result of your next collaboration, *Caddyshack*, that his death while hiking on a mountain in Hawaii in August of 1980 was most likely the result of a suicide. Do you agree with that theory?

Doug was not a happy person for many reasons. And *Caddyshack* was a big part of his life at the end. He was very disappointed with the movie, but I'd hate to spend the rest of my life thinking that I directed and co-wrote the movie that killed Doug Kenney. Ironically, since his death, *Caddyshack* has become a movie that people have embraced and cherished.

We were so arrogant and so deluded and maybe deranged that we thought everything we would do would be as successful as *Animal House*. And Doug knew only success. Maybe his career success was his greatest and most promising avenue to happiness or self-acceptance. And failing that, there wasn't much else to go on. But he had a miserable kind of psychological legacy from his family—not to blame them. Every family has its own kind of horrible dysfunction. There was a great tragic aspect with his situation. His brother died young, and Doug always felt that he was a disappointment to his family. Maybe that theme of disappointment, coupled with *Caddyshack*'s failure to launch, culminated in his whole humiliating sense of failure.

What's your opinion on the specifics of his death? Do you think he slipped or fell off that mountain?

I don't know. In a way, it doesn't matter. I never saw it as a perplexing mystery. Doug was sufficiently depressed. And, you know, having worked in a psych ward, I knew people who'd killed themselves. I've watched people process emotions on that level. About one-third of them succeed in getting better, one-third stay the same, and one-third get worse. Not everyone who feels suicidal kills himself. So I don't know how he died, but I've made a sick joke about this before: that Doug probably fell while he was looking for a place to jump. He was depressed, and he was intoxicated a lot of the time. And by that point in his life, he had cut himself off from the possibility of happiness.

How did *Caddyshack* come about?

Brian [Doyle-] Murray, Bill's brother and a writer and performer for *Lampoon,* had caddied when he was growing up, in and around Wilmette, Illinois. Brian would talk to Doug Kenney about his country-club experiences, and Doug could relate, because he had worked in a tennis shop, in a country club in Ohio. His father was the tennis pro. Doug came to the project from sort of the snobby member's point of view, although he was not from that ruling class himself. Brian understood it from the point of view of a poor Catholic kid in WASP territory. And I understood it from the Rodney Dangerfield point of view, which was the Jewish outsider. I was on the outside looking in—the unwelcome guest.

Brian and Doug started talking about this idea, but they were not the most focused people in the world, or the most disciplined. When they told me about the idea, I said, "What if we write it together? And I'll direct it?" We took it to Mike Medavoy at Orion, and it got launched. It was the first movie I directed.

How did the shooting script differ from what eventually appeared on-screen? Was it much different?

It started off as being about a Catholic kid from a large family, aspiring to join the fancy Bushwood Country Club. That was going to be the emphasis: this young, poor caddie who wanted desperately to join this high-end club. But once Chevy Chase, Rodney Dangerfield, and Bill Murray came on board, the emphasis shifted. Beefing up their parts was irresistible.

I would assume that's an advantage to being both a director and a writer. If you were just a writer of *Caddyshack,* you wouldn't have been able to flesh out those characters on the set. The direction becomes a continuation of the writing process.

True. And I probably felt more comfortable creating those characters than I did with the other characters in the movie. I understood how those three actors could be funny. The material with the young kid was not inherently funny, in and of itself. I've never seen a great comedy without a great comic performance. The actors playing the caddies were good, but none of them was a comedy star. So to count on them to carry the comedy could have been a little problematic—this all became apparent pretty early into the shoot.

Chevy and Bill were obviously adept at improvisation, which they did throughout the film, but how was Rodney as an improviser?

Terrible. Just awful. We were originally going to use Don Rickles, but at the time Rodney had just done a run of *Tonight Show* appearances that were hysterical. He was brilliant. Rodney was a joke comedian, and every joke he told was based on very precise wording and timing. His act had a specific rhythm that could not be violated. Every word and syllable was important. So there was no improvising with Rodney, unless it was him coming up with a line he had used somewhere in a past act of his. Or he would want to sit down every night and hammer out the jokes he would use the next day.

Often, he thought he was bombing on the set, because no one was laughing. He just didn't know from that world. He really knew nothing about the process of filmmaking.

How much of Bill Murray's performance was improvised?

Pretty much everything he did in the movie was improvised, except for the one big speech he gave on the Dalai Lama. But almost everything else—I would say 95 percent of his work—was improvised. The speech he performs as he cuts off the heads of the flowers with a garden tool was completely improvised. Only the action is indicated in the script: "The greenskeeper, Carl, lops the heads off tulips as he practices his golf swing ..."

With that particular speech, the "Cinderella story" speech, I had been out jogging one day, and one way I kept up my spirits was to be the announcer at the Olympics: "It's the end of the last lap of the marathon; let's see who's entering the stadium .... oh, it's Harold Ramis!" So I said to Bill on the set, "You know when you're pretending that you're a sports announcer and calling the play-by-play—" He said, "Don't say anymore. I got it." He started talking and improvising, and that speech was the result.

I had worked with Bill at Second City and then at *Lampoon,* and then we did *Meatballs* together, and I knew him to be the best verbal improviser I'd ever seen. He and Chris Guest were really two of the best at that. So I thought, Well, if I've got Bill, why not let him just talk? I would feed him motivation. I could think in all his character modes, having worked with him so much.

Improv is a tool for a director. But with any tool, I suppose, you have to know how to use it properly. Too much of it can be a bad thing.

Yes, that's true. And, also, it's the editing room that saves your ass. If you took all the improv from *Caddyshack* and did it on onstage, you'd bomb half the time. One thing I learned to do was to shoot enough improv so I could actually shape it in the editing room.

There are some Platonic and Aristotelian kinds of perfections out there. Waiting for the punch line or delivering a line too quickly won't work. There is a perfect amount of time you need to wait. You need a good ear. In fact, because my movies are largely talk, I do a lot of listening. I can practically edit with my eyes closed, at least as far as timing goes: when is the movement going on too long and when is it just enough? If you're cutting away on a joke, you're probably doing it because you can't top that joke. If the scene is still building and is still rich, you keep going.

How much footage was shot for the scene with Bill Murray and Chevy Chase in Carl's garage apartment?

It's hard to say. But because those guys are so good, it wasn't endless hours of it. I mean, we didn't shoot one thousand hours to get five minutes. They're very good.

Some reviewers at the time were critical of _Caddyshack_. They felt that it seemed too improvised, and that maybe it wasn't as tight as it could have been.

There was a _New York Times_ review of _Caddyshack_, and I think I'm quoting accurately, that said it was "an amiable mess." And that's fine. I knew it had some very messy elements. But that was the trade-off. The only way to get all that Bill Murray content into the movie was to settle for the fact that it was off-story and that it had nothing to do with the plot. Whatever arc there was to Bill's story was crafted later, when we shot the gopher material and everything else.

Do you think audiences are willing to forego perfection and craft if the characters are strong and the jokes are solid?

In any genre, viewers want to feel something. They want to have an experience. There are more well-made movies than good movies. That's sort of my new mantra. Plenty of people can shoot beautiful films. There are a lot of great editors, a lot of great designers. But where is the content? Who are the characters? Is it moving? You want the audience to feel something, and if it's comedy, you want them to laugh hard, even if it's at the expense of a better shot or a better edit. There are many times when the editor will say to me, "Well, that's not a real good cut." And I'll say, "Yeah, but it's funny. Let's just do it."

As a director and writer, you must have been happy to have had Bill Murray at your disposal.

I always tell students to identify the most talented person in the room, and, if it isn't you, go stand next to him. That's what I did with Bill. I met him when he was really young—in his early twenties.

The problem with that advice is that everyone thinks they're the most talented person in the room.

Yes, but if you're smart you know.

Bill Murray has a reputation for being difficult to work with.

Billy has that thing I've seen in only a few people in my life. Robert De Niro, whom I worked with in _Analyze This_ and its sequel, has it also.

It's a kind of penetrating intellect and a very intense kind of scrutiny. They look at you really hard, and you always feel that you're being judged for honesty and sincerity and clarity. You never want to hype those two or bullshit them in any way. It's as if you could be dismissed in a moment if they sense you're not a genuine or serious person.

People melt under that kind of stare. Chris Guest and Chevy also used to do it, but they did it almost as a tactic. They would just look at you without saying anything.

Almost as a bullying tactic?

In a sense, yes, bullying. It is intimidating. But with De Niro and Billy, it's not just a tactic. Billy just doesn't have time for fools or insensitive people.

Judge Reinhold, who acted in *Stripes,* said that the director, Ivan Reitman, was able to control the army and the tanks and everything else connected with the shoot, but the only thing he couldn't control was Bill Murray.

Well, you don't try. I mean, I never try to control an actor.

You understand the parameters and you work within them?

It's like that great saying, "You ride the horse in the direction it's going." Billy goes his own way. But he'll go my way if he thinks it's a good way. So my job is not to force the actor to do anything; it's to convince them. Billy was smart enough to know a good thing when he heard it. If I said, "Try this" or "Try that," and it was really funny, he'd do it.

Do you think there's any chance you'll work with Bill Murray in the future?

I highly doubt it. We hardly talk. I've just seen him a handful of times over the years.

Was it a specific falling-out? What was the reason?

No, it was just that his life changed. Both our lives changed in a big way. He left his wife, whom I knew before they were even married. He embarked on another life. Some of his old friends are still his friends, but he and I haven't spoken in years.

Was *Groundhog Day* always intended to be a comedy? From what I've read, it started out quite differently.

It wasn't anything broad. The first screenwriter, Danny Rubin, doesn't have a style that goes for big jokes. But it was touching. I got tears in my eyes after I read it. One of the differences was that when we first meet the Bill Murray character, Phil Connors, he's already repeating the same day, which has gone on for ten thousand years. There was a voice-over that explained how that came to be.

Ten thousand years? It sounds more like a horror story than a comedy.

That was one of the first big changes I made right away in my rewrite: to show how Phil Connors first found himself in this situation, rather than come into it after it's already been going on for so long. I think this helped ease the audience into the movie. And it was kind of a clever device. Actually, I had assured Danny that I wouldn't change that aspect of his original script. I told him, "It's so cool starting right in the middle. I'll never change that—I promise!" Of course, that was the first thing I changed.

I just thought, from a dramatic point of view, this would be a big moment to miss, the moment when the character first experiences the repetition—to show him going through those stages of disbelief and disorientation and confusion. Why jump past all that good material?

What I love about that movie is there's no explanation as to why Phil Connors finds himself in this situation. It just happens. Which is the polar opposite of most Hollywood films, where everything is overexplained.

Actually, the studio insisted on an explanation. So I wrote one.

What was it?

I wrote that Phil Connors had a disaffected lover who buys a book called *101 Hex Spells or Enchantments You Can Do For Free*. And she does some incantation, and she burns something and then smashes a wristwatch, which was obviously Phil's.

And the executives were happy with that?

Yeah, they were. But then the executive in charge at Columbia lost his job. A new executive came in, read the script, and said, "What do you need this for?" I said, "Okay, thank you." That was the last time we attempted to explain it.

Groundhog Day **has become very popular with religious audiences—of all faiths. And yet it wasn't an overtly religious movie.**

Everyone saw their own faith in *Groundhog Day*. And it was not really faith in a God, because there's no God postulated in *Groundhog Day*. It was a faith in humanity. And I'm nothing if not a secular humanist. You don't need religion to be a good person. Maybe there's a simpler way.

Do you think *Groundhog Day* is one of your films that came closest to the intended vision?

I think it's a film that I can stand behind on a moral, ethical, and spiritual level.

Are there any movies that didn't come close to your intended vision?

Sure. I mean, I've done some things that had no vision. I co-wrote *Caddyshack II*. I'm forever ashamed of that. We crawled out of the theater when we saw it—me and the other writer, Peter Torokvei.

How do you feel about sequels, in general?

In my experience, they cost twice as much and they're half as successful. But then again, I didn't make the *Star Wars* sequels. I'm sure George Lucas feels very good about sequels. But I haven't had much luck with them. *Ghostbusters II* cost more and did less well than the original, and it was the same thing with *Analyze That*. I'm not such a fan.

Do you have a target audience in mind when you write? Do you picture anyone in particular?

No, I write for everybody. Or, really, for anyone who can read and is not hopelessly fucked in the head.

Do you think today's comedies are less risky than those made in the seventies and eighties?

I don't think so. Comedies might be less risky politically, but taking political risks or going after sacred cows doesn't necessarily lead to good comedy. It may be well motivated and it may be well intended, but that doesn't mean it's going to be funny.

Director Ivan Reitman said something interesting about the difference between a comedy made twenty years ago and one made today. He said that if you looked at *Stripes* or *Ghostbusters,* the lead characters were much smarter than everybody else in the movie. Whereas today, the main characters aren't the smartest guys. A lot of the time, they're the *dumbest* guys. Would you agree with this assessment?

Yes, I can see that. But for me, it was never about my characters having more learning or technical ability. It was more about them being socially smart, cutting through all the pretension in the room and all the illusions and recognizing what's really going on. You know, just cutting to the most practical and realistic position right away. And it's not always the most heroic position. Sometimes characters may turn and run; they might not stick around and fight. They don't have to be the heroes, necessarily. But they should be intelligent.

A lot of your movies represented the comedic sensibility of the time period in which they were released—*Animal House* in the late seventies; *Stripes* in the early eighties; *Ghostbusters* in the mid-eighties; *Analyze This* in the nineties. Looking back, do you think that you captured the sensibility of the periods or created that sensibility?

I don't know. I just did what I wanted to do and what interested me. As I tell writing students, the only thing you have that is unique is yourself. You can write a movie that's like some other movie, and that's what you'll have: something that's completely derivative. But the only thing totally unique is you. There's no one like you. No one else has had your experience. No one has been in your body or had your parents. Yes, we've all had the same cultural influences. We've all lived at the same time, watched the same shows, gone to the same movies, listened to the same music. But it's all filtered through our unique personalities. And I honor the things that have influenced me. I'm grateful for whatever it is that became the particular lens that's allowed me to put out what I have.

Do you consider certain movies or a certain period in your career as having been your golden age?

No. I think I'm still waiting for my golden age. I really feel that way. I've had fun my whole career. Every movie I've made has been a wonderful experience in lots of ways. And right now I'm working on what I hope will be the best movie I've ever made.

Can't say it will be, but....

On February 24, 2014, Harold Ramis passed away at the age 69 in Chicago.

Getting Hired as a Sitcom Writer

An interview with Ken Levine, writer and producer of *M*A*S*H*, *Cheers*, *Frasier*, *Wings*, *Everybody Loves Raymond*, and *Becker*

What advice would you give someone hoping to break into sitcom writing?

The most vital piece of advice I can give is to keep writing and to come up with a great script. When producers staff a show, and I've been a producer for a few shows, it's like the Sorcerer's Apprentice—scripts just keep arriving, and then more, and then even more. You receive twenty scripts, and then in the afternoon, forty more arrive. It never stops. But every so often you find a good one, and you put it aside. Then you call the agent to ask about the writer, and nine times out of ten the agent will say, "Oh, he's already got a meeting with another show." What that tells me is that all of the producers in Hollywood have the same five hundred scripts, and everybody recognizes the same four writers.

What is it about these writers that you and other producers recognize?

Their scripts are funnier, they're sharper, they have a better command of the show. There's a kind of a freshness to them. There's a kind of nuttiness to the writing, where the jokes don't feel very stock. You get a sense of whether somebody is funny. I mean, look, it's an inexact science. I've rejected writers who went on to have very nice careers, but the majority you never hear from again.

Do you think that some of them could have perhaps succeeded if they were given a shot and had a chance to learn?

I can teach structure. I can teach dos and don'ts with a script. I can give various tips. But when you have to go into a room and write a scene, either you have a sense of what's funny or you don't. I can't explain it. It's just a god-given talent. I don't know how or why someone has it and another doesn't.

A lot of new writers take courses on sitcom writing, which I think is really unnecessary. Especially when the course skips a few steps and teaches you how to pitch. Before anything else, you have to learn how to write. And you learn writing by teaching yourself. When I first started, I went to a bookstore on Hollywood Boulevard that had TV scripts on a remainder table. For two dollars I bought an old *Odd Couple* script and just studied it. I thought, Oh, *this* is how it works: INTERIOR APARTMENT--DAY. I had no idea.

You figure it out. And then, through trial and error, when you finally have a script ready, you can pitch. My main advice is to try to have a story that stands out a little bit from the rest. Again, you're competing with a lot of other writers. One way to stand out is to write a holiday-themed script. There are two schools of thought on this: some producers don't like scripts that are too out of the ordinary, while others do. But, at the very least, the script will be different from the rest of the batch.

Scripts that are pitched will almost always have a story you've read a million times before. Years ago, I was trying to staff a show with writers, and I remember reading three sample scripts for *Everybody Loves Raymond* that all had the *same exact* story: Debra doesn't feel appreciated and Raymond has to take over the house chores for a day. Very obvious stories! I was beyond bored. Not one of those writers was hired.

Another piece of advice I'd give would be to avoid using lengthy stage directions in your script. The truth of the matter is that producers and studio readers just don't pay attention to stage directions. They see big blocks of direction and they fly through them. You need to be very,

very sparing. Doing this makes the script easier to read. And—let's face it—you are writing this script to be read, not for the script to actually be shot. So if a producer is just gliding along, page after page, he's probably going to like the script a lot more than if he's had to wade through detailed stage directions.

For instance, instead of writing "Jessica enters the room and sees this and sees that, and then notices that the contents of her drawers are strewn all over the floor," just make it: "Jessica enters." That's all you need. Describe the action quickly, and get on with it.

But you can sprinkle the scripts with inside jokes, such as: "Character orders a three-pound lobster (therefore breaking the show's budget)." Small jokes that will reward the reader.

Does a writer hoping to break into sitcoms stand a better chance by applying for a staff position on a new show rather than an existing one?

Yes, because when you apply for a staff job on a new show, you're not competing with returning writers. Your chances improve significantly.

How many sitcom writers do you consider to be top-notch?

It's a very small group. There are plenty of middle-tier writers who are just okay—it really depends on the level of the show.

When I was directing sitcoms, I would talk with the writers about what the script needed. Then I'd go home, and I would know that when I returned the next morning the script would be better—but it still wouldn't be great. I would just know; I could feel it. They were all perfectly nice, hard working writers who were willing to stay late, but they could not produce. They just didn't have the talent. The group didn't have the horses.

What does that mean, "the horses"?

The thoroughbreds—the writers who carry the rest of the group. I could have thrown those same notes at the writers for *Everybody Loves Raymond,* and I would just know they would turn out a much better draft the next morning. And they would have.

If you're not a top-notch writer, or at least not yet, can you still make a career out of writing for sitcoms?

You can, but it's harder. There's a great line I once overheard a producer at Paramount tell a young writer: "You need to make yourself indispensable. And if you are just a mid-range guy, you are not going to be indispensable." So, when I go on staff, I want the producers and everyone else to think, Man, we cannot do the show without this guy.

There's so much competition out there. You have to work at the top of your talent. If you don't, you're doomed.

Dan Mazer

A writer's worst critic (besides himself, and perhaps a reviewer or two) is, typically, another writer. So when a writer receives a compliment from one of his peers, especially glowing praise, it can be the most satisfying validation of his career.

In the summer of 2006, a group of respected comedy writers, including Larry David and Garry Shandling, were invited to a private Los Angeles screening of a new movie called *Borat: Cultural Learnings of America for Make Benefit Glorious Nation of Kazakhstan,* co-written by Dan Mazer. As the closing credits rolled, perennial *Simpsons* scribe George Meyer purportedly turned to Apatow and said, "I feel like someone just played me *Sgt. Peppers* for the first time."

Borat went on to become a critical and box-office smash, and was even nominated for Best Adapted Screenplay at the 2007 Academy Awards (losing to Martin Scorsese's *The Departed*). But, despite all the excitement, Dan Mazer did not become an overnight celebrity. Reporting on his Oscar evening for the U.K.'s *Observer,* he wrote, "I was with the elite ... and I was being regularly shouted at to get out of the way of the elite. Despite lingering for twenty minutes nobody took my photo or spoke to me." Such is the life of a writer even at the top of his game.

From an early age, Mazer demonstrated a skill for getting people to say and do things they might not have under normal circumstances. When he applied to become a law student at Cambridge University in the early nineties, his academic record was far from impressive. It was only after a college interview—in which he bonded with a Cambridge official by discussing their shared desire to play *Hamlet*—that he was accepted. "If we had talked about law for even a second," Mazer later admitted to *U.S. News & World Report*, "he would have uncovered me as a fraud and never given me a chance."

Though Mazer and comedian Sacha Baron Cohen first met as pre-teens, they did not begin collaborating with one another until 1998, when Mazer was hired as a staff writer for *The 11 O'Clock Show*, a late-night satire showcase on British TV that launched the career of Ricky Gervais, among others. Mazer recruited Cohen, and the writing duo soon created Ali G, a functionally illiterate hip-hop poseur who interviewed unsuspecting politicians, celebrities, and anyone else foolish enough to chat with him. The character became so popular that he was given his own show, *Da Ali G Show*, which ran first in the U.K. in 2000 and then on HBO from 2003 to 2004.

Ali G was the first of Mazer and Cohen's characters to make the leap to the big screen, with the less than warmly received *Ali G Indahouse* (2002). As Mazer and Cohen soon discovered, the appeal of their creations was in the apparent spontaneity. *Ali G Indahouse* was too obviously scripted, and fans preferred a film that looked and felt more like "realistic" comedy, which is why the Borat movie ultimately became such a huge hit. Although the movie was carefully constructed, with very little left to chance, it played like pure improvisation.

It's a testament to Mazer's role as silent puppeteer that the audience never noticed the strings.

First of all, thanks for doing this.

Before we begin, let me just ask you: How has it been going so far? Has it been fun to interview humor writers? Are they nice? Or are they humorless in person?

It's been miserable. Just a hellish experience.

You're joking ... I assume. But do you know what I find with most comedy writers, or at least the ones I know? I think a lot of them genuinely might have some form of Asperger's. Most of the comedy writers I know are complete disasters socially. You put them in a room together, and it's just a car crash. It's horrible.

What other similarities have you noticed among comedy writers?

They have the same type of childhood. Not necessarily unhappy childhoods so much as lonely ones. I think humor writers have either unbelievably tumultuous upbringings, which forces them to go into their own heads and develop and hone their humor and their own unique points of view, or they have just the dullest childhoods, which also forces them to go into their own heads and create their own universes.

I have a friend who writes sitcoms in L.A. When he was growing up, his mother basically did not want to deal with him. He was a nuisance to her. So to minimize this nuisance she told him that all children went to bed at 5:30 in the afternoon. Until the age of eleven, he went to bed at 5:30, because he thought that's what all kids did. He would sleep for fourteen hours.

That wasn't my experience. My childhood was very mundane and suburban; you know, perfectly nice and absolutely no trauma. There was no horror, almost to a fault.

You were raised in the suburbs?

Yes. It was middle-class ... actually, it was not even middle-class. It had aspirations toward middle-class, but it was slightly below that. I grew up outside London, where it was just incredibly twee, incredibly reserved, and very English. I had a protective mother who would cocoon me to such a ridiculous degree that she wouldn't allow me to go outside and ride my bike, for fear that I would ride straight into a lorry and kill myself.

Was there a great pressure to succeed?

No. None. My mum would have been proud if I were a serial killer. She would've boasted that I'd murdered thirteen prostitutes and left no forensic evidence: "He's the best of the lot!" There was no pressure from my parents to achieve or to be anything. And they kept me very close. I'd go out with my parents often, and I'd spend all my time with them. I was very introspective.

But your style of humor is not inward or introspective at all.

It's weird. I was always popular and had a lot of friends, but I didn't go out with them often. I still don't go out much. But I do think it's vital to leave the house and meet people and explore life, to get inspiration for your work. The scourge of comedy is when it eats itself—when comedy writers watch sitcoms and think, Oh, you know, such and such a show is great. Let's do something a bit similar to that. I think that's wrong, really. I think the idea is to live life and take inspiration from that experience, as opposed to just getting inspiration from other artists and their work.

When did you first meet Sacha?

When I was 11-years-old, at Haberdashers' Aske's Boys' School, outside London.

What was the school like? Was it similar to the British school portrayed in Lindsay Anderson's 1968 movie _If.... ?_

[Laughs] No, unfortunately not. There was no machine-gunning from the rooftops. But it's funny: Our school was, without a doubt, the making of my and Sacha's senses of humor. The school was full of very smart, but very cowardly, Jewish boys. If we had gone to the local school or, say, a less Jewish school, we would have spent a lot of time sharpening our instincts for fighting and avoiding fights. But we were all such nice, weak Jewish boys who were afraid to fight that we would spend most of our time honing our verbal instincts. Instead of pugilism, we'd resort to puns.

A lot of like-minded, smart, young Jews emerged from that school. Matt Lucas, the writer and actor from [BBC's] _Little Britain,_ was there. There's a very famous British stand-up comic, David Baddiel, who went there. Basically, as far as I can work out, half of the British comedy community is made up of ex-Haberdashers'.

By the way, I have this other theory on comedy. Specifically, why so many Jews are funny. At the age of thirteen—the most awkward phase of any young man's life—we're spotty, we're ugly, we're either just pre- or post-pubescent, and we are forced to get up in front of a group of those nearest and dearest to us—people we care about most—and not only give this great performance in a foreign language but also make a speech and be the center of attention. It's a baptism of fire, this Bar Mitzvah. And if you can face that at that age, then everything is pretty much downhill.

That's the most hideous ritual and rite of passage you can possibly imagine. Forget jumping over goat herds in Mumbai.

It makes cutting off your foreskin with a bamboo stick look easy.

That's exactly it. It's just horrific. After that, everything seems like a breeze.

Did your Bar Mitzvah ceremony have a theme?

Yes, "Barely Able to Afford the Bar Mitzvah." Around three hundred people were invited. I blanked out while it was happening. It was like Vietnam. I suffer post-traumatic stress just thinking about it. And, obviously, the photos are still on display in the Mazer household—the velvet tuxedo and all that.

The shame and the humiliation of it all was incredible. And, of course, I didn't have a girlfriend to invite, and lots of my friends did have girlfriends. I had lied to all of my friends about what my life was like outside school: "Yeah, I've got loads of glamorous girlfriends that you don't know or haven't seen, and my family is very comfortably off with a great sense of style and wit." The trouble is, it's all laid bare there on that day. There's no hiding from anything. Everybody sees your life.

Did Sacha come to your Bar Mitzvah?

Actually, he didn't. He was a year ahead of me at school. We knew each other, but we weren't necessarily great friends yet. And I didn't go to his Bar Mitzvah, either. We became friends a little later and attended the same university, Cambridge.

I read a few interviews with your former classmates from Cambridge, and in some cases you and Sacha and the rest of your friends were described as an "arrogant bunch."

Oh, yes. I mean, if you put that combination of Jewish and middle-class and Cambridge together, it's not a particularly savory thing. There are immediately three strikes against you right there.

Basically, the Haberdashers' school gave us this kind of self-assurance that we were special and destined to make our marks in life. That was just exacerbated by going to Cambridge, where we were told that we were the cream of the country's intelligentsia. Even as you arrive, they tell you, "In this room, there will be two future prime ministers, one future chancellor of the Exchequer, and two Nobel Prize winners." You're singled out for greatness.

At that age, you have a combination of cockiness and self-assuredness anyway, where you think anything is possible. So, if people are further gilding the lily and telling you all those great things, who are you to resist?

I was in the Cambridge Footlights, which was the university's theatrical club. We produced plays and satiric sketches. Apart from being a breeding ground for comedy, I think it's also a home for the most arrogant and unpleasant kind of young people in Britain. Occasionally, television crews would come and film us for whatever reason. And my mum, as you can probably imagine, diligently videotaped me anytime I appeared on TV. To this day, I live in fear of anybody seeing those tapes. Every single time my wife goes to my mum's house, she begs to see them—but if she ever did see them, she would divorce me.

What, exactly, is on those tapes?

Sketches on British morning TV, or interviews. The Footlights have this great legacy at Cambridge, so people assumed that some of us would go on to become famous, and they wanted to be the first to interview the next generation of Germaine Greers, Peter Cooks, Eric Idles, and John Cleeses, all of whom graduated from the Footlights.

You know, we were given this legacy and we just assumed that it's the most natural thing in the world following in these footsteps. Why wouldn't you think that? And it's just horrible. I was the most arrogant, unpleasant young man.

Don't you need a bit of arrogance in life? Especially in show business?

I think you need it to a degree. And I think that's the reason why people from Cambridge are successes. It's not because they're funnier than anybody else; it's just that they've been given the belief that they're funnier. Therefore, they're more unshakable on their way up. And in a kind of natural selection, they're less likely to fall by the wayside.

Can you remember any of the sketches you wrote and performed at Footlights?

Most of my sketches were dreadful and involved me getting naked or wearing few clothes—possibly just a Speedo. But I do remember one good sketch: a friend and I played alternative-therapy paramedics. We'd deliver holistic medicine but in a very aggressive way, almost as if we were performing an EKG on a heart-attack victim. In this case, we rubbed juniper onto a pimple. I can't remember the end of the sketch, but I'm pretty sure I got naked or wore a Speedo.

Your original major was law, wasn't it? When did you plan to switch majors from law to acting?

Originally, my interest in law came about because I liked the TV show *L.A. Law.* This isn't an exaggeration. I thought I could be a dashing Harry Hamlin–esque lawyer out to save the day. But then, within about two hours of my sitting down in my first law lecture and learning phrases like "bona fide purchases," "third-party equities," and all the rest of it, it occurred to me that the law wasn't quite as sexy as the creator of *L.A. Law*, Steven Bochco, was making it out to be. I realized, Well, hold on. I don't like law. I like television, and I've made a terrible mistake.

At the end of my second year—it's a three-year course—I told my parents, "Look, I'm not going to be a lawyer. I'm going to try and make a career in comedy." I think my parents just ignored it and pretended it wasn't happening, because it was just too traumatic for them. They already pictured me in a barrister's wig and had probably already told their friends that I was a lawyer.

Did Sacha ever make it into Footlights?

He never actually did. That's the terrible, terrible thing. And that just shows you the weird, arrogant, cloistered world of Footlights. It was such a horrible clique, that Sacha was considered too outrageous for it.

Did he try out?

Yes, he did—a couple of times.

What were his sketches like?

Loud, shocking, and vulgar. They just completely pushed the envelope. And the thing about Footlights is that it's quite sedate and chucklesome and always clever and satirical and smart. And always self-mocking. Of course, Sacha would come in and just be massive and larger than life. And that just wasn't done.

I remember one sketch Sacha wrote that was set in a suit shop, and it ended with someone ejaculating. I think we've probably since done that for the Borat character. There's an old adage about humor writers and comedians: no idea is never *not* used somewhere at some time.

What was your first writing job after you graduated from Cambridge?

I did stand-up comedy for about a year. I realized that I was fine but I was never going to be great. I would watch stand-ups who were exceptional, and I'd think, Okay, they've just got the stand-up funny bone, and they can do it. Meanwhile, I'm just workmanlike. So, I gave up performing and haven't done it since. That whole performing gene immediately went away, and now I'm petrified of it. It's just horrible—that constant pressure to be funny.

So, a year after college, I became a TV researcher on a show called *The Big Breakfast*, which was a British morning show. I started writing for two puppets called Zig and Zag. They were like Muppets, but they had a saucy wit to them. They were aliens from the Planet Zog, whose spaceship had landed in the *Big Breakfast* studios, and they would interview celebrities. One morning, they interviewed the rappers Ol' Dirty Bastard and Method Man.

How did that go over?

It was amazing. Ol' Dirty Bastard and Method Man both couldn't speak, because they were so freaked out by these two puppets and a spaceship; they genuinely thought they'd gone into space. They were also not sober.

I did that show for about a year, and then I worked on one show called *The 11 O'Clock Show*, which was a British version of *The Daily Show*, except that we wrote a lot more jokes about cocks.

When I got the job at *The 11 O'Clock Show*, I brought Sacha in and we began working together. One of the characters he performed was Ali G.

How was the Ali G character created?

Sacha already had a rough version of this character, but we really honed Ali G on *The 11 O'Clock Show*.

Initially, the character of Ali G was a sort of upper-class guy who thought of himself as a gangster rapper. The direct inspiration for that character were these preposterous people who were rich but pretended that they were very street. Similar to the sons of bishops in Britain who pretend to be from the Watts neighborhood in Los Angeles. It was all slightly ludicrous.

So, that was the basis of the character, but he was very cartoonish and not very believable. The key change came about when we put Sacha on television with real people—political figures, academics, people in the news. That made him more real.

Do you remember the first time you witnessed this change?

Yes, it was amazing. Ali G was interviewing an economist, Dr. Madsen Pirie. The interview actually never aired, because we didn't yet have the legal expertise and our release wouldn't hold up. But it was an amazing eureka moment. We thought, Holy shit! It's funny, it's different, it's satirical. And it's intelligent and stupid at the same time. It was just this incredible mixture of *Candid Camera* meets brilliant sketch comedy meets stand-up comedy meets political entity. It was an amazing thing, and the idea that this trick, this kind of jukery, could work was a complete revelation.

So you knew right away that you hit gold?

Immediately. It's such a rare thing for something like that to happen. It really is similar to gold mining. You find little bits here and there, and you toil away, and you do things you think are funny, and you make a nice living, and people might talk about something you wrote.

But occasionally you might find a nugget. You just find this thing that is completely different and special, and you have a moment when you just know. At that point, you have to trust that instinct and really go with it.

Happily, the channel we were on, Channel 4 in Britain, did trust it, and here we are—years later—still chipping away at that one nugget.

You mention *Candid Camera,* but there seems to be a major difference. At the end of each *Candid Camera* bit there was always a reveal: "Smile, you're on *Candid Camera!*" Whereas with Ali G, there was never a reveal. The participants found out about the joke only when the show was broadcast.

We were really keen to maintain the integrity throughout. But on a personal level, none of us could bear the embarrassment of the moment when we said, "Ha-ha! It's a joke." It comes back to the cowardly Jew. We just thought: Oh, God, we've got to get out of here. We never wanted to tell them that it was a joke, for fear that they might punch us.

We also felt that if someone complained long and hard enough, the channel would then be unwilling to broadcast it. If people liked it and thought it was funny, Channel 4 would be more willing to take a risk on it.

Was there ever a satirical purpose to the Ali G character? Or was the purpose just to make people laugh?

I think it absolutely, definitely had an unrepentant satirical purpose. We chose the people Ali G interviewed for a reason. It was either because we found something pompous or objectionable about them, or we thought we could make a point about society through them. We didn't just find little old ladies on the streets or people who worked in shops. We chose everybody for distinct and definite reasons.

To play devil's advocate, what was pompous or objectionable about professors or teachers who were just average citizens? Are they as worthy of satirizing as, say, political or media figures?

The people that you talk about were prepared to believe a societal point. They were prepared to believe that someone as stupid as Ali G could exist. It says a lot about generations and people's perception of youth. Ali G is somebody who can ask self-evidently idiotic questions that a 4-year-old wouldn't ask. And yet, there are people so pompous and with such a jaded view of youth that they would believe a young man could be capable of that.

On another level, there's a whole culture of people who appear on television just to appear on television. It's like, Look how important I am.

Would this also hold true for someone like the astronaut Buzz Aldrin? Ali G asked him if he was jealous of Louis Armstrong being "the first man on the moon." He also asked if man would ever "walk on the sun." It was very funny, but where was the satire there?

I think we hold a mirror up to people. We don't edit things to make people look more stupid or ignorant. A lot of people come out of the Ali G interviews looking great.

Ali G interviewed General Brent Scowcroft, the former national-security adviser [for Presidents Gerald Ford and George H.W. Bush]. We thought Scowcroft was going to be this evil ex-military, ultra-right-wing despot. But he turned out to be the most kind, avuncular, sweet, and gentle man, even after Ali G confused "anthrax" with "Tampax." And he came out of the whole thing wonderfully. He responded to Ali G in a not-at-all-patronizing fashion and actually tried to engage with him.

My all-time favorite Ali G interview was with a left-wing politician in Britain named Tony Benn. He just completely stood up to Ali G: "You treat women with a great deal of disrespect. You call them a 'bitch.' It's just like animals. You're calling them animals!" You know, he didn't take any of Ali G's rubbish, and he came out fantastically well. As a result, he had a real renaissance in popularity amongst the younger generation. He was re-introduced as a liberal hero to a whole new generation.

I think there was a satirical point in every interview, in terms of how people dealt with these attitudes. It's such a shocking situation for people that it shakes them out of their usual persona of how they deal with interviews and how they deal with the media.

The race card has also made a lot of interview subjects incredibly nervous.

God, absolutely. We were always very evasive about what race Ali G was and what he was supposed to represent. That allows people to draw their own conclusions.

We once had Ali G do an interview at West Point military academy, in New York, and it's the only place we've ever been thrown out. We set up the equipment, and then Sacha entered the room dressed in this big yellow outfit. And they said, "Okay, who's going to do the interview?" And we said, "Right over there—Ali G." And then a blind panic came across the room, including generals and media people. They had a confab and then came back to us and said, "No. I'm sorry, we can't do this."

What made them so nervous?

I took one of the P.R. people aside and asked, "Why? What's the problem?" And he pointed to Ali G and said, "We don't want *this man* coming in here with his canary-yellow suit and his *Harlem* ways." And I thought, You know, that's just so unacceptable.

Unfortunately, we didn't catch this on camera, but it just spoke volumes as to how people react to this character. There's always a great moment we fail to catch, when people realize for the first time that the character who is going to perform the interview is Ali G. And it's the very last thing they expect. I think that that speaks to peoples' perception of both race and youth.

On the other hand, race also affects people in the opposite manner. I'm thinking of the time when Ali G asked a policeman, "Why are you treating me like this? Is it 'cause I black?" The policeman, who had just been rude to him, becomes quite respectful.

[Laughs] Exactly, yes. It's amazing. And there's another incident in which Ali G refers to himself as a black man. And the subject nods in agreement. You just think, Look at this guy, for crying out loud! Ali G is not black! People's reactions to race are so powerful and weird and twisted; it's just an amazing thing to see.

Were you surprised by Ali G's success?

Oh, hugely. It's one thing to do something funny, and that's great, and all you can do as a comedy writer is to write funny things and hope that people find them. But the idea that so many people found this character and he became such a phenomenon is incredible to me. The furor over *Da*

Ali G Show when the show first came out in Britain in 2000 was amazing. He was on the cover of every newspaper and magazine.

It was both making news and causing controversy. Eleven-year-old kids were quoting it, and the Queen Mother was watching it and doing the Ali G hand-sign. Prince William and Prince Harry wanted to meet Sacha. It was a genuine pop-culture phenomenon. And I think if you try to go out and create something like that, it won't happen; it was just a weird confluence of events. It was a Zeitgeist-y thing that happened that really captured the mood of the moment. And so it completely blew us away.

How did Ali G capture the mood of the moment? What came together at that point, do you think, to create this level of success?

I think it came about at a time in English society when there were these weird cultural shifts. I think the nineties was a time when England moved away from a society that was motivated, influenced, and led by class to one that was actually more influenced by pop culture. And at that crossroads, that's where Ali G exists. The people Ali G interviewed generally represented the upper class, and Ali G represented kind of a weird mishmash of cultures. It said a lot about where Britain was at that time and what Britain's identity was and where it was moving. It was a generational thing. It was a sea change.

Were reactions to Ali G different in America than they were in Britain? Not from viewers, but from participants?

Not really, no. I thought they would be different, but they're about the same, when it comes to race and everything else.

One difference is that Americans are generally more polite. That is, up until the point when they snap. And then when they snap, they snap instantly and fiercely. There's just this moment, and then the switch flicks, and that's it.

Are you referring to any episodes in particular?

The one incident I remember the most wasn't with Ali G but with the character Borat. This was in the *Borat* movie, in the scene that took place at the southern dinner party. And here's an interesting incident of race playing a factor: the people at the dinner were very hospitable, very patient, very nice. But as soon as they saw a black woman enter the house, they just flipped. That was the last thing we expected.

And, actually, it was incredibly annoying. One of the big regrets of *Borat* was that we had written a great joke beforehand that we weren't able to do. Borat was supposed to take the prostitute into the bathroom and have sex with her while the other guests were sitting at the table eating dinner. The camera was going to be left on them as they heard sex noises coming from the bathroom.

Borat was then supposed to come out halfway through the sex act to borrow $20 from someone at the table. But as soon as the black woman entered their house, that was it—they weren't entertaining any thought of Borat staying any longer. We just never imagined that that would be the case.

You don't think the dinner guests were more upset by the fact that she was a prostitute than that she was black?
Maybe a little of both, but probably more that she was black.

And yet, these dinner guests hardly batted an eye when Borat brought out a bag of shit.
[Laughs] True. It became a case of "We'd much rather have a bag of shit than a black woman in our house." That was effectively the point of that scene.

How was the Borat character created?
Sacha already had a vague idea for an Eastern European–type character, but it took a while to get it right. The first thing we did with the character was to go out to Cambridge university for a May Day event. We interviewed some Cambridge students, and as one walked away, I heard him say, "Oh, what is that—some kind of rubbish version of Ali G?" And I just thought, Oh, god.

I think we probably chose the worst place to go, since the Cambridge students were the biggest fans of Ali G. It was a dumb place to start a new character. But that's half of the process; finding the right people to interview.

We did get some good material out of the Cambridge shoot, but it was really a process of evolution. We started off knowing that we wanted Borat to be a misogynistic character. Then we brought anti-Semitism into the equation a couple of weeks down the line, and that became one of his defining characteristics. Then we brought in the wife character and the wife-hating element.

Borat has been analyzed perhaps even more than Ali G. Did you have a larger satirical purpose for this character?

Oh, yes. Completely. Borat, being from a foreign country, reflects the attitudes and the values of the society that he's going into. He comes into situations without preconceptions and, because of that, people are much happier to reveal themselves to him. So the idea is much less about Kazakhstan than it is about whatever place he happens to be in, whether it's America or Britain or wherever.

People let their guard down around Borat. They think, Here is this kind of simpleton who knows nothing about us.

Were you surprised by the success of the movie *Borat?*

Beyond anything I could have imagined. It was just ridiculous. We knew it was funny, but there are plenty of funny things that simply disappear into the ether. And it was a difficult film in terms of marketing. I really thought it would be one of those movies that would kind of crack the Top 10, and, hopefully, make its money back—maybe develop a cultish DVD following, like *Office Space* or *Spinal Tap*.

Terry Jones from Monty Python came to the premiere, and he turned to a friend of mine and said, "My God, I'm glad Monty Python came before and not after this." That was astonishing to me, that one of the Pythons would say that. You think, Monty Python is saying that we've kind of re-invented the form?

The movie was criticized for making Americans look ignorant and occasionally violent.

I found that most Americans were just incredibly polite. Americans were welcoming and hospitable, and I think that's one of the edifying things that comes out of the movie. At the same time, it also shows that there are still incredible prejudices and preconceptions, as well as outdated and tasteless points of view held by people in your country.

Were there any scenes that were left out of the movie because they depicted Americans in too negative a light?

There was only one scene that was so revolting that we didn't put it in. It's now a DVD extra. There was a man in Texas who talks about the "final solution." And I just found that so unpalatable that I thought, You know what? We can't. That ceases to be funny and entertaining; it's just horrible.

But it seems that most of the people with whom Borat deals with aren't necessarily racist or anti-Semitic. They just go along with his crazy antics in order to be polite.

Yes, that's true. But I think there is a vast amount of difference between somebody volunteering a certain viewpoint, and one going along with it out of politeness.

How about the owner of the antiques store? Borat came in and "accidentally" destroyed his merchandise. Would he be on the same level as an owner of a gun shop who was willing to sell a gun to Borat that was perfect for "killing Jews"?

In the former case, we found a Civil War secessionist's antique shop. We tried to find the most unsympathetic antique store we could. That didn't bother me, and he was compensated very nicely for all of the broken merchandise.

The one thing I feel was the least justifiable in the film were the bed-and-breakfast owners. They were the only people I felt a little tinge of regret over. Subsequently, they were fine with it.

But, you know, there were instances in which we stopped filming someone midway through an interview. If we felt they weren't worthy of Borat's treatment, then we just stopped shooting and left.

How often did that happen?

Not very often. We had excellent researchers to set up these situations who knew exactly what we were looking for and who made sure the people fit the bill effectively. So it didn't happen very often. In fact, when it did happen, we moved on quickly and found someone else who was more fitting.

Did you write the "Throw the Jew Down the Well" song that Borat performed in an Arizona bar on *Da Ali G Show?*

I helped to write it, yes.

That's an incredible scene to watch. When you see a woman in the audience making the sign of devil horns after Borat sings, "You must grab him by his horns," it's just stunning.

Borat sang that song at three different bars. We weren't sure whether it would be better for the audience to be horrified or to go along with it. It seems a ludicrous thing to think about now, because it's so obvious that it's more interesting to see an audience actually enjoy a song like that.

Were the audience's reactions different each of the three times?

One audience was horrified. I'm not even sure they were horrified by what he was singing as much as by the fact that here's this strange guy on a stage, pretending to play a guitar. The other time we shot it, the audience was sort of mixed. Some were angry, some couldn't have cared less. In the final version, the audience loved it.

It must make it easy for you as a comedy writer to know that a performer like Sacha will never break character.

That's an amazing thing. Even when faced with arrest, Sacha won't break character. We were shooting a TV segment one time in Sedona, Arizona, and Borat was interviewing this New Age guy who was channeling angels through an "energized" cast-iron pyramid. The guy asked Borat to take off his clothes and lie down on a cot. The guy then began to chant and channel the angels. But while the guy was chanting Borat began to masturbate under the sheets, at which point this serene and gentle angel-channeler did that thing that Americans sometimes do—he just snapped. He went absolutely crazy. He screamed something like, "Why are you masturbating in my pyramid? This is no way to treat angels! You have contaminated my aura!"

Angels hate that.

They do. They're real sticklers for masturbating in pyramids. So we literally ran out in a Scooby-Doo way, grabbed our clothes and sprinted to our van—with its engine running, of course. We always had the engine running, just in case something like this would happen. Sacha had managed to grab his underpants and jump into the back of the van. We drove off and collected ourselves, and ended up shooting a segment at a drum circle not far away.

All of a sudden, we heard police sirens. The police stepped into the drum circle and said, "We've had complaints. We understand that you were masturbating in public and that's an offense here in Arizona, punishable by six months in prison." The police separated the director, and then me, and then Sacha to hear our individual stories. So I gave my story. The director gave his. And then I went over to Sacha, expecting to hear him say, "Look, I'm really sorry. I was just doing this for a television show." And instead I heard, "I do not understand what you mean 'masturbates.'" It was like he was doing a bit, but with no cameras. There was no way this was ever going to be seen by anyone, but nonetheless he was remaining steadfast in character. The police were so frustrated by their inability to understand him that they just said, "Okay, okay. Look, if you should leave Sedona now, we won't press any charges."

How often have you and Sacha been pulled over by the cops?

I think on the *Borat* film alone the official count was thirty-six.

***Thirty-six* times?**

Thirty-six times. In a lot of cases, it was just because Borat looked Middle Eastern. The FBI came and found us in Dallas. There were five separate reports of a group of Middle Eastern men traveling around in vans.

I supposed it didn't help that Borat was also traveling with a grizzly bear chained in the back of the van.

No, that didn't help either. But Sacha stayed in character each of those thirty-six times.

What does it take as a performer to do what Sacha does? What constitution do you need to have to stand before a rodeo audience in Virginia and mangle "The Star-Spangled Banner," knowing full well that you're likely to be nearly killed?

It's like getting into a prize fight. It's extraordinary the bravery that Sacha has. It's an amazing combination of bravery, brains, and humor. I think some performers have one or two of those things. Some have brains. Some are funny. And some are daring. But Sacha has all three. And that's a unique combination.

Because he is out there exposed.

Completely, yes. He's the one who's going to take the first punch, even if you have all the bodyguards in the world surrounding you. And they're not going to stop him from receiving that first punch or, potentially, even worse.

Has Sacha ever been punched?

No. Actually, he hasn't. He has an excellent instinct for recognizing when eyes are narrowing—when people are readying for a punch.

The Bruno character once asked a neo-Nazi if he used moisturizer. The Nazi had already said, "One more question and I will hit you." Actually, it didn't require one more question. He just got up and was getting ready to hit Bruno. As he stood up, we saw that he had a gun, so we just ran out.

The character of Bruno really upset a lot of people, and I think it was due to the gay issue. That is literally *the* red flag to most Americans. They just go completely crazy. We were at a University of Alabama football game, and Bruno began to dance with the cheerleaders. The crowd went insane, and we were all chased out.

To a van with its engine running?

Yes, of course.

Was this filmed?

No. We were too busy saving our lives to film it.

What is your writing process like? Do you write up to the point of shooting?

Yes. Right up to the point of shooting. Also, right in the middle of shooting. If I think of a funny line or idea, I'll write it on a piece of paper. The interviewee would never be able to see it, because I surreptitiously walk around with a clipboard in my hand. But Sacha will take a look at the notes, and he'll either use the suggestion or not.

How much of these filmed segments are written versus improvised?

We usually write about 75 percent to 80 percent of any given segment beforehand. We predict how people will respond, and we write to those imagined responses. We effectively navigate the whole conversation.

There was a scene in *Borat* where he was asked about his religion, and he says that he worships "the hawk." We didn't foresee that question coming, but we had built up such a completely thorough background for this character—we had written so many jokes in preparation—that Sacha was ready.

We're ready for anything. Our preparation is immense for each character. You ask me any question about Borat and I'll answer it.

When did Borat lose his virginity?

Eleven.

To whom?

His sister.

What were Borat's grades in school?

He didn't go to school. He was working from the age of seven.

Who is Borat's favorite Beatle?

The dung beetle. He's never heard of the Beatles.

How deep is the background for these characters? How many pages are we talking about?

We probably have a file of scripts and jokes that extends to about three thousand pages. We write so much material for each three-minute segment.

And Sacha is brilliant at keeping it all sort of filed together in his head. He's able to access any joke instantly and brilliantly. There are jokes from years ago that Sacha will be able to call on.

Does he have a photographic memory?

No, he doesn't, but he has an amazing memory for jokes and character material. I think you'll find that most comedians never forget a joke. I think that's one thing that keeps them going—I never forget a joke I've written. I'm able to recall one from five years ago and insert it into whatever I'm writing.

How important are the other elements for these characters? For instance, how much thought goes into picking out the costumes?

A huge amount. The outfits have to appear authentic for the characters. But at the same time they have to appear humorous and interesting. We test hundreds of outfits. We'll say, "No, that hat is too much." Or, "No, that ring is a little too eccentric."

Of course, with Borat it's a little different, because he's worn the same outfit for six years and not washed it. So the decision to wear that suit is difficult only because of the smell.

The suit has never been washed?

Never been washed. Sacha goes to extremes with each character. If he's playing Borat, he won't shower the night or two before an interview. It's an amazing devotion to detail. Even Borat's underwear is authentic for the character. It has a Russian label on it, so that if Borat strips and somebody catches him, his underwear won't say "Wal-Mart."

The level of authenticity is incredible. Even the shit in the baggy was real in the Borat movie. With considerable debate, we realized it had to be real. We didn't want to take a chance and have them call Borat's bluff. We didn't want them to say, "Hold on, this is fake shit." Then, all of a sudden, our cover would be blown. So one of us had to muster up some shit for the bag.

Who in their right mind would have called your bluff on something like that?

We weren't taking any chances.

Who provided the shit? The key grip?

It wasn't. It was a guy who worked on-set named Jason.

Did he receive a credit for his role?

Actually, he did. If you look in the credits, it says, "Mr. Baron Cohen's Feces Provided by Jason Alper."

His parents must be very proud.

From what I heard, they are.

Do you think it'll be harder to pull off these types of stunts in the future?

It will be more difficult, but we'll somehow manage to keep it going. Hopefully, we will.

Do you think Hollywood is going to copy this style of comedy?

It's an incredibly difficult thing—pulling off these stunts. It has taken us nearly a decade to get it right. It's as if we're terrorists or guerillas going into a place with a plan and methodology that we've honed over many years. I think it's inevitable in Hollywood that people will try and imitate us, but I think they'll find it very tricky. We try really hard to keep all of our characters lovable and sympathetic.

After the movie *There's Something About Mary*, there were lots of imitations with that gross-out style of humor. But they were less successful, because they lacked sophistication and heart. So, from my point of view, it's possible that people may try and do what they perceive as our brand of comedy, but I think they'll miss whatever part of the alchemy and the chemistry that makes it work.

Do you think you'll have to keep upping the ante—audiences expecting more and more and you having to deliver?

Yes, of course. I mean you always do that, and every performer does that. That's what keeps you going.

Do you have any advice for the budding humor writer?

There are two things I would say are the key to comedy. One is character. All good comedy comes from character. In my mind, jokes are one thing, but without a convincing protagonist and somebody you care about, your comedy is on a path to nothing. All my favorite comedies are character-based, whether it's George Costanza in *Seinfeld*, David Brent in *The Office*, or Woody Allen. Character, character, character.

Number two is to have a voice. Have an opinion. Try and say something. I don't think it's enough to just write trifling jokes. You should have a point of view. Have the confidence in what you think. Don't let the executives or your own self-doubt dilute what you want to say.

I've enjoyed what you've had to say. Thank you.

[Laughs] That's just my British accent. I can fool anyone in coming across as brilliant. Meanwhile, I'm just spouting off absolute and complete nonsense.

Getting Humor Published in Magazines

Advice from editors at *The Believer, Esquire, The Onion, Playboy,* and *Vanity Fair*

1. You don't need an agent to pitch a humor piece to a magazine.

2. Do not explain why a piece is funny. It either is or it isn't.

3. Do not copyright your work. No one's going to steal it. This is just a sign of being an amateur.

4. No fancy fonts.

5. The font should be no bigger than 18-point. In other words, don't make it huge.

6. Do not try too hard—or even at all—to be funny in the cover letter. Jokes in the story are fine. Jokes in the pitch are not.

7. When a piece you write is accepted, and the editor has "a few small changes" that kill your idea, go along with them cheerfully. There are plenty of writers out there. Editors do not like dealing with those who are deemed "difficult." As you die a slow death on the inside, you'll have more and more bylines.

8. Submit your work to the editors who are lower on the masthead; the editor-in-chief is not going to be interested in what you're pitching. Associate editors are a good place to start.

9. Always e-mail. The subject line should read "Story idea" and then the name of the pitch.

10. Never call, unless you already have a relationship with the editor.

11. Writers sometimes talk about the awards they've won. Don't.

12. A good idea is a good idea, and it's easy to spot. So that should be the first part of the pitch. The credentials should be at the end—unless you're dropping the name of a mutual contact. Obviously, that should be up front. There's no shame in vouching.

13. Don't use Mr. or Mrs. [last name of editor here]. Weird. Arcane.

14. If the story idea came out of a writers' workshop, keep that to yourself.

15. If you're pitching a draft on spec, do not include footnotes, embedded headers, or formatted bullet points. Also, do not use boldface or underscore. Just submit a document with characters that form words and sentences.

16. The basic rules of grammar and punctuation should be followed. Specifically:
Learn the difference between *its* and *it's*.
Learn the proper usage of *who* and *whom*.
Learn the difference between *their* and *there* and *they're*.

17. As far as *The Onion* is concerned, you sometimes have to pitch headlines for years before one is ever bought.

18. Be confident but not obnoxious. Be persistent but not overbearing. Do not bombard a website with submission after submission. After four or five unsuccessful tries, it might be good to take a break for a spell and get more acquainted with what the site is looking for before trying again. Pluck is good, but not when it veers on throwing whatever you have against the wall and hoping it sticks.

19. Most editors say they want more humor in their magazines, but not many do. What they really want is humor they find funny and that *they* would write if they could, which they can't, or else there would already be humor in their magazines. Consequently, you have to adapt your sense of humor to meet their sensibilities. It's very difficult. So if and when you find an editor who shares your sensibility, marry, adopt, imprison, or do whatever it takes to maintain that relationship. The other approach is to skip the pitch and just write it. You don't want to waste a lot of time waiting for an editor to evaluate the pitch. Just write it—either the editor will laugh or not.

20. Every writer, no matter how famous, will at some point be rejected. Do not become overly frustrated if you too are rejected. On the other hand, there might be a lesson to be learned. Take that lesson and apply it to a future submission.

Merrill Markoe

Born in New York and raised in New Jersey, Miami, and the San Francisco Bay area, Merrill Markoe spent her youth reading Robert Benchley and Dorothy Parker, as well as watching W.C. Fields for his "bizarre word choices." She attended Berkeley and, after receiving a Master's in Arts, in 1973, she tried teaching art at the University of Southern California for a year but found herself restless. She began auditing a few scriptwriting and filmmaking classes and, in 1977, landed a writing job for *The New Laugh-In*, sans Rowan and Martin. The show, to the surprise of nobody, was a disaster, even with (or because of) cast members such as Robin Williams and former child evangelist Marjoe Gortner. (Not familiar with him? Rent the 1972 documentary *Marjoe*—please.)

When TV proved frustrating, Markoe tried her luck on the stand-up circuit in Los Angeles, mostly at the Comedy Store and the Improv, where she became friends with such promising (if still unknown) comics as Andy Kaufman and David Letterman. After a few wildly successful appearances on *The Tonight Show*, Letterman was given his own daytime talk show on NBC in 1980, and he brought in Markoe (whom he'd been dating since 1978) as his head writer. The show didn't last long, partly because Letterman and Markoe's humor didn't translate to an early-morning crowd, and partly because they nearly burned the studio down (more on that later). Within four months, the show was canceled.

In 1982, NBC gave Letterman another chance, and, more important, a better time slot. *Late Night with David Letterman*—which came on just after *The Tonight Show*, hosted by Letterman's idol, Johnny Carson—was a perfect fit, and, thanks largely to Markoe's indispensable collaboration, it became a unique and inimitable comic creation.

Six years later, in 1988, Markoe abruptly left the show. As she's written on her website, she'd "plumbed the depths of [her] ability to invent off-beat, comedic ideas for acerbic witty white male hosts in suits."

Markoe moved back west, to Los Angeles, where she had little problem finding work. She wrote for TV shows as diverse as *Newhart* (1988), *Moonlighting* (1989), and *Sex and the City* (1999), and appeared as a writer/reporter on HBO's *Not Necessarily the News* (1990) and Michael Moore's political-satire *TV Nation* (1994). She also discovered a writing life outside of TV, contributing comedic essays and columns for *Esquire, Glamour, People, Rolling Stone, Time, U.S. News & World Report*, as well as *The New York Times* and *The Huffington Post*. She probably made the biggest impact, however, with her humor books, which have included such critical and fan favorites as *What the Dogs Have Taught Me* (1992), *How to Be Hap Hap Happy Like Me* (1994), *Merrill Markoe's Guide to Love* (1997), *It's My F---ing Birthday* (2002), *The Psycho Ex Game* (2004), *Walking in Circles Before Lying Down* (2006), and *Nose Down, Eyes Up* (2008).

You once described yourself as "one of those 1960s art-student types." Were you in any way a radical?

I was certainly against the war in Vietnam. And I attended a Black Panther rally once—by myself, I might add. I was one of the few white people there. What I was doing there I cannot exactly explain, except that I attended almost every event that was within walking distance at the time. But, me being me, I always left early. I left every important cultural event of the sixties and seventies early. Name any one. Altamont? I left before the killing. I felt compelled to attend these events, but I never really liked big, angry crowds, or drugs, or the smell of patchouli. By the way, everything smelled like patchouli back then! Even sweaty, knife-wielding bikers who drank Ripple.

One of the few events I did not attend was Woodstock. I wouldn't have enjoyed being a part of that big, happy, muddy, mellow community. I probably would have been standing off on the sidelines somewhere, in my beloved paint-splattered clothes, complaining about the weather and the sound system, and making snide remarks about all the embarrassing free-form naked dancing. Talk about a place that probably reeked of patchouli. No question I would have definitely left early.

So it wouldn't be a stretch to say that you felt like an outsider in the sixties?

I'm very consistent; I've felt like an outsider every single decade. Some of it is because I struggle to control my tendency toward contrarianism. If I know there is something I am supposed to be doing or saying or wearing, I feel compelled to resist—particularly with creative endeavors, like writing. If I see an obvious punch line or plotline driving toward me, I can't help but make a sharp left turn into the unexpected. I don't like to replicate what I've seen done before—I don't like to give people what they expect. I think it's my job to come up with a surprising angle or to add some personal twist.

You first met David Letterman when you were doing stand-up in Los Angeles in the late seventies. Would you say that one of his strengths as a comic, even at the beginning of his career, was the degree to which the audience felt a strong rapport with him—that they always felt they were in on the joke?

Yes, correct. He was always a crowd pleaser. Plus, he always had Johnny Carson in mind as his model. Dave always knew how to connect with an audience, even from the very beginning.

Both you and Letterman started in the trenches of showbiz. Can you tell me about the first TV show you worked on together?

Dave and I worked on a 1978 CBS variety show called *Mary*, starring Mary Tyler Moore and featuring Michael Keaton. I don't know if it qualifies as the "trenches" of show business, but I do know it was canceled after three or four episodes, even though *60 Minutes* was the lead-in and Mary Tyler Moore was America's Sweetheart. The show was an uncomfortable combination of old showbiz-style variety mixed with a miscalculated attempt to include some of that wacky, absurdist comic sensibility that the kids liked so much from that new program *Saturday Night Live*.

For example, the *Mary* show did a parody of the Village People song "Macho Man" that had Dave and Michael Keaton dressed in L.L. Bean-catalog outfits, in a setting that was made to look like a scene from *Deliverance*. I forget where the comedy was supposed to be in all this. I do know the powers-that-be didn't realize that "Macho Man" was a gay anthem. I also remember vividly that Dave was in real agony about this bit of levity.

What was the second TV show you both worked on?

Leave It to Dave. It was a 1978 pilot for Dave's own talk show, which never actually made it to air.

From what I've read, this is a notorious show. The set resembled a pyramid, and Letterman sat on a throne.

Because this was at the very beginning of Dave's talk-show career, he was sort of afraid to assert his point of view. There were people he hired and put in charge who supposedly knew all about the right way to execute a talk show. Unfortunately, one of their goofy ideas was to have a pyramid shape on the set that contained built-in benches covered with shag carpeting for Dave and his guests to sit on. No boring old-school desk and chairs for us! Better to look like the interviews were taking places at a "carpeteria" trade show at the Luxor Hotel in Las Vegas.

The set was not even the worst idea that came down that particular pike. I remember that one of Dave's managers wanted the guests to make their entrances by sliding down a chute and then landing on a sea of throw pillows. But even more vivid is the memory of how little blood there was in Dave's face when he was presenting the news to me. Somehow we succeeded in getting that idea shit-canned.

How did your next project, *The David Letterman* Show, come about? This morning show, a precursor to *Late Night,* was on NBC for only a short period in the summer and fall of 1980, but it became very influential with comedians and humor writers.

Around this time, Dave began appearing on *The Tonight Show,* and I was helping him come up with comedy material for those appearances.

Do you remember any of the jokes you wrote for him?

Here's one: "The commercial for Alpo dog food boasts that Alpo is superior because it contains 'All beef and not a speck of cereal.' My dog spends his days going through the garbage and drinking out of the toilet. Something tells me he might not mind a speck of cereal."

So Dave was getting a very good response from his *Tonight Show* appearances, and it didn't take long for NBC to offer him his own morning talk show. Ninety minutes a day. Live. At 10:00 A.M. This prospect seemed less appealing to me than it did to Dave, but by now I was in over my head with regard to both of Freud's two big areas: work and love. So, I just kept playing along.

Steve O'Donnell—a longtime writer for Letterman—once described the show's staff as those who really liked television but also kind of hated television. Was this true for you?

Yes, absolutely. I was particularly sick of seeing everyone on television doing that bigger-than-life, fraudulent, full-of-shit television persona— which was mainly how the shows all worked then. I welcomed the idea of a host being caught having real reactions to odd situations.

A lot of the segments on the morning show later appeared on *Late Night*. Can you tell me how "Stupid Pet Tricks" began? Was it meant to be a one-time deal only?

One immediate task—when we were determining how to construct a daily format—was to create segments that could be repeated. Since there was a horizon of future shows spreading out in front of us that seemed to stretch into infinity, it seemed to call for free-form thinking. Dave and I had two dogs and we wanted to do something with animals besides just having the guy from the zoo bring on the pygmy marmosets. I remembered how in college my friends and I would be hanging around in the evenings, talking and drinking. One form of constant entertainment was to put socks on this one dog. Everyone I knew did some version of a silly thing like that with their pets, so we ran an ad to see if we could pull a segment together like that.

When it succeeded, we mutated that idea into "Stupid Human Tricks." We also considered "Stupid Baby Tricks," but pulled the plug because— based on what we were seeing in the other two categories—we were afraid it would encourage child endangerment.

Were you responsible for "Viewer Mail"?

More or less. When we started "Viewer Mail" on the morning show, originally the idea was meant as a kind of parody of something *60 Minutes* was doing, where they'd show a mailbox and a magnified fragment of a letter. Their letters always commented on something of importance: "Regarding your piece on nuclear disarmament, I just wanted to say …"

I thought it would be funny to show the mail *we* were receiving, which was mostly pages full of scrawled non sequiturs from deranged people. By the time the show re-appeared at night, this had evolved into little sketches that played off the content.

Do any other particular moments stand out from the morning show?

It was pretty much nonstop bizarre particular moments. One highlight was when we decided to celebrate the 50th wedding anniversary of a couple from Long Island named Sam and Betty Kotinoff. We selected them from a group of people who wrote in and volunteered. Our plan was to show snippets of this big party throughout the regular broadcast, and we would check in with them to see how everything was going.

For music, we hired the Harve Mann Trio, a wedding band dressed in tuxes. We also hired a very flamboyant decorator and party planner to do the catering. He not only brought in ice sculptures, but he also staged a lovely finale, where synthetic rose petals would float down from the ceiling while all the revelers held sparklers and swayed in contented delight. So it came to pass that, as Dave signed off, the rose petals floated down and met the sparklers and created a number of small fires. As the credits rolled, the show ended with the Kotinoff family stomping out flames as stage-hands rushed in with fire extinguishers. Wafting from behind the clouds of smoke was Harve Mann still singing his closing song, "Can't Smile Without You." Dave and I were really mortified until we saw the tapes. Then we couldn't stop laughing.

What did you hope to achieve with this morning show? Did you feel that it was time for a talk show that reflected your own sensibility?

Yeah, both Dave and I felt that way. But Dave had more respect and passion for the history of TV talk shows than I did. Besides his love for *The Tonight Show*, Dave's favorite role model was always the old Steve Allen *Westinghouse Show* [1962–1964], which had elements of stunts, character pieces, and audience interaction. I liked some of Steve Allen's work as well, such as when he would jump into a vat of Jell-O or cover himself with tea bags so he could be dunked up and down inside a giant aquarium by a crane to make an enormous container of tea.

But to be honest, I never much liked *The Tonight Show with Johnny Carson*. Dave used to say that Johnny Carson seemed like the hip uncle whom he wanted to please. But to me, that show was a place where they never booked any smart women. I couldn't help but view it through the prism of my U.C. Berkeley Art School experiences, which boiled down to a simple "fuck that plastic showbiz shit."

What smart women in particular were missing from *The Tonight Show?*

Any smart women, of *any* stripe. Writers, reporters, producers, filmmakers, artists, scientists, eccentrics. No comediennes ever appeared on that show besides Joan Rivers and Phyllis Diller. Certainly none of the comediennes my own age appeared on the show.

On *The Tonight Show*, women were either amazingly glamorous actresses or they were booked to create cleavage-related humor and flirt with Johnny. I guess there must have been exceptions I am not remembering—the opera singer Beverly Sills, for example, or Carol Burnett.

But, as a whole, there never seemed to be any cerebrally oriented female content. I thought of it as one more example of the old showbiz sensibility that I was so sick of. Johnny reminded me of Hef in *Playboy After Dark*. Dave could look at Johnny and see a guy with whom he could joke and communicate. I would only see the kind of guy who would want no part of me and my kind.

Even though the morning show won two Emmy awards, it was still cancelled in October 1980. Why?

I remember a meeting where NBC executives showed me charts and graphs about what did and did not appeal to audiences when they tested the show. They said the audiences were okay with the idea of "Stupid Pet Tricks," but that they would have preferred to see the segment re-made with trained animals. I said, "You mean, like a horse that can count?" And they looked at me solemnly and nodded "yes." They also had research that made it clear that *Late Night* audiences did *not* want to hear live music.

To make things even more complex, Fred Silverman, then the head of NBC, had requested that we hire "a family" for the show, by which he meant regulars along the lines of a band singer, an astrologer, a beauty expert, a funny announcer, and an eleven-year-old fiddle player. Silverman's role model was the old *Arthur Godfrey* variety show, which none of us had even seen. Silverman saw Dave as a young Arthur Godfrey. Dave did not see Dave that way at all.

We pretty much ignored Silverman's edicts—at our own peril. Almost immediately, the show was cut from ninety minutes to sixty. After that, it was just a hop, skip and a jump to zero.

I remember fighting with executives about what women did and did not want to watch in the morning. I argued, "Don't tell me about women! I'm the *only* woman here!" But, of course, I was so much weirder than the majority of women in the audience. I had no idea.

If NBC didn't understand the morning show, why did they then give Letterman and you the opportunity to create *Late Night*, sixteen months later, in February 1982?

By then, it was a case of them having to line up an eventual replacement for Johnny Carson. And Johnny really liked Dave. Dave was a frequent guest host of that show and always a serious contender.

Were you surprised when Dave was passed over for *The Tonight Show* slot when Jay Leno took over in May 1992?

I guess so. I must confess that this was right after Dave and I broke up, so I wasn't paying a lot of attention to the dramatic arc of this particular opera. In fact, I was purposely doing everything in my power to be paying as little attention to it all as I possibly could.

You seemed to hit your stride so early with _Late Night_. I'm thinking in particular of the remotes, in which a camera would follow Dave as he wandered around New York.

Those remotes started on the morning show, so we had been doing those for a while. They came out of our mutual fascination with local news. I used to take the camera out into the hall and around the building and down the street and shoot things I thought were funny, like weirdly worded signs, misspellings, puzzling front-window displays, disputable business claims. I did a lot of research for these excursions by reading the yellow pages.

One of the early remotes I remember very fondly was "Just Bulbs."

The premise of the "Just Bulbs" remote was pretty much Dave acting as bratty interloper. We went into a store in Manhattan called Just Bulbs. Dave, very innocently, asked something like: "So, what all do you have here?" To which the woman working in the store replied, "Bulbs. We have every kind of light bulb you can imagine. Colored bulbs. Clear bulbs. Flickering bulbs. Every size and shape." To which Dave, after nodding politely, responded, "Great. And what else do you have?" And it kept going like that until the woman started to get irritated. At which point, in the editing of the piece, we switched to the second segment that took place at a store called "Just Shades." "So, what all do you have here?" "Just shades." "Yes, but what else do you have?"

I still am not sure why that strikes me as so funny. But it still makes me laugh—asking really obvious questions and then pinning people to the wall with them. Maybe it's my background. That was what it was like talking to my parents.

How much of these remotes were written versus improvised by Dave?

Before we hit the street, the premises were carefully constructed and equipped with a bunch of relevant questions that I felt predicted a pretty good outcome. A good premise required some idea of what you expected everyone to say. But Dave was free to add and subtract and ad-lib whatever he wanted. Then, in post-production, I would go through all the footage and create a script. Somehow it would eventually be arranged into a coherent whole. I was very scrupulous about never putting words in anyone's mouth except for David's, via voice-overs. Everyone else was free to respond honestly to whatever stupidity we were hurling their way.

There's a story that after the initial success of _Late Night_ the writers for Johnny Carson were told to come up with more "Lettermanly" material. If that's true, it's a major compliment.

I remember that phase, when Johnny was doing bits that looked like our show. It was weird and kind of sad. That style of humor didn't fit him, and it didn't look right on him. It was as if Tony Bennett or Barry Manilow suddenly decided to start recording rap songs. Or when Pat Boone was doing heavy metal.

When we began _Late Night,_ Johnny had the right to approve Dave as keeper of the time slot after _The Tonight Show._ And with this privilege came a couple of basic rules that we inherited on day one. We were told, "There cannot be an announcer/sidekick who sits down to chat with the host." Also, Dave was told not to do an opening joke monologue.

Johnny didn't want Dave to do a joke monologue to open the show?

No. He thought the monologue was _The Tonight Show'_s distinctive signature.

Is this why Dave made his monologue shorter and called it his "opening remarks"? Was this in response to Johnny's request?

Yes, exactly.

How did Dave feel about this?

I think it was initially confusing for him. Dave was a stand-up comedian.

And what were your thoughts about this at the time, being less a fan of Johnny than Dave?

I thought, If they don't want us to imitate _The Tonight Show_ too closely, big deal. _The Tonight Show_ consisted, as far as I could tell, of a few distinct elements that they repeated endlessly: the monologue, the guests sitting beside a desk, Johnny's several repeatable characters, and a segment called "Stump the Band." That left us with, oh, let's see ... about a million other things we could do.

There was a real explosive, subversive nature to those early *Late Night* shows, specifically with the frequent appearances by Andy Kaufman, comic-book writer Harvey Pekar, and Chris Elliott.

That was the hoped-for idea. In the beginning, I used to make a lot of noise about booking a different kind of talk-show guest. And I made quite a lot of those delightful noises for a number of months until I realized how hard it was to actually book a nightly show. Guests were always backing out. You had to find credible replacements right before airtime. As Peter Lassally, the executive producer of *The Tonight Show*, once explained to me, "There comes a point in the week where Charo starts to look really good to you." So I lightened up about it after that.

Chris Elliott, however, wasn't exactly a subversive when we met him. He was about nineteen and giving tours of Rockefeller Plaza. Dave and I were both fans of his father, Bob Elliott [of Bob and Ray], and we liked Chris instantly. So Dave hired Chris with no idea of a job definition for him. Chris's first task was to make and then post FREE FLU SHOT signs all around the 30 Rock building. I remember seeing one of these really sad little hand-printed signs Scotch-taped next to the elevator buttons.*

As for Andy Kaufman, he was a big fan of the morning show and appeared on it quite a few times. He came back to my office early on and told me he liked what we were doing. I remember we once had a first-grade class on the show to perform their Columbus Day pageant. Andy really loved that sort of thing.

How well did you know Andy Kaufman?

He was one of the first people I met when I moved to L.A. in 1977. I had seen him on *Saturday Night Live* and related to him in a big way, because his pieces seemed so art school—esque to me. So we hung out a little. He had started to do a weekly midnight talk show at the Improv in L.A., which he was calling "Midnight Snacks." At that time, Andy was calling me his "writer," which I found flattering, since I hadn't yet managed to get myself hired for real as a writer anywhere else. But no matter what anyone tells you, no one really wrote for Andy Kaufman. He was a one-man band, his own *force majeure*. You could agree with him, maybe say something like, "You should fill the cup with Pepsi instead of Coke," and possibly he would consider that. Or, just as likely, you wouldn't be able to tell if he'd even heard you.

My favorite element of Andy's pretend talk show was the set itself. He had his desk mounted on a platform that placed him a good five feet above his guests. That was pure Andy, and it still strikes me as the most brilliant and completely hilarious vision of the talk-show format I have ever seen.

Dave's famous comment about Andy was, "When you look into his eyes, you get the feeling that someone else is driving."

Someone else *did* seem to be driving. Dave was right. But that someone else was Andy—and Andy knew exactly how to do his comedy with that other guy. He was always in control. That's why Dave really loved having Andy as a guest on his show. He knew Andy would only go so far and no further.

It seems that quite a few *Late Night* guests tried to imitate Andy's bizarre behavior. I'm thinking in particular of the infamous Crispin Glover interview in July 1987, when the actor, on the show to promote his movie *River's Edge,* wore a blond wig and platform shoes and performed a karate kick, nearly missing Dave's head.

I seem to recall that Dave was a little concerned about getting kicked in the head. But as a rule, Dave didn't mind any attendant brouhaha inflicted by guests as long as he thought the elements of chaos were being handled and controlled. That was why he loved having Andy as a guest. Andy's little circus was always being controlled by Andy.

How picky were you and Dave with material from the show's writers? What was the acceptance rate for jokes? I've been told that it was very, very low.

Dave and I had a very intense collaboration that went on day and night when we lived together. But, in most cases, he only liked a portion of the jokes or ideas anyone suggested. Your odds were slightly better if Dave was in on the original thought. Don't forget, Dave started out as the writer of his own material.

Were there any writing rules on *Late Night?* Anything that you wanted the writers to avoid, such as comedic clichés?

We wanted them to avoid *every* comedic cliché, unless the point of the piece was to showcase how something was a cliché. We didn't like anything maudlin and we didn't want anything with a sentimental core—unless we were trying to make fun of coy, manipulative sentiment. Otherwise, we were up for anything we thought was interesting and funny, and anything that had an original or authentic quality to it.

Dave and I both really liked words. That was actually the first bond I felt with him. Seriously, I remember admiring his choice of nouns. So when we hired writers, we looked for people who liked to use language very carefully.

Why weren't there more women writers for Letterman over the years? There has only been a handful, including you.

I was also guilty of not hiring women in the few batches of writers I hired. But in my own defense, this was for a very particular reason: it was my task to hire writers who could replicate Dave's voice. I was kind of hiring Dave replicates. We were a new show, and I didn't feel like I had any margin for error. I needed to hire people who could write for Dave the way Dave would have written for himself if he'd had the time. I always felt like I had a gun to my head down there in the bunker. I also didn't receive very many submissions from women. I was just as picky in hiring men, but their odds were better just based on numbers. I was looking for writing that was a very specific combination of cerebral and silly. The funny submissions I did get from women were often funny in ways that didn't fit. I didn't need writers who could create hilarious characters. Dave didn't do characters. I needed a very specific attitude, use of language, and sensibility.

I had Dave's voice all analyzed and figured out, because not only did I live with him, but I was preoccupied with creating a show that would please him. Nowadays we call that sort of thing "co-dependence." But in those days I simply called it "being head writer."

Did you have any idea at the time the influence *Late Night* was having on pop culture?

No. None whatsoever.

Really? No idea?

No.

In the eighties, especially the mid-eighties, the show was a sensation. It was featured in practically every major magazine—from *Rolling Stone* to Time. Were you in the eye of the hurricane, so to speak?

Dave always felt we were on the verge of going down with the *Titanic*. He always felt that we were doomed because our ratings weren't good enough. Sometimes I would argue that he was being hysterical and pessimistic, but I couldn't win those arguments because I also kind of believed him. How did I know if he was right or wrong? He seemed very certain, and I had no idea.

If we were ever experiencing success, I definitely missed it.

Can you appreciate the show more now?

No. Although this interview is kind of making me sound interesting—even to myself.

Why did you leave *Late Night* in the late eighties?

How to phrase this for public consumption? My personal relationship with Dave was becoming unmanageable. So I had the uniquely unfortunate circumstance of having to back down from a position of power to a position of limited power, all in a misguided attempt at fixing the relationship. Thus, I went from being the head writer to other, lower-profile tasks, such as segment-producing all the remotes. There were such indistinct boundaries between the personal and the professional that none of it really worked out the way I meant for it to. My addled, little brain then imagined, Maybe if I don't work on the show at all and just pursue other things, everything will be okay.

In interviews, you've described "reconnecting" with your writer's voice after you left _Late Night_. How did you manage to reconnect? And how was it lost to begin with?

A good collaboration is a melding of sensibilities, and my voice was only lost in the same way that fans of _Seinfeld_ probably couldn't sort out what was Jerry Seinfeld's voice and what was Larry David's. It all became more clear when _Curb Your Enthusiasm_ appeared, and you could see, "Oh, that's Larry David's." In our case, this was Dave's show, not mine. Dave had his name in the title of the show. He was entitled to be the final arbiter of what material got on.

But when I started writing essays and articles and I didn't have to seek Dave's counsel or endorsement, I could finally hear my own sensibility. Now there was no one to please but myself. That was a really delightful feeling. Next thing I knew, Viking [Publishing] asked if they could publish a collection of my magazine columns. That became my first book, _What the Dogs Have Taught Me_ [Viking, 1992].

Since you left the show, you've written seven books, both fiction and nonfiction, and have contributed numerous articles to magazines and websites. Do you find writing for print as rewarding as writing for TV?

It's less exciting, but I guess it is more rewarding artistically. A piece of writing on the page is entirely by you. An editor gives you notes designed to make it be as much about your style as it can be. That rarely happens in TV.

I should probably add that it's about one-tenth as rewarding financially—at least for me. You can win an Emmy for a script that has your name on it and have only contributed a couple of lines. A friend of mine calls TV writing the "golden handcuffs." You get hooked on the idea of making big money as a reasonable and worthy trade-off for lack of artistic control. So you stop worrying about whether you are meeting your own needs for self-expression and just focus on the size of your bank account.

Some of the experiences you write about in your books are down-right frightening. I'm thinking in particular of the chapter in *Merrill Markoe's Guide to Love,* when you consulted a "love channeler" to help find and keep a boyfriend.

That was very spooky. I showed up at this love channeler's apartment, and I knocked on the door, which opened to reveal a man sporting a Captain Kangaroo haircut and dressed in an ill-fitting Snoopy T-shirt. To make it more perfect, there was harp music playing on the stereo. *Music to Be Strangled By.*

When I see weird ads in the paper, or things where people make strange claims, I think, Bingo. Perfect! I can get some great comedy from this!

But then I arrive at the place, all by myself, and no one even knows I went there, and I can hear that scary narrator inside my head intone, "It all started out as a prank...."

When I was a TV reporter for KCOP in Los Angeles, in the early nineties, I loved to cover weird events. I was the only reporter to attend the opening of a yogurt franchise Mickey Rooney was somehow associated with. Mickey was *not* amused by my questions. He turned hostile and started making fun of my stammer. And then he stared at me with the cold, dead eyes of a chicken and said, "Look, honey, don't mess with me. I can get really nasty, and I don't want to have to do that, because I love you too much." I remember thinking, Whew! Okay, I'm definitely glad that you love me, because I'd hate to see how you'd be acting if you didn't.

What sort of questions were you asking him?

"How did you get into the frozen-yogurt business?" "Is this an old Rooney-family recipe?" "Is this connected to Mickey Rooney's Weenie World?"

Mickey Rooney's *Weenie World?*

It was a chain of restaurants that Mickey once owned that specialized in Weenie Whirls, round hot dogs on a hamburger bun, with mustard in the central hole. I remember seeing one of the last ones on Long Island when I was out researching remotes for Dave's show. I always planned a visit but never got around to it. Mainly, I was attracted to the term "Weenie World," as any self-respecting person would be. How can you not love a place called Weenie World?

Awkward segue: Are you insulted when certain critics invoke the adage that women aren't as funny as men?

It is very annoying, especially since it is so patently untrue. I don't understand what is wrong with these guys. I assume we are talking about Mr. Christopher Hitchens, whom I rather admire, and Mr. Jerry Lewis, the man who brought us my very favorite horrible movie, the exquisitely painful *Hardly Working* [1981]. It almost seems beneath me to argue this point. It would be kind of like saying, "People should not own slaves." For the record, there are a lot of funny women around these days. A lot. *Many*.

I think a sense of humor is something that certain people take on as a protective adjustment to the difficulties of childhood. And when it seems to be working, it's a hand that they keep playing. I can tell in just a couple of seconds if I am going to find someone funny. It has nothing to do with gender. It's all attitude and the right kind of brain cells.

It may also be an intimidation factor. If a man can't keep up with a woman who's faster and more quick-witted and who has a higher "humor I.Q.," he might lash out.

This is certainly true. Our culture as a whole is very ambivalent about funny women. But, then again, they do let us get driver's licenses and learn to read and wear shorts, so I guess, relatively speaking, we shouldn't really complain. I'm hopeful that the Tina Fey/Amy Poehler surge has turned the opposing army around once and for all.

What do you not find funny?

Comedy with a maudlin center is the opposite of funny. Anything that is meant to trigger both a laugh and bring a tear to the eye has departed the comedy arena for me. Like in a catalog I just received that sells a sign that reads: "Who needs Santa when you've got Grandma?!" Same goes for the apron that says, "Pinot Noir Envy."

Any other comedy pet peeves?

Well, I hate puns. I never find them funny. To me, they are all about, "See what a clever boy or girl I am." I can't even make the edges of my mouth curl up a little when someone puns at me. I wind up glaring at them.

I also hate jokes that are made up ass-backward. Someone thinks of a clever piece of verbal gymnastics and then takes the long way around to justify it with a complex setup. The example that comes to mind is a joke that ends with the punch line like "carp-to-carp walleting." Also, for the most part, I would rather not even read forwarded Internet jokes.

I hate stock improv-group characters that seem to be based not on observations about people but on other famous and beloved stock improv-group characters. Two that come to mind are the theoretical Sean-Penn-in-*Fast-Times-at-Ridgemont-High* surfer dude and the hair-tossing Valley Girl. If a prototype of these people *ever* existed, the people now perpetrating the offense never met them. There's a certain kind of old-timey reverend character that is also in this category. And a certain kind of seventies lounge singer. How many of these can we pretend we find amusing?

This gripe includes hating anecdotes about any kind of stereotypes that don't seem specific enough to have ever been real human beings. And my complaint cuts across all racial and gender lines. Real human beings don't behave in big broad strokes. They behave with tiny, exacting, site-specific details. *Your* stupid McDonald's employee should be different than *mine*.

I hate any clichés. Comedy clichés are as big an offense as Hallmark-card clichés, because in both cases they are trying to manipulate you into a response with something prepackaged. If you're going to get a response from me, I want to hear an individual point of view. If you do an impression, I don't want to see another version of the same film clip everyone else is using. I don't want to see the *same* Jewish mother or black church lady. I want to see the one *you* know.

I hate plots that hinge on amazing coincidences or overheated misunderstandings. I don't like to see life remade as too perfect or adorable.

I hate people who talk in buzzword cues they've heard other people use and now think amount to humor shorthand. The example that comes to mind is: "He gives good phone."

I hate anyone who is wise beyond their years. I don't mind precocious children if they come as a side order with W.C. Fields.

I don't much like parody songs ... the Weird Al genre. And I find the category even more offensive when they're supposedly political. Like "Hark! The Harried Republicans Sing." Hopefully, there is no such song. I don't mind funny songs. Or political songs. But, such as with everything else I've mentioned, I want original thought.

And as a rule I hate tit jokes. I think every reasonably funny version of the average tit joke was wrapped up and put to bed about 1720. Same with double entendres. I've seen all the melon and hot-dog confusion I need for one lifetime.

How about things that *do* work for you? Any advice for novice writers—technical tricks you've found helpful?

Where rewriting is concerned, I always think, The bologna rises to the top.

When I am in the midst of writing, I tend to hear my words in a sort of sing-songy verse and chorus that's almost musical. But once I put the work down for a while and then return to it, I have forgotten the melody I was using and I can read what I have written with the ears of a stranger. You need to find a way to get enough distance from yourself to effectively edit and rewrite your own work. And I do a lot of editing and re-writing. A *lot.*

Don't be overly attached to every syllable and detail of your work. Your commitment is to making the *whole* thing work. So you have to allow yourself to throw out sections you may love if they block the flow or seem unnecessary. Tell yourself you can save them and use them elsewhere later. Even if you never do, lie to yourself if it makes it easier.

On a related topic, take a moment to imagine how you will feel when your work is published. Anything that you think will make you uncomfortable or ill at ease ... get rid of it. Lose anything that makes you cringe, anything you think is questionable. If you are writing about someone you know in real life and are worried that you are being too mean or that maybe you will feel bad and regret it, change or get rid of it. But, at the risk of confusing you entirely, I have also found that sometimes the pieces I write which cause me the most pain and embarrassment are the pieces others like best. Sometimes it is by working through areas of personal discomfort that you stumble to where your own growth is taking place.

You have to allow your first draft to be really bad. Just throw a lot of things out there and get it on paper. The hardest part of the process is just getting a first full draft. The fun part, if any of it can be considered fun, is when you start to improve the piece through the editing and rewriting. That is definitely where the art is; knowing what to save, what to throw out, what to embellish.

In the end, nothing works except sitting down to write. And then, even sadder, actually writing. Robert Benchley wrote a funny piece called "How to Get Things Done" [*Chips Off the Old Benchley,* 1949]. In it, he explains his premise: "Anyone can do any amount of work, provided it isn't the work he is supposed to be doing at that moment." He describes putting up shelves, clipping magazines, sharpening pencils. You don't get any writing done, but you get all this *other* work done. At the very least, it's not a complete waste of time.

You have a very strong and distinct comedic voice. How does a young writer of humor find his or her own voice?

One easy way would be to sit down and write a bunch of material that includes the personal pronoun "I." Even if you keep a journal, you are hearing your own voice.

Another way would be to begin to analyze *why* you like what you like. When you can isolate and put your finger on the mechanism you can try to duplicate it in an original way and then apply it.

Count on the fact that, yes, almost everything has been done before, but not necessarily informed with your perspective and details that will make it different.

You just used the word "mechanism." What does that mean exactly?

Everything has an underlying structure, some kind of a formula, and leave it to me to analyze and identify it. I do that with everything I see or hear. I also do it with everything I read. Consequently, I drive very abstract people nuts.

You see a piece of written work as having structure—like, say, a blueprint or a machine would?

You don't? I see an underlying structure in everything, everywhere on the planet—including random remarks, bad behavior, and this interview.

In that case, can you see a good way to end this interview?

Yes, but we'd have to start from the very beginning.

Famous Last Words (of Advice)

David Rees, cartoonist, *Get Your War On, How to Sharpen Pencils*

I made cartoons off and on my whole childhood. Then, later, after college, I had a bunch of temp jobs in Boston where, if there was nothing to do, I would just make cartoons using Microsoft Powerpoint, and I started selling these cartoons on my own, on consignment. The first good career decision I ever made was when I started selling a comic on consignment to a comic book store in Boston called The Million Year Picnic. They were selling a ton of copies. So I asked if I could take the store owner out for coffee to just pick his brain about self-distributing comics, how it all worked. I knew nothing about it, really. And he recommended other stores around the country that he thought would be good.

Something that's really important—and that I should definitely do more of—is to ask people for advice. Just very straightforwardly say, "Can I buy you a beer or a cup of coffee and pick your brain about this particular thing?" Not something like, "How do I become funny?", or "How do I become a cartoonist?", but more like, "I'm in this particular situation, and here's what I want to do next. How do I do that?" Most people are flattered to be asked specific questions as long as they don't feel like it's this huge thing, like: "Read twenty jokes and make them funnier for me!"

I would mail book-sellers a sample comic and say, "My cartoons sold this many copies in this store, and this many copies at this store, and I would love to send you some and see how it does in your store." And I was my own distributor. I did all my own invoicing, all my own printing, shipping, all that stuff. And then after 9/11, I started *Get Your War On*, just as a personal project, and then it was just one of those web things that people forward around. That was a weird situation. I was very lucky in a way, because I made something for myself that a lot of people got into. I was not especially thinking about how to monetize the comic or how to get it to the right people, it's just one of those things that grew out of control. I've had other times where I have very deliberately tried to make something that I thought would appeal to people, and it's been a complete disaster. I mean, when I think about it in the broadest possible terms, if you want to be a working artist, the single most important thing is to learn how to live cheap, and don't take on debt when you're in college. Because any time you have to do something for money, you've already lost leverage over your creative life. The best possible position to be in is where you can figuratively and literally afford to do whatever you want. Now, if you don't have a trust fund, that's going to be difficult. But in some ways, I found the experience of just having a temp job that paid the bills, and then having my evenings or my slow hours in the office to create whatever I wanted, to be the most creatively fulfilling.

Get Your War On eventually got picked up by *Rolling Stone*, and there was a period where I could support myself just cartooning. If you'd told me that that would have been possible when I was 11-years-old, it would've been my ultimate fantasy.

Some days you don't do anything. You get home from the office and you're spent, you don't have the energy to want to create anything. But then again, that also describes a lot of my days now as a self-employed creative person. [Laughs] Some days are more productive than others. You have to have a healthy mental attitude. You have to have structure, and you have to be disciplined, but you cannot let that discipline mutate into this self-destructive, debilitating beating up on yourself: "Why didn't I work as hard? So and so's more successful than me." The whole point of doing this type of work should be because it's fun, and it helps you grow as a person and makes you more aware of being alive.

I have a friend who's a self-employed musician, and we've been talking a lot about the idea of play in our creative life: when you just start fucking around in a completely different mode without any thought as to whether you're going to be able to sell anything, if you're ever going to share it, if it's ever going to advance your career; you just do it to stimulate different parts of your brain. I think that's a part of overall life, but that's also an important part of your creative life if you want to be a working artist.

One of the things I try to keep in mind as I struggle with self-employment, making my own hours, hitting up editors, pitching TV shows, all the grind that comes with being a working creative person, is this great quote, I can't remember where I read it, but it's, "The opposite of play is not work. The opposite of play is depression" [from *Play: How it Shapes the Brain, Opens the Imagination, and Invigorates the Soul by Stuart Brown*, Avery Trade, 2010]. You have to have a sense of play in your life. Frankly, this is the opposite of what *Get Your War On* and political cartooning turned into for me. It just became a job like any other job. It was the same sense of anxiety and stress, the same sense of resentment if I couldn't come up with anything I thought was funny, the same sense that I was just doing it for the paycheck, which is not how you want to feel about your creative work. So I moved on to other projects.

I've done very little comedy writing outside the cartoons. The good thing about the three-panel cartoon, or any short cartoon, is that you don't have a lot of time to waste. You kind of have to make your point and move on, although a lot of those *Get Your War On*s, at least the ones I liked the most, were almost anti-humor. They didn't have traditional joke structures, or there were no jokes, it was just ranting. Really, the good thing about it is, if you're a cartoonist and you're on a schedule, even if you're a webcomic guy who just makes your own webseries, if you make the pledge to update every Tuesday and Thursday, you just do it. You learn how to make deadlines.

With comedy, you can't be too precious, you just have to produce content, and you don't have time to overthink it. And a lot of times, your first impulse is usually your best impulse, especially if you're just blazing through something trying to make yourself laugh. The sad fact is that I'm not super productive and I'm not super disciplined. I've never made a lot of money. My career is fine, I'm really happy about the success I've had and all of the nice things that people have told me about how the cartoons I've made have affected them, but it's not like I'm a major player or anything. I'm always stressed about where my next freelance gig is going to come from. But I feel really lucky that I don't have to commute to an office every day. Some days if I just want to watch YouTube videos—or if I want to stay up until four in the morning working on a crazy project because I'm in the zone and I'm a night person—I can just keep my own hours and really get lost in something, and that will lead to a project I can share with people or use to make my friends laugh, or something.

The big thing for me that I still haven't tackled is, How do you just end your workday and be off the clock? Even if I'm just watching a Netflix movie, it's like, "This is *kind* of my job." That's where the sense of play comes up. You have to stimulate your mind in a way where you don't have any idea of where it's going to fit into your gig. Just stimulate your mind for its own sake. The fact that your mind is being stimulated and poked and prodded, it's going to lead to new ideas, and you're just going to grow as a person. It sounds so simple and obvious, but for some reason I had a hard time with that concept for a while.

When I look back on my own career, the things I've done that have been the most successful are the projects I just did as a lark. They were the moments when I decided not to worry about the future and to just let the project be what it was. When I did that, they were more pure and more particular, and became more engaging than anything that I could have attempted to reverse-engineer.

Dick Cavett

As a host on various talk shows that have run for a record-breaking five decades on networks such as ABC, CBS, PBS, and CNBC, Dick Cavett did what few of his contemporaries bothered to even attempt: he had *conversations*. Never one to simply sit behind his desk with a knowing smirk, waiting for his guests to finish promoting their latest projects so he could wrap things up with a well-crafted zinger, he listened to what they had to say, and he asked them questions that weren't prepared in advance on 4-by-6 cards by assistants. It was just two (sometimes more) people talking about whatever came to mind. When the laughs came—and they almost always did—they were genuine and true, never manufactured.

It could very easily not have happened. In 1961, Cavett—a few years out of Yale and a copy boy for *Time* magazine—boldly walked into the RCA Building in New York City (where *The Tonight Show* was filmed), found host Jack Paar in a hallway, and handed him an envelope of jokes. He was hired as a *Tonight Show* writer soon after, and eventually wrote for Johnny Carson when Carson took over the show's hosting duties in 1962.

Cavett's job security on *The Tonight Show* depended on his producing solid one-liners night after night. As it turned out, the small-town boy, born in Gibbon, Nebraska, had a talent for writing comedy on the fly. And, even more impressive, he could write for any specific performer, tailoring each joke for that person's unique tone and mannerisms. Whether he was writing for Paar, Carson, or Jerry Lewis, Cavett's jokes always matched the meter and rhythm of the particular host.

Cavett got his own chance at the spotlight when Carson called in sick in 1962, and he was recruited to temporarily replace his hero. His debut as a talk-show host was, to say the least, controversial. During his opening monologue, he explained that Carson was resting at home, recovering from a severe case of "Portnoy's complaint." His reference to the Philip Roth novel was not lost on the NBC censors, who recognized a masturbation gag when they heard it—one of Cavett's very first jokes on national TV, and he was already being bleeped.

ABC offered him his own talk show in 1968, and, from the very beginning, *The Dick Cavett Show* seemed almost destined for failure. Its time slot flip-flopped from daytime to late night to prime time and back again—and yet, somehow, Cavett attracted a loyal audience, mostly among the hipper, more "with it" generation. He was widely referred to as "the thinking man's Carson," if only because his show was unapologetically intellectual and openly accepting of his (barely) younger generation's counterculture.

Cavett was smart, dangerous, and willing to bring on guests who had something to say, rather than just to promote. Case in point: John Lennon appeared with Yoko Ono three times, and most of their conversations dealt with charities and political causes. Charles Bukowski, the underground poet who made Skid Row seem sexy to those who would never live there, once claimed that he would appear as a guest only on Cavett's talk show. Appearing with Johnny Carson or Merv Griffin or anyone else, he said in his six-hour documentary *The Charles Bukowski Tapes*, would be "like eating your own vomit.... If you ever catch me on a talk show, you can shoot me.... Cavett's the only guy I respect." Then again, only moments before, Bukowski had muttered, apropos of nothing, "Let's go to Paris and burn the town down, man."

Perhaps Cavett's finest moment occurred in 1968, during an hour-long interview with one of his comedy idols, Groucho Marx. Cavett and Marx had been friends since their first meeting, in 1961, at the funeral of playwright George S. Kaufman. During this interview—one of Groucho's last memorable TV appearances before his death in 1977—he discussed shoplifting at Bloomingdale's as a child, being knocked unconscious for thirty minutes (also as a child), and the Vietnam War. About a third of the way through the interview, just prior to complaining about the nudity in the Broadway production of *Hair*, Groucho turned to Cavett and said, most earnestly, "You know, you're one of the best and wittiest conversationalists."

No small compliment from a performer who was once quoted as saying, "I find television very educating. Every time somebody turns on the set, I go into the other room and read a book."

It seems you had a tremendous hunger to escape the Midwest and make it in show business. What did you want to escape from?

I don't know. I wasn't one of those kids whose life was a nightmare until he escaped into showbiz or comedy. I never thought of it as escaping a terribly unpleasant place. There was never a feeling of "I can't stand it here another minute." I just knew there was another place I wanted to be. I probably could have stayed and lived in Nebraska, but it never would have happened. I wasn't a suffering child, except when my mother died, when I was ten.

Do you think your mother's death affected your comic sensibility?

I've never even thought about that.

Really?

I'm not sure I have any reason to think that it did. But my mother was probably more responsible for my becoming a performer than anyone else. She got me hooked on applause. When I was very young—almost in my pre-conscious existence—she would prop me up on an easy chair to perform soliloquies.

Almost like the young Mozart.

At these recitals I got my first big laughs and didn't know why. I learned later that what made my "act" so popular was my habit of saying at the end of each selection, "Everybody clap." But I had a slight speech problem with the letter "l," causing it to sound like "Everybody crap." This feature probably netted extra bookings—in every living room in Gibbon, Nebraska.

My mother really was a huge fan of show business and entertainment. She loved going to shows and would even direct dramatic scenes starring the neighborhood kids. And she instilled that love in me.

Did you perform comedy when you were in school?

In my magic acts, I did. I would join extracurricular clubs I didn't give a shit about, such as student council, just for the opportunity to get up onstage and give a speech. The other candidates would give dreary, straightforward speeches, and I would write a funny poem and get virtually every vote available.

A lot of humor writers and comedians seem to have taken up magic as kids. Do you think there's a connection between comedy and magic?

Only that most writers are shy when younger, and magic gives them an opportunity to be funny while hiding behind props.

It's that perfect crutch. I used to get paid up to thirty-five dollars for performing magic at neighborhood birthday parties and for friends. One time, I was booked into a thousand-seat auditorium at a state fair to open for Ed Stibe and His Wonder Horse. Do you know how many people showed up to see us? None. I never went on. And I don't think the bastard even paid me.

What did your parents do for a living?

They were teachers. My father actually taught in the same high school I attended. How I envy people who had his class! I still run into his former students all over the world, and they tell me how great a person and teacher he was. But I was such a self-conscious little twerp. I was embarrassed with the idea that my father taught in my school. My father used to laugh, because between classes I would pass his classroom, and I would always avert my eyes for fear of anyone making the connection.

Why do you think students loved your father so much?

He was terribly smart, and he was also very funny. He had this important trait of making people like him and making people feel liked. He was a great man. He attracted the most forlorn loser types. People would say, "Al Cavett was the only person I've ever liked in the whole world." This even extended to Charles Starkweather, the serial killer from the late fifties.

Charles was our garbageman. I was at Yale when the murders happened [and which were later fictionalized in the 1973 movie *Badlands*], and I was walking past a newsstand one morning when I saw the headline, "Lincoln, Nebraska Murder." I called home, and my stepmother said, "Yeah, your dad used to talk to Charles every single time he picked up our trash. Charles didn't talk to very many people, and your dad felt sorry for him."

It turns out Starkweather slaughtered a gas-station attendant about five blocks away.

So your father took in Charles Starkweather like a stray puppy?

I guess in a way he did—if a puppy can slit throats. My father had always said that Charles was a pitiful person, misled and kind of lost.

You once pointed out that the Midwest has produced its fair share of serial killers; not just Charles Starkweather, but also the *In Cold Blood* murderers, Dick Hickock and Perry Smith. Have you ever figured out the connection?

I don't know what it is. I really have no idea. But, you know, the Midwest has also produced its share of talk-show hosts. Johnny Carson grew up in Norfolk, Nebraska, which is not too far from where I grew up.

As a kid in the forties, I saw Carson perform as "The Great Carsoni"— that's what his magic act was called—in a church basement in Lincoln, Nebraska. Years later, he was amazed when I told him about this.

How did Carson treat you in that church basement?

I went backstage, and I saw him setting up for his show. This is something that usually upsets magicians, because they want to be left alone before a show. But as soon as Johnny learned I was a fellow magician, he became very kind. After his performance, I watched him step into his car and glide off into the night—he told me years later that it was a second-hand Chevy. He was a huge star, headed back to Omaha, where he had a fifteen minute television show.

Did Carson have stage presence that early in his career?

Oh, God, yes! He was famous around the University of Nebraska community. He would perform at school events and at other functions. He was a local celebrity.

Johnny really loved me, and I think it was the Nebraska connection. He invited me out to dinner once in the early eighties—this was after I wrote for him. We were in a booth, and we were swapping stories about old shows and about our early experiences with the opposite sex. He started talking about a TV special he had just done in Norfolk, Nebraska. This was *Johnny Goes Home* [NBC, February 1982]. It hadn't been aired yet, but it had just been edited. When he went to his old school, all his old teachers were lined up waiting for him. They applauded him. He teared up telling me this.

He had the reputation for being very aloof with most people.

I loved going on *The Tonight Show*. One time, as he was introducing me, he said, "Dick Cavett is here tonight—we always have sort of a fatherly feeling toward Richard."

When I watched the show later that night, I could see that he said this with genuine—almost tearful—affection. We were so attuned to each other on the air that a staff member once told me, "You're the only guest Johnny has on where he allows himself to lean back in his chair."

Once, at the end of the show—there were four of us on the couch by then—Johnny asked what we were doing. Everybody had a movie or a play or a TV series to plug. I had nothing. He had brought me out first, so I was farthest down the couch, next to Ed. I hoped he wouldn't get to me.

I was praying to the gods of comedy, when I heard, "And you, Richard?" I heard myself say, "I'm working on a new sitcom. It's a humorous version of *Gilligan's Island*." The laugh was cyclonic. Johnny did his "off the chair" thing he did when genuinely convulsed. I wish I had a copy of that show.

As for him being aloof, he couldn't endure the small talk and social chitchat that he faced offstage. One day he slipped away from some tourists who had cornered him in the hallway outside his studio. He came over to me and said, "What makes the average person so goddamn boring?"

I loved it. The way to Johnny's heart was to produce a deck of cards and ask, "Could you teach me how clean up my double lift?"

Let's jump back a few years to your first writing job, which was for *Jack Paar's Tonight Show*. The story about how you landed this job in 1961 has become legendary.

Listen, if we had lived in an age of security in the early sixties I never would have pulled this off. After graduating from Yale in the late fifties, I began working for *Time* magazine as a copy boy for sixty dollars a week. I noticed an article one day in the *Time* office, about how Jack Paar wasn't happy with his monologue—that he was worrying about the quality of the jokes. I just happened to see this article with the words "Jack Paar" in heavy type.

I wrote some jokes for a monologue and stuck them in an envelope with "Time Magazine" stamped across it. I knew where *The Tonight Show* studio was, from having snuck in several times. I walked over to the studio, and I entered as if I belonged there. Just by chance, I saw Jack leaving the men's room and walking down the hallway toward me. I could tell that he noticed "Time Magazine" on the envelope. He was feuding with *Time* then, so those words really jumped out at him.

I handed Jack the envelope and then took a seat in the audience, waiting to see if he told any of my jokes.

It's almost a story from another age—from a Dickens novel.

It really is. The number of events that had to fall into place for this to have worked was too contrived by half. I often think about that. If I hadn't seen that article, or if a guard had rightly kept me from going into the building, or if I hadn't seen Jack in the hallway, I would now be a plumber. Not that there's anything wrong with being a plumber.

Did Paar perform any of your jokes that night?

I was sitting in the audience, watching his monologue, and he didn't use one of my lines. It nearly killed me. I thought, Well, that was a dumb idea.

But after the monologue, Jack took a mic into the studio audience. A woman asked him, "What do you think about those people on the pirate ships?" There had just been a story in the news about a Portuguese ship that was being held by pirates. He responded, "Wouldn't it be great to hear a voice coming over the loudspeaker: 'Attention! This is your pirate speaking.'"

This was one of the jokes I had written, and it got an enormous laugh. Then he used more of my lines. After the show, we got in the same elevator. He said, "You want to write, don't you, kid?" I told him that I did. I got the job shortly thereafter.

What was it like to write for him? He was known for being somewhat mercurial.

When he hired me, he said, "Better be funny, pal!" Can you imagine the pressure?

The staff always wondered what mood Jack would be in each day. Would he be up? Would he be down? That was always a problem with him. Jack was the most fascinating neurotic I ever met on this earth. But that was the key part of his magic: a sense of danger that made him exciting to watch.

The British theater critic Kenneth Tynan once said that if Jack were talking to a guest—even if the guest were Cary Grant—you would never take your eyes off Jack. You were always afraid that if you did take your eyes off him, even for a moment, you would miss a live nervous breakdown on your home screen.

But does a viewer of late-night television necessarily want to see a near breakdown night after night? Doesn't it become exhausting?

It was a little extreme night after night, but I don't know if it was exhausting. In a lot of ways, Jack really made it all look effortless. When I left his show, around 1968, to host my own show, he gave me the best advice I ever received: "Kid, don't ever interview anybody. That's just David Frost with a clipboard. Make it a conversation."

As hard as this is to believe, Jack never used cue cards or a prompter for his monologue. Before each show, he would write out the monologue in long hand, with a very nice fountain pen. And he would look at the jokes a few times, and that was it. He would sometimes forget, but rarely.

Did you work for Jack Paar when he walked off *The Tonight Show* in February 1960, because censors didn't allow a joke to be aired that involved a "water closet," or toilet?

No, I wasn't writing for him yet, but I did watch that show as an eager viewer. I think it took place in 1960. I just thought it was wonderful. And I noticed he said, "I'm going to leave *The Tonight Show*." Interesting that he referred to it as *The Tonight Show*, rather than "my show" or *The Jack Paar Show*. It was always *The Tonight Show*.

It was an institution, and he knew it, and he was willing to leave it. When he returned about a month later, his first words were, "As I was saying before I was interrupted ... "

Do you remember any jokes you wrote for him over the years?

I gave Jack one famous line. It was a joke borne of exasperation and some anger. Jayne Mansfield was going to be a guest on the show. It's hard to remember now, but she was almost as big—in all ways—as Marilyn Monroe. She was a huge star at the time, and Jack was very excited. He rejected all the intros as inadequate for this magnificent event. He said to all of us, "You guys haven't written me an intro I could use in three months!"

I put a single sheet of paper into the typewriter and typed out an intro that went: "Ladies and gentlemen, here they are ... Jayne Mansfield."

It's become a classic line.

It's been stolen many times, actually. Not too long ago, a journalist sent me a letter from *Harper's*, speculating on where that joke first came from.

It's funny, but I really wonder how I even came up with it. It's not at all like any other line I ever wrote. It's subtler than a joke really needs to be.

It's so pristine. You cannot improve on that joke.

Every part fits. I've always maintained that your first wording with any joke is always the correct one. You should always go with that first version. When you start asking questions like "Should I slow down the punch line by another beat and a half?" or "Should I add something to make it a little clearer?" well, you should never, *never* do that.

I once wrote a joke for my stand-up act that went, "I don't know much about caviar, but I do know you're not supposed to get pictures of ballplayers with it." It always got laughs, but I then overthought the joke and changed it to: "I don't know much about caviar, but I suspected something when I noticed that this caviar came with pictures of ballplayers."

The joke didn't need that over-explanation. I'm not sure why I even felt the need to change it. The first and simpler version was better.

Have you ever understood why jokes come so easily to you?

The whole thing is a mystery—how one person can read a newspaper article and come up with ten jokes instantaneously, while another person could never—not in a hundred years—come up with a single joke.

Beyond that, it's also a mystery as to why some humor writers can write in ways that other humor writers can't. It's making that leap from a perfectly acceptable joke to one that just shines. There are plenty—more than plenty—of humor writers who are unable to make that leap. Many simply do not have an ear for jokes, just like they don't have an ear for music. They're comedically tone-deaf.

How would a beginning writer even know if they had an ear for humor? I would think that it would be like smelling your own breath—a difficult, if not impossible, feat.

Sometimes shows would "audition" a writer for thirteen weeks. There was one writer, I can't quite remember his name, let's just say Joe Connor, who would have a tendency to spell out every joke. It became so bad that his name became a verb among the other writers for ruining a joke: "Have I Joe Connored this joke too much? Or maybe I should Joe Connor this a little, because I'm not sure the audience will get it." It was sad. I had to change the wording on his jokes whenever I had the chance.

Once your name becomes a verb, I suppose it's time to leave your chosen profession.

Either you have it or you don't. I would almost get high writing jokes. It wasn't so much meditating as a feeling of exhilaration. Something would thrill in my veins, and I couldn't stop once I was in this place. The jokes would just start to roll out from under my fingers. They would just keep coming and coming.

One of the things that interests me about humor writers is that with other professions—say, doctor, electrician, bank manager—there's very little mystery; you learn the trade, and then you perform it for years, becoming more and more proficient along the way. But it seems that a lot of veteran humor writers find their craft just as mysterious as they did when they first began.

It's just as inexplicable to me now as it was when I was a kid. And I don't want to analyze it too much, or think about it too much, for fear of it disappearing for good. It's such a blessing when it does happen—your angel has appeared once again.

I remember visiting relatives when I was nine. The adults were all sitting around a table. I loved to hear adults joke and talk. One of the adults was talking about a friend, and she said something like, "Well, that was a long time ago. My friend was just a babe in arms." I then said, loud enough for everyone to hear, "And now she's a babe in someone *else's* arms." The adults laughed, but they also gave me some very strange looks.

Several years ago, I played the narrator in a Broadway production of *The Rocky Horror Show*. I was given the opportunity to do two comic monologues in the show—it could be about anything in the news, anything current. I had my hand in my pocket one night up onstage, and a voice from the audience yelled, "Hey, Dick! Ya playin' with yaself?" And I heard myself say, "I have people who do that for me." I don't think I had ever used that line before. It was almost as if I were on humor automatic pilot and I was hearing this joke at the very same time that the audience heard it. It was out of my mouth before I even thought about it. The angel had appeared to me again—with a little help from a jackass in the audience.

After Jack Paar left *The Tonight Show* in 1962, you stayed on to write for Johnny Carson. Did you find it easier to write for Carson than Paar, since you were closer to Carson? Was Carson's persona easier to capture than Paar's?

Actually, that's not entirely accurate. I had left *The Tonight Show* to write for Merv Griffin on his daytime show, *The Merv Griffin Show*. It's funny to even think about now, but a lot of people forget that Merv's show and Johnny's *Tonight Show* debuted on the same day [October 1, 1962]. And Merv received almost *all* of the positive reviews. There was even a rumor that Merv might take *The Tonight Show* away from Johnny. But then Johnny hit his groove.

To really succeed as a comedy writer, you have to be able to write in different comics' voices. As far as finding it easier to write for Johnny or Jack Paar, I knew both their sounds. I knew how they thought, and I knew how they talked. It was easy for me to write in a comedian's voice. One night, someone had written down on an audience-response card that their hometown had cleaner streets than New York. I gave Johnny a line that went: "Pompeii, after Vesuvius went off, had cleaner streets than New York." I could just hear it in his voice. Can't you? It's essential to hear the comics in your head when you write jokes for them. If you can't do that, you'll never make it as a comedy writer. Mort Lachman, who was Bob Hope's head writer for years and years, told me this: "You turn 'em on in your head, and they do the work for you."

So, no, it wasn't necessarily easier writing for Johnny than Jack. But I never wanted to let Johnny down. One day I wasn't feeling very well, and it was one of those days when I just didn't care very much. I gave Johnny the minimum, probably four jokes per page. I kind of spread them out to look as if they had filled both pages—maybe eight jokes total. Johnny called me on the phone and said, "Richard, I think you're capable of a little better monologue than this." And I died. It gives me the chills to think about now. It felt like I had just let a favorite teacher down. But it was very good of him to do it that way. He jolted me out of my miasma.

You eventually left *The Tonight Show* in 1964 to try stand-up comedy. What made you want to give up writing to perform? Were you not happy strictly as a writer?

I can't remember the specific moment when I decided to get the lumpy ball rolling, to borrow a Fred Allen phrase, by quitting my job writing for Johnny to go into nightclubs in the Village, such as the Bitter End, and brave the onslaught of stand-up audiences.

It was always a big thrill when I heard Jack or Johnny get a big laugh with one of my lines. But I have to admit that it eventually dawned on me: I wonder if I could have gotten that same laugh?

Was it a smooth transition—from writing for others to writing for yourself?

I thought this would be the easiest thing in the world, because I was turning out material every day for comics. That turned out to be an inborn fallacy. You don't hear your own comic voice; it's much more difficult. Certainly, I could have written the same type of jokes for myself that I had written for Jack Paar or Carson—and I knew I would get some laughs with them—but it seemed like the wrong thing to do.

Woody Allen gave me encouragement and advice. He said, "You know how to write comedy, but writing for yourself is different. I can sometimes go for an hour or more without being able to get a single joke out."

I thought, God, if Woody has to sit there for an hour to think of a single joke …

What was your reaction when you first saw Woody perform his stand-up act?

It was at the old Blue Angel [New York nightclub] in 1961. I had heard that Woody had written for Sid Caesar when he was just a teenager. I felt I had to meet this guy—quickly.

When I saw him, I knew that this was an astounding talent, although the audience didn't realize it yet. They talked during his act. His great lines went literally over their heads, to me, standing in the back. It was just clear that his level of intelligence was great. Every line was a gem. There was not a single feeb. That's what we used to call a feeble joke—a "feeb."

Woody didn't have an easy time onstage, did he?

No, he had a hard time. I don't know what made him keep at it. Somewhere in him was this desire to be a performer, but I'm not sure how he stood it. I'm not sure if he literally vomited before going onstage—it was reported that he did—but he struggled to get up there.

One day, the legendary Jack Rollins, Woody's manager and mine, said that putting Woody onstage "may not be one of our genius ideas." Rollins soon changed his mind.

Did you enjoy the stand-up lifestyle?

In some ways, the life of a stand-up was better than the life of a writer. You could affirm that a joke was funny right away. You didn't get that sitting in front of a typewriter.

I bombed horribly the first time I went onstage, at the Bitter End, in '64. But after that first time, it was always much easier to go on. Also, it helped to find a character, which I eventually did. I was sort of "the rustic at the Ivy League." Sample joke: "My Nebraska clothes set me apart. I remember I actually wore brown-and-white shoes. But they were impractical. The white one kept getting dirty."

You wrote a few classic jokes for your stand-up act, such as the Chinese restaurant joke.

That joke was stolen so many times! It killed me. It showed up on *Laugh-In* once. That was the joke that went, "I went to a Chinese-German restaurant. The food is great, but an hour later you're hungry for power."

That was a really solid joke. If that joke didn't get a laugh in my act, nothing would. But that's the funny thing—you can have the same joke on any given night. One night it would kill; the next night, nothing.

So, you don't believe that all audiences are created equal?

No, you can easily get an audience full of dumb clucks. It's just them gaping at you.

Is it true that you once told an entire audience to get the hell out?

Yes.

Did they comply?

They didn't, no. But once, two women had their boots up on the stage, and I kicked one of them off. Both women stood up, and when they reached the door, one of them turned back. I said to her, "No refunds." And she replied, "We'll take a chance." She got the laugh, and I didn't.

Eventually, I was lucky enough to perform on *The Ed Sullivan Show* in the mid-sixties. And as I stood in the wings, it felt as if I had come through the looking glass. It felt like my younger self was lying down on a couch in the basement of my house in Lincoln, Nebraska, with some peanut butter and graham crackers, watching my older self perform on television. It was like an out-of-body experience.

In the late sixties, you became the host of your own daytime and then nighttime program on ABC, *The Dick Cavett Show*. It's amazing to watch these shows now on DVD. You conducted real conversations with the guests, who weren't on the show merely to shill a new product or a new release.

I've been reading some of the DVD reviews. A common theme seems to be that I had a genuine interest in the guests and that the conversations were evident of that. I think I can agree.

I can remember early in the daytime show's run [in 1968] when I had James Mason as a guest. By the way, all of the videotapes for my daytime shows—not my nighttime shows—were erased to make room for the taping of *Let's Make a Deal*. Everything is lost. Anyway, James Mason and I were talking, and I suddenly realized, Oh my God! I am on the air, and they are signaling me something. The conversation had become so interesting and spontaneous that I almost forgot where I was. When something like that happened, it was really good; it was a real conversation. On the other hand, I could also fake that, too.

Johnny Carson once asked me if I ever forgot who my guests had been on that day's show. He used to do that all the time. He would go home after a show, and his doorman would ask who his guests had been that day, and Johnny would forget. It happened to me sometimes. I went home one night after a taping, and there were some people over. One of them asked, "Hey, how did the taping go?" And I said, "Fine." They said, "Who was on the show?" And I said, "Ummm...." They sat there waiting for my answer to bubble to the surface. I'm not sure it ever did.

How could you possibly forget who the guests were from that very day's episode?

Johnny and I sort of agreed on this later: that it's not really completely *you* who's out there in front of the cameras. At times, it can be—especially when the conversation is so damned interesting that you have to be frantically waved to do a commercial. But at other times, it's similar to those Broadway actors who do the same speech night after night and their minds just wander.

So, it was almost as if you were playing the role of a talk-show host.
Sometimes, yes. You become your own doppelgänger.

It's fantastic to see some of the comedy greats who appeared on your show. It's a bridge to another time and place: Bob Hope, Lucille Ball, Groucho Marx, Jack Benny.
I received some criticism that went something like: how many times can you gush and say, "I can't believe it's you! I can't believe you're sitting here! I can't believe I've met you!"? I may have done that too much, but it was genuine. I mean, I really couldn't believe it. On my daytime show, during a commercial break, I once looked backstage and made sure that Bob Hope was really standing there. I was about to introduce him, and it all seemed like a dream.

Years later, I got to be in a sketch on a Bob Hope TV special. I played a reporter, and Hope came out in some sort of costume. I can't remember what he was supposed to be playing, but I was just thrilled as he came out and did that thing he always used to do: walk a little to the right and then around in a circle, like a model showing off his outfit to everybody. We performed the sketch three times, each time to total silence. And I thought, I am in heaven. Nobody is laughing, but I don't care. Of course, laughter magically appeared when the sketch eventually aired.

What was it about Bob Hope's style and comedic voice that you liked growing up?
I have this childhood memory of Hope on the stage of the Lincoln Coliseum in Nebraska: "Now, here is the star of our show," and then the theme song. And my friend next to me said, "God! There he is!" Hope ambled onto the stage with that great Hope walk. And I thought, Jesus,

there's that nose from the movies! Afterwards I said, "Fine show, Bob." And he said, "Thanks, son." That was a formative moment for me. A large part of my life began right there.

Hope happened to have a sound he was born with that became a part of him. It just said "comedy" in a mysterious way. It was the same thing with Groucho and Jack Benny. Almost anything Groucho said was funny. Almost everything Benny said was funny. Both had those voices of the "funny man" that always make you laugh.

As for Hope, he was slick, and he was impertinent. He was glib in a hilarious way. He just seemed inexhaustibly funny. Just naturally funny. He could ad-lib very well. I once asked him if he was going to make another *Road* picture with Bing Crosby. And Hope instantly replied, "We gotta find somethin' that's downhill for Bing." It was instant. I laugh every time I remember that.

These comedy greats really seemed to have taken a liking to you. It was a genuine affection.

They did, and I'm not sure why. They would tell me stories that I don't think they told anyone else.

Like what?

Groucho once told me about a nightmare flight from New York to L.A. He said, "I got to the luggage area to get my bag, and there's an old Jewish woman standing there. She says, 'You're Groucho Marx, aren't ya?' And I said, 'Yes,' and she said, 'You know, you weren't very funny on the plane.' And I said, 'Go fuck yourself.' "

Something similar happened with Jack Benny. I was riding down in the elevator with him, and the other passengers must have asked him seven trademark Benny questions: "Do you really not pay Rochester much? Do you really have a Maxwell? Do you still have your vault?" On and on. He smiled patiently and nodded. We all got off the elevator, and everyone rushed off to tell their friends that they had just met Jack Benny. Meanwhile, Jack put his hand on my shoulder and said, "You know, sometimes you just want to tell them to go fuck themselves." Hearing him say that in the same voice that had come through our old Majestic radio, in Nebraska, well, it was surreal.

Did you ever interview your favorite humor writers?

I interviewed S. J. Perelman a few times. He co-wrote two of the Marx Brothers movies, *Horse Feathers* and *Monkey Business,* and wrote humor pieces for *The New Yorker* for many years. But Perelman was not totally at home in that sort of TV setting, truthfully. He once said that he would give anything to be able to run around a musical-comedy stage the way Groucho could. He was such a perfectionist when it came to writing humor. He was notorious for spending a lot of time re-writing his pieces. He used to call writing "lapidary work." He saw writing as similar to polishing and shining gemstones. If you look at Woody Allen's writing, you can really see how deeply Perelman influenced him—attention to detail, the value of each word.

One of my biggest regrets over the years is not having interviewed James Thurber, who was a hero of mine. I never did meet him, although I did once see him across [New York's] Algonquin Hotel lobby as he was getting into an elevator. I was too fucking dumb to go up to him then, or to later see him perform his own work in *A Thurber Carnival* when it was on Broadway [in 1960]. If you can believe it, I actually did see the show later—but after Thurber died.

"Ladies, and gentlemen, James Thurber will not be performing in this evening's show. Taking his place ... Tony Danza!"

"But there's no reason to be disappointed. Please do *not* make your way to the exits; they have all been locked."

It's hard to imagine now, but when you befriended a few of these comedy legends, they weren't necessarily still being lauded. In fact, in some cases, they had almost been forgotten. I'm thinking of Stan Laurel in particular.

I sought out Stan Laurel when I was a copy boy at *Time*. There was a big manila folder on him in the archives, and I took it out for some reason and read it.

Did you ever get any work done as a copyboy at *Time*? It seems that you spent most of your efforts researching and then seeking out comedy legends.

Actually, no, I never did get any real work accomplished. [Laughs] But the job paid off, didn't it?

Back to Stan Laurel. I didn't even know if he was still alive, but I wrote him, and he wrote back. He invited me to his apartment, and I went to visit him.

Just as easy as that?

Yes.

Do you think he was at all aware of the reverence people still felt for him?

No. He knew that the young audience, or "the kids" as he called them, was aware of him and liked him. But he would tell me, "I'd hate for the kids to see what I looked like now."

That's why he didn't want to appear in the [1963] movie *It's a Mad, Mad, Mad, Mad World*. Stanley Kramer, the director, asked him to be in the film, but Stan didn't want his fans, especially the younger ones, to see how he looked. You could have passed him on the street and not recognized him, but once you knew who he was, you would know who he was. When I walked into his apartment, I checked his ears—his famous ears—and they were the same. The voice was also the same. He had that speech impediment on the letter "s."

This was at the Oceana apartment building in Santa Monica, California. The building is still there, by the way. I sometimes drive past it.

I wonder how many people who are now in that building realize that Stan Laurel once lived there.

How many people knew or cared *then?* I entered the building and asked a resident where he lived. "Mr. Laurel? Oh, I think it's apartment ... Oh, where does he live? 2C? Or 5G? I'm not sure."

No one could convey to either Stan Laurel or Oliver Hardy how much they meant to people. Stan used to complain all the time about how his films were edited for television. That drove him mad. You know, he wasn't paid one cent for those films when they ran on television, even though millions of dollars were made from them. But it wasn't the money that bothered him as much as the cutting. The films were edited in such a way that they stopped, as he put it, "on the way to the gag." That killed him. He actually wrote to one of the TV stations and asked if he could re-cut the films for them. He told me they never even bothered to answer him.

Oliver Hardy was quoted once—this was in his later years, when he was hideously fat and unhealthy—as saying, "I don't really see that my life's amounted to very much. Just pulling some funny faces in front of a camera." And he was an artist to his fingertip.

By the way, Woody once had an interesting observation about Laurel and Hardy—Hardy was simply a better screen comic than Laurel. His delicacy of movement and gesture was the right size for the screen. Stan, who had come from the stage and music hall, often played a little too broadly for the camera.

I never even thought about it until Woody pointed that out. It certainly didn't distract me from how much I loved Stan—but I agree.

Speaking of Woody Allen, in preparation for this interview, I watched episodes of *The Dick Cavett Show* in which he appeared as a guest. In one episode I saw something I had never, *ever* seen before: Woody Allen laughed. In all of his films and in all of his appearances, I don't think I had ever seen him actually laugh.

I remember that show [October 20, 1971]. Woody was very animated. It's a real eye-opener for so many people now. I mean, some of the younger viewers never dreamed that Woody was once a stand-up comedian. It's even more amazing for them to see how funny and likeable he was. By the way, he still is both.

On another episode of your show, Woody came very close to performing a few push-ups at the suggestion of an audience member. That would be another thing I've never seen him do before.

Oh, yes. Woody could have, but he was guarding his image. He was a first-rate athlete in school and in the Brooklyn neighborhood where he grew up—with track, especially. We really did have fun together on the show.

[Pause] Did I ever tell you about the time I was almost in a threesome with Marlon Brando and a beautiful woman?

Let me think about that. No.

Marlon and I were eating dinner at the Russian Tea Room, in Manhattan. A young woman walked up to our table and said, "I'm just crazy about the both of you. This is just too much of a dream for me, and I want you to know that I'll do anything—absolutely *anything*—with the both of you. The only problem is that I don't have very large breasts."

Brando didn't see this as a problem. He delivered a monologue that went something like [in Brando voice], "Listen, honey. I've been to bed with girls with big breasts, little breasts, saggy breasts, breasts that you can tie together, cross-eyed breasts—it doesn't make any difference. You are just fine."

She was very happy to hear this.

So did anything happen?

No.

Why not?

We hadn't finished our meal.

The only thing that came between you and a threesome with Marlon Brando was a bowl of borscht?

It pains me to say this, but yes.

Well, at the very least, that anecdote shall now provide a perfect segue to my next question: How troublesome were the censors for you?

There was a censorship issue when John and Yoko appeared as guests on the show in 1972. They sang "Woman Is the Nigger of the World," and the censors were upset by the title. I mean, the song's meaning was so obvious that I just thought, Don't you get it? You have to ask yourself sometimes, Who is the target of the joke?

The meaning of that song was the exact opposite of what the word represented.

Absolutely. I mean, it was ridiculous. The network wanted it out, and I refused. Everyone was so afraid that there would be protests, and letters would come pouring in. And the letters did pour in. But they were mostly calling me a "cop-out" for having to read this disclaimer before the song. Things like, "Don't you realize that we are mature enough to not have to listen to a disclaimer like that?"

ABC had cobbled up a sleazy, chickenshit disclaimer about "possible offense" and inserted it into the show. Protests came in, but they were all about the "mealymouthed" statements you "made Dick read."

That actually gave you hope for America—a hope that so long ago vanished. Or maybe not. Can I play you something? It's from an audio recording that someone handed to me the other day out in California. This man told me he got it from a woman who's a professional in the field of forensic archiving. I want you to guess who the main participants are:
[*Audio recording*]

First man: "What the hell is Cavett?"

Second man: "Oh, Christ, he's, he's ... he's terrible. He's impossible ..."

First man: "Nothing you can do about it, obviously?"

Second man: "We've complained bitterly about the Cavett shows."

First man: "Well, is there any way we can screw him? That's what I mean—there must be ways?"

Second man: "We've been trying to."

It's kind of difficult to make out. Richard Nixon and Kissinger?

Close. Think crew cut.

[Long pause] Nixon and H. R. Haldeman?

Go to the head of the class. Thousands of hours of Nixon's tapes were just released. I think this particular recording comes from the summer of 1971.

Assuming that the recording is indeed authentic, why do you think Nixon wanted to clamp down on you in the early seventies?

At the time, John Kerry had just been on my show as a guest—he had recently returned from Vietnam. I also interviewed John O'Neill, who would much later become the spokesman for the Swift Boat Veterans for Truth. Charles Colson, who was Nixon's special counsel, later admitted to grooming O'Neill to represent the White House side of the Vietnam War issue. So I suppose both Nixon and Haldeman were none too happy that they had put all that work into O'Neill, and I wasn't buying what they were selling.

A kid from Nebraska, now being talked about by the most powerful man in the world.

It's very, very strange. I once upset Nixon on another issue—I had a White House representative on my show who was pushing for a certain treaty. And I said, "Well, it was nice to have you on, but I certainly hope the treaty is defeated." Soon thereafter, the IRS audited my entire staff—from the secretary to the ashtray emptier. The "Wonder from Yorba Linda" was at it again.

I once attended an event at the White House, and I spoke to Nixon in the reception line. I remember being struck by the appalling width of his nose. I also remember him asking me, "Who's hosting your show tonight?" I responded, "Joe Namath." And Nixon asked, "How are his knees?" Mr. Light Conversation. He'd been briefed, I suppose, and he knew to ask specifically about Joe's knees.

Then again, it wasn't just top government leaders who hated me. After I had Jane Fonda on the show in 1970, I received a telegram from Waco, Texas, which read, in part, "Dear Dick. You little sawed-off faggot Communist shrimp." I wrote back, "I'm not sawed-off."

The Dick Cavett Show **is infamous for many highlights, but perhaps none more so than for an episode that never actually aired. Can you tell me about the Jerome Rodale incident, from the summer of 1971?**

I saw a videotape of that show about a month after it happened. A lot of what occurred was already wiped from my memory. I had forgotten that Rodale, who was a fitness guru and health expert, as well as the publisher of *Prevention* magazine, had been bragging on the show about having "never felt better" in his whole life. He said that he planned to live to be one hundred. He also said that he was in such good health that he had fallen down a long flight of stairs the previous week and laughed all the way. A few minutes after telling this anecdote, he slumped over, dead.

Is it true, according to legend, that you then asked him, "Are we boring you, Mr. Rodale?"

I don't know. I wonder about that. If I did, I couldn't hear it on the tape. You know, when Joey Bishop would be on a talk show with Buddy Hackett, one of them would invariably snore while the other was talking. It was kind of a standard gag. That's how it looked with Rodale, and that's how the audience took it.

They really did think it just had to be a part of the fun.

How long did it take for the audience to realize that this wasn't just part of the fun?

It didn't take long. It soon became very obvious. Watching that wave of awareness once the audience realized that something was wrong was a very curious thing. I never saw anything quite like that. It's strange to think about now, because traumatic moments are a difficult thing to remember. But I do remember getting up and holding Rodale's wrist and then thinking, What in the hell am I doing? I'm obviously in charge, because I have to be in charge, but I don't know what his wrist is supposed to feel like or what I'm looking for here.

Of course, that episode never aired—but a half-dozen people a year still believe they saw it! I think I own the master tape, although I'm not sure. I've said many times that I would check on that, but maybe after this interview I finally will.

The ABC version of *The Dick Cavett Show* went off the air in 1975, when you were only thirty-nine. Was there ever any sense, from your standpoint, that your gifts were tailor-made for the talk show? And that maybe your talents weren't sufficiently highlighted in other realms?

I was made for the talk show—too bad my tap-dance skills have had to take a backseat.

It was never my goal to host a talk show. My career was never—not even for one moment—planned. I often wonder what would have happened if I hadn't noticed the article in the *Time* office that mentioned Jack Paar being unhappy with his monologue. I don't remember standing there and thinking, I shall write him a monologue. I just went home and [snaps fingers] tapped out two pages of jokes. Then the odds against running into Jack at the studio, the odds of me even being let into the building ... it's like the chance of any individual human being born—if any one of the other spermatozoa had somehow gotten into the egg, someone other than you would now be here.

When I was just a teenager back in Nebraska, I would often appear on a fifteen-minute children's show called *Story Time Playhouse*. One day, after the show was finished, I was leaving the theater and ran into a local radio star. He was a tall, good-looking blond man with a voice that I knew very well. His name was Bob Johnson. He stopped me in the hallway and said, "I was thinking about you the other day. You know, you're gonna get up and out of here."

I didn't know what he was talking about. Was he talking about where we were standing in the hallway, or out in the world? And he said, "No, it's true. I have a feeling that you're going to get up and out of here just like Carson did." By this time Johnny was in New York and was already a bit of a success. I looked at this guy, this fifty-ish man, and realized that he wasn't going to be Jack Benny's announcer, or another Carson, or any of the things he dreamed of becoming earlier in life. He had gone as far as he was going to go—and he knew it. It really hit me, and I've never forgotten that. I do realize how lucky I've been.

To misquote both you and Fred Allen, it's now time to stop this lumpy ball from rolling. Any advice for humor writers hoping to have a career as successful as yours? Beyond, of course, walking straight up to you and presenting you with a big ol' packet of their jokes?

[Laughs] Oh, God, the number of times that I've heard the phrase, "I am asking you for the same favor that you once asked of Jack Paar...."

You know, it's such a different time now anyway. The savvy legal advice is to never even open one of these packages, for fear that they'd later want to sue you.

As far as writing advice, just put down anything you think is funny. Don't think about what purpose the writing has to serve—just put the words down. Write anything that you think is funny for any reason. You can then go back and make it perfect, if necessary.

Also, if you want to write for other comedians or anyone else, well, you can have a pretty nice career doing that too.

One more thing: When faced with the choice between a bowl of borscht and a threesome with Marlon Brando, always choose the latter.

Perfect advice for any young writer. Follow that and you can't go wrong. And write it up afterward. Good luck.

Finding a Literary Agent for Your Humor Book Idea

Advice from literary agents at Writers House, L J K Literary Management, Mendel Media Group (Scott Mendel), the Carol Mann Agency

1. Do your research. If an agent doesn't deal with the genre of humor, why waste your time sending your pitch out? A modicum of Googling on most agents will turn up a website with submission guidelines. That's always the best approach.

2. Take the time to write a personal note to the agent. Show the agent that you're not spamming the entire industry.

3. Do not send props with your submission. If you can't make the words on the page funny, then photos of yourself wearing feather-accented nipple clamps won't make you more appealing; I have actually received such a photo, as well as other personal objects. I've never taken on such a client.

4. Do not expect that your headshot will matter much. If you're too beautiful, it will just make the prospective literary agent hate you. As a rule, we're a pretty nerdy-looking crowd. If you're not too beautiful, then the prospective agent will file you under "Not Media-Genic." Welcome to the land of the double-bind—a classic scenario of comedy writing and performance.

5. Do not expect the brilliance of your material to make up for a sloppy, poorly edited submission. A disregard for literary agents' professional expectations just signals to prospective agents that you'll be a high-maintenance client.

6. Do not call to check on the status of your pitch. Let us call you after we read your work and decide that we want to represent you. If we haven't called, we either haven't read it yet or we are not the right literary agency to represent your work.

7. Perhaps what matters most is having an exciting, original voice. It's also important that the writer have a platform or credits to his or her name: television, magazine, newspaper, or stand-up. It's not impossible to sell a book without published clips, but it's much more difficult—especially if it's humor.

Todd Hanson

Todd Hanson's Five Easy Steps to Becoming a Professional Comedy Writer

1. Start out life full of intelligence, talent, and wide-eyed enthusiasm.

2. Be slowly beaten down by the indifference of the universe.

3. Maladapt by developing a horrifying pathology of freakish narcissism paradoxically combined with masochistically low self-esteem.

4. Eventually give up hope, curse God, and abandon your dreams.

5. You are now ready to start writing comedy.

Authors tend to joke that they ended up in a writing career because they didn't have any other marketable skills, but for Todd Hanson, longtime head writer and story editor for *The Onion*, this was literally true. Aside from writing comedy, Hanson's only other meaningful employment was minimum-wage menial labor—dishwasher, floor mopper, cashier. And, by his own admission, he wasn't very good at any of it.

Since 1990, the writers at *The Onion*—billed as "America's Finest News Source"—have been responsible for some of the most brilliant and influential comedy of the last two decades. While it's often mistaken for mere newspaper parody, *The Onion*—like *The Daily Show* and *The Colbert Report*—is not simply mimicking the sloppy reporting and questionable ethics of tabloid (and, yes, mainstream) journalism. The headlines alone are mini–satirical essays and stories, ruthlessly critiquing everything from religion ("Church Group Offers Homosexual New Life in Closet") to economics ("Neither Person in Conversation Knows What Hedge Fund Is") to education ("Nation's Educators Alarmed By Poorly Written Teen Suicide Notes") to orgies ("Orgy a Logistical Nightmare").

Like the best comedy institutions, *The Onion* has always been non-partisan, bashing both the right ("Republicans Call For Privatization Of Next Election") and the left ("Adorable Democratic Candidate Actually Believes He Has a Chance"). And, above all, they've remained consistently controversial. A headline such as "Los Angeles to Siphon Water from Minorities' Bodies" may have raised some eyebrows, but Hanson and company are unrepentant and unapologetic, determined to stay true to their satirical roots, whomever they might offend.

When Hanson first enrolled at the University of Wisconsin at Madison in 1986, he didn't foresee a future in humor writing. Madison was, after all, by no means an epicenter of entertainment or comedy. And Hanson was not exactly the university's most ambitious academic. He personified the "slacker" image, so popular at the time with the media. He may have kept his dorm mates laughing with his caustic zingers, but the deans and professors did not find his act (and lack of schoolwork) as amusing. After dropping most of his classes, Hanson stuck around campus anyway, drawing cartoons for the college newspaper, *The Daily Cardinal*, and hanging out with people who shared his sardonic and disaffected sensibilities.

When two of his *Daily Cardinal* colleagues, Scott Dikkers and Peter Haise, decided to take over a newspaper parody called *The Onion* in 1989, originally created to promote a local pizza establishment, Hanson signed on as head writer. The rest of the writing staff consisted of friends from their small social circle, which Hanson once described as "a disparate group of odd and often misguided underachievers."

In the beginning, putting out *The Onion* was merely a way to pass the time. They never expected anybody outside of Madison to read it, but it didn't take long for word to spread, first to Milwaukee, then to

Denver, Boulder, Chicago, and, ultimately, with the launch of their website in 1996. Their breakout moment occurred on April Fools' Day 1999, with the release of the best-seller *Our Dumb Century*. The bare-bones satirical rag thrown together less than a decade before by a small group of friends in a basement and published with little or no budget had transformed, seemingly overnight, into a worldwide comedy juggernaut.

Now in the national spotlight, *The Onion* soon eclipsed *The Harvard Lampoon* as the country's number-one resource for comedy-writing talent. Many of *The Onion*'s pivotal contributors were lured away to write for television for fat paychecks. Ben Karlin and David Javerbaum ended up writing and producing for *The Daily Show;* Richard Dahm helped create *The Colbert Report;* and Tim Harrod joined the writing staff of *Late Night with Conan O'Brien*. Hanson, on the other hand, remained stubbornly loyal to *The Onion*.

Hanson and *The Onion* team moved from Madison to New York City in early 2001, where they soon grappled with Hollywood over movie deals, published a series of *Ad Nauseam* book collections, and launched *The Onion News Network* (featuring online videos), as well as *The Onion Radio News*, which currently airs daily on more than sixty stations nationwide. But despite its fame, *The Onion* hasn't evolved into a publishing behemoth. The newspaper's headquarters is now located in a posh Manhattan office building and its staff numbers in the hundreds, but the creative core is still (more or less) the same dozen or so snarky outsiders who have been with the paper since the early nineties, putting out a weekly product for the sheer love of it.

You've been a writer for *The Onion* for more than twenty years. Do you feel at all constrained by the paper's format?

Yeah, of course, I do—sure. You can't do the same thing for that long without feeling somewhat constrained. But not really by *The Onion*'s format. When people say, "Why do you want to keep working at *The Onion* when you could have left and gone to do this or that?," I always answer, "Well, because you can't make child-molestation jokes about the Pope anywhere other than *The Onion*."

So there's no interest in branching out and moving beyond writing for print?

Listen, if I had wanted to make a quarter-million dollars a year writing for a sitcom, I could have done it. I could have gotten one of those staff jobs. But I didn't do it. I just didn't. Maybe I'm the dumbest guy in the world. But it seemed like, "Why would I leave *The Onion* when it's clearly a once-in-a-lifetime thing?" Actually, scratch that. It's not a once-in-a-lifetime thing. It's a never-in-almost-anybody's-lifetime thing.

How many people can say that something like that happened to them? That they and their friends have this little group in which they did this little fun thing together and then it ended up becoming internationally respected? Most people go through their entire lives without ever having anything like this happen. They get married, they have kids, they grow old, and die. And nothing like this ever happens to them. But it happened to me. That's amazing. What are the chances it's going to happen twice? I'm going to go out on a limb and say probably zero.

But don't get me wrong. I still complain every day.

Why—are you not happy with your lot in life?

[Laughs] Am I happy? I am absolutely miserable!

Are you clinically depressed?

Yes, and I've been my depressed my whole life. My entire adult life, anyway.

Do you think this unhappiness expresses itself in your writing?

I think so, sure. If I hadn't found dark humor as an outlet, I don't know what the hell I would have done. I'm known for writing really, really black humor at *The Onion*.

Can you give me any specific examples?

I wrote an article that was called "Local Man Might as Well Just Give Up." I don't think I came up with the headline, but I wrote the piece. Another piece was called "Doctors Find New Way to Prolong Meaningless Existence."

Let's see, there are so many: "U.S. Populace Lurches Methodically Through the Motions for Yet Another Day," "Study: Depression Hits Losers Hardest," "Utter Failure to Spend Rest of Day in Bed." I was actually in the photo in that last article. I was the loser in the bed.

You once said that *The Onion's* humor is about one thing: life's nightmare hellscape of unrelenting horror. I suppose those articles are a good example.

Well, like many of the jokes I make, that was said to get a laugh, but it was also true. That line was actually used in the "Utter Failure" article. That was an honest joke. That's kind of my rule about jokes. I don't think there is any point in making a joke that is not an honest joke. And I don't find jokes funny if they're not honest. Unfortunately, the truth usually hurts.

How did you become involved with *The Onion?*

I first met Rich Dahm, who later became a writer for *The Onion*, in a dorm during my freshman orientation at the University of Wisconsin. This was in 1986. We had this icebreaker exercise in which you had to state your name, your major, and what kind of car you'd be if you were a car. It was some idiot's idea of an icebreaker, you know. And, of course, I'm sitting in the group area of the dorm, just feeling like a moron. All the guys tried to sound cool by naming expensive sports cars, and all the girls tried to be sexy by saying things like, "I would be a little red Corvette." And then it was my turn, and I said I couldn't decide between the modified Jaguar hearse from the movie *Harold and Maude* or the magic bus from the song by The Who. People laughed.

Then it was Rich's turn. He said he would be the Wagon Queen Family Truckster, which was the fictional car from *National Lampoon's Vacation*.

How many of the other freshmen understood that reference?

A lot didn't. It was a strange thing. I felt a connection right away. We became friends. We'd sit up all night in the dorm making each other laugh, just being silly.

Scott Dikkers, the longtime editor of *The Onion,* was going to the University of Wisconsin at this time. Did you know him?

Scott is not a social person, but I met him because he had a brilliant comic strip called "Jim's Journal" in *The Daily Cardinal*, which was the university's newspaper. I thought it was absolutely hilarious, totally deconstructed. It received some criticism because it wasn't a stereotypical cartoon with a gag at the end. It was anti-humor. That's the shorthand word that we used to throw around all the time on *The Onion* staff: anti-humor.

I was also doing a cartoon for *The Daily Cardinal* called "Badgers and Other Animals." It was kind of a cross between "Doonesbury" and Lynda Barry's "Ernie Pook's Comeek," and it was basically about me dropping out of school and doing nothing. I did this for four years, from 1988 to 1992.

How were you supporting yourself at this time? Just through your cartoons?

Hell, no. I only made $4 a strip! I was doing odd jobs, like washing dishes or working at an answering service, where I would answer phones for doctors and take messages. Or working at a convenience store. I worked at a comic-book store for a little while. That was the best job I had, because I could draw signs for the store with cartoon characters on them. On the other hand, I did manage to get myself fired within a year or so.

It wasn't like I just dropped out of school and that was that. It was gradual. I would take a class now and then, but eventually I did drop out completely. Basically, I was just hanging out at *The Daily Cardinal*. And that's where I met all these people who later became associated with *The Onion*.

Who originally started *The Onion* before Scott Dikkers and Peter Haise took over?

Two guys—Tim Keck and Christopher Johnson—in 1988. They were advertising majors at the University of Wisconsin. They created the paper just to sell pizza coupons. And rather than produce an actual newspaper, Tim and Christopher figured they'd just get some friends to make up stories. The papers were distributed in record stores and delis and other places like that.

About a year after it began, Scott Dikkers and Peter Haise bought the newspaper from Tim and Christopher for around $16,000.

The Onion was a very different paper in the early 1990s than it is today.

Right. At first, it was a parody of a *Weekly World News*–type tabloid.
A lot of the early stories were so great and silly, like "Dead Guy Found,"
which was written by my old roommate, Matt Cook. Or a huge front-page
banner headline that read "Pens Stolen," with the subhead "From Dorm
Study Area." We still do those kinds of satires; a recent article has the
headline "Rubber Band Needed."

But even then the paper sort of exhibited an anti-establishment attitude.
Tommy Thompson, the former Secretary of Health and Human Services,
used to be the governor of Wisconsin. And the paper ran a headline
like "Governor Declares November Masturbation Month." Thompson
complained and demanded the paper run a retraction, which we did. The
retraction read something like, "We previously reported that the governor had said that November was Masturbation Month. This was untrue.
In reality, November was Sodomy Month. *The Onion* regrets the error." I
believe that is the only actual retraction *The Onion* has printed.

**Was there ever any thought on your part that it would one day become
what it's become?**

Are you kidding? Everyone on the staff felt that it was just something
to do where we would feel less like we were wasting our lives. Nobody ever
had a goal of getting paid, let alone thinking we were going to become
media figures or have our work read all over the world. It was just something you did two nights a week when your shift ended. We got together
and worked on this little free paper in Madison, Wisconsin.

I think *Onion* writers are a completely differently breed. They're just
a bunch of weirdos. Mostly shy, mostly geeky. That's them in a nutshell,
but I don't know if that's really an adequate description. We never thought
we were going to have careers, period—let alone *this*. And here we are,
twenty years later.

The Onion now has a huge readership for a humor publication.

It's not as big as you might imagine. I think our current audience is
about five million readers, which is a lot, but that's not enough to keep
a network TV show on the air. That's not even *close* to enough to keep a

network TV show on the air. If you only had five million viewers, you'd be canceled immediately. *The Onion* is not really part of the showbiz mainstream. You may think it is, but it isn't. But I don't care if we are outside of the mainstream—I prefer it that way. And I think that's why the people who like it really like it. That's what makes it unique.

Besides, how many millions of fans do you really need? If I were a stand-up comedian and I went on the stage and there were a thousand people in the audience, I would be like, "Holy shit! That's a lot of people!" And yet, there are about five million people out there who read *The Onion* every week. That's ridiculous. That is beyond the wildest dream that I ever would have had.

How many years did you work for *The Onion* without being paid?
The first seven years.

Seven years?
When I say not getting paid, I mean I was paid maybe $10 a meeting. There were two meetings a week. So that was $20. And then, at one point, there was this big leap forward when writers made $15 a meeting. So I then made $30 a week.

So from 1990 until 1997, you were working for about $120 a month writing humor? That would come out to, what, about $1,500 a year?
[Laughs] Well, you're not taking into account all that big-time dishwashing money I was earning. Getting paid to write for *The Onion* was never a goal. It was just something to do for fun, like being a part of an intramural volleyball team. Not that I would ever be on an intramural volleyball team for fun, but you know what I mean. Everything that we've achieved is gravy. I had no idea how long I was going to be washing dishes for a living. Five years? Twenty years? I would have a panic attack when I thought about it. In fact, when I think about it now, I have a panic attack.

One thing that really annoys me is when I'm on a panel or giving a talk and I have to take questions from the audience. People will often ask, "How do I get a job writing comedy?" And I just ... it just annoys the fuck out of me. I always answer: "You do it for free for ten years and then, if you are really lucky, you get to write humor as a full-time job." And then they look at me like, "That's not what *I* want to do."

How is it different now with the younger writers who work at *The Onion?* How does their sensibility differ from yours when you were starting out?

I think some of the younger writers have the same sensibility that I had in the early years, but I also think some of them are actually more of the type A, ambitious variety. Not that there is anything wrong with that. It's probably a much better way to be. But it is interesting. The people we hire now are twenty-two, and you get the feeling that they are kind of like, "Oh, this is awesome. I got a great job." As opposed to, "Hey, I have to go wash dishes in a couple of hours. I better think of something fun to do in the meantime."

Also, they grew up reading *The Onion.*

That's just the strangest thing to me. When people say, "I've been reading *The Onion* since I was ten," I don't even know how to respond to that. It's very strange.

Any advice for those readers who dream of writing for *The Onion?*

Start your own paper. Do your own thing. That's what I would recommend to anybody who wants to do anything, not just write for *The Onion*. Do it for free and have fun. Whether it's writing comedy or making music or painting or performing interpretive dance. If you want to do something creative, you should have a better reason for wanting to do it than to make money. If you want to make money, my advice is to sell shoes or go into banking.

Let's talk about your influences. You've spoken in past interviews about your admiration for *Late Night with David Letterman*. What was it about the sensibility of that show that appealed to you so much?

When I was 8-years-old, going on nine—this was in 1977—*Star Wars* was the big paradigm shift for me and my generation. It blew everybody away. You didn't have to be a sci-fi nerd to appreciate it. It was just the coolest thing that anybody had ever seen, by far. But then all of that changed at some point, and I forgot about *Star Wars*. There was this new generational paradigm shift, and that was *Late Night with David Letterman*.

That show changed everybody's attitude—at least people my age. Everyone just started trying to imitate Letterman's attitude, that sarcastic persona. It was powerful—this ironic voice really became the touchstone for my generation, what people would call "slackers" or "Gen X."

What do you mean by "powerful"?

I just mean it gave us a certain power to ... it wasn't like I was this little nerd who got picked on or anything. I was the little nerd who could talk himself out of being picked on. I would crack wise, and the tough kids were too dumb to get it. I had this ironic distance that enabled me to kind of set myself above all of the bullshit and yet still participate. It became this thing where I could simultaneously mock everything and appreciate it at the same time.

Later, when I was living in Madison, Wisconsin, we all loved *Late Night*. There was a certain shared sensibility. Everybody used that ironic voice all the time. And that was the voice of *The Onion*. It was just the way we always joked with each other. I still find Letterman amazing—his timing, his whole persona. He's just a machine. He's like this honed, brilliant genius. Merrill Markoe, the show's first head writer, deserves a lot of credit for that voice, though she rarely receives it. She's amazing—one of the only people who can do the Letterman voice just as good as he can. I love her.

Do you remember the first headline you wrote for *The Onion?*

I remember it very well. I came up with the headline in the fall of 1990 and it was called "U.S. Signs Peace Treaty with Canada." The idea was funnier than it sounds, because it was written just before the first Gulf War. I think I probably came in with a list of headlines, and they picked that one and let me write it.

Readers of *The Onion* might assume that it's a fun product to put together week after week. Is it?

No.

Is it difficult?

Not difficult—tedious. On a tedium scale of one to ten, it's a ten. That's not just me being my usual depressive self; that's how everybody feels. It is rewarding, though, when you write articles and jokes no one else would ever publish and the readers love it. Comedy is extremely hard. It's not just like, "This is so great!" It's a hell of a grind.

Why is the process at *The Onion* so tedious?

Because it's so time-consuming, and there's such a high attrition rate. We have these long, long meetings where the writers and editors go through and evaluate a huge list of headlines. And then maybe five get picked. It's probably not an exaggeration to say that at this point, with so many different contributors, there might be five hundred headlines for every one that eventually makes it into the final product. We always choose the headlines first, and then write the story.

And what's done with those headlines that are not chosen?

They are thrown away.

Never to be used again?

They are gone.

Can they be saved and then used later for individual jokes within a piece? Or maybe for a chart or a graph idea? It seems like such a waste.

If a joke or a headline idea doesn't make it through the selection process, it disappears for good.

Does it bother you that the individual voice is eliminated? That your byline won't be on the story? That readers won't know who wrote what?

Not really, no. It's like being in a band or being in a comedy troupe, as opposed to being an individual comedian or being a solo singer. It's all toward the common good—making the product as good as it can be.

I'd like to talk about *The Onion* and Hollywood. Over the years there have been a few *Onion* movie projects that never got off the ground.

At least three.

Is there a disillusionment with the Hollywood process for you?

Hmm, how can I possibly answer that question in such a way as to convey the full extent of what I mean? The answer is not only yes; the answer is "fuck yes." The answer is even more than "fuck yes." My disillusionment with the Hollywood process started at the very beginning.

Which was with *The Untitled Onion Movie* in the mid-nineties?

No, that came later, but that's a good example. That was actually going to be called *The Onion's Major Motion Picture: Now a Major Motion Picture*, which I still think is a great title. But it went nowhere. Five years of frustration. That project was our big attempt to interact with the larger entertainment industry. And it didn't exactly work out—at least on the big screen. It was later released on DVD.

What happened?

We really thought that project was going to be great, because we had a deal with David Zucker, who produced *Airplane!*, a movie we all loved. But Hollywood and *The Onion* just aren't a good match. If we were to try to make a movie again, I think we would try to do it independently.

Was it the creative frustration of not being in charge?

Partly. As you know, we're from Wisconsin. So we're not part of the entertainment industry. On the other hand, we're not idiots. We sort of knew that there would have to be a lot of compromises. But we had no idea. Even the most cynical attitudes that we could have had going into Hollywood would have proven inadequate to the reality. Our worst-case scenario paled in comparison to the actual-case scenario.

It was just a series of compromises that began literally from the very first conference call and just continued and continued and continued. And we kept compromising and compromising and compromising. And, eventually, we got to the point where we had the script, but none of us liked it. The script had gone through all these compromises. And then somehow the script got greenlit and we were like, "No! Don't greenlight that! We don't like it!"

At that point, we did all this emergency rewriting and tried to fix the script. The movie that was eventually shot incorporated some of our changes, but not all of them. The movie wasn't horribly bad or anything. It just wasn't great. And we really, really tried to make a great movie.

How much did the studio spend on the movie?

$10 million.

It was supposed to be released for the big screen in 2004. Why was it only released on DVD in 2008?

Almost from the very beginning we felt, Oh my god, we don't want a movie to come out with *The Onion*'s name on it that we don't like. We were very lucky to have an agent who had worked into our contract final script approval. But even that gets you only so far. Eventually, we heard it was just never going to be released. That was so disappointing, after all the effort we'd put into trying to fix things—all those rewrites. There were supposed to be reshoots that would incorporate all those fixes, but it never happened. Anyway, by that point, it was almost a relief that it wasn't coming out.

With the limited amount of interaction I've had with Hollywood, I've noticed a very strange thing. Scott Dikkers put it very well. Hollywood people will say, "I love what you do. Would you come over and work for me and do what you do?" And you respond, "Sure, I'd love to do that." And you go over to Hollywood, and they say, "I'll tell you what. Why don't you *not* do what you do? Why don't you do what *we* do?" Then you're like, "But the whole reason I'm here is that you like what *I* do." And they're like, "Yeah, but just do what *we* do." I don't even think it's anyone being an asshole or anything ... it's no one's fault. I think it's just the way Hollywood works.

Tell me about *The Onion*'s move from Wisconsin to New York in January of 2001. Why did the staff feel a move was necessary?

First of all, when *The Onion* made the move to the Internet in 1996, we had no idea how quickly it would become popular nationwide. There was no reason to believe it would ever happen. It wasn't an active goal. It's almost like when you're in a garage band and you say something like, "Wouldn't it be great if we were famous and rock stars?" But that doesn't mean that anyone thinks it's really going to happen.

Before we went online, the paper was only available in a few cities, including Madison and Milwaukee. The most ambitious thoughts the business staff had up to that point was to put the paper in more cities and sell local advertising space. There was never any thought of it being a national media presence. Then we got the book contract for *Our Dumb Century,* and the book eventually reached number one in 1999, which just blew everybody's mind.

So it wasn't as if we were moving to New York for any reason other than we just wanted to make a move. One of the writers, Mike Loew, said in an interview that the staff just wanted to walk down a couple of different streets in our lifetimes. We were ready. We weren't in our young, formative years anymore. I was already thirty-two. Most of the other writers were about my age, and most of us were now staffers and no longer had day jobs. And *The Onion* was already a full-formed adult entity. The move was more a reward for us than any type of goal. You know, just from a personal standpoint, I felt that it would be really nice to go see a live comedy show at a club that didn't suck.

There was some concern that *The Onion* would change once it moved to New York. Was that ever a concern of yours?

It was. We all wondered whether the humor would change, but we self-consciously decided we did not want that to happen. There was a lot of attention when we first arrived, but then there was a period of quiet when not much was written about us. Then these articles came out that implied we had moved to make a big splash, and we had failed to make any splash. What these journalists didn't understand was that all we ever wanted to do was the same thing we had been doing in Madison. We never intended to become anything big and new and different. And I think that just sort of confounded certain people.

The media sort of figured, Well, isn't that what people come to New York to do? You come here in order to re-invent yourself or to move up from one level to a higher level in terms of social status or fame. We never wanted any of that. We just wanted to meet and hang out with people with a like-minded comic sensibility. It's not as if we arrived here so that we could hang out with celebrities.

That being said, the company has changed in the past few years. There's been a lot of growth, and it's starting to feel like an actual business instead of some slackers in a band.

How were you treated when you first arrived?

I have to say we've really been accepted by New York. There were a few journalists who wrote about us in a weird way. One reporter from *The New York Observer* took me out to a few nightclubs and basically tried to make me look like a hick. Which is not so far from the truth. You really didn't have to stretch the truth too much to explore that angle.

But, overall, most people really showed us respect, including people we admired, like David Cross and Conan O'Brien and the Upright Citizens Brigade. They've all been incredibly nice to me. I once found myself in the elevator with Conan. He somehow figured out I was from *The Onion,* and he complimented me and the book *Our Dumb Century* for five minutes. It was nothing but superlative praise. I just stood there looking up at him, because he's very tall, you know. I alternated between daring to look up at him and then looking down at my shoes. I didn't know what to say; it was just so scary.

That's one of the strange things about *The Onion* coming to New York. The standard pattern was reversed in our case. Usually you become a big fish in a small pond and then you make the leap to New York and suddenly you're a little fish in a big pond. But it was the opposite for us. Nobody in Madison really gave a shit about *The Onion.* And then we moved here, and we began to meet people we really loved and who loved us back. It was very, very strange.

Why? You didn't feel that you deserved some of the accolades?

To this day, most of us don't feel like we're part of the New York–show-biz world. We were always, and are still, blown away when people show us respect. How do I put this? It's kind of like growing up watching what's on television, and you get the sense that there are two worlds: there's the world on your side of the screen which is the reality, and then there's the world on the other side of the screen which is from some other planet, where the people are rich and famous and get to be on television. And it never occurs to you that those people are on the same planet and that you don't have to take a spaceship to get from where you live to wherever they live.

You moved to New York nine months before the events of September 11. What was that time like for you and the rest of *The Onion* staff?

Like it was for everybody else. It was fucking horrifying. I saw the buildings burning from my apartment window. It was certainly the most awful thing I've ever witnessed, and I pray to God it's the most horrible thing I ever do witness. None of the staff was feeling irreverent or ironic or saying, "Well, this is our chance to make some really edgy humor." We were absolutely stunned and emotionally blank. I was absolutely out of my mind.

September 11 was on a Tuesday. We immediately decided we weren't going to do an issue that week. It was too soon, so we just ran a black banner on the website. But to begin working on the next issue, we had to start the following week. We phoned each other and started talking. At first we were like, "I guess we'll just have to do something lighthearted and non-topical and something that doesn't have anything to do with this." But the more we talked about it, the more we realized we had to address it head-on, because it was the only thing on everyone's mind.

It was really risky, and we knew that some people might be offended, but we had to do it. Normally, we love to offend people. Usually, that's our favorite thing to do. That week, though, nobody felt like offending anyone. But I should point out that we didn't set out to do something historic. It wasn't our intention to do something that no one else had the guts to do. We just sat down, tried to do our jobs, and ended up with that issue.

What was your contribution to that first issue after 9/11?

I wrote two stories: the article with the headline "American Life Turns Into Bad Jerry Bruckheimer Movie" and the piece "God Angrily Clarifies

'Don't Kill' Rule." I cried when I wrote that "God" piece. And, in the piece itself, God ends up crying.

There was no room for error in that issue. If you failed, you would have failed on a grand scale.

Absolutely. I remember one of the writers, Carol Kolb, wrote a perfect story. It was called "Not Knowing What Else To Do, Woman Bakes American-Flag Cake." That was a very touching story. Very effective. Hit the right notes. Not one of us felt like taking anybody down. It's hard to feel anti-establishment when the establishment is lying in smoking ruins at your feet.

Did the staff have any idea as to what the reaction was going to be to that issue?

The first e-mails began to arrive the day of publication and we looked through them. Some of the e-mails said things like, "It's too soon. How can you do this?" But 90 percent were positive. Then they just kept pouring in. It was incredibly humbling and incredibly touching, just the outpouring of support that we got from people for that 9/11 issue. They were really moving in their praise. They were saying things like, "God bless you."

The paper seemed to become a bellwether of whether it was okay to laugh again. Even professional humorists looked to *The Onion* at that time. In my interview with Dave Barry, he said, "God bless *The Onion*."

We were just trying to reflect what everybody was going through, what people were feeling. We were trying to be honest about how we felt. And I think that's why people responded so much to that issue. We were getting a lot of fan mail at that time. The same thing sort of happened after we did the issue about the Columbine High School shooting in 1999. I personally was really, really freaked out when Columbine happened. That hit me really close to home, because that's the kind of kid I was in high school. Wearing the black trench coat and getting picked on by other kids and feeling like an outsider. That's who my friends were.

What article did you write for the Columbine issue?

"Columbine Jocks Safely Resume Bullying." It was an article about how everything was supposedly great again in Columbine. You know, "We've got metal detectors and it's all safe and we can just go back to everything the way it was before." Again, it was very sad. I was really afraid of how readers would react. We did get some angry letters from people who were offended. But, on the other hand, we got more fan mail for that issue than for any issue we'd run up to that point.

And then the 9/11 thing happened, and it was the same thing, except to the *nth* degree. People still talk about that issue when they meet me. They often say that it was a work of genius. That it was one of the greatest things they've ever seen in comedy. I don't know, I'm just really humbled whenever I think of people's reactions to that. The massacre was definitely the most Zeitgeist-defining thing that's happened since I've been alive. And the fact that our little paper was important to people during that time, it's just so humbling and so sad that I don't have words to express how I feel.

Do you regret having written any particular articles over the years?

I've never actually thought about it before. But I believe the honest answer would be no. There were articles I worried about and thought I might regret, but no, nothing I've ever regretted writing.

Are there any subjects that are off-limits for you?

When *The Onion* does "irreverent humor" about subject matter some might consider inappropriate for humor, I take it very, very seriously. And I wouldn't make a joke that was dishonest or that had the wrong target. People say you can't make a joke about certain things. We all know certain things aren't funny, such as rape. That's just understood. But in our book *Our Dumb Century* we had an article—I can't remember who wrote it—but it was set in 1919, and it was about a new study that found women were only at fault in 85 percent of rapes, not 97 percent, as previously believed.

Do you think the joke works because it was set almost one hundred years ago?

That's an honest joke about what people believed at the time. The target is the attitude toward rape; the target is not the rape victim.

Anything can be done—it just depends on what your target is. You can't make a genuinely funny joke at the expense of a rape victim. Is rape wrong? The answer is obviously yes. Are things that are wrong deserving of ridicule? The answer is obviously yes. Are things that are really, really wrong even more deserving of ridicule? The answer is obviously yes.

A lot of humor writers might be afraid to even tackle it from that angle, or from any angle.

It depends on what your attitude is toward the purpose of humor. If you think the purpose of humor is to cheer people up, that's one way of looking at it. I don't happen to have that attitude. Maybe it's because I'm an unbelievably depressed guy. Satire is the ridicule of human folly. There's certainly plenty of that to go around.

I'm not a cognitive scientist. But what I understand about humor is that it's a form of a startle reaction. It's the processing of fear. I certainly know that in my life humor has been all about sorrow and horror. Mark Twain said, "The secret source of humor itself is not joy but sorrow." He also said, "There is no humor in heaven." That's one of my favorite things that anybody has ever said.

Why?

Because you don't have to be an expert to figure out that humor is connected to the fear response. You know what I mean? Even the smile response of baring the teeth is a fear response in primates. It's a way of processing all of the terrible realities that, if you couldn't laugh at, you'd want to roll over and die.

Look, man, I'm a college dropout. What the fuck do I know? I'm just saying you don't have to be a genius to figure out that humor is connected to pain.

Writing for Sitcoms

Advice from Ian Gurvitz, writer for *Wings, Becker, Wonder Years, Get a Life, Frasier*

#1. If this is what you love to do, you should do it.

#2. Just realize there are going to be propeller blades that you're about to walk into.

#3. Don't have a soft heart. Get a strong stomach. Make a friend of heartbreak. Learn how to spend a few months on a script or a year on a script with it not being bought.

#4. Avoid "clammy" jokes, meaning jokes so old that they have a slimey film over them (for example, the spit-take joke).

#5. Avoid "clammy" plot ideas. (For example: "The Cabin Show," in which a group goes away on a trip and gets stuck in a cabin after a snowstorm. They have no food or water, but they are going to *learn* something about each other.)

#6. Avoid "schmuck bait," meaning story ideas that are so preposterous that only a schmuck would believe them. (For example, a woman going through labor in a stuck elevator.)

#7. If you don't have to write, then you shouldn't be doing this. Do not get in it just for the money.

#8. If you do happen to be hired on the staff of a great show, it's like riding a wave. It's the best job in the world. You're paid a criminal amount of money. You hang out with other writers and you make up stories and you tell jokes and you make each other laugh and people bring you food. Is there anything more fun than that?

#9. But, again, only do this if this is what you love to do. Otherwise ...

Paul Feig

Life, especially before the age of twenty-one, is filled with mortifying and embarrassing moments. And while most of us would just as soon forget them, Paul Feig has been writing down his bad memories and welcoming—even *encouraging*—the world to laugh.

Feig's body of work, which ranges from TV shows to humor books, has been described by *Relevant* magazine as its own genre—that of the "masochistic memoir." It's sometimes painful to read his stories, because Feig never sugarcoats his past or spins even the worst personal humiliation into a tidy lesson. As frequently as you cringe at the unspeakable horrors Feig has endured, and it can happen frequently, you still find yourself laughing. If he has accomplished nothing else, he's proved a universal truth about human nature: Tragedy is when something bad happens to you; comedy is when something bad happens to somebody else. Or, as Mel Brooks so eloquently put it, "Tragedy is when I get a hangnail. Comedy is when someone falls into an open manhole and dies."

Feig began writing down his life stories in the eighties, when he was fresh out of USC film school with few prospects in Hollywood. Broke and out of ideas, he signed on as a contestant for Dick Clark's *$25,000 Pyramid* game show and earned enough ($29,000) to support himself while he launched his stand-up career. After six months on the comedy-club circuit, he had generated so much material—much of it about his awkward high-school years—that he decided to write a memoir, which he tentatively titled *School*. The project was subsequently shelved.

Then, in 1999, thanks to a short-lived but critically beloved TV show called *Freaks and Geeks,* Feig became, if not famous, at least more well known than he had been during his stand-up days. Although the show—about a group of teenagers (both cool and geeky) living in Michigan in the early 1980s—was technically fiction, Feig has admitted that many of the story lines were at least partly autobiographical. There were the obvious similarities: the show was set in small-town Chippewa, Michigan, similar to Feig's hometown of Mount Clemens, a Detroit suburb. But the parallels ran deeper than geography. All of the characters, particularly the "geeks," were in some fashion composites of Feig's younger self. And the plots were often based on his (and the other writers') actual high-school experiences. When gawky nerd Bill Haverchuck (portrayed by Martin Starr) dressed up as the Bionic Woman for Halloween, it was inspired by Feig's own experience with cross-dressing.

Freaks and Geeks was canceled after just twelve episodes (six were later seen on the ABC Family cable network and then, later, on DVD), but it continues to have a loyal cult following even today, with fan conventions and viewing parties held across the country. At a cast reunion at San Francisco's Sketchfest in 2008, Linda Cardellini, who played brainy, unsettled, Lindsay Weir, admitted that she initially didn't believe the show was anything but the product of a very active imagination. "Then you would look at Paul," she told the website BuzzSugar.com, "[and] you'd see the earnest look on his face and the sadness in his eyes, and you'd realize that most of this happened to [him]."

In 2000, a book editor and *Freaks and Geeks* fan from Random House recognized this same sadness, and Feig was soon a published author, with the 2002 memoir *Kick Me: Adventures in Adolescence,* and then, in 2005, *Superstud: Or How I Became a 24-Year-Old Virgin.* Readers learned that Feig's youth was, to put it diplomatically, hellish. Whether it was his classmates demonstrating how easily "Feig" turned into "fag" or his first kiss, with a girl who had just puked at a school dance, things never came simply for him. Even masturbation, the only dependable bright spot in even the most miserable teenage existence, was ruined after Feig heard a radio preacher warn that "each time you masturbate, God takes one day off of your life."

Feig still occasionally writes for TV, but his main focus, as always, remains creating stories about his past. He's working on another memoir, the third in his "trilogy of shame," which will include, among others, an essay about his short-lived day job as Ronald McDonald.

One can only assume that things don't end so well for Ronald.

When I read memoirs, especially those written by humor writers or comedians, I often get the sense that much of it is fictionalized. When faced with a choice between going for the laugh or the truth, comedy writers usually choose the former. But I didn't get that feeling with your books.

I'm very much a purist about memoirs and the truth in stories. As far as I'm concerned, a memoir only gets its power when it's true. At some point during a story, especially if it's a funny one, a reader or viewer should be thinking, I can't believe that happened. I can't believe he or she did that. But if you're ever thinking, No, that's fake, then it just neuters the whole thing.

I mean, look—I can think of a lot of funnier endings for everything that's ever happened to me in my life, but that's not the point. Most of the experiences I've written about were just awful. They were painful and upsetting and horrible. And yet that's the great thing about humor. You can take those experiences, and if you recount them in a funny way, and if they're truthful and real, they will always become funnier.

That sounds like the sensibility of *Freaks and Geeks*.

Well, exactly. I've never considered myself to be a writer who's great at making up stories and plots. What happens when you make up a story is that you tend to fall into this standard set of *A leads to B leads to C*. We're all used to a standard trajectory for television and the movies; there's a typical route that a writer can go in a story.

When we were doing *Freaks and Geeks*, we always wanted to avoid that typical route. Real-life experiences are rife with bad decision-making. And bad decision-making is, in a lot of ways, the key to comedy.

I go through such a rigorous process of not making up material in my memoirs that my wife gets mad. She yelled at me when she read my manuscript for the longer version of *Superstud*—the one that didn't make the final cut. She told me that I didn't have to be so honest, that I didn't have to tell these stories exactly as they happened.

But if I did that, I might as well have written a novel.

Considering the stories you put into *Superstud*, I shudder to think what was left out.

[Laughs] Well, here's one story I left out: When I was about nineteen or twenty, I went out on a date with this younger girl who was really cute. We went to this bar, and we were sitting in a booth talking. My date excused herself to go to the bathroom. The booth was close to the bathroom, and I could hear this girl urinating. And it sounded like a fire hose.

We actually wrote that scene into a *Freaks and Geeks* episode, but we ended up taking it out. It was one of the times when the Sam character was getting close to dating Cindy. They were on a date, and Cindy had to go to the ladies' room, but it was out of order. So she went into the men's room, with Sam standing guard outside the door. He heard her urinating, and it really upset him.

Your wife had a problem with that story making its way into *Superstud*, but not some of the other stories? Such as when you attempted to give yourself a blow job as a twenty-something and nearly broke your neck in the process?

Oh, that she will not talk about! When I first showed her that chapter, she said, "You absolutely *cannot* publish that! Just don't!" So I thought, Yeah, maybe she's right. I called my publisher and told her to take it out, but the publisher said, "It's too late. Sorry. That's the sample chapter I sent out to all the booksellers."

What was the reaction from your family and friends after they read that self-gratification scene?

I mean, that's the risk you take. It was scary for me. Would readers relate to it? Or would I be the only person in history who's ever done this? That's the strange thing about being a writer. At first it's just you and your computer, or you and your pen and paper. And no one is going to read it.

You think, I'm just going to be honest. I'm just going to have this confession with myself. And you put it down. And then off the manuscript goes to the publisher, and there's always that moment when you think, Oh my god! Now it's out there. But if I think too much the other way, I wouldn't put out half the stuff that I do.

I grew up in a religious family. My parents never talked about sex, even though this was a time when people were very sexually promiscuous—the seventies. In our house, that was obviously not the case. My father abhorred the whole sixties and seventies sexual freeness. It was not a comfortable topic. And to this day, I don't like talking about sex. But that's why it's fun to write about.

The way you depicted your parents in both of your books is refreshing. Most memoir writers are so negative when portraying their parents, but you seem to have a real affection for yours.

I think that holds true not just for memoir writers but for almost everyone in comedy. It's clear that most comedians and humor writers hate their parents. I loved my parents, and we got along great. But that's really just how I approach humor. I prefer the humor of optimism. I naturally go into a situation thinking everything is going to be okay and everything will be really good.

Is that a Midwestern sensibility?

I think so, but it's hard to say. Maybe there is that sensibility from the Midwest—where you just hope and want for everything to turn out fine in the end.

What I do know is that people in the Midwest seem to be a little more emotionally honest—maybe their bullshit meter is higher. And I think that the Midwestern sense of humor is about honesty and realism.

When I first arrived in Hollywood and started writing comedy in the late eighties and early nineties, I found that executives would always react more positively to over-the-top characters. They preferred the nerds with the big glasses, who snorted and laughed really loud. And I hated that. It was fake and wrong.

Such as *Revenge of the Nerds?*

Yes, exactly. Those were the types of characters the executives were looking for. People always ask me, "Don't you just love that movie?" I always think, Actually, no, I sort of hate that movie. It feels ridiculous.

The kind of comedy I don't like is when the performers and writers are winking and basically saying, "I know this is stupid and you know this is stupid. I'm not really this dumb, but I'm playing as if I am." And that's fine, I suppose, but it's dishonest and it's kind of mean to the characters.

With that said, I don't mind a broad comedy when I believe what's going on and when the characters are authentic. That's what we tried so hard to accomplish with *Freaks and Geeks.*

How did *Freaks and Geeks* come about?

I wrote the spec script in 1998 and showed it to Judd Apatow, who loved it. Judd had a deal with DreamWorks, which bought the script, and the executives loved it. DreamWorks sent it over to NBC, and they also loved it, to the point where they said, "Don't change anything." This is all unheard of, really. I was very lucky. This happens very infrequently.

At that point, when we had the go-ahead, we started thinking about the cast.

We wanted to avoid the typical beautiful actors you find in most high-school TV shows. We didn't want models. We didn't want characters who were going to take off their glasses and let their hair down and then, all of a sudden, they're gorgeous.

Also, there was another element of casting that was very important: when you cast actors and actresses, especially in comedies, you often look for what you've envisioned in your head. So, when an actor comes in who's just so weird and different and not at all what you envisioned, there might be a tendency to say, "No, I'm sorry. You aren't what we had in mind." But I think that's wrong. More exciting things can happen when you take chances.

There were a few instances when we hired actors who were different from our original vision, and it just lent so much more substance to the show. We actually ended up including the actors' personalities in their characters' personalities.

Which characters in particular?

The actor who played Harris Trinsky [Stephen Lea Sheppard] is a good example. This was somebody we discovered in Canada, and we knew we had to add him to the cast. Seth Rogen, who played Ken Miller, we found in an open call in Vancouver. His character was barely in the pilot. Also, Jason Segel, who played Nick Andopolis—originally, his character was this little weaselly stoner. When Jason came in to audition, he was this big, strapping guy who was a basketball hero in real life. We later funneled that into the show.

The Sam Weir character was originally based on me. He was supposed to be a tall, gangly kid who was attacked by bullies smaller than him. That happened to me when I was in school. All of my bullies were two feet shorter than I was—it was just ridiculous. But when John Francis Daley, who played Sam, came in, he was just so real and so funny and so heartbreaking that it was not a problem to jettison that initial idea and change the bully aspect.

Once we started hanging out with the actors, the show started to write itself. We put a lot of real elements in, even specific moments. If two actors were mad at each other on the set, something similar would end up in the script. There was a moment during the shooting of the "Looks and Books" episode when Linda Cardellini, who played Lindsay, and James Franco, who played Daniel Desario, weren't getting along. So we worked that into the scene where Lindsay screams at Daniel after she wrecks her parents' car. It's funny, and it's real, and that's what makes these characters seem like your friends.

To me, that's really the difference between television and movies. I feel that movies are mostly about spectacle and huge stories. There are exceptions, but I find that that's usually the case. On the other hand, TV is about assembling a group of friends that you visit and hang out with every week.

One of my favorite characters in TV history is Jim from *Taxi*. He's a completely outrageous character, but you buy it because, as nuts as Jim is, there's a humanity about him. He's not winking and nodding. There's this sense of, I'm a weird guy, but this is just who I am.

Freaks and Geeks **is one of the most honest depictions of child-hood and the teen years that I've ever seen—on television, anyway.**

One of my pet peeves is when comedy writers write for kids and there's this attitude of, "If I knew *then* what I know *now*." That's why you get all these portrayals of wisecracking kids who put down the bully and the bully goes running off. That's all bullshit. That never happens—except in fiction.

It's almost as if comedy writers, who were most likely geeks in high school, now want to spin or sugarcoat their experiences as teens. They didn't get laid in high school, but they make sure their characters do.

That's just it. I've never been ashamed of my childhood. But I think a lot of comedy writers are ashamed of their younger selves. And I think that's why a lot of these people go into humor in the first place: the only thing you have to hide behind is comedy.

There's a lot of anger there, too. I did stand-up for a few years, and a good number of comics I met were extremely angry people. They were not pleasant. That's actually one of the things that drove me out of stand-up. I didn't like going on the road, because you never knew if you were going to get stuck with a head case or not. And I noticed one thing: comics love to be laughed *with*, but if people laugh *at* them, they fucking lose their shit.

I've seen more comics storm off the stage and yell at people, slam their mics down, and do weirder things than you could ever imagine. There's a real insecurity that comes with being funny. You're on a razor's edge. Comedy is an attempt to control things, and it just so happens that you're trying to control people through laughter. But laughter can go off the rails at any given point.

It all goes back to childhood. You can make the cheerleaders laugh, but if you say the wrong thing they're going to laugh *at* you and not *with* you. This can happen very quickly. Horribly quickly. So all this weird anger and resentment builds up.

Another realistic element of *Freaks and Geeks* is that the kids actually sound like real kids.

That's another thing that drives me crazy. I hate it when kids talk like adults; it drives me insane. Kids who actually talk like real kids are much funnier. The idea of even trying to jam adult thoughts and jokes into their mouths is just ridiculous.

This especially holds true with jokes. How many fifteen-year-olds are capable of coming up with jokes as sharp as those of a professional comedy writer?

Absolutely. There aren't too many kids who can come up with a hilarious joke. The characters in *Freaks and Geeks* often make unfunny jokes that could have been easily fixed by the writers. But that, to me, is much more amusing. The Sam character is very much based on who I was as a kid and as a comedy fan. I did so many unsuccessful comedy routines for friends when I was young. I used to dress like Groucho, and all that.

When you're a kid, your only refuge is through the comedy of successful people. All you do is quote lines from funny Hollywood movies.

What did Hollywood represent for you as a kid growing up outside Detroit?

It was like a magical fairyland for me. I thought every actor I saw on TV lived in a mansion and drove a Rolls-Royce. They were all rich and wore tuxedos all the time. When I first saw the reality of it, it just depressed the hell out of me. I first came out here in the early eighties. I drove onto Hollywood Boulevard, and the first thing that happened was that two hookers jumped onto the hood of my car. And I've never forgotten the shock that I felt with that.

Are you still friends with them?

I am, actually. They're coming over for dinner tonight.

What were some of the jobs you worked when you first arrived in Hollywood?

I worked as a tour guide at Universal Studios. Many of us guides were these deluded actor wannabes who thought that we were going to be discovered. It was ridiculous.

I almost died because of that job. I was giving a tour, and a woman was dangling one of her clogs over the side of the tram, and the clog fell

out just as we were passing the mechanized shark from *Jaws*. When I went
to retrieve her shoe, I fell into the water and almost got sucked into the
shark gears. I thought, I am going to die in front of this tour group—killed
by a fake shark.

Probably not the most ideal way to leave this earth.

No, not at all. But it would have made for a hell of a story back in
Detroit. Anyway, after that job, I went to USC film school, and when I
graduated, I worked as a script reader for the producer Michael Phillips.
He had produced *The Sting* and *Taxi Driver.* I was in charge of reading
the scripts that were submitted to his office and passing along the ones I
thought were good.

Actually, that experience was much more valuable than film school.

How so?

Film school was so theoretical, and there were so many rules that really
fucked me up. There was one rule in particular they were always teaching,
and it was right out of good old Syd Field's [1979] book *Screenplay*. And it
had to do with "theme." The theme of the movie is always *this* leads to
that. "Jealousy" leads to "downfall." One thing leads to another, which
leads to another, which leads to the end. Everything is set up in a logical,
well-thought-out manner.

But I couldn't do that; I was just unable to break down a movie that
way. It messed me up for years. I couldn't even get out of the gate, because
I couldn't make anything work. I would get hung up on semantics and
minutiae. And because I'm such a rule follower, when I first started out
this killed me, because it was so theoretical.

Another thing I learned as a script reader was that 99.9 percent of
the scripts that are written are basically terrible. This just blew my mind.
It actually gave me a lot of confidence. I was reading scripts supposedly
written by the best writers in the business, people who made a career of
screenwriting, and I thought, If these are the best writers in the business,
and they're producing this shit, then I can do just as well—and hopefully
better. It gave me the confidence to say, Okay, this is not a mysterious
kind of skill.

My whole life, I've always looked at things and thought they were more complicated than they really were. I would see writers portrayed on TV or in the movies, and they would sit down and type out a manuscript and it would turn out brilliant. That, for me, was how writing was supposed to be.

You thought that a writer had to produce a flawless piece of work quickly and easily?

Yes. A piece of writing had to come out perfectly or you were not a writer. Well, the process became a lot less mysterious to me after I read those scripts. It freed me up to write what I wanted.

***Freaks and Geeks* was only on the air for one season, 1999–2000, before it was canceled. What happened?**

When I created that show, I honestly thought, Who *wouldn't* relate to something like this? Who *wouldn't* want to see true stories from their past shown in a funny, realistic way? And maybe I didn't bank on the fact that there were a lot of people who didn't want to re-experience those years. But I found out pretty quickly.

Here's a good example: I was talking with a TV critic when the show was on the air. We were discussing the episode "I'm With the Band"—this is when the Nick character auditions as a [rock] group's drummer. Nick is terrible and embarrasses himself in front of Lindsay, the girl he wants to impress. And the critic said to me, "When Nick walked into that audition, I had to leave the room. I knew everything was going to go wrong, and I couldn't deal with it."

I remember when the movie *Independence Day* was coming out. I was sitting in a theater, and the preview for that movie came on. And it showed a huge spaceship blowing up the White House. I remember thinking, Well, this is going to be the biggest movie ever. It hit the pleasure center of the audience's brains. The problem with *Freaks and Geeks* was that it didn't hit that pleasure center. It played in the pain center.

How about the pleasurable-pain center? Can't a comedy play in that part of the brain?

How many people enjoy that part of their brain?

A lot, I would think. The show eventually found a huge audience after it went off the air, particularly because of DVD.

There's a large DVD audience, true. But in the grand scheme of things, that show was a blip on the radar. Hollywood is a numbers game. And that's not to say that Hollywood doesn't care about quality but that they only want the quality when it's going to bring in money. Nobody in Hollywood wants to do something that they're proud of but that nobody is going to see.

For so many weeks, we were one of the lowest-rated shows on NBC, and we were not a cheap show. We were on Saturday night at eight. We got knocked off the air constantly. We were pre-empted for baseball playoffs. We were off the air for two months at one point. In the end, only twelve out of the eighteen episodes were ever shown during that first run. Later, all of the episodes were shown on the Fox Family cable network. And they're now on the DVDs, of course.

Do you think the show could have found its audience if it had stayed on the air longer?

It never got to that point. The president of NBC at the time, Garth Ancier, hated the show. Absolutely hated it. Judd [Apatow] met with him once, and Garth was complaining about the "Girlfriends and Boyfriends" episode, in which Sam finally gets a date with Cindy Sanders and all she does is talk about this jock she has a crush on. And Garth dressed down Judd. He was like, Okay, you have the hero. And he's finally going on a date with the girl he loves. And she tells him that she's in love with somebody *else?*

This just blew his mind—that it was taken to that level and then, worse, there would be no payoff. He wanted a victory at the end of each episode. My feeling was that there are no victories when you're a geek. Actually, I take that back. There is a victory: you still have your friends, and you've gotten through the experience alive. That's the biggest victory you can have in high school.

You really got away with some edgy material, especially for a show that aired prime time. I'm thinking in particular of "The Little Things" episode, in which the Ken Miller character learns that his girlfriend is a hermaphrodite.

For a show like *Freaks and Geeks*, you come up with a million ideas and every one of those ideas will fit somewhere in some episode. But you need the show to be grounded. When it's grounded—when the characters are living, breathing, *real* people—then you, as a writer, can do practically anything with them. But you have to treat the characters and the ideas with respect. We're not saying that this young woman is a Martian. We're not saying that she's half-donkey. There are hermaphrodites and transgender people out there in the world. So, what if one of these people—this living, breathing person—walked into our lives? What would happen? And if you face it that way, the only challenge is keeping it real.

Your natural instincts with an idea like that is to make fun of the situation. But I always prefer to defend the underdogs. I have great empathy for people like that—and that's really why I have the hardest time writing about characters who are kind of cool and on top of their games.

But weren't the "freak" characters, such as Daniel and Kim, at the top of their games and considered cool?

They were, but they were still outsiders. That was really my whole motivation for making *Freaks and Geeks*. In high school, I was afraid of the freaks. But I ended up befriending a few of them, and I found that they were on the periphery—just like I was as a geek. I realized, Oh, these people are just like me. They're just going about it in a different way. The geeks used comedy and Dungeons & Dragons to hide, whereas the freaks used drugs and sex to hide. There were other differences, of course, but there was overlap, and both groups could talk the same language.

In other words, one high-school clique can bleed into the next, as opposed to *The Breakfast Club*–style cliques, which are so delineated?

Right, those are sort of caricatures. Real life doesn't work like that.

The anchor of *Freaks and Geeks*, Lindsay, was very well written, very well defined. This is another aspect that one doesn't find too often in television shows about high school—a very strong, exceedingly intelligent female character.

I feel closest to Lindsay. I wanted to create a character who saw the world of high school for what it was. So, what's the best way to do that? It's with a girl who is more mature and smarter than everyone else at the school. But I didn't want this character to be wisecracking. I wanted a real character who was stranded. She's sort of our tour guide, because we've all been stuck and stranded in high school.

We've all been in the jail that Lindsay now finds herself in. Some people liked that situation; some people didn't. Some had varying degrees of resignation to it. Lindsay sees it for what it is, and that, for me, becomes the best type of character.

That's interesting. It's almost like the Peggy Sue character in *Peggy Sue Got Married*. Lindsay is both removed from and living through the experience at the same time.

Right. The big difference is that she's still that age and she's still susceptible to it. And that's what I love. It's that dichotomy of feeling above it all while, at the same time, getting drawn into it.

That's why I love the "Looks and Books" episode, where Lindsay's new friends convince her to take her father's car, which then gets smashed. She thinks, I'm supposed to be the smartest out of all you people, and I turned into an idiot. And now I'm in the biggest trouble of my life, because I forgot who I was or who I think I am.

But at least Lindsay knows she'll escape. For some characters, such as Nick, there is no escape. He realizes, even at this young an age, that he probably won't be going to college and achieving the success that Lindsay likely will achieve. That's a very melancholy theme for a prime-time show about teens.

That was a really important element for me, because I grew up in the Rust Belt and I saw people like that, these kids whose fathers were in, say, the auto industry. And there was a real sense from a lot of these kids that they had to go into the army or into a factory and they wouldn't be able to go to college. They knew, even at that age, that there was no escape. This is a serious matter, and to portray that realistically was very important to me.

Back when I was going to college, *The Cosby Show* was popular. And NBC would broadcast these public-service announcements. The Cosby kids would say things like, "Don't do drugs, because you've got a lot to live for." And I used to think, Well, okay—it's easy to say that, but some people are sitting at home and aren't from a rich family and might have no future. And here's a kid actor making shitloads of money, and he's telling everyone they have a lot to live for? It's hypocrisy on the grandest scale. Seeing something like that was always a motivation for me to create something more realistic.

That was one of the things I dealt with in the "I'm With the Band" episode, where Nick auditions to become a drummer. Lindsay tells Nick, "You've got to follow your dreams! You can be anything you want to be!"

When I wrote that episode, it was my way of saying, "Actually, no. That's nonsense. You might have that attitude, but that's not the way the world works."

In almost any other TV show, Nick would have performed wonderfully in the audition and then made the band.

And even if he didn't make the band, they would have told him, "Hey, man. You're really good!" There would have been a wink of encouragement in the end, and he would have walked out of that audition thinking, Yeah, maybe I *can* do this.

But that's not interesting. And it's also not funny in that heartbreaking way. The cruel side of me likes creating situations where people get buried deeper and deeper. I find that really amusing—the fact that Lindsay starts out encouraging Nick to follow his dreams and then ends up feeling sorry for him and making out with him and then getting stuck with this nightmare boyfriend, well ... that's real life to me.

You've said that good writing is when characters don't always say what they feel. Would this be an instance of that?

Yeah. Lindsay doesn't tell Nick how she really feels, because she wouldn't in real life. You want characters to respond as they would in real life. They're saying things quickly without thinking about them. But when you write, you can take months to finish a script. So everything the characters say has been so well thought out that it becomes almost perfect. But that's just fake.

And sometimes characters don't need to say anything at all. Just a look or an expression will do.

Some of the funniest jokes in *Freaks and Geeks* are just expressions. When Bill looks off to the side and makes a face, that's the punch line. It's not a Neal Simon—y kind of joke with clever wordplay. You don't need that. You can get away with a lot by having just a simple expression. In the last episode, when Lindsay is getting on the bus and leaving her family for two weeks, supposedly to go to an academic retreat but really headed off to follow the Grateful Dead, what would she really say in that situation? When I was writing that scene, I thought, What would she say when she was looking back at her mother? Nothing much. You don't want to break your mom's heart, so you just smile and get on the bus.

How extensive and detailed were the backstories for each of the *Freaks and Geeks* characters?

I actually wrote a huge character bible, about eighty pages. That's not to say we used all of these backstories, but it really helped me as a writer. If you create character background, there's less chance of writing details that don't feel germane to the character. Even if it's something as specific as what clothes they wear and what music they listen to and what type of furniture they have at home, it becomes very, very helpful.

How much care went into the writing of each episode?

Tons. Tons! You know, there was a side of me that was relieved when we got canceled. I was just exhausted.

When you're working on a television show, the pace is just nonstop. You work so hard to get an episode perfect, and when it's done, you then have to deal with the next forty-five. [Laughs] It's overwhelming. That's why a lot of TV probably isn't as good as it could be; there just aren't enough hours in the day.

We did only eighteen episodes. I really don't know how you do it season after season. To me, it sounds nearly impossible.

Did the writing change when you knew you were on the verge of being canceled?

The pace accelerated, because we had all these stories we wanted to do, and we didn't have much time to do it. We wanted to have Sam date Cindy, and then for their relationship to slowly fall apart. But because we were going to be canceled, we had to push that story through very quickly. I feel that poor Cindy Sanders was completely kneecapped. We set her up as a straight girl, and then, in one episode, we turned her into a monster.

Fans of this show were very loyal, and a lot were quite upset when they weren't able to learn what happened to these characters. They took it very personally.

Oh, yes. A lot of people were very upset. But my feeling is, Do you know what happened to 90 percent of the people you went to high school with? And do you *want* to know? Quite frankly, I don't. I don't want to hear a potentially sad story. I want to remember them as they were. Mystery is sometimes a good thing.

In a sense, that's what I liked about the show ending so suddenly: loose ends are never tied up in real life.

But doesn't life contain enough mystery and loose ends? And isn't that what fiction provides: a tidy ending that you can't always find in life?

I'm not saying that it wouldn't have been fun to have created a second season, but I'm happy with the way things ended, especially for the geeks. In the last episode, "Discos and Dragons," the coolest guy at the school, Daniel, spends a night playing Dungeons & Dragons with the geeks, and he becomes a part of their world. I really liked that validation for the geeks.

But, yes, it would have been fun to have done something with the characters after they all returned from summer vacation. After summer, everyone comes back different. Some of my friends in high school were these super-nerds, just really awkward guys, and they would return from summer vacation as these enormous stoners, to the point where they never talked to me again.

Summer is the perfect time to re-invent yourself.

You find your vices. You get laid. You become cool. You go on a trip, and that changes your life.

It would have been fun to have a second season, because we were going to really play with that element and explore how some of these *Freaks* characters would have changed. We were going to have Bill Haverchuck [Martin Starr] become a basketball player. We were going to deal with little Sam Weir becoming really tall and handsome, which happened to John Francis Daley in real life. Where would he go? Would he stay with the geeks? Or would he start hanging out with the popular crowd?

I really wanted to have Kim [Busy Philipps] become pregnant. Neal [Samm Levine] was going to join swing choir. We were also planning on having Coach Fredricks marry Gloria Haverchuck, Bill's mom. But, again, loose ends are never tied up. Even if Coach Fredricks did marry Bill's mom, you know, the day after they got married they could easily have broken up.

Do you think Lindsay would have left town after graduating?

She would have definitely gone away. To me, Lindsay is such a free spirit. I've always joked that she would end up being a performance artist in the Village for about ten years, and then, after that, she'd become a lawyer.

From time to time, I've toyed with the idea of doing a show with Lindsay as an adult. And who knows? I talk to Linda all the time. It could still happen.

How would the writers have dealt with the characters if they had stuck around and graduated? Would you have shown the characters in college? Or working their jobs?

I've always said that this wasn't a show about high school; this was a show about a small town. It was not going to be a show in which, six years later, everybody is still in high school. Every year would be a school year. And certain students would graduate, and we would have to deal with what jobs they were doing and who went to community college and who went away.

There are two books of *Freaks and Geeks* scripts, and with both you did something rare. Instead of publishing transcripts of the finished shows, you published the shooting scripts. I don't know why more writers don't do this. It's much more interesting and informative to the readers, especially if they, themselves, want to write.

Publishing those shooting scripts was a reaction to Woody Allen's *Four Films*. When that book came out [in 1982], I rushed to the store and bought it. But when I saw that they were only transcriptions of his movies, I thought it was the biggest rip-off ever. There were literally lines in the book like, "Ah, ah, ah, I just, ah ..." I was never happy with books like that. They never helped me as a writer.

There's a very, very small group of people who are going to read a book of scripts. So it might as well be a textbook and show the readers what the process is truly like. The majority of the people reading a book like that are going to be people who want to write scripts. So let's make it truthful.

Do you think you could create a show like this again? Or are there too many elements that have to come together to duplicate that type of magic?

I don't buy that theory. If there's any magic, it only exists to create a chemistry within a group of talented people—actors, writers, directors, producers—who are willing to work together and allow each of the others to do their best work. I personally don't think that's a hard mix to create again. It's not always going to work, but I think it could work if enough talented people with a vision are willing to make it work.

At the end of the day, none of us is that different. Freaks, geeks, jocks, whoever. The events we experience as human beings are fairly similar. The circumstances are different, and the surroundings and the social strata are different. But, you know, insecurity is insecurity. And loneliness is loneliness. And the basic human circumstances are all the same. If you're telling honest stories that are done in a special way, magic can definitely be duplicated.

I hope. [Laughs]

Famous Last Words (of Advice)

Dan Gregor, writer for Adult Swim's *NTSF:SD:SUV* **and** *How I Met Your Mother*

Becoming a comedy writer is fundamentally a battle with yourself to stop being awkward. I know a lot of people who want to become writers because they think it'll make them appear funny, interesting and cool without ever actually having to demonstrate those things in front of living human beings.

But it won't. Being a professional writer is as much about your ability to collaborate with others—from other writers on your staff, to producers and executives, to actors and directors—as it is about your ability to come up with funny jokes on your own.

Irving Brecher

"Time wounds all heels."
—Groucho Marx, *Go West*

The Marx Brothers apparently never subscribed to the philosophy that "too many cooks spoil the broth"—at least when it came to screenplays. The brothers often employed anywhere from five to eight different writers for a movie. And that should come as no surprise: a Marx Brothers comedy featured such seemingly disparate elements as Groucho's intricate wordplay, Harpo's high-energy physical shtick, and plenty of musical interludes, both amusing and sincere. In the Marx Brothers' twenty years of starring in movies, only one of their screenwriters ever worked alone and received sole credit—Irving Brecher.

Brecher likes to say that Groucho Marx was initially dubious of his gag-writing abilities. But over the course of two movies, *At the Circus* (1939) and *Go West* (1940), Groucho quickly changed his mind and began referring to Brecher as "the Wicked Wit of the West." Brecher crafted some of the Marx Brothers' most hilarious moments, comic feasts for the eyes *and* the mind. Some of his jokes were outlandish, such as the famous scene in *Go West* in which the brothers tear apart a moving train to provide it with enough fuel to keep running. And then there were the more subtle gags, slipped in as rewards for audience members who paid close attention, such as jokes about Hollywood's unpopular Production Code.

Based on his work with the Marx Brothers alone, Brecher would go down in history as one of the greatest screenwriters of Hollywood's heyday.

But this poor kid from New York, born in Manhattan in 1914, went on to achieve much more—creating shows for radio and television, writing award-winning movie musicals, and becoming one of the forefathers of the television situation comedy in 1949 with *The Life of Riley*. Over the course of his career, Brecher has written for no less than Jack Benny, George Burns, Jackie Gleason, and Ernie Kovacs.

The first to recognize Brecher's innate talents was Milton Berle, who hired the nineteen-year-old to write gags for his stand-up act. Berle eventually moved Brecher out to Hollywood to write for his long-running radio show, *Gillette's Community Sing*. After "punching up" the screenplays for *New Faces of 1937* (1937) and *The Wizard of Oz* (1939), Brecher was recruited by MGM, which kept him busy for much of the forties, penning not only his two Marx Brother movies but a string of comedies such as *Shadow of the Thin Man* (1941), *Best Foot Forward* (1943), and *Ziegfeld Follies (1946)*. By far his most successful effort, however, was the 1944 blockbuster *Meet Me in St. Louis,* a nostalgic take on the 1904 World's Fair, seen through a Technicolor prism, and starring a twenty-two-year-old Judy Garland. The film was so well received that it led to Brecher's first and only Oscar nomination (Best Writing, Screenplay).

Although a trailblazer in the movie industry, Brecher had his biggest impact on the small screen. *The Life of Riley*, which he originally created as a radio show, was so popular during its seven-year run (1944–51) that NBC hired him to retool the series for television. It starred William Bendix as Chester A. Riley, a hapless working stiff and family man. From 1953 to 1958, *The Life of Riley* became one of NBC's biggest hits and a template for half-hour TV comedies for generations to come. You can see its influence on practically almost every subsequent TV show, particularly in sitcoms featuring working-class families who live in the city, each with a lovable lummox of a father-husband/best friend.

Your first major writing gig was for Milton Berle in the thirties. How did that come about?

I was an usher at the Little Carnegie Playhouse on Fifty-seventh Street in New York. That was one of only two art houses in the city at that time—this was 1933. I was nineteen then; I'm now ninety-three. We would screen movies from Germany and France, and that's really what made the theater exclusive. Actually, we had many anti-Semites as customers, some of whom were actual Nazis.

At this time, I was working six-and-a-half days a week for eighteen dollars. Occasionally, I would send a funny one-liner to the newspaper columnists Walter Winchell and Ed Sullivan. When they would print one, I'd get a big kick out of it.

I was taking tickets at the movie theater one day, and a reviewer from *Variety* came in. His name was Wolfe Kaufman—"Wolfe" with an "e." He knew me because he came to every movie that premiered. He said, "I heard a couple of your jokes last night. I saw Bob Hope at the Loew's [Paradise] Theatre and he used a couple of your lines."

I said, "No kidding. Really?" I was a little naïve. "They laughed like hell," he said. "Listen, schmuck, people get paid for doing that type of writing. Why don't you take out an ad in *Variety*? Maybe you'll make some money." I said, "Gee, that's a good idea. How much is an ad?" He said, "Fifteen dollars an inch," which was really much more than I could afford. He knew this, so he told me, "Just write up an ad, and I'll give you one inch of space. You can pay me back when you can."

I was very appreciative—but kind of bewildered. Later, when I was on my lunch break, I wrote an ad that read, "Positively Berle-Proof Gags. So Bad That Not Even Milton Would Steal Them. The House That Joke Built." Berle was known to steal jokes, so I was playing off that. I also published the phone number of the theater—which I still remember, by the way.

I can't even remember my number from a few years ago.

Circle 71294. I have a remarkable memory. It's weird.

When the theater closed that night, I walked down to the *Variety* office, which was in the Times Square area, and I dropped off the ad with the right person.

The next week the mail arrived, and I quickly looked for my ad in the weekly *Variety*. I was thrilled! A few hours later, the theater's phone rang. I said, "Little Carnegie Playhouse." A voice said, "Irv Breecher?" He pronounced it "Breecher." That was not the way my name is pronounced, so I figured it was my friend Lee, who always liked to fuck around on the phone. I said, "Lee, I'm busy," and I hung up.

The phone immediately rang again. I picked it up and said, "Little Carnegie Playhouse." I then heard, "No son of a bitch hangs up on Milton Berle!" I thought, Maybe this is for real? Berle said, "Are you the guy that took out the ad?" I said, "Yes, sir." He said, "If you're so smart, bring over some material, and be at the Capitol Theatre tonight at eleven. Go backstage. You'll be sent up to my room. Bring something funny."

I got the newspapers—at the time there were half a dozen of them—and I wrote some topical gags. I had about ten or twelve by the time I was finished. With great trepidation, which I can't even describe, I walked to the Capitol Theatre and entered the backstage. I had never been backstage at any theater, let alone a theater this big. I walked up the stairs to a room with a star on it. I knocked on the door, and a naked man opened it. I knew it was Berle immediately. I had already heard that he had the biggest cock in show business.

A firsthand account! So, the rumors were true?

Have you ever seen a salami chub? Yes, they were true. They were more than true. Anyway, I said, "Mr. Berle, you wanted me to bring some jokes—"

"—Yeah, yeah, yeah," he said. "Whatcha got?"

I handed him my gags, and he told me to wait a minute. He closed the door, and I just stood there. I can't tell you what I was feeling—but it was mainly terror and worry. Also, fear of failure. I was really petrified.

About five minutes later, he opened the door again. Now he's wearing a bathrobe, and he said, "Some of these jokes are pretty good, so I'll tell you what. You know where the Park Central hotel is? It's six blocks away. Run there, and go up to an office on the second floor where my agent works. He'll give you a check. Then come back, because we're going to work all night."

I ran to the hotel, and his agent handed me a check. I looked at it. It was more money than I'd ever seen in my life: fifty dollars. When I returned, Berle and I worked practically all night. I would write a joke, and if he liked it, he'd tell me to write it down. If he didn't like it, he would just say no.

We had worked up a monologue by around six the next morning. The first performance was going to be at 11 A.M. I remember sitting in the auditorium, waiting to hear my jokes. It was like a nightmare. Beyond scary. I was filled with strange tensions, all of which immediately vanished once Berle took the stage. He was dynamite! Just an incredible performer! He came out and practically attacked the audience. The monologue went over very well, and when he got to my lines, he received tremendous laughs.

And I remember thinking, I'm gonna be rich!

When the show was over, I walked up the stairs to Berle's room, and I'm about to knock on the door, when I hear a voice of a man—not Berle—screaming, "Listen, you bastard! If you use any of that material again, you're out of here! You'll never work in this theater again!"

Berle was imploring this guy, "Please, *please*! I got some laughs. What's wrong with the jokes—"

"—Shut up!" the guy screamed. "You heard me! *Never* again!" The door opens and L.K. Sidney, the manager of the theater, and later a very successful Broadway producer, walks out. His son, by the way, was George Sidney, who later became a movie director [*Annie Get Your Gun, Bye Bye Birdie, Viva Las Vegas*] and a friend of mine. I timidly walk in and ask, "What's happening?"

Berle said, "That son of a bitch of a manager! He doesn't want me to ever use a few of our jokes again. Can you believe it?"

What were the jokes the manager wasn't happy with?

There were two jokes in particular. Now, remember, this was 1933. The first joke had to do with the economic situation back then—a lot of banks were closing—and it also had to do with the actress Marlene Dietrich, who was really one of the first women to wear pants. The joke went something like, "People around the country are really desperate for money, and they can't do anything about it. In fact, when the banks closed in California, Marlene Dietrich was caught with her pants down." This got a belly laugh.

The other joke had to do with the former mayor of New York, Jimmy Walker. He was a womanizer, and there was a strong rumor that he had a mistress named Betty Compton. Everybody knew about this, but he wouldn't divorce his wife, because he was a Catholic. He was investigated by Congress, and during his testimony he said, "I can match my private life with any man's." That quote was published in many newspapers, and it became famous.

So Berle's joke went: "You see what's happening with Jimmy Walker. They put him on the stand, and he told them, 'I can match my private *wife* with any man's.' " Again, the audience screamed.

Those jokes seem pretty tame. Were they considered too blue in 1933?

It was a different time. They were considered off-color. Few performers even said "damn" until Gable finally did it in 1939, you know.

So what made you think you could get away with them?

I didn't even think about it, really. I just thought they were funny. I didn't know any better.

The next day, I quit my job at the movie theater. I mistakenly figured that Berle would need new material as he performed from one city to the next. I didn't realize he used the same jokes over and over and over again. But Berle, to his credit, mentioned my name to a couple of third-rate vaudevillians, and I started selling gags, at five to ten dollars apiece.

This was just before vaudeville disappeared.

It was in the process of disappearing.

But it disappeared quickly after you began to write for it, correct?

Yes, that's right. Radio made it easy for people to stay at home. Motion pictures were taking some of the vaudevillians away, too. One of those movies was *The Jazz Singer* [1927], which was a huge hit. A few years later, by 1933, when I first started working, vaudeville was already fading. The theaters were becoming picture houses—it was vaudeville with a movie. It was no longer straight vaudeville.

Were you a fan of the Marx Brothers before you began writing for them in the late 1930s?

It's a very funny thing. When I was a kid, years before I ever met them, I would dress as Groucho, with a burned-cork mustache and big eyeglasses and a rubber cigar. My cadence and voice were already exactly like his. It was no effort for me to imitate Groucho—none at all. I would make my friends laugh with my Groucho routines and monologues.

What in particular did you like about him?

I liked the fact that Groucho was anti-establishment. All of the Marx Brothers were nihilistic—they destroyed the powerful, those in charge, the big shots. They were iconoclasts. They pricked the big balloons, and I had always done the same thing.

Up to that point, I had seen Charlie Chaplin, and I loved the way he attacked the so-called Establishment. But the jokes, obviously, did not involve dialogue. There was nothing to quote. There was nothing to repeat for your friends.

I had seen other comedians in the movies—but I never saw a comedian flip lines for the sake of amusing themselves more than Groucho did. He told jokes just to satisfy himself. He was a huge influence for other comedians. [1930s comic actress] Carole Lombard began to throw her lines like Groucho, as did Rosalind Russell [*His Girl Friday, Auntie Mame*]. A lot of performers picked up on Groucho's style.

Groucho would also look directly at the camera—and at the audience. I don't know if this started with Groucho, but I had never seen it before. And I loved it. I later had Groucho do the same thing in the two films I wrote for him.

How did you get the job writing for the Marx Brothers?

By 1938, I was under contract at MGM, and I received a call from Mervyn LeRoy, a producer [and director] for the studio. He told me, "You're going to write a movie for the Marx Brothers." This would have been *At the Circus*, which came out in 1939.

I was shocked. I just couldn't believe it. I was going to meet the performer I imitated and loved! Incredible. The next day I went to LeRoy's office on the MGM lot, and you can only imagine how excited I was. Terrified, really. I couldn't believe I was seeing the real Groucho. Just couldn't believe it. And there he was, standing in the office. A screen image come to life!

LeRoy said, "Groucho, this is Irv Brecher. He's going to work on your next movie. He's a very funny writer."

"Hello, Mr. Marx," I said, trying to be polite. Groucho said, "'Hello, Mr. Marx?' Is that supposed to be funny?" I said, "No, sir, but I heard you say it once in a movie." Groucho just stared at me. Finally, he said, "I'm going to take you to lunch."

For whatever reason, he liked me, and we quickly became friends.

Groucho had a reputation for not being easy to befriend.

He was not easy to be with—that's true. He was a very withdrawn person; he was not outgoing. He was a bit of a curmudgeon. He was basically an unhappy guy. He went through two or three failed marriages, and he didn't have too many friends. But he did like me and my writing, even from that first meeting. He became a big champion of mine, and I was always very grateful for that.

Groucho told interviewers that if he had a choice, he would rather be a writer than an actor. So why did he need screenwriters? Was he not capable of writing a film script by himself?

I don't think Groucho could have done it. He did have a wish to be an important writer, but he wasn't really capable of writing an entire movie script alone. I don't know if he ever tried to write a movie script, actually. He did co-write one play in the forties, called *Time for Elizabeth*, and it was terrible. Groucho made his living as an actor. He was paid to act, and that's what he focused his attention on.

Groucho *was* very involved with the scripts and the details that went into making a movie. He was much more involved than the other two brothers.

Harpo was creative, and he would suggest a joke or two—he would even occasionally get involved with the rewriting. But Harpo was only interested in his *own* shtick. We would have meetings in my office, where we would both go over certain jokes or scenes, and maybe add a little something here and a little something there.

I remember this one time in particular, I came up with a Harpo bit for *Go West*. Harpo was in a face-off with another cowboy. It was our *High*

Noon situation, where they both slowly walk toward each other, but at the last second, Harpo pulls out a whisk broom and dusts the dandruff off the cowboy's shoulder. The broom then accidentally fired. It diffused the tension and got a big laugh.

How was Chico to work with?

He paid no attention. None. He showed up for shooting when he could remember it, but his mind was really only on gambling and women.

Groucho was truly the spokesman and the front man for the rest of the brothers. You could even say he was a type of producer, because the actual producers never really had anything to contribute—from a comic standpoint. I would read the producers the script, and they might say, "A little long, trim this part a bit." On the other hand, Groucho would carefully read each joke, and by the end, when he said, "That's good," then that was that. That was the version of the script we shot. Once Groucho approved a script, he almost never questioned a line when he was on the set. Groucho respected what was on the paper—at least when I was involved. I don't know how he was with his other screenwriters.

So the Marx Brothers never improvised scenes or dialogue on the films you worked with them on?

Never. Groucho always sounded like he was making up a joke on the spot—that was his talent. But his jokes were always very carefully written. Then again, he wasn't against telling me, "This line is a little hard for me to say. Can you rephrase it?" And I would do as much.

Were the Marx Brothers directed? I imagine they knew exactly what they wanted and weren't necessarily open to suggestions.

The Marx Brothers were not hooligans. When a director would say, "I think that if you do *this* a little over here it might be better," they really did appreciate it. They were not out to kill the director, necessarily. However, they had no respect for Edward Buzzell, the director of *At the Circus* and *Go West*. The brothers went through their paces on those two pictures—and nothing more.

In my opinion, the kind of work that Buzzell did with the Marx Brothers was not the type of work that made them better. Sam Wood, who directed *A Night at the Opera* and *A Day at the Races*, directed them differently—and more effectively. He shot the films dead-on straight, as if they were dramas. He didn't have the actors mincing around acting cute, which is what Buzzell did.

Can you give me a specific example?

Take a look at *A Night at the Opera*. That film was very successful because opera is a damn serious subject. And that only made the comedy funnier, having that anarchy bumping against the serious. It wasn't as easy to pull off with *Go West* or *At the Circus*. The circus is funny on its own. And when you throw in more funny, it becomes too much. You need a solid framework.

How did Hollywood's Production Code, adopted in 1930, affect your writing? Did you feel hamstrung by the limitations it set forth?

It's strange what the Hays Office [which ran the Production Code] would and would not accept. When it came to a line like, say, a joke that had to do with violence, it was okay. When it had to do with sex, it was often not okay.

Even with the Production Code, you did manage to sneak some very dark jokes into your Marx Brothers movies. I'm thinking in particular of the scene in *Go West* in which Groucho asks a stranger in a bar: "Didn't we meet at Monte Carlo the night you blew your brains out? Oh, how we laughed!"

You had to play games with the type of material you could get into a film. It's much easier now—there are far fewer restrictions.

But you really had to be clever in the way you went about writing certain jokes. There's a sequence in *At the Circus* where the actress Eve Arden plays a character who walks on the ceiling. She's the girlfriend of the crook who's stolen a wallet with ten thousand dollars in it. Groucho suspects her of being involved with the theft, and he very openly accuses her. He then watches as she puts the wallet down her cleavage.

I needed a line for this moment, to bridge the action, so I wrote a line where Groucho looks directly at the camera and says: "There must be some way of getting the money back without getting in trouble with the Hays Office."

The director was mortified to insert that line—he just wouldn't do it. He was replaced and the joke made the cut. A few weeks later, an audience watched a sneak preview, and the biggest laugh in the movie came with that line. Groucho later said it was the biggest laugh he had ever received in his career. The audience laughed so long and so hard that extra footage was added after that joke. Otherwise, the audience would have drowned out the dialogue that followed. That happened sometimes—when we were lucky.

So the Marx Brothers films were shown to audiences and then tweaked in the editing room?

No, not the films. The brothers would travel around the country performing the script live. They did this for all of the films, I think, except for *At the Circus,* which would have been impossible. But I do know they did this for *A Night at the Opera.* Four or five of the writers, including George Seaton, a friend of mine, traveled with the production and managed to get some added jokes into the movie. They also cut out some dead wood on the road, which only helped.

Go West went out on the road, and I would stand in the wings as it played in these vaudeville theaters. The brothers would perform the script, and singers would come out between sketches and perform. An emcee provided the audience with the plot. This was done four times a day.

It's incredible the amount of work that went into honing these scripts.

In most cases, the jokes worked. But if a joke didn't work, I would replace it in time for the next show, and certainly in time for the movie. Chico, of course, couldn't remember a damn thing, so we had a guy in the wings who would read out his lines. If you were sitting in the theater, you could have heard this guy behind the curtain, whispering out the jokes before Chico said them.

Yes, it was a good way to sharpen the movie. It was a good technique.

Beyond the language issue, how do you think comedy has changed from when you first started writing?

Comedy these days takes on subjects that have some sort of importance in the cultural or political life of the country. Now a writer can now talk about abortion, the death penalty, immigration. I don't even know if I would have wanted to deal with the abortion issue and other issues when I was writing, but it would have been nice to know that I could have touched on something real if I had wanted to.

Here's another major difference: I had to create a lot more material than today's comedy writers. When I wrote for *The Life of Riley* in the early fifties, I had to write most of the twenty-six episodes—by *myself.*

My point is that there are writers in Hollywood now who make a quarter-million for writing five fucking jokes per episode. I'd be a millionaire if I were starting now.

What's your opinion of the romantic interludes in the Marx Brothers movies?

Personally, I hated them. Just hated them. The difference between the Marx Brothers movies that I was involved with and the movies that came before was that Irv Thalberg, the producer of those earlier movies, cast very good actors and actresses for the romance portions. What I got was garbage. The two young actors who played the lovers in *At the Circus*, Kenny Baker and Florence Rice, had as much chemistry as Metamucil.

The romantic interludes were really an intrusion. However, the audiences at the time did like them.

I know quite a few fans in the present day, including myself, who can't stand them.

Like I said, I hated them, but they were in the movie for a reason. It gave the Marx Brothers a reason to do something besides running around and cracking jokes. If you look at the so-called plotting in *A Night at the Opera*, or in my specific case, *At the Circus*, the brothers are trying to help a young couple out. In *Go West*, they're doing it for Diana Lewis, because the bad guys want to take away her land. You see what I mean?

You don't think the movies would have been as popular without those subplots?

If you cut out the subplots, why would you be interested in what the Marx Brothers were doing? Who would they be doing it for?

Themselves?

No. A selfish gain? They have to act altruistically. You need certain things in film. You need that romance. But you also need a villian in movies. Do you remember the scene at the end of *Go West* when the Marx Brothers are riding a train, and they want to escape the bad guys, but they run out of coal? And they start to burn the wood from the train itself? If you can believe it, the producers wanted to take out that sequence. I said, "If you take that out, you have no end to the goddamn movie!"

Why did they want to take it out?

It was going to cost too much.

So the long romantic interludes could stay, but not the funniest scene?

Right. Eventually the producer came around, and told me, "I just don't know how we can cut it." So it stayed.

How confident were you, as a writer, that a joke would work on the screen?

This is certainly immodest, but I was almost positive every time. Now, that's not anything I'm bragging about—it just happened to me. It doesn't mean I'm a genius. It only means that somehow I had a way of doing this without any courses or college or teachers. What happened, happened genetically—that's the only way I can explain it. I don't take bows for that, but I am happy about it.

Can a writer learn such a thing, or is it merely instinct?

See, that's where I may be wrong, but I don't believe you can teach that. I don't believe you can teach anybody to be a top comedy writer. If anything, you have to teach yourself.

Why did you stop working with the Marx Brothers in 1940 after *Go West?*

I didn't want to keep writing for the Marx Brothers. I just figured that it was enough already. I wanted to work on other movies, do other things.

One of which is a long-forgotten little film called *The Wizard of Oz.*

For that movie, I was brought in to spike up a few lines of dialogue between three of the main characters: the Tin Man, the Cowardly Lion, and the Scarecrow. Mervyn LeRoy, the producer, thought the script could use more comedy. For about a week I gave each of the three characters new lines, which LeRoy approved.

Do you remember the jokes you wrote?

It was so long ago I don't remember the specific lines, but one had to do with Bert Lahr, the Cowardly Lion, boxing and saying, "Put 'em up! Put 'em up!"

Did you have any idea at the time that *The Wizard of Oz* was going to become such a big hit?

Not really. I did love the songs. I knew the songwriter Harold Arlen and the lyricist Yip Harburg. I was friendly with Harburg, and I ran into him one day on the studio lot. He said, "We just finished a song, and we like it. Do you want to hear it?"

I said yes and walked into a room with a piano, and this little girl was standing there. I had no idea who she was, but I later learned that her name was Judy Garland. They played the song, and this girl sang it, and I just knew it was wonderful.

You were one of the first people to ever hear Judy Garland sing "Over the Rainbow"?

I was one of the first, yes. And I just knew the song was special.

Let's talk about some of the other humor writers who were out in Hollywood at this time. Did you know George S. Kaufman?

I loved him. I befriended Kaufman when I came out to California. He was already Groucho's friend, and he had already written Broadway musicals, as well as the script for *A Night at the Opera*. He was a genius.

When I was with him, I was always happy to be in the presence of someone who was this good. I loved George, but he was a sour man—as most humorists are.

How about S. J. Perelman?

I thought that Perelman was a wonderful humorist in his books and in his short pieces for *The New Yorker*. But, as a person, he was not so nice. He seemed antisocial.

Dorothy Parker?

Only a hello. I saw her at the Round Table at the Algonquin when I had lunch there once.

Who else was at the Algonquin that day?

Harpo. Alex Wolcott. Edna Ferber [author of the novels *Show Boat* and *Giant*]. Harold Ross. I've forgotten who else.

What was Harold Ross, the founder and first editor of *The New Yorker,* like?

He was kind of a crotchety guy, but sharp. I'd only talked to him one time. I said, "Mr. Ross, I'm an avid reader of your magazine, and I'm curious: it seems like your movie reviewers really dislike movies." In a drawl, he said, "I wouldn't have a reviewer that *liked* the goddamn movies!"

He had scorn for the cinema. Now, that didn't mean that there wasn't a staff reviewer who didn't rave about movies, but Ross, the top editor, didn't like them at all.

Many of the readers of this book weren't born when you started writing humor. In fact, many of the readers' grandparents hadn't yet been born. If anyone in this book is entitled to give young humor writers advice, it's you.

I would say that if you think you're funny, then do it. As long as people genuinely respond to what you produce, keep at it. If their laughs seem genuine, keep writing. And don't stop. *Never* stop.

On the other hand, if nobody likes what you create, well ... find another profession. Like interviewing.

Thank you for your time. I hope to speak to you again one day.

Don't wait *too* long.

Thirteen months after this interview took place, Irving Brecher passed away at the age of 94 in Los Angeles.

Writing for Stand-Up

A list by comedian Myq Kaplan, *The Tonight Show with Conan O'Brien, The Late Show with David Letterman, Comedy Central Presents, Hang Out with Me*

#1. Carry a notebook or digital recorder everywhere you go. Or your brain, if that's your thing.

#2. If you see something, say something into your recorder. Or write it in your notebook. This can be anything you think could be funny. It doesn't have to be just seeing, either. You can hear things or smell them or just think them.

#3. Go on stage and say the things. Don't be sad if the audience is sad. They were probably sad anyway. It's not you.

#4. Record your sets and listen back. See where things went well. Edit the things that didn't go the way you wanted them to go.

#5. When you're starting out, don't force it. In fact, never force it. And by that I mean no rape jokes. Unless it's the best-ever rape joke. But it's probably not. I mean, go for it if you want, but why bother if it can't be the best?

#6. Keep repeating these steps. Hope that the spark of talent that exists within you—which may be impossible for anyone to see for years—will eventually ignite and explode.

Bob Odenkirk

Bob Odenkirk's Three Rules of Writing

1. Finish *all* errands and chores before picking
up pen and paper!

2. Put down pen and paper—computers are
where it's at nowadays.

3. Play computer games.

There's an urban legend about Bob Odenkirk that goes something like this: In the late 1980s, when Odenkirk was a staff writer for *Saturday Night Live*, Al Franken—also a writer on the show—pitched his Stuart Smalley character to the entire cast. Franken insisted that *he* was the only person who could possibly play Stuart. Odenkirk listened quietly, and then raised his hand to ask the question everybody at the table was thinking but didn't dare voice.

"Here's an idea," Odenkirk suggested. "Why don't we let one of the *actors* do it?"

Depending on which version of the story you hear—and there are at least two—Franken either leaped across the table and punched Odenkirk in the face, or he kicked his own chair and injured himself so badly that he couldn't perform at all.

If either of these stories is true—and even if they aren't—there's a lesson to be learned. Writers write, and the best of them are satisfied solely by tackling the often near-impossible task of putting words down onto the page in a coherent fashion.

Although Odenkirk hasn't always adhered to this truism—most notably when he performed in his comedy cult classic *Mr. Show with Bob and David*—he has proved time and again that, at heart, he's a comedy writer, perhaps one of the most brilliant in television.

In 1990, Odenkirk briefly joined Second City in Chicago, where he appeared in a critically lauded sketch revue called "Flag Smoking Permitted in Lobby Only or Censorama." While most of the cast were interested in showcasing themselves as performers, Odenkirk was busy coming up with ideas for others. For his friend and castmate Chris Farley, he created the character Matt Foley, a motivational speaker who scared teens with a warning about his own disastrous situation: "Thirty-five years old, thrice divorced, and living in a van down by the river!"

When Farley was hired by *Saturday Night Live* that same year, he took Foley with him, who became one of his—and the show's—most recognized and popular recurring characters. He gave Odenkirk full credit, of course, but the glory belonged to Farley.

Odenkirk's career has been filled with successes and failures, obscurity and slight notoriety. After leaving *SNL,* he joined the writing staffs of such short-lived shows as Chris Elliott's Fox sitcom *Get a Life,* in 1991, and the critically beloved *The Ben Stiller Show* for its only season, also on Fox, in 1992. He briefly wrote for *Late Night with Conan O'Brien* in 1993, but left to join forces with David Cross (another *Ben Stiller Show* writer) to create, in 1995, *Mr. Show* for HBO.

Mr. Show was one of those rare comedy masterpieces, such as *Monty Python's Flying Circus,* that managed to break the rules while making it all seem easy. With skits about Satanism, cock rings, and mentally challenged parents—all loosely connected by a narrative thematic thread—*Mr. Show* was consistently more intelligent and irreverent than anything else on television. But despite critical raves, Odenkirk and Cross's style of humor failed to attract a mainstream audience (or what counts for one on Monday mornings at midnight), and, in 1998, HBO axed *Mr. Show* after four seasons.

Since then, Odenkirk has remained mostly behind the scenes. He's written for animated sketch shows, such as Tim and Eric's *Tom Goes to the Mayor;* non-animated shows like *Tim and Eric Awesome Show, Great Job!;* and webcasts like *Derek and Simon: The Show.* He's also directed films both independent (*Melvin Goes to Dinner,* 2003) and studio-funded (*Let's Go to Prison,* 2006).

How early did your interest in comedy begin?

Very early. I got into comedy when I was a little kid. I would goof around with my brothers and sisters at the dinner table. My brother Bill and I would imitate the people we met in the course of a day, while the rest of my family ate dinner and laughed. Bill used to write for *The Simpsons.* Then, in junior high, I would write and perform sketches for school projects. I would do these sketches in various classrooms, and not just in my classes—the school would let me go around and do them in other rooms too.

So, that's really where it all started, but I never thought about writing and performing comedy for a living until I went to college, at Marquette University and then at Southern Illinois University. I wrote radio shows at both schools for three years—live performances and sketches every week. My friends and I performed them in the studio with no audience.

But it was a really long and slow process for me to ever think that I could do this sort of thing for a living. I just didn't know anything at all about show business, or how one gets a job in it. It wasn't a legitimate field. There was nothing real about it.

I take it that you or your family didn't know many people in the showbiz world?

No one. This was Naperville, Illinois. My parents didn't even watch movies. My mom's probably seen fewer than one hundred movies in her entire life. Show business was just not a thing that was talked about in my house.

It's actually a shame, because my father was a really funny guy, and he could have been a happier person earning a living as a comedy writer. He could have done it, I think. Instead, he made business forms for major corporations and hospitals and other companies, which you can now make on your computer in a second, but back in those days you had to hire somebody to design them for you. I think he was very unhappy—which, of course, is one of the reasons I am in comedy.

Who were your comedy influences?

My strongest influence was Monty Python. After that comes the Credibility Gap and Bob & Ray. Also, *SCTV* and Steve Martin's first album, *Let's Get Small* [1977].

What was it about the radio personalities Bob & Ray that you liked? Were they even on the air when you were growing up? They were very popular in the late forties, fifties, and sixties.

They were doing a lot of commercials, and I think I only heard them on records. My friend had a copy he'd somehow found. I loved their little individual sketches. Like the one about the guy who swam across the country by buying a semi truck with a pool on it and swimming the length of the truck, back and forth, back and forth, as the truck creeps along the highway. Brilliant, loopy stuff.

What in particular did you like so much about Monty Python?

I loved Python. People always tell me that they can see *Mr. Show* being similar to Python. In particular, with the way the sketches flowed into each other. But to me the primary attribute of Python was that it had something on its mind and, at the same time, was laugh-out-loud funny. Python actually made you laugh. It wasn't just intellectually funny or clever.

You also had different actors, with very different sensibilities, that blended very well. Once you got to know the show, you could tell who did what, like a John Cleese–Graham Chapman sketch versus a Terry Jones–Michael Palin sketch. You could even see how each of the sketches was different. But that's only after you got to know the show really well.

Mr. Show was similar. We had different actors, but it came together well. We had a shared sensibility. We worked really hard to make every sketch as good as it could possibly be. I think that's what happened with

Python too. Everything had to be approved by the whole group. The quality was very, very high.

How difficult was it to create the Python-esque segues for *Mr. Show*, in which each sketch would be seamlessly linked to the next?

I think that's one aspect of the show that's overrated. I'm glad we did it that way. It made all of the shows hang together. Sometimes it was a very clever trick. But sometimes those segues were not very clever. Our rule was that transitions had to work on their own merit, but they also had to somehow comment on the next sketch. That was very hard to do, and we just couldn't do it all the time. When we were really stuck for a transition, we would do something simple, like pan to a poster with a few words that summarized the next sketch—and then we just panned back.

One of the things we experimented with in the second season was abandoning this idea of thematically tying together the show.

Why? Wasn't that one of the aspects that made *Mr. Show* unique?

It became too difficult to pull off. We thought that it would be a neat thing to do, and it turned out to be a drag. And besides, we soon learned that the best *Mr. Show* episodes were the ones that contained scenes that were vastly different in subject matter and comic sensibility. One scene might be physically comic, and the next more verbal. It was really fun to jump between things that were as different as they could be in presentation and also in subject matter. In the end, you didn't really need to have those strict segues between sketches.

What would you look for in a sketch idea? Did a sketch have to meet certain criteria with the writers?

We would ask ourselves about every sketch, "Is it funny? Really, *truly* funny? Or do we just *think* it's funny because we really *want* it to be funny?" That doesn't sound very scientific, but I think there's an important truth there. We took this very seriously. It was very, very important to us.

Second: What is this sketch about? That was a little challenging some-times, because we'd have an idea that seemed funny, but the sketch didn't really have anything to say.

Does every sketch need to say something?

No, but it's nice to know the underlying meaning. If you have a sketch that's a bunch of taglines that are stupid and funny, that can just be a list of funny jokes. But if you can think of a unifying point of view for them—something you are clearly commenting on while you're listing a bunch of funny taglines—that's even better.

You've said that quite a few of the sketches from *Mr. Show* sprang from real-life experiences, including the sketch in which you parodied the *Mr. Ed* television show. In that particular sketch, you played a talking junkie who "spoke" just like Mr. Ed.

Yes, the "Talking Junkie" sketch. I had a meeting about writing a movie script for *Francis the Talking Mule*, which was a really dumb idea. I thought, What did the executives see in my past work that made them think I'm the perfect guy to write this? It then made me think about talking mules and what's at the core of that type of comedy. People are just fascinated by something that talks that shouldn't be talking. The notion occurred to me that junkies are just so weird, almost like a different species. So that's how that sketch came about.

Here's another sketch that came from reality: the "Great Hemingway" sketch, from Season Four. It was about an explorer who tells his friends about his amazing adventures to Africa, but he only uses descriptions in relation to his scrotum and ass. I've always loved Hemingway, and I remember reading an issue of a magazine that had an excerpt from a lost Hemingway fictional memoir [*True at First Light*, 1999]. And one of the first sentences in the excerpt was "You cannot describe a wild lion's roar.... you first feel it in your scrotum.... " And I thought, Now *that's* bad writing.

Not Hemingway's best line.

Just bad writing. Now, in Hemingway's defense, who knows if he would have kept that sentence in the book had he lived, but that's just trying way too hard to be cute in a really strange way. And so the sketch came from that.

Another instance of a sketch coming from real life was our "Fartin' Gary" sketch. The character Fartin' Gary was a professional farter, or a "fartist." That was his act: he would fart. We based him on a real performer named Mr. Methane who was at the Montreal Comedy Festival when David [Cross] and I performed there in 1997.

It's a living, I guess. Or maybe it isn't.

You have a reputation for being a perfectionist. Are there any *Mr. Show* sketches you're still not happy with?

I can think of two sketches that were among our worst, but I wish to hell they were our best. One was called "Clumsy Waiter." It was from Season Four, and it was about a waiter, played by me, who spills food on a patron's suit. The maître d', played by David, insists on paying for the restaurant's mistake, but only for *half* the cost of the cleaning. It almost devolved into vaudeville, which is what it felt like when we were rehearsing it. It didn't work, but it could have been a good one.

What do you think that sketch needed?

It needed exactly what I pitched and what no one would do. No one would do it! Dino Stamatopoulos, one of the writers, told me, not long ago, "We should have done what you wanted, and I wish I would have backed you on it." What the sketch needed was a little stopwatch in the lower-right-hand corner of the screen with "Time till end of sketch" and a countdown.

Wouldn't that have called attention to the fact that the premise for the sketch was weak, and that even you, as the writers, knew it was weak?

Yes, it would have implied that we thought the sketch sucked. But it doesn't matter. It would have made the whole thing funny. I believed that, and I fought like hell. But that's something I didn't win.

Why did the other writers not want to do it?

They said things like, "Come on! Some people might like the sketch. Don't do that to them. Don't steal their joy if they are going to enjoy it." But—goddamn—that would have been funny, wouldn't it?

I think it would have been. I've never seen anything like that on a sketch show.

It would have worked on so many levels. It would have said that the sketch wasn't working and because of that, we're now giving you exactly what is needed to improve it. Which is a countdown to the end of the sketch.

What was the other sketch you're not happy with?

The "Philouza" sketch.

The sketch was a takeoff on the relationship between Mozart and Salieri in Amadeus. Two nineteenth-century composers of marching-band music—one a genius, the other an idiot—compete for the attention of a beautiful woman.

To me, that sketch just never worked as well as it did on the page. I think maybe it was miscast. We were trying to be clever by having me play the sillier character and David play the angry guy—not that we were some kind of traditional comedy team who had the prescribed roles, but I would often play the person who got angry about the craziness going on around him. And with that particular sketch, it just didn't work with us in those roles.

Dino and I wrote that sketch, and, from the first draft, everyone who read it said, "Wow, that's perfect. Just do that." Troy Miller directed it and did a great job. It's very well executed in every way, but it just isn't that funny. Maybe the concept is a little too rich or something. Just a little too pleased with itself.

You're so honest with your assessments of your work. There's no sugarcoating.

To me, honesty is everything; it's an honesty about life and people and the way we all act and the way in which we are pompous or hypocritical or ridiculous. And for me, that translates into being honest about the work, too.

I think I've tried to become more forgiving about things in the last few years. I don't know if that really helps your work, though. But I'm always trying to stretch myself and grow. I think another thing that I've been really trying to do in the last few years is to be a little less ironic and do some things that are more honest and straightforward. That's always hard for anyone who starts in comedy.

How did the writers' room work at *Mr. Show?*

Very few ideas were not accepted by all the writers by the time a sketch got on the air. You would have to prove it to the group, and certainly to David and me. We both had to like everything. Neither of us wrote things off. Neither of us said, "Well, you like it, but I hate it, so just go ahead." We just didn't work like that. If I didn't like something, I would say to David, "I just don't like it yet." And he was the same way.

Also, I'd come from *Saturday Night Live*, and a lot of what I did at *Mr. Show* was a direct response to things I thought were done poorly at *SNL*.

Like what?

Like very little interaction and very little guidance for the first two days of the week before the show—and then all of the material is suddenly brought to a rewrite meeting in the last fourteen hours. By that time, everyone's wiped out. Another thing I was reacting to was the way in which ideas were abandoned after one reading at *SNL*. If the ideas didn't go over well at the first pitch meeting—for whatever reason—they were thrown away, even if they were good ideas. You couldn't pitch them again, because they had already been done once and they didn't have the surprise element to them. They weren't new to the people in the pitch room the next time they read them.

How often did that happen to you at *SNL?* When you felt that you had a good, solid idea, but once it was rejected it was never used again?

There were quite a few times when that happened. There were jokes and ideas I used at *The Ben Stiller Show* that I'd written for *SNL*, like "Three Men and an Old Man," which was a takeoff on the movie *Three Men and a Baby*. In the sketch, three men cared for an old man as if he were a baby.

I pitched that idea at *SNL* and it didn't get anywhere. We later used that idea on *The Ben Stiller Show*, and it was that episode that actually won the show an Emmy in 1993.

I saw that happen often at *SNL*, but probably more so with other people's ideas that I thought were really good. There would be a reading of a sketch in front of everyone, and it didn't go over well, and then that was the end of that. And I thought, Well, why get rid of it so quickly? If you had done a rewrite, you could have ended up with a good sketch.

Another thing that used to happen at *SNL* was that if you were a new writer and a little tentative, you may not have pitched things well. I remember pitching ideas when I was new. And I would get my ass kicked. I would wonder, What am I doing here? You liked my writing samples. And now you won't listen to me. I'm not that good at pitching. I'm new to this. Give me a chance—help me pitch it.

So I was really averse to quickly rejecting ideas on *Mr. Show*, and I guess I even took it to a torturous extreme. When writers would pitch ideas at meetings, and I think the other writers can attest to this—with very few exceptions—I would talk at length about every idea. Because when you shit on a writer's idea quickly, they either clam up or they pitch ideas just for the sake of pitching them and just to sort of waste time. They know everything is going to get shit on, and they're more apt to pitch something that even *they* don't believe in. So you get this list of shitty pitches that are being bandied about.

I tried to avoid that at *Mr. Show*, and some of the best sketches came out of that process.

Like what?

The "Titannica" sketch.

A speed-metal band named Titannica meets one of its fans in the hospital after the fan hears a song called "Try Suicide" and does exactly that—tries suicide, but fails. Not an idea one would think of as being funny, but it worked.

That sketch is a perfect example of what I'm talking about. One of the writers, Brian Posehn, pitched it in the writers' room—and it got no response at all. At first, it was about a kid who jumped into a vat of acid and was burned from the neck down. The sketch didn't have a comic core to it. It was just kind of mean-spirited. After we finished reading it, we set it aside and I said, "So what's funny about this idea?" The rest of the writers looked at me sort of like, "You *asshole*! Nothing is funny about that! Don't even say that it's funny!" Brian then put aside the script and said, "Oh well, it didn't work. So what?"

In the writers' room at *SNL*, no one would have heard that idea ever again. But my feeling was "Brian, you are a funny guy. You wrote this because you saw something funny here. What is it? What was funny to you? Because if we can all understand why you thought it was funny, then maybe we can make it great, or maybe we can all agree that it is not very good. But you didn't intentionally just write a piece of shit."

After discussing this Titannica idea for a while, I thought of having the kid's body just be a puppet, shriveled and looking like a wrinkled hot dog. I also wanted to make the kid very upbeat. And that changed everything about it. Then everybody grasped the attitude of the sketch: that this kid has a really good attitude. He's done a horrible thing to himself, but he's still really happy to meet his heroes, these incredibly stupid heavy-metal musicians.

So those two aspects of the sketch came together and it worked great. It just took time to make it work.

A lot of *Mr. Show* characters were losers or physically disabled.

Yes, but by and large they were happy and upbeat. And that's actually a lesson I needed to relearn in the course of making movies, I think.

How so?

When you feature a physically or mentally disabled person just to feature them, it becomes mean-spirited. More importantly, if it's not funny enough, there's nothing to save it. There is no reason to like what you're seeing.

That's very important: to have a good feeling, an upbeat feeling. There are very few comedies that I can name that don't have "dog" jokes in them, or "dog" scenes—meaning just awful jokes and terrible scenes. But in the good comedies, you excuse those bad scenes and bad jokes because you just don't care; it doesn't matter. They blow by you—they're not weighed down, and the good things are still worth waiting for.

Was this one of the problems with *Run Ronnie Run!*, the 2002 feature-length movie that involved Ronnie Dobbs, a *Mr. Show* character? You've talked in the past about your unhappiness with that film.

To its credit, the movie has a few scenes that are really funny. It has as many funny scenes as can be found in numerous hit comedies. But the problem with it is that the unfunny scenes are such tonal shifts that they drag the rest of the movie down. They *really* weigh on the rest of the movie. The trick is to have a consistent tone throughout. If you can accomplish that, then the scenes that don't work can just be excused. You say, "Well, whatever. That didn't work."

In *Run Ronnie Run!*, there is a really funny scene with Jack Black. He does this takeoff from *Mary Poppins*, in which he plays a chimney sweep and sings a song in a terrible Cockney accent on a roof. Now, if we had put that scene in *Mr. Show*, it would have been a huge hit. It would have killed, and it would have fit. But in *Run Ronnie Run!*, it doesn't fit with the rest of the movie.

Does that theory hold true for *Mr. Show*—that even if one sketch didn't work, the rest of the show would still work, as long as the tone remained consistent?

Yeah, I think so. Just take a look at *The Ben Stiller Show*. The show was really a great experience for me, and it's something I was really happy to be a part of. And yet the tonal shifts in that show are very noticeable. The scenes don't complement one another and the show doesn't have what Python had and what *Mr. Show* hopefully had, which was that shared sensibility. Even though a lot of the individual pieces were very good, I think the show dragged and didn't work as well as it could have—in particular, the segments between the sketches, when Ben would walk around the sets and talk with the guests.

A lot of *The Ben Stiller Show* sketches were brilliant, such as the one you wrote called "Manson," a parody of *Lassie*. You played

Charles Manson as a lovable, shaggy-man-creature who lived with a 1950s family and had many fantastic adventures.

You really have to give Ben Stiller and Judd Apatow, two of the creators of that show, a lot of credit. It's so hard to get a sketch show on the air, and it's even harder to make a *great* sketch show. They were really young, and it was a great experience for me and the rest of the actors on the show, like Janeane Garofalo and Andy Dick.

But I was never completely thrilled with that show. In fact, I always felt it was a bit of a disaster. None of the episodes were cohesive—the tone and voice were different from one sketch to the next. There were some brilliant moments, but overall the show was a mess.

Maybe another reason it didn't gain a huge audience was that it wasn't exactly typical family fare, and yet it was first broadcast Sunday nights at 7:30.

Absolutely. Part of the success of a show is that you have to be on a network and in a time slot in which you belong and can do well. That show was never going to succeed on that network at that time.

It also didn't help that we were up against *60 Minutes.*

Was that part of the problem for *Mr. Show* and why its ratings weren't higher? That it was on HBO at midnight on Monday morning?

I think the time slot was a problem, but the biggest problem was that it never really had the full support of the network. I do know that two executives—Carolyn Strauss, later the president of HBO Entertainment, and Chris Albrecht, later the chairman and CEO of HBO—were fans. They really made the show happen in the first place. But beyond those two, there weren't many executives at the network who understood the show or liked it at all. In fact, I think a lot of people really actively disliked it.

Have the executives at HBO since changed their tune now that the show has been released on DVD and has done extremely well—at least with comedy fans?

No. You know, this is true of sketch comedy, and maybe it's becoming less true, but I think sketch comedy is about concepts and new ideas. To me, the best sketch comedy, like Python, is not about recurring characters and situations but something different and fresh. And viewers might have a lot less patience for that than they would with the tried and true—with the familiar. Audiences like the same characters and the same ideas week after week. It makes them comfortable.

Why do you think that is?

I think people are looking at entertainment not for ideas; they are looking at it for an easy kind of distraction. And I think this especially holds true as viewers get older—when there's less patience for being challenged. They reach a point where they don't want to look at a show and have to ask themselves every two minutes, Where are we now? That's exactly why high-school kids and college kids, whose brains are orgasming with ideas, are thrilled by sketch comedy.

If you go to colleges and see how many goddamned sketch troupes there are, it's insane. It's like, Calm down! There are sketch festivals in which fifty groups are going to perform in three days. What the hell is going on? There can't be that many people who want to do this. But that's where you are headed at that age. Then people get older, and they just don't want to hear a new idea. They want to sit back and watch the same people do the same thing they did last week. That's what TV exists for—it exists to be a mild sedative.

We've been talking about Monty Python. Fans might assume that *Monty Python's Flying Circus* was hugely popular when it was on the air in the late sixties and early seventies, but, like *Mr. Show,* the Pythons didn't necessarily get the credit, or the ratings, they deserved at the time.

Yeah, that's true. I saw the guys from Python when they reunited to receive an award years ago, and John Cleese got up and said that he wished Python had received the award back when they really needed it. He said, "No one watched the show when we made it." And now I think about how hard it's been for David and me to get a *Mr. Show* sketch-movie made, and how we really had no control in the making of *Run Ronnie Run!,* a film we both really think is subpar. And it occurred to me that Python had a benefactor—George Harrison.

If you're going to create a comedy like Python or *Mr. Show*, you need a benefactor. No one's going to take a chance on that type of comedy otherwise. If Python hadn't had George Harrison, they never would have made any movies. It's not like a studio wanted to make a movie with them.

But there has to be at least one Hollywood executive out there willing to make a *Mr. Show* movie. Fans have been clamoring for one since *Mr. Show* went off the air in 1998.

Mr. Show is very much a cult success. Our fan base and our awareness level really goes to a certain place, then stops. And unless we get a benefactor or somebody in a rock band who makes millions, someone who loves us and says, "Here, make a movie," it's just not going to happen—no one who runs a studio has ever heard of us. It's hard for our fans to understand that, but it's really true. It's funny that I say that, because one of the producers of *Mr. Show* was Brad Grey, and he now runs Paramount. But did he ever see *Mr. Show*? I don't know. I'd be willing to bet he never saw an entire episode.

It was only a half-hour.

That's just show business. When you are talking about making a movie, you are talking about needing somewhere in the neighborhood of at least two million. And who has two million to just spend?

People ask us all the time: "Why aren't you making a *Mr. Show* movie? What's wrong?" And we tell them that basically we need money, and it's very hard to get. David and I have talked about it, but we just don't feel right asking for it.

Why not? The script is already written, right?

I just don't feel comfortable asking for money. But I certainly do tell the studio executives I happen to meet that the sketches are really funny.

Any sketches that you can tell me about?

There's one called "The Attack of the One-Eyed Aliens." It's a takeoff on 1950s sci-fi films, where the aliens look exactly like giant penises. All of America is in fear. Europe is okay with them, however.

France especially.

Right. Europeans have no problem looking at them, but Americans are running and hiding. Then the army is sent after them, and it's like a horror movie. Another sketch is called "Stripper Town." It's our version of *The Stepford Wives*, only all of the women are strippers who string their husbands along. Champagne flows out of the faucets, and you have to pay your Champagne bill every month.

One of the things you seemed to avoid with *Mr. Show* was using topical material. The material has remained very fresh.

We tried to avoid topical material. That was another thing from Python. We would also try to avoid repeating characters. Python had two or three characters that came back a few times, but that was about it. I never liked the recurring character thing on *SNL*, although it works for that show. When I left *SNL,* I really wanted to get past that sort of thing.

***Mr. Show* also refrained from using too many catchphrases. *SNL* is notorious for doing just the opposite.**

I am not a fan of the "Pump You Up" and the "Making Copies" type of thing. I don't like that very intentional philosophy of "We are going to grind this catchphrase into your head and you are going to like it."

But you did write a sketch on *SNL* with a catchphrase of sorts: the "van down by the river" line, in Chris Farley's motivational-speaker sketch.

I first wrote that sketch at Second City, and I wrote it very quickly. There've been very few things that I've written over the years that just flowed out of me, that were just really strong and pure. And that was one of them.

It may also be one of the strangest sketches I ever wrote, because it's not really funny. It's only funny with Chris Farley doing that character. It has a catchphrase, but it's different. That character is telling a story with that catchphrase. It paints a picture; the phrase has a lot more meaning to it than just a catchphrase that stands alone.

It's a sad story, too. Here's a motivational speaker whose job it is to give advice, and yet he's an absolute disaster.

It's very sad, you're right.

So why do you think it worked so well?

It was a perfect marriage of an idea and an actor who made it real. Chris just made that guy come to life. Chris had a real sad side to him, and he somehow used that side to make that character work. As an actor, he was very sympathetic onstage, and very charismatic. Audiences really liked him.

That particular sketch contains a very strong idea: that this guy uses his own tragic career path as fodder for his motivational-speaker bit. But there is a lot more to it when Chris did it, and he made that character whole. It's not a gimmick. You felt like there was a real person in that character. I wrote the idea, and Chris performed it the way it was written and he really made it very popular. They even wrote subsequent sketches after I left the show.

That character became a lot more cartoonish after you left. The writers seemed to replace the sadness with easy laughs.

I told Chris and the writers, "Look. Whatever you do, the one thing to remember is: don't start from the ending. Start from the beginning, so that you have somewhere to go." Almost every time Chris did that sketch after I left *SNL*, he started by breaking the table.

It just became one of those dangerous examples of becoming addicted to the big laugh. You become addicted as a performer to that big moment, and you ask yourself, Why am I not just doing my big thing that gets the big reaction? Why am I not just standing up there and doing that?

You mentioned earlier in the interview that you found the writers' room at *SNL* forbidding, but you did manage to get other great sketches on the air.

I'm trying to think of some of the sketches that I don't hate. I wrote the Dana Carvey character Grumpy Old Man. I helped write "Mr. Short-Term Memory" for Tom Hanks, which was a Conan O'Brien idea. I remember working on the "Drill Sergeant" sketch when Matthew Modine hosted, which was a takeoff on the boot-camp scene in *Full Metal Jacket*. And I helped Robert Smigel with his "McLaughlin Group" sketches.

Robert actually got me on the show. I knew him from Chicago; this was in the mid-eighties. He lived in an apartment with three roommates, and I knew one of them. I then moved into Robert's apartment and became one of his roommates. We shared a room.

You've said in the past that Robert Smigel helped you become a better sketch writer at *SNL*.

I don't understand where Robert got his instinct for sketch comedy. I had written many sketches before I got to *SNL*, but he taught me a lot. He used to talk about finding the core joke of your sketch, which was something that struck me as a great lesson and one of the first things that a writer should think about when it comes to sketch comedy.

A sketch starts off as an idea, or a point of view. You then take it and you twist it and play with it and try to find an ending for it. But each sketch needs an idea. Robert just had a sense of what the core idea for a joke should be—what mattered in a sketch and how to construct the sketch around what matters. He was very aware. He wrote a lot of sketches that were definitive for our time, for our generation. For instance, the *"Star Trek"* sketch from 1986, in which William Shatner tells the Trekkies to "get a life."

Robert wrote a lot of amazing sketches. "Da Bears" was his idea. Just so many things. I've said in the past that he saved that show, and I really think he did. He gave that show, I think, the strongest and smartest sketches that it had for a couple of years. When Robert arrived, stand-up comedy was really at its peak, and sketch-comedy was not happening. *SNL* was kind of a mess. But he definitely helped change that.

There were just so many limitations placed on the writers at *SNL*, like writing for a host each week. That was a creativity killer.

A lot of the show's hosts are not actors at all, but athletes, musicians, or politicians. And even if the hosts *are* actors, a lot aren't fluent in comedy. Did you work on the infamous show hosted by Steven Seagal in April of 1991?

Yes, I did.

That was a notoriously difficult week.

Steven Seagal was insane. He was a tree that spoke. He was unbelievable. He kept saying all week that he had never seen the show; that
he didn't even know what we did there. I mean, who could even believe
that? He was obviously just pretending he had never heard of the show.
He was a scary presence. I was sitting in a dressing room with him and
Dana Carvey, and I thought, This guy could really hit me.

That week was a nightmare. I was helping write a "Hans and Franz"
sketch and Seagal said to me and some of the other writers, "If I do this
sketch—*if* I do this sketch—I'm only going to do it under one condition:
I have to win."

Win what?

The fight. Hans and Franz were going to challenge him to a fight.
And he wanted to win it.

He thought it was going to be a real fistfight?

I don't know what he thought. The whole thing was so bizarre. He
was also involved in the worst sketch ever done on *SNL*. On behalf of the
environment, Steven Seagal gets in a fistfight with a bunch of corporate
guys. It was about eight minutes long, and it had three sets. It ended with
Seagal having to fight live on TV, just as clumsy and awkward as can be,
where he beats up these guys, these stunt people who were brought in. At
the end of the sketch, Seagal turns to the camera and says, with no sarcasm
or irony, "That's what you get when you *mess* with Mother Nature!" Or
maybe it was, "That's what you get when you mess with *the Earth!*" I don't
know. The audience—their jaws just dropped. They did not know where
to turn. They couldn't back out, and they couldn't leave, because the doors
were locked. It was the only time where the APPLAUSE sign came on
and the audience just looked at it and squinted and refused the request.

**How was your experience on your two major-studio films, *Let's Go
to Prison* and *The Brothers Solomon?* The first was released in 2006,
the second in 2007. Did you have the creative freedom you had on
*Mr. Show?***

No, of course not. This is Hollywood. I had total creative freedom at *Mr. Show*; David and I had complete power over the script, the production, and the delivery.

Both of those films were made with a team of producers and a script written by other people—all people I like very much and with whom I'm proud to have had an opportunity to work—but they were decidedly mixed experiences compared with *Mr. Show*.

The reviews were quite negative for both movies. Do you think this will hamper your chances of making another film?

I wish those films you mentioned were successes on every level, but they clearly were not. Films are difficult—it's a challenging business. I have learned a lot from my experiences on those films, and my next movie will benefit greatly from what I consider my apprenticeship in the movie industry. I just hope the industry is able to conceive of it as an apprenticeship. If not, I will wrestle that stupid behemoth industry to the ground and kick it in the balls until it gives in.

I fear that the failure of those two projects will hamper my chances of taking chances in the future. Basically, to be blunt, I am in "director jail" when it comes to features. The box-office returns weren't good, and that will bite me in the ass for most future projects. These projects were very much about not taking chances. Both movies would have been made without me, and it's not my usual way of working. I like to work on the fringe.

I am now "relegated" to this work the critics seem to like much more. I will work my way back into a place where the industry is willing to take another chance on me. I'm good, and that's coming from someone who hates me more than anyone else could.

How often do you watch your work? Say, old *SNL* sketches or *Mr. Show* episodes?

Not often. I just don't do it. I have two kids, and I play with them. I'm busy writing or directing, and I have plenty to think about and to work on. Occasionally—maybe every five or six years—there's some reason to watch *Mr. Show*. And then I'll watch it. It makes me happy. There are small things that bother me about it, but overall it's certainly something

I'm very proud of. We knew when we were doing it that this was exactly what we wanted to make and, by and large, it came out how we wanted it to come out.

I tend to think way more about the sketches that didn't go right over the years—or the movies that didn't go right—than I tend to think about the things that *did* go right. And *Mr. Show* is one of those things that went right. So what's the point in watching and examining it? I'd rather think about the future. And all of my many mistakes.

Getting Your Cartoons Into *The New Yorker*

An interview with **Bob Mankoff,** cartoon editor of *The New Yorker*

In a typical week, how many cartoon submissions do you receive?

The number of cartoons that arrive each week, over all, approaches a thousand. From our regular cartoonists, probably three or four hundred. Each regular cartoonist will pitch about ten to fifteen ideas a week. We also receive hundreds that are unsolicited from other cartoonists. From all of these, I take about forty to the Wednesday cartoon meetings with [editor-in-chief] David Remnick. From these forty, there will be fifteen to twenty cartoons that might get picked for publication.

So after looking and judging thousands of cartoons, week after week, how does the editorial process not simply become white-noise?

I do tend to look at a tremendous amount of cartoons, probably more than anyone else alive. But there is a way of doing it. Does it work for the magazine? Is the illustration a good match with the joke? There are many things to take into consideration, and I've just become proficient at it, by necessity.

Do you ever laugh out loud while reading submitted cartoons?

Very, very rarely. Those tend to be the jokes from out-of-left-field, some of the crazier ones. But for most cartoons—for the vast, vast majority—I don't laugh out loud.

You're not only the cartoon editor for *The New Yorker,* but also a contributor of cartoons. Who picks the cartoons that you, yourself, write and illustrate?

I'll submit a batch of my own cartoons to David Remnick, and he'll decide which, if any, are used.

For someone who dreams of getting a cartoon into *The New Yorker,* would one style be more advantageous than another style? For instance, would a young cartoonist have a better chance with a character-based cartoon rather than with a straight gag cartoon?

All styles are acceptable, although simpler styles tend to work best for gag cartooning, and more realistic styles tend to work best for cartoons that are rooted in reality. The pendulum has probably swung a bit away from naïve styles in general, but the nature of pendulums is to swing, so that probably will come back again.

The most important thing is for a cartoonist to be capable of producing funny cartoons over time; not just one funny cartoon, or two or three. But batches of great ones month after month, year after year.

From what I read, it took you around two thousand submitted cartoons before you made your first *New Yorker* sale. This is such a specific talent and so difficult to learn. You were willing to stick with it. But how many young cartoonists—now or down the road—will be willing to do the same?

Off the top of my head, my estimate would be none. That's why we're probably a little more open these days to buying a cartoon from someone who demonstrates potential, in order to encourage them, and to see that potential realized.

How long did it take you, as a cartoonist, to develop your particular voice? Did it take as long as your first sale to *New Yorker*?

I think I discovered my voice before I made my first sale to *New Yorker*. It took a couple of years. I have a rather all-purpose comic intelligence which is nice, but in my early years I tended to mimic cartoonists I admired rather than trying to develop my own voice.

How would you recommend that young cartoonists discover their voice? Is perseverance the only way to develop a singular voice as a cartoonist?

Not all cartoons demand a singular voice. For some it is essential, like Roz Chast, but for others who deal in straight gags, just a bit of distinctiveness in terms of tone and style is what is required. But, in either case, whatever degree of individuality that is required will come through by way of doing a lot of cartoons. There is no shortcut to that.

You've said in the past that the difference between a professional and an amateur cartoonist is that the amateur thinks everything they do is good, while a professional thinks most of what they do is crap. Do you notice this with young cartoonists?

Well, I exaggerated a bit for effect when I said that, but it's basically true. It varies depending on the cartoonist. And it's probably necessary to have an ample reservoir of misplaced confidence in your own work to get you started. One thing I would say for young cartoonists is that the cartoons, the drawings, shouldn't monopolize his or her attention. A cartoon lives or dies on the strength of the joke, not the illustration. A great joke with a mediocre illustration will always be funnier than a mediocre joke with a great illustration. Of course, the ideal is to have both.

You've also been quoted as saying that two things have to come together for a successful cartoon: "The normal and the abnormal." What does that mean exactly?

Well, by normal, I mean what we expect from a particular situation. By the "abnormal," I mean an intruding image that is unexpected.

As a specific example of a cartoon that we once ran in *The New Yorker*, it's normal or expected to see an image of a gallows that has steps leading up to it. On the other hand, to have a ramp for the handicapped is unexpected and abnormal in that situation. Another term that could easily substitute for abnormal is incongruous. So, in many humorous situations there is something that exists or something that is happening that violates the way we think the world should be. That may be a necessary condition for humor but it isn't sufficient. Lots of other factors are needed to seal the deal, among them an attitude that is playful and accepts that whatever is happening—even though it may be incongruous, abnormal, weird or whatever—is not threatening.

In past interviews, you've spoken about the creative process for cartooning being almost similar to a dream state. Would this be similar to what you're talking about?

Yes. Creativity is our default modus operandi for dealing with existence. Everyone has this ability and uses it every day to solve the most ordinary problems. Honing it into something that can be used on a professional level is another matter.

There are fewer and fewer publications putting out single-panel gag cartoons. For a cartoonist, is this even a viable occupation anymore?

A good question without a good answer.

Really? There's no good answer?

There's no doubt that despite it still being championed by *The New Yorker*, the single-panel cartoon is an endangered species in print. The use of this type of cartoon in magazines has dwindled over the years, and now magazines themselves are dwindling. So the future is not so much online as *offprint*. That could be on the web, phones, or technologies yet to be developed. Maybe one day a cartoonist will merely have to think of the joke and it can be telepathically transmitted to his subscribers. I do believe gag cartoons will survive and even have the opportunity to thrive as never before as new technologies create new opportunities.

What's the preferred method of first submission for young cartoonists? E-mail or hard copy?

If you want to submit, mail your sketches to us at *The New Yorker*, Cartoons Submissions, 4 Times Square, New York, New York, 10036. We only ask that you don't send originals.

Be honest: Do you actually look at the hundreds of unsolicited cartoons sent your way every week?

We look at *everything* that is submitted. Submit away.

Robert Smigel

The first time you watch one of Robert Smigel's cartoon shorts, it's easy to forget it's merely parody—he perfectly captures the choppy animation and stilted acting of most children's television. It looks instantly familiar, and anybody who grew up watching Saturday-morning cartoons can't help but feel nostalgic. And yet there's a pretty good chance that the similarities between Smigel's comic universe and your childhood memories exist only in appearance. *TV Funhouse*—which aired on *Saturday Night Live* and later as a series on Comedy Central—has featured everyone from the X presidents, a crime-fighting team that includes Jimmy Carter and Richard Nixon, to the Ambiguously Gay Duo, a pair of superheroes with a curiously close relationship.

Smigel's best-known character is probably Triumph, the cigar-chomping insult comic who speaks with a vaguely Hungarian accent. The canine hand puppet, voiced by Smigel (always lurking just below the camera or behind a podium), was originally conceived as a one-joke bit for *Late Night with Conan O'Brien* in 1997. But Triumph soon became an audience favorite, thanks mostly to his utter lack of self-censoring and crude sense of humor. Whether he was interviewing big-time celebrities or just fanatics lined up to see a *Star Wars* premiere, Triumph said things that were so unexpectedly rude and even cruel that he was practically begging to get punched in the face. But when such vile insults came out of a dog's mouth, particularly a *puppet* dog's mouth, it was impossible for anyone to defend themselves without looking foolish, especially after Triumph half-apologized with his favorite catchphrase, "I keed. I keed."

Triumph (and, by association, Smigel) has managed to stir up plenty of firestorms. He was banned from the Westminster Kennel Club dog show (for "humping" a few of the dolled-up canine contestants), was nearly assaulted by Eminem at the 2002 MTV Video Music Awards (for approaching the rapper and his entourage unannounced), and was publicly condemned by Canada's parliament (for a taped segment in which he mocked French Canadians for their supposed obesity and for not speaking English). For a writer like Smigel, it was the best of all possible worlds. He could say whatever he wanted, sparking outrage and upsetting almost everybody he came into contact with, all the while maintaining relative anonymity. Smigel gets to have all the fun and a hand puppet takes the blame—the perfect situation for any writer. Or, for that matter, anyone.

Not surprisingly, Triumph's success begat an entire collection of vulgar animal puppets on Smigel's short-lived Comedy Central show, *TV Funhouse* (2000). Smigel (with co-creator Dino Stamatopoulos) introduced the world to his Anipals, a ragtag group favoring gambling, booze, and casual sex. If his work on *SNL* and *Late Night* was occasionally profane and daring, then Comedy Central's *TV Funhouse* was a celebration of bad taste, pushed to extremes to shock and offend. The animal puppets had (mis)adventures in a Mexican bordello, a rooster got married to a monkey hooker, and host Doug Dale learned how to achieve weightlessness by taking laxatives. Interspersed amongst all this wildly obscene behavior, Smigel premiered many new cartoons, including two that featured the jaw-dropping titles "The Baby, the Immigrant, and the Guy on Mushrooms: Construction Site," and "Porn For Kids: Silence of the G.A.M.S."

Sometimes Smigel's comic genius has been appreciated, such as when he was hired as the first head writer for *Late Night With Conan O'Brien*, in 1993, where he created some of the show's most popular bits, such as the talking-lips celebrity interviews, "In the Year 2000," and, of course, Triumph. Sometimes his genius has not been appreciated, such as when he was hired as an executive producer for *The Dana Carvey Show* in 1996 (which was canceled after seven episodes, although one additional episode was shot), and helped shape some of the show's most universally loathed (or, in some cases, loved) bits, one of which involved President Clinton breast-feeding a gaggle of puppies.

Don't remember that one from the Saturday-morning cartoons?

Is it true that you almost became Dr. Robert Smigel?

[Laughs] Well, I had no idea what else I was going to do with my life. My father is a dentist; he still practices.

More than thirty years ago, he developed the cosmetic tooth-bonding technique. He's much more important to dentistry than I could ever be to my own profession. You really should be interviewing *him*. And your book should be about dentistry. It's only right.

My father's actually very funny. He has his own odd bedside manner. I've seen him ask patients who have cotton in their mouths non-sequitur types of questions, like, "If you were forced to save only one of your grandchildren, which one would you pick?"

Do the patients appreciate his *Sophie's Choice*–type questioning?

That's where the cotton in the mouth comes in. The patient can't answer, so they kind of become a prop in his act. Jon Lovitz goes to him, and he's always telling me how my dad's funnier than I am.

I actually worked in his office for a couple of summers when I was considering dentistry. He has a very thriving practice, and it seemed ridiculous for me not to consider becoming a part of that business. I was funny to my classmates as a kid, but I never assumed I could make strangers laugh. It wasn't really until I was at the end of my rope with pre-dental in college that I just—as a lark more than anything else—entered a stand-up contest that was being held at NYU, where I was attending, in 1981. I wrote a routine for the contest just to see what would happen, and I ended up being one of the winners.

Do you remember any of the jokes?

I was a big fan of Andy Kaufman's. So I was into testing the audience with anti-performance stuff. I would come onstage in full Orthodox Jewish garb. I would wear an overcoat, a tie and a hat, and I fashioned a big beard out of cotton candy. I would also bring out a large religious book called the Pentateuch, which contains the five books of the Torah, and I would then do what the old men in our synagogue used to do when they were trying to find a prayer. They would very slowly and deliberately turn each page, one at a time, and lick their fingers. I would do the same thing onstage until I got a laugh, and then, when the laughs died down, I'd start to eat my cotton-candy beard. It would become a rhythm. I'd lick my finger, pull a piece of the beard, eat the beard, lick the finger, back to the page, pull the beard, and so on.

How did your parents react when you made it clear that there wasn't going to be another dentist in the family?

My father was understanding. He had sort of been led into dentistry—his father was a dentist—and he never enjoyed it until he made it interesting for himself with dental aesthetics. My mother was somewhat horrified but still supportive. I sort of crawled to the finish line at NYU. I even tried to finish pre-dental, but then I flunked organic chemistry.

A few weeks later, during the summer of 1982, I left for Chicago and joined a Second City offshoot I'd heard about called the Players Workshop of Second City. I also joined an improv group called All You Can Eat. I didn't name it, by the way. We put on a show that we produced ourselves called "All You Can Eat and the Temple of Dooom [*sic*]," which grew to be very successful. We would split the profits each week, which came to around $300 for each of us. I lived with two friends in this group, in a filthy apartment, and our rent was $450. It was probably the happiest time of my life. Chicago is still a great place to start out in comedy; it's cheaper than most cities, and there's a huge community of people doing improv and sketch comedy. It's not hard to find like-minded people.

What sort of sketches did you perform in the stage show?

There was a range of silly ones. I don't think it was the most inventive comedy group that was out there at the time, but we tried to do clever material, and we became very popular. It was actually good preparation for *Saturday Night Live*. We didn't do improv onstage, just sketches. At the time, I thought improv was great as a writing tool, and I loved watching people at Second City develop scenes in improv sets. But I was not a fan of watching improv games.

In fact, one of our more interesting sketches was a parody of an improv game. So for our sketch, we'd ask the audience for the typical improv suggestion, like, "We need an occupation, and we need a period of time, and we need a location." Then we'd have a plant in the audience who'd start making weird suggestions. Every time we'd freeze the scene, the plant would highjack it, coming up with stranger and more convoluted suggestions: "Okay, so now you just grew a tree on your arm, because you find out that she had an affair with Hall and Oates's mother, and you're all going to sing a song about orange puppies." Most of the audience loved seeing the improv game ruined, although some of them probably felt a little ripped off.

At what point did this stage show lead to *Saturday Night Live?*

Al Franken and Tom Davis, two of the great original writers for *SNL*, were shooting a movie in the Chicago area called *One More Saturday Night* [1986], and one of the members in our improv group, Dave Reynolds, just happened to be cast in a major role. Franken and Davis became friendly with Dave, and they came to see our show, and they really liked it. We hung out with them afterward at a goofy German bar. And I thought, Well, that was fun, and that's the end of that.

About a month or so later, I read in *TV Guide* that Lorne Michaels had gone back to *Saturday Night Live*, after a five-year-hiatus, and that he was hiring Al and Tom as producers. It was about the closest that I'd ever come to literally hitting the ceiling. All of a sudden, there was a possibility that I could actually be doing what I most wanted to do, and it felt completely alien. I was never the kind of person inclined to go after things aggressively. I once contacted *Late Night with David Letterman* before it premiered, to see if they were hiring writers, but I never sent them anything. I was so naïve that I simply called the show and asked if I could submit material. They said, "No," and I said, "Okay," and I never thought about it again. To give up, that was all the rejection I needed.

For a job as a writer at *SNL*, did you have an advantage over those writers who didn't grow up in New York City? You were closer to the showbiz world than others, and might not have found it as mysterious.

That's true on one hand, but there was an extra layer of awe. *Saturday Night Live* meant that much more to me *because* I grew up in New York.

As big a phenomenon as it was around the country, it was much, much bigger in New York. To have grown up in the city watching the show, and, having experienced the media craziness that surrounded those early years, I was maybe more intimidated than a writer from the Midwest might have been.

Having been such a fan of *SNL* growing up, did you find that you had an easy time with the writing once you were hired?

No. In the beginning, I didn't have an easy time writing for that show at all. I was freaked out just being there. I mean, when I met people on the staff I already knew all their names from watching the credits every week. "Robert, this is Edie Baskin." "Yes! Hi! I love your hand-tinted portraits of the cast!" "This is Akira Yoshimura." "Hi! Yes! You played Sulu on the [1976] Michael O'Donoghue *Star Trek* sketch! Whuh? Oh, okay, see you later." I was only a nerd, though, not a stalker. I lacked the confidence to be a stalker.

There were other circumstances beyond my control that created an atmosphere of panic that first year. This was 1985 and the ratings had plummeted and the critics were savaging the show. I think Lorne felt a bit of insecurity coming back to the show five years older, and maybe he wanted to demonstrate he was still in touch with what was funny. So he very consciously hired some very young performers who were all brilliant and funny, but who weren't classic sketch performers.

Robert Downey Jr., Anthony Michael Hall ...

Right. And Joan Cusack and Randy Quaid. You know, Joan and Randy were probably as funny as anybody I've ever worked with, but as performers they were different than Phil Hartman, Jan Hooks and Dana Carvey. When you have actors like Phil, Jan, and Dana—who can pretty much play anyone—then all of the other performers around them can shine at what they do best.

For instance, I think Joan Cusack probably would have had a very long and successful career at the show if she had been teamed with Nora Dunn and Jan Hooks; she wouldn't have been forced to stretch to such a degree and go outside her wheelhouse. But there was an edict for change after that '85–'86 season and she didn't get a fair chance. She had to settle for getting Oscar nominations [for *Working Girl* and *In & Out*] when she could have been working on a Morgan Fairchild impression.

Did that place limitations on you as a writer—to have at your disposal actors who were funny but who weren't necessarily solid sketch performers?

I can tell you that when the new cast arrived the next season, in 1986, the change was palpable from the beginning of the first show. All of a sudden, it just became much, much easier for the writers.

One of the first sketches was a takeoff of a game show, in which a psychic was a contestant and knew all the answers beforehand—a nice, simple premise that would have done okay the previous season. But Dana Carvey was the psychic, Jan Hooks was the other contestant, and Phil Hartman was the host. And the sketch just sailed in a way we weren't used to seeing. Everything changed all at once, and it suddenly felt as if the show was in the hands of total pros who could sell anything.

It's interesting, because the show was criticized for its writing the previous season, but we really had a very talented staff. Quite a few of those writers were fired that summer, and I barely escaped being fired myself. And some of the fired writers are now legends, like John Swartzwelder, who's probably the greatest *Simpsons* writer ever. He's written more than fifty *Simpsons* episodes. He's absolutely brilliant.

Why was he fired?

I think the show was under so much pressure to make changes that they fired writers who wouldn't have been fired under normal circumstances. Swartzwelder and I actually shared an office. I don't feel like I did any better than he did, necessarily, but a few of the show's actors were fans of mine—Jon Lovitz, Dennis Miller, and A. Whitney Brown. They all spoke up for me over the summer, and I think that that's why I made the final cut. Also, I might have displayed a little bit more affinity for writing for performers than Swartzwelder did, being a performer myself.

At the time, that mattered to Lorne.

Did you, as a writer, ever purposely set out to create a catchphrase that would stick with audiences?

Oh, no. Definitely not. I think the best catchphrases happen accidentally, because they're honest and organic. You can't purposely send a catchphrase out into the world with the intent that it's going to be loved and adored and repeated endlessly.

I wrote the "Da Bears" sketch with Bob Odenkirk [in January 1991], but we never set out to create that catchphrase. It sounds like an aggressive attempt at a catchphrase, but it wasn't. We liked the rhythm and the attitude of saying "Da Bears!" But in the first script, the line actually appeared as "the bears." The "Da" stuff was started by Chicago D.J.s that played clips of the sketch, as well as Chicago fans writing DA BULLS on banners.

How about the "*Star Trek* Convention" sketch you wrote in 1986, when William Shatner tells the *Star Trek* fans to "get a life"? You had no intention of creating a catchphrase with that line?

I didn't, no. But I have to say that popularizing that phrase was maybe the most far-reaching thing I've ever done as a writer—for better or worse. I remember pitching that sketch idea to William Shatner, and he really liked that phrase. He kept repeating it—"Get a life." He had never heard it before. And, actually, most people had never heard it before, either. So when I pitched that phrase around, everyone really responded to it. I have no idea where or when I first heard it.

Now the phrase has been abused to the point where it's become shorthand for mocking anyone who's very passionate or knowledgeable about *anything*—not just *Star Trek* trivia. Our culture has become so dumbed down that if you know anything a *little* specific, you quickly get cut down to size. "Did you know that Gerald Ford was our only non-elected president?" "*Sheesh!* Get a life!"

Was William Shatner even aware of his own kitsch factor at that point? His career really seemed to have a resurgence after he appeared in that sketch.

Yes, I think he was aware of the kitsch factor, to a degree. I mean, you have to remember that it was already fifteen years after *Star Trek,* and the guy wore a ridiculous toupée, and the Trekkies had been around for a long time. I think he knew what he was doing.

Bob Odenkirk has told interviewers, including me, that before he joined *SNL* he didn't know how to properly write a sketch. He said that it was you who taught him how.

I don't know why Bob would say something like that. I think if anyone taught all of the young writers how to properly write a sketch, it was Jim Downey, who had been with the show, off and on, for more than twenty years—he was the head writer for a number of years.

What in particular did Downey teach you?

It was never a Robert McKee [screenwriting lecturer]–type of thing. Downey never actually sat down and taught me that every sketch needed to have a character to root for, and that every sketch needed an arc, and that every sketch also needed to have a payoff. He never imposed his own style on us, and he appreciated different kinds of writing. What he *did* do was set standards.

What do you mean by "standards"?

Downey would let us know how important it was to not necessarily write a sketch with what he called "first-idea premises," especially if we were writing about something topical. You had to challenge yourself and make sure that the premise of a sketch wasn't something that would be the first or most obvious thing an audience would think of. He would explain that by the time the show aired on Saturday night, all of the TV comics would have already had their shots at the current stories. We would have to tackle these stories by another route; we'd give the audience another take.

Downey once summed up *SNL* sketches this way: actors love to act in sketches about a crazy person in a normal situation, and writers love to write sketches about normal people in a crazy situation. And, of course, the ideal is to have a balance. He also made a point of not beating the audience over the head with a political opinion. He felt it was lazy, since most humor writers tend to be liberal anyway. But he also thought the audience resented the heavy-handed stuff. Downey left the show in 1998 and returned in 2000. In the time he was gone, *SNL* swung much more obviously to the liberal side.

Downey's standards had a huge effect on the quality of the writing. And he's a brilliant writer himself, so all of the writers wanted to make him happy. To be honest with you, I don't think the bar has ever been as high as when he was running the place.

Many writers have complained over the years that the environment at *SNL* does not foster an atmosphere conducive to creativity—that it's not a place where the best comedic writing can be accomplished.

I think the difference between me and Bob Odenkirk, for example, who has been a critic of the show and who describes his time at *SNL* as being unhappy, is that Bob really didn't have a lot of reverence for the show. Bob was his own entity who would create characters for himself; he was someone who could do stand-up and perform in a one-man show, which is something he did when he wasn't at *SNL*. On the other hand, I truly revered *SNL*. It just meant everything to me. And I did my best to fit into the show's parameters, while also trying to come up with smart and interesting material.

SNL is its own entity, and Lorne Michaels tries to make the show a comedy gumbo. There are a lot of different tastes going on, and the audience isn't going to necessarily be of one mind. There's a lack of a safety net for a show like that. It's a different beast than *Mr. Show*, where the audience is all of one mind and where everybody wants and expects one kind of comedy—and they're going to get it. *Mr. Show* was outstanding, and I loved it. But there's a reason why certain sketches that will kill in a closed format like *Mr. Show* might eat it on *Saturday Night Live*.

I have a lot of respect for alternative comedy, but it's a different challenge to survive and get laughs on mainstream TV while still being hip and smart. It's a lot more difficult to be a rebel in a sweater.

Meaning what exactly—that it's more difficult to sneak subversive ideas into a mainstream show such as *SNL*?

Yes. It's incredibly satisfying to slip something strange into the mainstream and have it work.

All of my comedy heroes when I was growing up were performers like David Letterman and Steve Martin and Andy Kaufman, and later Larry David. These guys were every bit as smart and extreme and inventive as any performer or writer who cultivated a reputation as being too cool for the masses. But they were just so brilliant and smart that they figured out a way to do what they wanted to do on network TV. I have a lot of respect for that.

Do you think you've gotten away with more subversive material on *SNL* because much of your work is animated?

For sure. There are certain images that are just easier to swallow in cartoon form.

As an example, I wrote a commercial parody in 1992 called "Cluckin' Chicken." It was about an extremely happy cartoon chicken who explains in great detail how he will soon be butchered and then eaten and then digested in a customer's gastrointestinal tract. If he wasn't animated with googly eyes—if it was just a guy in a suit—it probably would have been much more disturbing.

I'd agree with you on that.

There were certain jokes in the "X Presidents" cartoons—about former presidents now acting as superheroes—that only worked because of this. When George H. W. Bush was called away to be a superhero, he was always having wild sex with his wife, Barbara, either in bed, or in the shower, or on a swing. And there's no way on earth that I could have gotten away with that with actors. I'm still a little shocked that I got away with it at all, quite frankly.

Similarly, I suppose you wouldn't have been able to get away with the "Ambiguously Gay Duo" shorts if they were live-action and not animated.

Actually, I think I could have. Maybe not every visual joke, but a lot of the jokes were just *this* short of being overt. "Ambiguously Gay Duo" is one of my favorites because of its slyness—because it's all about what's *not* being said as much as anything else. The villains are always sharing suspicious glances with each other in the presence of Ace and Gary. We're all perversely obsessed with everyone's sexuality.

Especially those of superheroes.

Even more so, yes. We love taking down celebrities. Imagine what we'd do to superheroes.

You've talked about your love of cartoons when you were a child. What were your favorite characters?

I loved Bugs Bunny. Very little entertainment matches up to the best Bugs Bunny cartoons. They've got great sight gags and plenty of cynicism—and not the pop-culture-self-referential kind that's gotten so overdone. Bugs Bunny villains are all hilarious embodiments of unfettered greed, vanity, envy, rage. They were all very broad characters, but they have great internal moments that are played with subtlety. By today's standards, it's very sophisticated material for kids.

On the other hand, I despised Mickey Mouse. Just hated him. For one thing, he was never funny. It always felt corporate to me. I was a cynical kid who didn't like to be addressed like a baby. Those cartoons felt like they were selling brain death—the "Hey, kids! Everything is great!" approach. They made you feel like a Stepford Kid, even though *The Stepford Wives* hadn't been written yet.

But what affected me the most was "Peanuts." My father gave me a Charlie Brown book when I was 7-years-old—one of those tiny paperbacks that had the collected strips in them. It was summer, and I started reading the book, and I was up until three in the morning. I had never done that before in my life; I'd never stayed up that late for anything. I was just alone in my room reading and giggling and being completely taken over by this other world.

What was it about Charles Schulz's work that affected you so deeply?

I guess I connected with the melancholy. As much as I loved Bugs Bunny, I didn't identify with him as much as I did with Charlie Brown and the others. There were no winners in those "Peanuts" strips. The kids always had problems, sometimes adult problems. I learned a lot of words reading "Peanuts," most notably "anxiety."

Charles Schulz is famous for saying, "Happiness is not funny."

So Mickey Mouse sucks. That should have been the whole quote. Actually, it's a very realistic take on childhood. Every age has its share of misery and anxiety. But, you know, there were a lot of surreal elements with that comic that I loved just as much as the sad stuff—pioneering visual jokes that no one ever talks about. I remember one specific panel [originally from June 28, 1956] that made me laugh harder than I ever laughed. It was from my first "Peanuts" book. Linus is about to shoot an arrow that he wants Snoopy to retrieve. Linus seems to be excited about this, but as he pulls back the bow and releases it, Snoopy just leans forward and chomps down on the arrow in midair. The look of disappointment on Linus's face is beautiful. So it was a great combination of darkness and goofiness. A lot of cartoons have been influenced by "Peanuts," you know, with semi-cynical ensembles of kids and so on. But they don't go the distance. They're all morality plays. Everyone always has to learn something, and I think that's kind of sad.

You've used the "Peanuts" characters in at least two of your "TV Funhouse" cartoons, including a takeoff on the 1965 _Charlie Brown Christmas_ special.

A Charlie Brown Christmas was a very brave move for television. Every other Christmas special at that time was all about peace on earth and good tidings to your neighbor and every other cliché imaginable. But Charles Schulz saw the Christmas special as an opportunity to say something new, and he made a very adult social commentary about commercialism that kids could understand.

If that weren't enough, he also had the courage to take it a step further and actually inject real religion into a Christmas special. It sounds like a joke, but no one had done it before. The CBS executives in 1965 weren't going to allow the Charlie Brown special to be shown at all. They weren't happy that Jesus was even mentioned. But a drunk animator stood up at the screening and said, "If you don't show this special, you're crazy! It's going to become a classic!" And he was right.

When Linus speaks up on that stage, the sight of an innocent child reading a passage from the Bible is so simple and powerful that it kind of knocks you off your feet. You're moved, and yet you don't feel like you're being taught a lesson or a moral. I'm Jewish, but this is a message that goes far beyond the specifics of religion and into a plea for simple humility.

In my own Christmas "TV Funhouse" cartoon—this was in 1997—Jesus returned and was horrified by the hypocrisy of people using his name for their benefit. The only thing that did not annoy Jesus was seeing Linus's speech in the *Charlie Brown Christmas* special. As he was watching it, Jesus began to tear up, and then dance like the "Peanuts" kids. I expected his tear to get a big laugh with the studio audience, but just the opposite happened: the audience was touched, just as they are when they watch the real special.

It seems that you have a rarified position at *Saturday Night Live*. You've had the freedom over the years to write whatever you wanted, in any format, whether it was animated shorts, commercial parodies, or political sketches, such as *The McLaughlin Hour parodies*.

The *McLaughlin* sketch was definitely a high point. The first of those sketches may be one of the funniest things I ever got on *Saturday Night Live,* and it was exhilarating to write something that was that silly, and to have it kill as hard as it did. It was definitely one of those milestones where it added to my confidence and made me want to go for more of that type of thing. A few months later, we did the Sinatra Group sketch. Instead of the usual *McLaughlin Group* panel members, there was Frank Sinatra as the host, with his guests, Billy Idol, Sinead O'Connor, Luther Campbell [of 2 Live Crew], and Steve and Eydie Gorme. And that sketch became more famous than the original—but I don't like it as much.

Why?

Well, it was a funny idea to have Frank Sinatra say a million rude things in an incredibly rapid fire setting. He would shout out lines to Billy Idol like "I've got chunks of guys like you in my stool!" For the audience it was a bigger hit because it had some topicality on top of the goofy structure. But for me it wasn't as interesting. It was a comedy game that wasn't as sophisticated; Frank's insults were funny but not as crazy as the *non sequiturs* we wrote for McLaughlin.

Is that what you wanted to achieve with your sketches? Sophistication?

No, not always. Sophistication is fine, but more importantly, a sketch has to be funny. If you can have both sophistication and humor, then that's even better. That's why a chimp in a smoking jacket is the apex.

With all of the freedom that you were afforded on *Saturday Night Live*, why did you decide to leave the show as a full-time staff writer in 1991?

I left for a little while, but not for long. I would have left for good if a sitcom pilot called *Lookwell* had been picked up by the networks in the summer of 1991. I co-wrote it with Conan O'Brien. It starred [TV's Batman] Adam West as an incompetent detective. Only the pilot was broadcast.

***Lookwell* is one of those mythological "lost" comedy projects that has a real underground following among humor fans—especially now that the pilot is available on YouTube. How do you think the show would have played out in the long run if it had been picked up by the network?**

It seems really cocky to say this, but that show was probably a few years too early. It was a single-camera comedy, which was almost a nonexistent form at the time, and it was kind of commenting on reality in a coy way, which started happening later with *The Larry Sanders Show*. I've sort of come around to *Lookwell*, because for a long time I was like, Is this really any good? Do people like it only because my name and Conan's name are on it?

I watched it recently, and I have to say that I think it's funny and I'm glad we did it. But, you know, while we were working on *Lookwell*, I wondered if we could really sustain a show like that, week after week. There are so many strange elements to the show. And, of course, the protagonist is practically insane. Would viewers want to see that every week? I'm not so sure they would have.

There were a few neat ideas that might have helped. If you remember, Lookwell taught an acting class where he showed old clips of his 70's crime show. If Lookwell had stayed on the air, I was hoping to have a marginal celebrity each week playing themselves taking the class, in hopes of stretching out their fifteen minutes of fame. For the pilot we asked Donna Rice, the woman who had an affair with the '88 Democratic presidential candidate Gary Hart, to do it. She actually came very close to saying yes. Marla Maples—Donald Trump's former wife—said yes, but after we'd already cast the part with another actress.

Do you think that actor Adam West was in on the joke? It doesn't look like he was cognizant at certain points during the pilot.

Definitely. He knew he was being made fun of, and he had been self-deprecating in the past about his role as Batman. At the same time, there was a little part of Adam West that was still innocent and naïve enough to be incredibly sweet-natured about the whole thing. I remember one day he ran into our office, and he was wearing shorts and a straw hat—but not as a gag. It was just the way he dressed. And he announced, "I've got it!" He was dancing on air. He told us that he had been walking on the beach and he'd thought about everything and he finally understood the part. He had cracked the code, kind of like Batman would. He knew exactly what we wanted to do and he was exuberant. He was like a kid.

When the show wasn't picked up, he was very disappointed, and there have been times over the years when he's called to ask if we could reconsider bringing it back to television. But I wouldn't want to do it without Conan. The basic idea and story elements were mine, but Conan had an amazing ear for the main character, and he lifted it to the next level with some of the best lines.

So, it was only after _Lookwell_ wasn't picked up that you then decided to leave _SNL_ for _Late Night with Conan O'Brien_ in 1993?

I was offered the head writing position on _Late Night with Conan O'Brien_, and I decided to do that for a while. But I never really left _SNL_—at least not for good. To this day, I still have an amazing setup, and one that is unique in television. I think I'm the only person who gets to be an important contributor on some level to two major late-night shows. Also, I don't have to go to either show each day. I can work from home, alone.

But is that a good thing—to work alone? Doesn't it help to bounce ideas off others?

It does get lonely, truthfully. Writing by myself is something I rarely did as a staffer at *SNL*. The time crunch dictates that it be a very collaborative show. I really do love writing and working with other writers—the neurons fire faster. And it's good to have more input and to not have to work in a vacuum.

How difficult was it for you as the head writer to deal with the criticism for *Late Night* in the early years? The show didn't have an easy time with critics or executives. Tom Shales, of *The Washington Post*, wrote in 1993 that Conan should "resume his previous identity, Conan O'Blivion."

I didn't really care about negative reviews, but it did piss me off when critics were lazy and wouldn't even give us credit for being new. When someone would say, "It's a low-budget Letterman rip-off," it kind of reminded me to take it all with a grain of salt—because I knew, if anything, we definitely weren't that.

So many of the main elements of the show were already in place from the first week: the "Clutch Cargo" bits, "In the Year 2000," "Actual Items," and others. The core of the show was already there. The show struggled for a while, mostly because Conan—and he's said as much—needed to learn how to be funny on camera the way he was funny in real life. He needed to look relaxed and confident, and he wasn't necessarily a natural at the beginning. If you're an audience member, you really have to have confidence in your host. And I don't think audiences felt that at first.

But there was this whole other audience that didn't care that Conan was green, and they were the ones that caught on right away. They were a younger audience, and they saw what the show was supposed to be. Conan was very likable, and that's extremely important—maybe *most* important. The audience has to like a host. If they don't, the show will fail no matter what you write.

What was *Late Night* supposed to be? What did you want to create with the show?

There's a theory that when you're young, you define yourself by what you're not. And I've done that many times in my life and in my career. But it's not as simple as just rejecting convention. You have to come up with an alternative. In the case of *Late Night*, creating new alternatives was tricky. Letterman had already done the ultimate "fuck you" to talk-show conventions; he changed everything. To me, that was probably the most important period of comedy in my lifetime—that time between the late seventies and the early eighties when irony took over. Performers and writers were being funny in a completely different way.

What I wanted to do on the Conan show was to go in the other direction and not break that fourth wall, and not comment on being a talk show. I wanted a show that would commit to a fake reality with fake characters. And it's not like that hadn't been done earlier; I always say we stole the part of Steve Allen's show that Letterman hadn't already stolen.

Steve Allen's *Tonight Show* was a wildly inventive show in its time—this was the mid-fifties. Allen did the "Man on the Street" sketches and "found" humor that Letterman ended up taking to another level. But Steve Allen also had an ensemble of actors, like Tom Poston [*The Bob Newhart Show, Mork & Mindy, That '70s Show*] and Don Knotts, who would come onto the show and play characters.

Also, I came from a sketch background, as did Conan. That's what I saw as a fresh take on the format. If you look at all of the failed talk-show hosts who preceded us—Pat Sajak, Dennis Miller, and all the rest—they tried to do the ironic reality-based material. In my mind, no one was going to do that as well as Letterman. So why even try?

You mentioned the TV critic Tom Shales. Well, he eventually came around to enjoy *Late Night* quite a bit. But critics never did represent our target audience. The day after the first show aired, we received calls from so many comedy writers—including George Meyer of *The Simpsons*, who's known to be a high critic of anything that isn't top quality. And he said, "You solved it. You figured out a new way to do a talk show." George wrote for Letterman's original *Late Night* show, so for him to say that meant absolutely everything.

Critics may not have represented your target audience, but, even so, the negative comments from that first year must have stung.

It wasn't just the critics. Warren Littlefield, the then-president of NBC Entertainment, hated certain elements of the show, including Andy Richter as the co-host.

Was Littlefield the executive who called Andy a "big fat dildo"?

No, I don't think so. I think you're getting Andy confused with an actual big, fat dildo. [Laughing] I kid Littlefield.

But, you know, we didn't really care about the reviews or the critics too much, because we felt—at least I did—that we were on the right track. But it was certainly bumpy at first.

What's interesting is that eight weeks into the show I got married and went on my honeymoon. And I watched a rerun of the show. There were some great moments—some great bits that I was proud of—but there were also a number of times when there was deathly silence. Conan didn't quite know how to pull himself out of those situations. It made me realize that the power of those moments is so significant. One doesn't see that kind of death on television often. It's very jarring for a viewer—and I could see how it could color a critic's whole perspective.

You saw it differently watching it on a TV than you did from the studio monitor?

Yes.

I wonder how many late-night writers have even bothered to do just that? You would almost think it would be a necessity. It reminds me of how Elvis would insist on listening to his singles on the same type of record player that his teenage listeners would use.

I think writers should. You see a show differently than you would otherwise. You see the show with fresh eyes, just as a home-audience viewer would—which is how you really should see it.

Another thing, too, is that late-night shows are not like sitcoms. They're not sweetened with laughs. They go out in front of a regular audience, and they just live or die. And on our show, we were trying all kinds of stuff.

We weren't shy; we were taking a lot of big swings. But there were more homers and strikeouts than singles and walks.

Wouldn't you rather go for those flashes of brilliance, even if you might earn some uncomfortable moments?

Yes, absolutely. I view that type of failure as a very positive type. If we hadn't been that bold and tried to stretch, then the show wouldn't have the unique identity that it does. I call it our "flailing period," and it was a necessity.

And, by the way, it was thrilling. It was the best job I've ever had, and the one I'm proudest of.

Let's talk about Triumph the Insult Comic Dog. Why do you think people love him so much? Even Terry Gross, the host of NPR's *Fresh Air*, is a huge fan—she's had Triumph on the show quite a few times.

Triumph made her snort on the air. It's funny what makes you proud. I think the reason that Triumph works on everybody's level is because he's protected by his own layer of irony. I mean, the character was born as a completely ironic joke. It was spun off from an old bit that I had done on the show for a number of years, in which we had realistic dog puppets play Westminster show dogs who competed against each other by doing Jack Nicholson impressions or singing "I Will Always Love You," the theme from the [1992] movie *The Bodyguard.*

And then on one show—maybe four years into the bit, around 1997—I suggested we bring out an insult comic. I just thought of the phrase "For me to poop on." But if you watch that first bit, the joke is 90 percent irony; a dog isn't going to be a good insult comic, because he has a limited repertoire.

After Triumph very quickly became a hit, I realized that he could provide a kind of cathartic reaction for the audience when Conan had goofy guests on the show—like John Tesh or David Hasselhoff or William Shatner. Here was this ridiculous puppet who could say what everyone else might have been thinking.

Also, the fact that it's a dog puppet mitigates the meanness and the shtickiness. It reminds you that on some level you're supposed to think this act is ridiculous. And it permits you to laugh at the straight, nastier insult jokes that you might not have laughed at if they were coming from a human. So the character becomes a little more mainstream than, say, a comedian at a roast.

How many of Triumph's jokes are written as opposed to improvised?

A few remotes have been mostly improvised—it really depends on the situation—but we generally write jokes in advance, sort of imagining the kinds of people or situations we're going to encounter.

I always do improv, too, and we usually bring a writer or two with me to help out. When Triumph visited fans in line to see a 2002 screening of *Attack of the Clones*, one of our writers, Andy Secunda, came up with the best line. I'd seen the first three *Star Wars* movies, but I didn't know the details too well. One adult fan was dressed as Darth Vader, and I asked Andy, "What's that shit on his chest?" Andy quickly came up with a joke that will probably be the funniest line Triumph ever utters: "Which one of these buttons calls your parents to pick you up?" It's overwhelmingly the line I hear the most.

Triumph really seems to fluster celebrities and performers, even professional comedians who normally know how to play the role of straight man.

I always tell people, "Don't try to top Triumph." That's the first thing. You shouldn't do that, because you're going to look like an asshole. If you're smart, you'll just sort of smile. And if you're even smarter, you'll just laugh, because nobody's expecting you to say anything if you're too busy laughing. You're covered; you're just being a good sport. Once in a blue moon someone reacts in a funny way—a lot of the *Star Wars* fans were funny because they were natural and reacting honestly. But, usually, we just cut to the next joke.

We were talking earlier about how *Lookwell* is a "lost" comedy project that has an underground following. You were the executive producer for another lost project that is now much loved and respected, but was only on the air for a short amount of time in 1996: *The Dana Carvey Show.*

Any show is capable of becoming a lost project. I mean, if the executives had not given Conan a chance, we'd now be talking about *Late Night with Conan O'Brien* as a lost project. But the problem with *The Dana Carvey Show* was that it just didn't belong in the 9:30 time slot, which was during prime time, after *Home Improvement*. It was a sketch show with a late-night sensibility. We were trying to be the rebels with the sweaters, but following *Home Improvement*, even the sweaters were too much. We needed to wear Mickey ears.

In the first episode, Dana Carvey told the audience that the show was for "baby boomers who really want counterculture humor."

That's how we felt.

It looks like they didn't want it.

Oh, no, they did! There just weren't as many who wanted it as we thought. What I didn't realize was that *Home Improvement* was a show that parents watched with their kids. I knew Pamela Anderson had been on it, and I just assumed that it was a guys' show. Later, I found out that it had a huge audience among children. If I'd just had the common sense to watch *Home Improvement* before we went on the air, I probably would have been a little smarter about everything.

I suppose the very first sketch on the first episode didn't help your cause.

Right. That was the sketch in which Dana Carvey played Bill Clinton. In order to prove that he was compassionate—that he was both a father *and* a mother to the nation—Clinton fed babies, then puppies and kittens from his lactating breasts. *Real* puppies and kittens.

We basically killed ourselves then and there. Maybe if we hadn't done that sketch, the audience would have given the show a little bit of a chance, and we might have figured out some sort of compromise that would have made people okay with it.

Do you think the reaction would have been different for that Clinton sketch if the animals had been puppets, instead of real?

I just think that so many people found the idea of portraying a sitting president in that way to be disrespectful. Even though it was Clinton, the image was gross and dirty. It had everything going against it.

We actually had planned to start off with a different sketch, a *Nightline* parody. But we chose this one because it featured Dana exclusively—well, him and the animals. Louis C.K., who was head writer and producer, said to me, "You know what's great about doing the suckling sketch? It's gonna draw a line in the sand right away. It's gonna tell people that this is the kind of material we're going to do—either you're with us or against us." For some reason, I agreed with that logic, but I should have known better. We put it on, and we paid the price.

We received tons and tons of angry phone calls and letters. Taco Bell, who was the sponsor, acted like they didn't know anything about it—they didn't want to get in trouble, and they sort of disowned that sketch. But they knew all along. They had their name attached to that individual episode, "The Taco Bell Dana Carvey Show," and the executives had seen the taping.

What's rarely mentioned is that not only did the first episode have the Clinton sketch, but it also had a sketch that featured the character of politician Pat Buchanan eating the live heart of an illegal immigrant.

[Laughs] That was much easier to take after the breast-feeding. The heart image was extreme, and probably not ideal for what we were trying to accomplish, but I think we could have gotten away with it. On the other hand, there's just something about the combination of a tiny animal and a man's nipples that tends to upset viewers. Isn't that an old comedy saying?

The writing staff for *The Dana Carvey Show* was incredible. Besides Steve Carell, Stephen Colbert, Louis C.K., Spike Feresten (who wrote the "Soup Nazi" *Seinfeld* episode), and Dino Stamatopoulos, who wrote for *Mr. Show,* you also had Charlie Kaufman, who would soon write the screenplays for *Being John Malkovich* and *Adaptation.*

Charlie kind of got screwed in the end. We hired him to write weird, interesting stuff, but we received a lot of pressure very quickly to try to make the show more acceptable for families. We didn't really have the confidence at that early stage to take a lot of risks with his kind of material.

For instance, Charlie wrote a sketch about a guy who owned his own postal service, "Manny's Postal Service." And he was competing with a neighbor who also owned a postal service. It was very dry, and it only got titters in rehearsal, so we didn't air it. If we had just had a little more success and a little more confidence from the network, we could have aired sketches like that one, because we knew they were funny.

In doing research for this interview, I read quite a few articles in which you and your humor are described as "intellectual." Do you think that's an accurate description?

If I'm an intellectual, I'm a very limited one. I read, but I'm definitely not well read, as far as fiction or big fat books in general are concerned. I'm not that great a wordsmith, either. Those aren't my strengths. But I think I am intuitive enough to be able to write material I think is smart. A lot of writers I work with were English majors or liberal-arts students, and they received a more well-rounded education than I did. I wasted a lot of time in college, and I didn't go to a very good high school.

How good of an education does one necessarily need to become a humor writer?

You mean an academic education? You don't necessarily need one. What's just as important, I suppose, is to be self-educated—to read and soak in as much as you can from the world at large. Del Close [Chicago teacher of improv comedy] once said, "The more you know about, the more you can joke about." And he had way funnier heroin material than I've ever had.

Your work has also been labeled "edgy." Do you think that's accurate?

For me, that word is clichéd. It's kind of an embarrassing word. I prefer "dangerous." No, I don't. That was me being "ironic."

Do you think journalists feel this way because you juxtapose very adult themes with children's formats, such as animation and puppetry? It's a heady mix.

Sure, I can see that. This is where the word "edgy" gets embarrassing, simply because there's been a lot of shock comedy in which something cute getting bloody is supposed to be enough. I may have written material that could be viewed as being a little dark or dirty, but I hope the humor goes way beyond those basic juxtapositions. And I don't think my stuff is that angry, either—which a lot of "Edgy 101" comedy seems to be.

Hopefully, my version of edgy feels more original than that. Obviously, my *SNL* material gets into subjects and areas the sketches wouldn't be able to get into. Besides the cartoon factor, Lorne once told me that the material that I do on *SNL* with "TV Funhouse" has a little more leeway because it doesn't reflect the show's sensibility. My material is an independent element *within* the show. I even created the format to reflect that—I have the animated dog tearing away the *Saturday Night Live* bumper and Lorne running after it.

Then again, by doing something like that, *SNL* is protected and I'm not. I'm exposed. If the audience likes it, they know it was me who wrote it. On the other hand, if they hate it, they also know that I wrote it. It's my neck and reputation that's on the line.

Dave Chappelle was visiting the show one week in 2007, and he saw a cartoon I had written called "Torboto." It was about a robot invented by the military to torture Muslim prisoners, since human soldiers were no longer allowed to torture. It was very dark. And Dave had an "oh, shit" look on his face throughout the whole cartoon. Afterward, he came over and said, "You got balls." That was impressive coming from Chappelle. Still, I would have preferred, "That was hilarious."

It almost sounds as if you think you get too much attention.

I do think that I get an inordinate and disproportionate amount of attention, truthfully. I've worked with plenty of hilarious writers who have written amazing things that people have never heard of. Sketch writing is generally good money and little attention. When *SNL* put my name out there with the cartoons, that was a big break. It's made it a lot easier to get other TV and film opportunities, even if I have blown most of them.

It could have very easily not happened for me. And the evidence I have is that there are a lot of writers and performers I worked with twenty years ago in Chicago who were absolutely brilliant. And yet, as far as I can see, they still haven't had the success I thought they deserved. Some are still waiting tables. When I hear that sort of thing, I'm just stunned. It's a cruel profession where there will probably never be enough work for people who are truly funny.

Did that sound discouraging? Okay, high note. High note! I feel I did get lucky, but maybe eventually I would've found my way in anyway. If you think you have some talent, just try to find opportunities. Find like-minded people and keep writing. If you're good, and maybe lucky, it'll probably work out. And you won't hate yourself for not trying. Just have something to fall back on.

Dentistry is a good option.

Getting Your Comic Book or Graphic Novel Published

Advice from Eric Reynolds, editor, Fantagraphics Books

#1. Do not submit a plot synopsis. Send finished work.

#2. I prefer to see as much of a finished piece as possible. It's not absolutely necessary for you to send a large amount of material, but it does enable me to appreciate the work as a whole.

#3. The cover letter should not be lengthy. It should, however, contain what you want to achieve with your work—a comic book series, or a graphic novel, or something else.

#4. I don't need plot synopsis, I don't need a marketing plan, I don't need your resumé, I just need to see the work. If you don't have enough of the work to show, I don't want to see it yet.

#5. For better or worse, I don't want to know why your book will be an easy sell to Hollywood. If I like the work, and want to publish it, then we can discuss ancillary concerns down the road as we craft a publishing plan.

#6. You do not need an agent to publish a graphic novel or a comic book.

#7. It is better to mail in your submission. If you want your work returned, include a self-addressed stamped envelope: Submissions Editor, c/o Fantagraphics Books, 7563 Lake City Way NE, Seattle, WA 98115.

#8. But I'm also open to email pitches: fbicomix@fantagraphics.com.

#9. We receive about 15 to 25 submissions a week, more than 3,000 a year. Out of these, we might buy two or three unsolicited manuscripts. But if you are talented, you will be noticed. We discovered the Hernandez Brothers this way, as well as R. Kikuo Johnson [*Nightfisher*]. Good luck.

Marshall Brickman

Fans of writer-director-actor Woody Allen like to refer to the mid-to-late 1970s as his career's high point, his cinematic heyday. It's when Allen stopped making movies that were merely funny and started making films with substance. But three of his most critically lauded films during that period—*Sleeper*, *Annie Hall*, and *Manhattan*—were co-written by another Jewish kid from New York, the lesser known, but multitalented Marshall Brickman.

Brickman may have looked like an overnight success in 1978 when he walked onstage at the Dorothy Chandler Pavilion to accept the Academy Award for best original screenplay for *Annie Hall* (which he shared with Allen), but he was far from a novice to the comedy-writing game. He was already an accomplished television scribe, a former head writer for *The Tonight Show* (a job he received at the relatively young age of twenty-seven), and a staff writer for *Candid Camera* and *The Dick Cavett Show*.

Brickman was also one of the key writers of a little-seen pilot in 1975 called *The Muppet Show: Sex and Violence*. It was a risky venture to combine *Sesame Street*–type Muppets with adult content, but Marshall somehow managed to make it work, with irreverent yet oddly innocent gags, such as the "Seven Deadly Sins Pageant" (appropriately, the character of Sloth arrived just as the end credits began to roll and asked, "Am I late?"). Brickman didn't stick around when *The Muppet Show* was picked up for its first season, but he did leave a lasting influence. Without him, the world might never have enjoyed a bushy-eyebrowed Swedish Chef howling, "Bort! Bort! Bort!"

After helping Woody Allen win his first Oscar, Brickman went on to write and direct many of his own projects, including *Simon* (1980), *Lovesick* (1983), and *The Manhattan Project* (1986). He co-wrote *Manhattan Murder Mystery* with Allen in 1993, directed a TV adaptation of playwright Christopher Durang's Catholic satire *Sister Mary Explains It All* (2001), and co-wrote the Broadway hit *Jersey Boys* (2005), a musical about the popular early-rock and roll quartet the Four Seasons.

It's not a coincidence that Brickman would write about a singing group. During the early to mid-sixties, shortly before making a living as a writer, he was a member of the folk trio the Tarriers, then later the New Journeymen, which included a pair of musical visionaries named John Phillips and Michelle Phillips, who would soon go on to form the Mamas and the Papas.

Perhaps Brickman's biggest hidden talent is his bluegrass roots. He played guitar and banjo (along with banjo virtuoso and Juilliard graduate Eric Weissberg) on the 1963 album *New Dimensions in Banjo & Bluegrass*, which would find a huge mainstream audience nearly ten years later as the soundtrack to the wildly successful John Boorman–directed movie *Deliverance.*

It's almost impossible to ignore the inherent irony that the banjo picking of *Deliverance,* which so many people associate with the stereotypical Hollywood-created Southern rednecks and "mountain folk," was at least partly created by a future *New Yorker* comedy writer and Woody Allen cohort. It's just another example of how Brickman can be so wonderfully and unexpectedly subversive.

What was it about bluegrass that appealed to you growing up?

I first heard it when I was about eleven. My friend Eric Weissberg had been playing the banjo for a few years, and he was kind of a genius at it. It was a thrilling sound—it just knocked me out.

But I've never been able to satisfactorily answer why this particular music appealed to guys like us, from Brooklyn, urban Jews. Especially back when the idea of doing this type of Southern local music was so associated with things that we had a lot of suspicion about—politically, socially, culturally. It was so alien, in a way. Maybe that was part of its appeal. Or maybe it was the type of percussive, masculine sound that pre-adolescents enjoy so much.

The *Deliverance* soundtrack has an interesting history.

Eric and I made a record called *New Dimensions in Banjo & Bluegrass* in 1963 and it sold about five thousand copies. It was a kind of experimental album—we were developing a style of playing that was a combination of traditional Earl Scruggs–style picking and something more fluid and melodic. Other guys like Bill Keith, and later, Béla Fleck, did much more impressive developing of that kind of playing, but we were among the first.

Anyhow, now it's 1971 or so and John Boorman, the director of *Deliverance*, had this idea for the sequence in *Deliverance*—or maybe it was James Dickey, the author of the book and the screenplay—when one of the characters plays a duet with a little kid. So Eric and Steve Mandell then recorded the "Dueling Banjos" track. I really had nothing to do with it—I was already working on *The Tonight Show* as a writer. Warner released it as a single and, for some crazy reason, it became a big hit in Detroit. But Warner needed a whole album, so they re-mastered our old *New Dimensions* album. They released the record as the "soundtrack from *Deliverance*," which it certainly is not, but it took off and it's been a steady seller for thirty years now.

How did you get involved with your first folk group, the Tarriers? Was this after college?

I graduated from the University of Wisconsin with degrees in music and science. Eric had already been with the Tarriers, but he felt they needed something else. They were a trio at that point. And he asked me, "Why don't you join the group? We'll become a quartet."

What did you bring to the group?

I played a bunch of instruments—bass and country fiddle, and guitar and banjo. Since I could tune up pretty fast and had a little background in comedy, it defaulted to me to do the between-song patter—de rigueur for folk groups of that era. I was the guy who stood up in front of the group and told jokes.

Do you remember any of the specific patter?

Thankfully, no. I would guess that the material, while appropriate for a coffeehouse audience of 1966, might suffer and die from exposure to print—even if I could remember any of it.

Who else was in the group besides you and Eric Weissberg?

Bob Carey and Clarence Cooper. Two black guys and two Jews.

An integrated group—that must have been a rarity.

We couldn't play south of Washington, D.C. We couldn't get booking for the same hotels.

What year was this?

1964 or so.

This was around the time of the British Invasion.

Yes, but as folk purists, we never felt we were in the same world as the Brits—or the Roger & Roger groups that were vying with the Brits for space on *Billboard*'s Top 10.

How did you end up joining forces with John Phillips?

"Join forces"—that's an interesting way of putting it. It was more like John ingested me whole, like a python. John had a group called the Journeymen. In the early sixties he met a spectacular-looking young woman named Michelle Gilliam, and promptly fell in love. We all became friends, and we formed the New Journeymen. A clever name, no? John, Michelle, and me.

Were you ever in the running to become a member of the Mamas and the Papas?

On the contrary. Leaving the group—which I did after an eight-month wild ride—was, for me, the equivalent of escaping from a burning building. John was into drugs of all kinds; experimental, over- and under-the-counter. John was wonderfully talented and charming, but I was this kid from Brooklyn and really couldn't tolerate that lifestyle. It was madness.

We'd come into some town to perform, and I'd keep saying, "We have to rehearse! We have to do a sound check!" And John would say, "Chill out." And he and Michelle would take off and do interesting things like buy two motorcycles and ride around town. Whereas I would stay back at the hotel and write bass charts. [Laughs]

Did you keep in touch with John after you left the music scene?

We did remain friends. Later, I quit the music business and went to write for *Candid Camera* and later for *The Tonight Show*. By this time, John and Michelle had hit it really big, and they were living in Bel Air in ['30s and '40s film actress] Jeanette MacDonald's old house, a spectacular chalet with a giant pool and peacocks strutting around the grounds—like a drugged-out Versailles. It was quite a scene. I used to work all day at NBC in Burbank, and then, at the end of the day, I'd switch gears and call John and ask, "Okay, what have you got for me tonight? What's going on?"

One Friday in 1969, I called John to see what the plan was, and he said, "We have a choice. There's a party over in Malibu. Or we could go over to Benedict Canyon."

You have to understand that as head writer for a daily show like *The Tonight Show*, one is always looking for material. I used to read every magazine and newspaper I could get my hands on, in a never-ending, desperate attempt to find material for the show. I had read earlier that day, in the science section of the *Los Angeles Times*, that there was a colony of phosphorescent plankton that had drifted into Malibu from the Pacific, and that every time a wave crashed, it looked like a big neon tube lighting up the entire beach. So I opted to go see the plankton. That's the kind of fun guy I was. I told John: "Let's go to Malibu."

We show up at this party—hosted by this Brit director Michael Sarne, who had gotten a little heat from a 1968 film called *Joanna*, and who later directed a train wreck called *Myra Breckenridge* [1970]. Anyhow, we showed up, and it was like Caligula's Rome. There was a big pile of white powder on a table, which turned out to be mescaline. People would casually stroll by, lick a finger, dip it into the power, and lick it off. Who was I not to do this also? Out on the beach was a huge bonfire, and everyone was singing and playing and doing other things not suitable to mention in a family publication, and at one point my hand started to strobe in front of my face. Understand that up to that time I was, pharmaceutically speaking, pretty much a virgin. Maybe a little grass in the dressing room. So, as a Jewish control freak now out of control, I started to panic. I said to John, "My hand is strobing." He looked at me for a full twenty seconds, his pupils teeny little black dots, and finally said, "What?" And I yelled, "My hand is strobing in front of my face!" And he said, "God gave you a gift, man. Why don't you enjoy it?" So I immediately called a friend of mine and told her, "Get me the fuck out of here."

My friend picked me up and deposited me back at the hotel on Sunset Boulevard, where *The Tonight Show* put up their staff, and I put the Do Not Disturb sign on the door and went to sleep. When I awoke, there were about six dozen messages waiting for me. You're probably ahead of me, but that was the night of the Manson murders. The horrible events took place at the other party I could have gone to—the one in Benedict Canyon. The first victim they had discovered was a young man about my age who was shot numerous times. All my friends thought it was me.

My god, it could have easily been you.

Absolutely. Then again, maybe if I had been there, the murders wouldn't have taken place. But, most likely, I would be dead. And we wouldn't be having this conversation.

What can we learn from this? Perhaps: Stay out of Los Angeles.

The music scene was just never for me. There used to be a mirror on 57th Street in New York, a little distorted, like a fun-house mirror. One day, as I was carrying my banjo and my guitar, I looked at this strangely-shaped person in the reflection, and I thought, Is this why my father escaped from Poland? So I could become an itinerant musician with a squished head and spindly legs?

So I gave up the music scene entirely and eventually got a job as a writer for *Candid Camera*. This was before writing for *The Tonight Show*.

How did you get the job for *Candid Camera*?

I auditioned for Allen Funt, the creator of *Candid Camera*, by writing a couple of pages with ideas for those hostile, hateful little stunts he used to do. I guess you could say that *Candid Camera* was one of the first reality shows.

Compared with what goes on today, those stunts were very sweet.

I know. Nobody had to eat tarantulas.

What was Allen Funt like to work for?

Kind of eccentric, and when he walked into the room there was an aura of tension around him. I was fired after about seven months, which was par for the course. Pretty much every writer was fired from that show at one point or another.

What sort of ideas did you come up with for the show?

One of the ideas—I think it was mine, but it's been a long time—concerned a dry-cleaning establishment. A guy would drop off his suit to be dry-cleaned—this took a little planning, of course—and we would manufacture an identical suit, but in a tiny size, like for a chimpanzee. When the guy returned for his suit, the clerk would bring out the tiny version and explain that it had shrunk, and he was really sorry, but the customer should have read the warning on the back of the ticket. And some people accepted it and some people became very angry, and so on.

I recall one customer didn't respond very well. It turns out this guy was caught once before by *Candid Camera*. He was in a city he wasn't supposed to be in, with someone he wasn't supposed to be with. So after he was caught for the second time, and after he was told "Smile, you're on *Candid Camera*!," instead of smiling, he went berserk. He spotted the hidden camera and picked up a glass ashtray weighing about six pounds and hurled it at the camera operator and broke the two-way mirror the camera was hidden behind. Then he decked the clerk, who was, of course, an actor working for the show. Lots of good, wholesome fun. Needless to say, he didn't sign the release. But the footage was a big hit at the show's Christmas party.

Did this happen often?

Not as violently, but the ratio of filmed segments to segments that actually aired was something like twenty to one.

It must have been tough to pull off those stunts. The cameras were huge compared with the ones today, and I assume you needed a tremendous amount of lighting.

You're absolutely right. One of the crises on the show was the phasing-out of anything that was in black-and-white. They had to start using color film, which needed about five times the amount of light as black-and-white film. So they had to put these two-thousand-watt bulbs in the lamps in the fake offices or other places we used. Most of our "locations" were more like movie sets than offices. The walls didn't even go up to the ceiling. And there would be some poor person earning $4.10 an hour, hired as a temp, sitting at a desk. The "manager" would tell this temp, "Look, I'm going out for twenty minutes, so just answer the phone and take messages." And then a man in a gorilla suit would run through. And then the "manager" would return and say, "I'm back from lunch. Did anything happen?"

And the temp would often say, "No, nothing."

People don't notice what they don't want to notice—either that, or they don't trust their own senses. More likely, they were afraid that if they were the only one to have seen the gorilla, they might be locked up. It was like that famous experiment conceived by the Yale psychologist Stanley Milgram, detailed in *Obedience to Authority* [*Journal of Abnormal and Social Psychology*, 1963; HarperCollins, 1974]. If a person in a white lab coat tells someone it's okay to hurt someone else, then it becomes accepted. Someone in a position of authority can remove all rationality from a person's responses.

That's especially true when you're a temp.

You don't want to rock the boat.

How did you get the job writing for *The Tonight Show?*

My friend Dick Cavett, who was a writer on the show at this time, the early sixties, was leaving to try his hand at stand-up. And I was bouncing around after *Candid Camera*. So I said to Dick, "Let me see what your stuff looks like when you hand it in to Johnny." I had this idea that if Carson saw material submitted to him in the form that he was used to, he would think I had already worked for him. Or deserved to work for him. Anyhow, he hired me.

That's the key to life, isn't it? Acting as if you belong where you want to end up.

"Assume a virtue if you have it not," as Shakespeare wrote.

How did you become the head writer for the show?

I didn't have an office when I started, just a rolling typewriter stand with an old Royal on it. And I would push my stand to an empty part of the office and write my jokes. Walter Kempley, who later wrote for *Happy Days*, was then the head writer. He had a disagreement with the producer over a raise, and he left. Walter called me into his office and said, "Congratulations, kid. You're the head writer." He gave me half a box of cigars and his joke file. I got his office—a nice office with a window—and a backlog of four or five years of jokes.

How long had you been on the show?

A month or two.

You skipped over all the other writers to become head writer?

The other writers didn't want the job. They were smart. The monologue writers, like David Lloyd, who later wrote for *The Mary Tyler Moore* show and *Cheers* and *Frasier*, merely had to deliver a monologue to Carson every day by three o'clock. I shouldn't say "merely," because writing a daily monologue can be a terrifying task. But the head writer, in addition to running the writing department, had to write all the sketches, the little interview pieces, the comedy spots.

Such as Carnac the Magnificent, Aunt Blabby, and "The Tea Time Movie"?

All that shit. I have piles of it, cubic feet of it, stored somewhere.

They were very vaudevillian, those sketches.

Johnny loved to do characters. And the advantage we had was, as a nightly show, the material didn't have to be timeless—or even very funny. But if you had timely references, it usually worked. And Johnny was quite skillful. The audiences loved him.

TV's a monster. It just eats up material.

It's impossible to be continuously good. That's why I'm amazed when I see a TV show that's good consistently, night after night, week after week.

One of the things that I'll go to my grave having to apologize for is having invented the "Carnac Saver."

Which was what?

Every time Johnny's character Carnac the Magnificent told a joke that bombed, he would have a line that would save him. Like a "heckler-stopper." And we would give Johnny a page of these jokes: "May the Great Camel of Giza leave you a present in your undershorts." I can't believe we were paid for this.

Was there a lot of pressure for you on *The Tonight Show?*

I didn't experience it as pressure. It was a good stress. I was young, had a lot of energy. I was what—twenty-six, twenty-seven?

What are your feelings about Carson? What was he like to work with?

He was an avuncular figure to me, even though he was probably only forty when I started on the show.

He had a reputation for being difficult to write for, very aloof.

Aloof, I guess. He wasn't a touchy-feely type of guy. But appreciative and loyal. And a good boss.

What were his strengths, from a writer's standpoint?

He knew how to deliver a joke. He was a good reactor. He was perfect for television. He never gave a whole lot away. But in terms of delivering comic material, he had that glint.

He knew exactly what would work for him.

He had a good arena instinct, a solid sense of what the audience would accept from him. Not only in terms of the kinds of jokes, but how far he was willing to push it politically. He was a kind of barometer. When he finally did a joke about Johnson or Nixon or whomever, then it became okay to think about those things in a different way. I've always thought that television exists for the audience as a kind of parental entity. If it's on TV, then it's been certified by someone, somewhere. And if Johnny did a joke about Nixon or the mayor or whomever—then it became okay to do jokes about that person.

We were constantly trying to push Johnny—by we, I mean Jewish, liberal-left-wing writers. We would always try to have him do jokes that were a little stronger than what he wanted to do. But every once in a while he'd sense when the time was right. That was his strength, really. He was like a tuning fork. He would vibrate with what he perceived was the mood of the country.

So he could sense when the time was right to tell a certain joke?

Yes. Without losing his constituency.

I think of Carson as representing this Gentile, Middle America persona. Did you have trouble tailoring your humor to that world, being a Jewish writer from Brooklyn?

No, it's easy to write for someone who's already established a persona. It's easy to write for a Bob Hope or a Jack Benny or a Groucho Marx. Those characters have already been developed.

It's the hardest thing to develop a persona. That's why movies and plays about fictional comedians are almost never truly convincing. Because it takes years for the audience to help a comedian shape a comedic persona.

A case in point: Woody Allen's act was all over the map at first. I remember, early on, he had one of those "what if" premises. For instance: "What if Russia launched a missile and it was going to hit New York? And Khrushchev had to call Mayor Lindsay and warn him about it?" And then Woody would get on the phone like Bob Newhart and be Mayor Lindsay's half of the phone conversation. It was funny, of course—because he can make anything he touches funny. But then he eventually started to explore more personal things—subjects about his psychiatrist or his marriage. Initially, people were kind of shocked that he was willing to be so intimate onstage—it's hard to believe this now, in the current environment of public confessionals—but they didn't know what to think. And a lot of times they didn't laugh. Woody would say his jokes for twenty minutes, and the audience would just stare at him, as if he were an oil painting.

Because he was so new? Too new for the audience?

I don't know. I would stand in the back and think, This guy is a genius. It was like discovering a new author, such as Fitzgerald or Faulkner. The material was so great, so imaginative and audacious. Even early on, when he was still finding his voice.

He found a whole new area of insight: relationships of a certain kind, psychoanalysis, and the creation of the so-called loser—mostly with women. To some extent, the loser-with-women character was someone Bob Hope would play, but in a much more general and mainstream way. Woody's character was more ethnically and culturally specific.

It takes true genius to develop a comic character like that.

It does, but it also requires a collaboration with the audience. It's the only way you can do it. You have to get out there and do a variety of material. Over time, certain things, statistically, will continue to work, and other things will drop away, and the audience will tell you what seems correct for you—for what you project onstage as a personality.

But even with that said, you can work for twenty years and never connect with the audience half as much as Woody Allen.

That's right. That's the genius. Creating something that somehow resonates with an audience that strongly.

Why do you think people feel such a strong connection to his work?

Because it's true. [Playwright] Tom Stoppard has said that laughter is the sound of comprehension. So when an audience laughs, it means they really understand and, by implication, identify with the material. Woody's work will still be around to be read and enjoyed by generations to come.

When did you first meet Woody?

He opened for the Tarriers at the Bitter End in the early 1960s, and we were represented by the same manager, Charles Joffe. He thought

Woody and I might be able to write together, and as I said, I was the one in the Tarriers who was the front man and told jokes. It turned out Mr. Joffe was right.

You once said that Woody is very intuitive, while you're much more analytical and logical.

I would always try to back into something logically. And he would always make an intuitive leap.

Is that your science background? You mentioned earlier that science was one of your college degrees.

No, it was just a lack of confidence. Because at that time I was young and new, and was sort of going to school with Woody. I was just feeling my way. But I don't think I'm that way anymore.

There's a great exchange that I remember. It's always stuck with me. Woody and I were walking down a street around the time we were writing *Annie Hall*, and this guy was walking toward us—someone both of us knew. And I said, "He looks terrible." And Woody said, "Yeah, he just went through a very bad divorce." And I said, "Didn't he used to have a mustache?" And Woody said, "Yeah. His wife sued for the entire face but settled for the mustache."

Woody's able to do that. That's the leap. I mean, how many things have to fire in your brain in one-twentieth of a second to come up with that?

He has a reputation for not being an "on" comedian.

He's not "on," but he's always thinking. When you're with him, he's not performing. But in the right environment, the right situation, you can see it working. And I got to see it a lot.

How would you write together?

Just like you and I are doing now. A dialogue. Then he'd go off and write a scene and give it to me, and we'd trade it back and forth. Or we would play "What if this?" or "What if that?" like Woody used to do when he first started in stand-up.

One of us would say something and someone would say something else. You know, if you're loose enough, you can make it work. That's the trick. It's hard to do. It's like an actor who's in the part but who's also looking at his own performance at the same time. Then you can come up with the right material. A lot of it is intuitive, and it's hard to get your internal editor out of the way. The editor is always sitting there and editing before you say it.

You once said in an interview: "Every writer harbors two personalities: the infant who generates the raw material and the editor who evaluates it. Both are crucial to the process and each is inescapably at war with the other."

That sounds so pompous. But I think it's true. You generate the material and you also edit it. Sometimes it's simultaneous.

For a writer who's just starting out—who doesn't have a writing partner—how does he or she find that balance?

It's hard. When I first started writing by myself, I would actually type out dialogue on a typewriter. I would write as if someone else was in the room. I would literally try to write as two different entities within myself. "What is this about?" "Well, it's about two people in love with the same girl." "Okay, well what happens now?"

I really did miss the presence of other writers.

Collaborations can often be tricky, though. In the end, who ultimately decides what's funny and what's not?

I don't think there's ever a totally equal collaboration. There has to be one dominant intelligence or creative force that informs the process. You have to have one person who is making those decisions, so that you wind up with something that has a little consistency and integrity.

Can you give me a specific example of your creative process with Woody?

Our first movie was *Sleeper*. We first wanted to do the movie with an intermission. Talk about arrogance! We wanted the beginning of the film to take place in contemporary New York, where a guy who owns a health-food store goes in for an operation. And then there would be an intermission, and you would come back and this character would be defrosted and in the future. We thought there would be no speaking whatsoever in our version of the future. We wanted to do a purely visual comedy. And we tried to figure out why in the future there would be no speaking. We decided that in the future it was a privilege to speak, that only certain classes of society had the right to speak, that everyone else had to be quiet.

So we wrote a whole scenario in which none of the things that we were good at as writers, like dialogue and jokes, were in the second half of the movie. Fortunately, we soon came to the conclusion that this was a bad idea. It eventually became what it became, the movie that everyone knows, but it had to go through that exploratory process first.

What are some specific jokes that didn't make the final cut of *Sleeper*?

One early joke was that the president of the future exploded and Woody had to reconstruct him. But the only thing left was his penis. That was later changed to a nose.

When you're loose and intuitive, you're vulnerable to a variety of peripheral influences. We were working on the screenplay during the 1972 Fischer-Spassky chess match, in Reykjavík. We were both chess fans, and we were watching a lot of it on TV. So we wrote a chess sequence in which the pieces were played by actual human beings—knights on horses, the whole deal. Woody filmed the scene out in the desert on a giant chessboard. He was a white pawn, and he was trembling. One of the other players, who was the voice of God, muses, "Hmmm ... should I sacrifice that pawn?" Woody starts to argue with God, and then finally breaks all the rules of chess by running off the board, with the other chess pieces chasing after him.

That scene never made the final cut. It was like what later happened with *Annie Hall*. A lot of material was taken out because the audience just doesn't care how clever the authors are. They only want a good story. And they're right.

Are there jokes in *Sleeper* that you now regret? Any that you feel are too dated?

I try never to regret anything. But the Albert Shanker joke is one that might need some explanation to current viewers.

At the time of the movie's release in 1973, Albert Shanker was the very powerful president of the United Federation of Teachers in New York.

The joke was that Shanker had somehow gotten his hands on a nuclear bomb and destroyed civilization. How do you feel about that joke now?

I love that type of stuff. I think it really grounds it in its time and place. If people don't get it now, too bad. I think you always have to be as specific as possible; that's the only way you can achieve the universal. But that's the problem with TV—it tries for the universal and gets nothing.

It's like E. B. White's advice about writing: Don't write about Man, write about a man.

Exactly.

You once said that humor came so easily for you that you were suspicious of it. Do you still feel that way?

Woody used to say that comedy sits at the children's table. But I don't agree, and I don't think Woody really believes that, either. I think humor is a way of getting to an essential truth. If you can get an audience to laugh together, it does a whole lot of great things. It solidifies them; it gives them a mystical experience of being in a crowd. It socializes people.

Do you think comedy is equal to drama?

Look, if you're trying to write a dramatic piece that encompasses the deepest aspects of what it is to be a human being, you're probably not going to be able to do it in a comedy. Drama is a more profound medium. But I think comparisons are odious. I mean—so what? Now that we know that, what do we know? We need both of them.

Charlie Chaplin did both comedy and drama, often in the same movie. When he puts on a mustache and plays with the world as Hitler, is that any less profound than anything else that might have been said at that time?

Maybe even more profound, because the whole world can understand it.

Yes. It's so compressed, so quintessential.

Let's talk about *Annie Hall*. From what I understand, it started as a book.

Woody might have started it as a book. I'm not sure. After *Sleeper*, we decided to do something else. We were working on two ideas for movies simultaneously: one was this kind of weird literary piece, which turned out to be *Annie Hall*. The other was a more conventional period comedy.

For me, trying to decide which one to finally do was like being in a desert between two mirages. As you got closer to one idea, it would start to break up, and you'd turn around, and the other idea would look very nice from a distance, and you'd approach that one, but then that one would start to disintegrate. We went back and forth for a while, until, one morning, Woody said, "You know what? The movie that could really be a breakthrough hit is the kind that nobody's tried before. So let's do the crazy one, the literary one." Which was *Annie Hall*.

The French had tried it a little bit, talking to the camera, breaking the frame. Very Brechtian, always reminding the audience that they were watching a movie, with split screens and cartoons. Nobody had really tried anything like that in American cinema, however, and we really couldn't have done it anywhere but at United Artists. They were enthralled with Woody, and they gave him carte blanche.

What was the first version of *Annie Hall* like? Was it different from what eventually ended up on-screen?

It was full of brilliance. It was very long—about two hours and forty minutes—and it really didn't have Annie as a significant character. She was just one of the women in his life, among the others. If I remember correctly, she didn't come from Wisconsin; she came from New York. But that was just in the first draft of the screenplay. By the time the movie was shot, she was from Wisconsin.

When we saw the initial screening, we thought, There's no story here. In the first scene of the original version, Woody came out and looked at the camera and said something to the effect of, "Well, I just turned forty and I've been examining my life. How did I become who I am?" And it went on from there, in a ruminative and associative fashion.

After watching it, we thought, "Where's the relationship?" When people come to me with ideas, sometimes they say, "I want to do a story about a war" or "I want to do a story about a hospital." And I'll always say, "Tell me the story in terms of a relationship." So, with *Annie Hall*, we knew what was missing. It didn't focus on a relationship.

Audiences don't really care how bright you are as writers and how many literary associations you make and how brilliant you come off. When you're showing off, it becomes a little exclusionary to the audience. You're just being precocious.

That's why the movie was called *Annie Hall* and not *Anhedonia* or *The Second Lobster Scene*, which were two working titles.

Didn't the movie have a few working titles, such as *Roller Coaster Named Desire*, *Me and My Goy*, and *Me and My Jew*?

Not to my recollection. Those sound like jokes, not titles.

What were your thoughts upon first seeing that two-hour-and-forty-minute cut?

I was very inexperienced. I didn't realize that a rough cut is exactly that—rough. There's a Yiddish phrase: "Never show a fool something half-finished." Well, I was the fool in that situation. And I don't even know why they bothered to show it to me. I thought, "Uh-oh." It was like a nightclub act, like a riff.

Later, after the drastic edit, were you upset that a lot of the brilliant material never made it to the screen?

Oh, no, no, no. Because when I saw the final cut, I thought, *That's it.*

It went through a lot of reshoots, didn't it?

A few. The ending took a while to get right. But who knows why that film works? I have no idea. It's a film where you can learn nothing as a screenwriter or as a director, because it's so eccentric. It's such an odd, idiosyncratic, personal thing, and that's probably part of its appeal. And, not to take anything away from Woody's performance, which is very skillful, but I think that a lot of the success and charm of the film is due to Diane Keaton, with her endearing eccentricity and the way she appreciates Woody and grows as a character. She was—and is—a delight. She sort of inhabits the whole movie. And I think that's what you leave with, that glow from her performance. But again, who knows, really, why it works? It's a mistake to think that what you're seeing up on the stage or on the screen is what the author intended. It isn't. It's always the result of a hundred compromises and accidents, both good and bad, and if you're lucky, you get lucky.

People feel such a strong attachment to _Annie Hall_.

It was, among other things, a reasonably accurate record of what it might have been like to live in New York at that time. In a way, it's an anthropological document. It was sort of at the tail end of the new Hollywood, the revolution that started, I guess, with _Easy Rider_, when the Young Turks from USC film school took over Old Hollywood—those years when Elliott Gould was in every other movie. There was an air of promise, an aura of possibility. It was sort of like the cultural equivalent of what happened socially in the sixties, when you felt that there was a possibility for something new and exciting. And I'm not sure that exists anymore. I think there's a kind of nostalgia for that now, when everything's become so corporate, so homogenized and controlled. That generation in the seventies used movies as their way of defining themselves culturally, the way kids now use music. Film for us was really a very important cultural experience. We loved foreign films by Bergman, Truffaut, Resnais, Fellini.

What were your thoughts when you saw the first cut of _Manhattan?_ The same as _Annie Hall?_

I never saw the first cut. I just saw the final film. I thought it was fine. And it looked wonderful. I did have one discussion with Woody about a scene. It was the only time we ever had a real disagreement. In this particular scene, Woody lists Groucho Marx, Louis Armstrong's "Potato Head

Blues," Flaubert's *Sentimental Education*, Mozart's "Jupiter" Symphony, and a few other things that make life worth living.

And I thought, Why *Sentimental Education*? Why not *Madame Bovary*? And how do you pick the Jupiter Symphony over another Mozart symphony? Woody was doing the same thing he accuses Diane's character of doing in the movie—ranking works of art. Plus, isn't that a tad myopic? How about things that *really* make life worth living? Kids. Family. Love. Sacrifice. Yes, it can be argued that this is the *character's* view of the world, but I thought it was dangerous—the line between who Woody was in life and the characters he was playing in his movies was pretty fuzzy. And I said, "The critics are going to kill us! It's a pretentious, narcissistic, solipsistic view of the world that you're offering up." And he said, "Nah, you're crazy, nobody's going to say anything, it's going to be fine."

And he was right. The only person who criticized us was Joan Didion in *The New York Review of Books*. She said something to the effect of: "Who in the hell do they think they are with their things worth living for?"

I've always felt that that particular speech was essential to the broader theme of the movie—that an obsession with minutiae takes our minds off the bigger issues.

Maybe you can extract a theme from that dialogue, but, honestly, we were not writing to proselytize a point of view like that, although I guess it's sort of inherent in the movie. None of that was really in the air when we were writing the screenplay. Most of what we talked about was conversation and plot.

To me it's a very dark movie, with these over-educated, anxiety-prone characters looking for meaning in life. It had a much darker tone than *Annie Hall*.

Yes, it's dark. But it's a much more conventional film than *Annie Hall*. Technically, it's a romantic farce that's based on deception.

When you look at *Manhattan,* can you tell who wrote what? What scene or joke you came up with and what Woody came up with?

Sometimes, but the great rule I learned from Woody is that when you get in a room with another person, you're both responsible for the result—assuming that there's a reasonably equal level of talent. This is not as coy an answer as it might appear. Even though a great line or idea might be uttered by one person, it may have been triggered or stimulated by what the other party said. This happens all the time in collaborations, so the safest and fairest way of attributing ownership—though probably less satisfying to the curious—is to attribute everything to both parties.

It sounds like _Manhattan_ was a lot easier to get right than _Annie Hall_.

Manhattan has a much more traditional structure. It proceeds in logical time, and there are no flashbacks. Also, the style is totally naturalistic, and the logical demands are greater than in _Annie Hall_, which established a style that allowed the movie to go anywhere. _Annie Hall_ jumped around in time and used many alienating devices, such as direct addresses to the camera, subtitles, split screen, and a cartoon. A lot of the material in _Annie Hall_ could be shuffled and re-arranged without too much damage to the structure; that would have been harder to pull off in _Manhattan_.

How did you eventually write for the Muppets?

I was an enormous fan of Jim Henson's; I really thought he was a genius. I was finally introduced to him by a mutual friend, and when Jim was given the green light to develop a pilot for ABC, he asked me to work with him. This was the 1975 TV special called _The Muppet Show: Sex and Violence._ The Muppets were making fun of sex and violence on television, complete with a beauty pageant featuring the Seven Deadly Sins. The humor was somewhat mature for a show featuring puppets.

As evidenced by the following two jokes: "What's black and white and red all over? The Federalist papers!" Also: "Knock knock. Who's there. Roosevelt. Roosevelt who? Roosevelt nice, but Gladys felt nicer." Did you write either of those jokes?

I don't remember, truthfully. But I did create, or help to create, a few of the Muppet characters, like the two old men in the balcony, Statler and

Waldorf, and the Swedish Chef. Somewhere out there, there's a cassette of me speaking in a mock Swedish accent that Jim Henson listened to in order to capture the mood for that character. Maybe it'll show up one day on eBay.

You wrote and directed a movie called _Simon_, released in 1980. The plot involved a think tank that performed a social experiment on a character played by Alan Arkin. The purpose of this experiment was to convince Arkin's character that he was an alien.

I always looked at _Simon_ as being a film for the seventies. It was satirical of the culture at the time—especially TV and faith in science. All of that seemed to be in the air then.

In one scene, a group of believers pray before a giant TV set. I take it you're not such a fan of television?

TV is just a medium. What I'm not a fan of is how TV has replaced more meaningful cultural values and experiences—like reading and group activities. Watching TV is an isolating, rather than a socializing, experience. It creates passivity in the viewer. Most of TV is a sales tool; the culture and entertainment aspects are just a means of delivering markets to merchandisers.

Do you have any interest in writing more humor for the page? You've written a few pieces for _The New Yorker_, but not in a long while. It's been more than thirty years.

I'd love to. In college I was introduced to the writings of S.J. Perelman, Robert Benchley, and the whole _New Yorker_ bunch. What they were able to do with the written word had an effect on me similar to when, at the age of eleven, I first heard Eric Weissberg play Scruggs-style five-string banjo. It was like watching someone levitate.

The first thing I ever wrote for _The New Yorker_ was actually published. It was called "What, Another Legend?" It involved a fake press release for a fictitious, 112-year-old black clarinet player. But those pieces are not so easy. They take some time to get right. I am forever indebted to my editor at _The New Yorker_, Roger Angell, who led me through my overwritten stuff and edited it down to what finally appeared in print. At one point, many years ago, some-one from *The New York Times* took me to lunch and asked me if I would be interested in taking over for the columnist Russell Baker. And I said, "You're crazy. I could never do that each week!" Baker, as I recall, did two columns a week. I couldn't imagine doing that. Besides, I didn't really have a voice then.

How would you describe your voice now?

I don't know. If it's anything, I suppose, it's anti-sentimental.

Can you give me a specific example?

In *Jersey Boys*, there's a scene in the second act when the two members of the Four Seasons who are left, Frankie and Bob, are sitting and having a cup of coffee. And Bob says, "Look, I think you need to go out on the road." And Frankie replies, "You want me to go out by myself? What if they don't like me as a solo singer?"

Originally, the next line was: "Frankie, this is your time." And it never sat right for me. So I changed it to: "Frankie, what makes you think they liked you *before*?"

It's a nice little change, because it defines the relationship between these characters very quickly, that they're able to deal with each other like that. Also, it's funny and it's not sentimental. What I like to do is to turn ninety degrees from something that's headed towards sentimental and undercut it.

That's a very Jewish sensibility.

The Jews have always had something amusing to say while they're getting the shit kicked out of them.

I can attest to that.

Right. So it's the abhorrence of unearned sentiment, I guess. Which is defined as asking the audience to feel more for the characters than God does. By the way, I still can't believe I wrote *Jersey Boys*.

Why did you? What was it about the story that appealed to you?

When I heard that the Four Seasons had sold about 175 million records here and abroad, I blinked. And then, when I finally met with Bob Gaudio and Frankie Valli and they told me the story of their rise from blue-collar New Jersey—with their involvement with the Mob, with being poor, to finally making it, the whole arc of success and failure—I realized that this was not only a true story but it was a very good story.

Are you a fan of musicals in general?

Some, like *Guys and Dolls*. But not a fervent aficionado. I'm more of a movie guy. That's where I was for twenty years. But when musical theater works, there's really nothing like it. You almost never get a movie audience to stand up and cheer, because they realize on some level—not a very deep level, actually—that what they're seeing on-screen *has already happened*. In a very real sense, movies are dead. In live theater, the audience gets to bond through the live event with live actors and singers. It's all happening in real time in front of their eyes, and it can be a deeply moving and socializing experience.

How is writing for the stage different than writing for the screen?

It follows the same general rules about character and action, of course, but in many ways writing for the stage is a totally different animal. For instance, initially, I'd write a scene and then end it with, "Then we cut to ..." And I would have to be reminded that in live theater you don't "cut" to anything. So it's a different set of rules—how to get people on and off the stage, how to make smooth transitions, remembering that there are no close-ups or reaction shots. The audience looks where it wants to look, and it's the job of the author and director to make you, in the audience, look where you *need* to look.

Because of the fluidity and freedom of theater, you can do many things without apology—and without being necessarily naturalistic. Great productions of the classics have been done with minimal sets and props—a table, a drop, some lighting. You couldn't get away with that in a movie, in which the "contract" with the audience is different. Movies are, on a certain level, documentary.

It's time to end the interview, so I'm going to pull out one of my stock, yet extremely popular, questions. Do you have any advice to the aspiring comedy writer on how to discover their voice?

Search your roots and your heritage, your ethnic background, the way people speak. Most great comedy comes from minorities—ethnic, social, economic. If you think about it, most comedy ought to function as a corrective—against one or another social or cultural or economic inequity. Perhaps I should modify that to read "real or imagined" social or cultural or economic inequity.

Then there's the issue of language and style, which gets into the equation somehow. But even that definition doesn't cover the entire waterfront, as it doesn't exactly include parody or other literary forms, such as with Benchley and Perelman and others. And yet, it's a good start.

So, by searching your own roots and using what you have at your disposal, does this make the comedy more authentic and true, and thus more real and funny?

I really have no idea as to why something is funny. I know it has something to do with the correct matching of performer and material, or some set of commonly held assumptions about the world, or an attitude. I get dizzy trying to deconstruct it. I do know that when I can match a comic performer or writer with some sociological turf, then the comedy has, for me, a better chance of landing: Jonathan Winters and his characters from the Midwest. Or Woody Allen, from a Jewish-urban landscape. Or Chris Rock, from the upwardly mobile, urban-black perspective. And so on. I do know that those performers who seem to come from the Land of Media have a more difficult time making me laugh—the exception is David Letterman, much of whose humor is deconstructionist and exhibits, or tries to conceal, a hilarious rage against the various forms of media, like advertising, political doublespeak, and so on. So there are exceptions.

Any advice for the comedy writer on how to succeed in the movie or TV business?

My feeling is that there are already too many comedy writers. What we need is people in health care. Learn CPR and how to fill out a certificate of death.

And if you're not into CPR and still want to pursue humor writing?

Have an uncle who runs the New York office of the William Morris Agency.

And if you're not lucky enough to have an uncle who runs the New York office of William Morris?

Then you *must* go into health care.

Getting Your Humor Piece Published in *The New Yorker*

An interview with Susan Morrison, articles editor

On average, how many submissions do you receive each week for the Shouts & Murmurs section?

I'd say around one hundred.

Do you read submissions from the slush pile?

My assistant reads all of them, and then gives me the promising ones. We have found a number of new writers this way.

What should a writer include with their pitch?

A short cover note is fine—it's not that important to me. Also, pitches and queries don't really apply with humor pieces: it's better to just write the piece and submit. As an editor, you have no way of knowing whether a piece is going to be funny until you read it.

What sort of mistakes will doom a writers' chances?

A writer once tucked a submission into a flower arrangement. I like flowers, but I found that pretty creepy.

I see a lot of obvious parodies of things that have already been done—for example, the *New York Times* wedding announcements. Or sometimes the approaches are just too schematic. People write listy, high-concept pieces in which you get the joke right off the bat and then it just chugs along without enough surprise. When Madonna published a children's book, I received a lot of submissions about other children's books written by celebrities.

What's your preference: e-mail or hard-copy submissions?

E-mail to the Shouts & Murmurs submission address: shouts@ newyorker.com. Also, keep in mind that if you're submitting a topical piece, it's a good idea to write "time-sensitive piece" in the subject line.

Do you need an agent to be published in Shouts?

No. In fact, I feel that dealing with agents on short pieces is a nuisance.

How often is a humor writer discovered on the Web?

Not too often. I have contacted a few writers I've read on blogs or on McSweeney's, but I can't think of any that we've then published.

A more common move is for me to ask a funny screenwriter or television writer, such as George Meyer, Paul Rudnick, or Andy Borowitz, to try writing a piece for the magazine.

Jack Handey has said that his pieces are rejected about one-third of the time. Does that hold true for other regular Shouts contributors?

I think that rate sounds a little high for Jack, but maybe he's right. Every writer will have a piece rejected now and then—even pieces by Johnny Carson or Woody Allen. The first time Carson submitted a piece he enclosed a self-addressed, stamped envelope.

Did you end up publishing it?

Yes, we ran that piece and a couple more of his. I rejected one or two later.

Do you remember what you rejected?

I think I rejected one that was a modern update on classic fairy tales.

You feel no pressure to accept a piece by a Johnny Carson or a Woody Allen?

I don't think you're doing anyone a favor—not readers, not the writer—by publishing a piece that isn't up to snuff. Usually there is a particular reason—the concept isn't fresh enough, for example. But if a piece is just not up to par in a general way, I'll simply say that it didn't do anything for me.

What do you mostly edit for on a typical Shouts & Murmurs piece?

I trim when the piece is too long for the space we have or because the concept doesn't quite sustain itself. I probably subtract jokes more than I add them; I tend to make pieces dryer rather than wetter. I also like to clarify a narrative throughline when there is one. I prefer pieces that tell a story with a beginning, middle, and an end to pieces that are just some kind of a list.

Who has to approve a manuscript before it's published? Just you, or are there other editors involved?

I have to like it, and then [the editor in chief] David Remnick has to like it, too.

How often does David Remnick reject a piece that you recommend?

David has final say, but he and I have pretty similar tastes. If he doesn't love something that I feel strongly about, I might poll a few colleagues and then ask him to reconsider. It's pretty civilized, and I can't recall any specific piece I really adored that was later rejected.

For those humor writers eager to one day be published in *The New Yorker,* what advice would you give?

Reading back issues of *The New Yorker* is always good. You get a sense of the sort of pieces that work here, what the ballpark length should be, and what subjects we've already covered. Mostly, though, it's important for a writer to have an original voice and a distinct sense of what is funny to you. There are certain writers whose work you'd always recognize, even without a byline, because the sensibility is so distinct. Also, doing a great job with a topical, newsy subject will always get our attention.

Mitch Hurwitz

It's not easy being Mitch Hurwitz, especially when so many people regard you as the comedy equivalent of Thomas Edison.

In August 2004, when his Fox sitcom, *Arrested Development*, had just finished its first season, *The New York Times* ran a story about Hurwitz with the daunting headline: CAN THIS MAN SAVE THE SITCOM? Apparently it wasn't enough that his Little Show That Could had won several major awards and narrowly avoided cancellation. He was now marked as someone attempting to "re-invent the rules of the half-hour" sitcom by creating a "new kind of comedy." It was never explicitly stated, but the unspoken implication by the media was that *Arrested Development*'s failure (and, by association, Hurwitz's) would mean the fall of sitcom's last great hope.

Of course, we already know how that story ends. Despite numerous Emmy Awards, a cult audience, and having been named by *Time* magazine as one of the "100 Best TV Shows of All-Time," *Arrested Development* was canceled, effective February 2006, after just three seasons. History may very well judge this cancellation as one of the biggest injustices in television, but while the media and the show's legion of fans and bloggers never recovered—"I cry myself to sleep at night when I think about [what] could have happened," wrote one anonymous Internet griever—Hurwitz seemed to accept it all with a shrug. Even when the show was offered a second life on Showtime, Hurwitz took a pass. "I'd be happy to [act as a consultant], but I've gone as far as I can go [as a writer and producer]," he told *Variety*.

Born and raised in Orange County, California, Hurwitz attended Georgetown University, in Washington, D.C. After graduating in 1985, he moved to Boston and tried his luck as a writer, penning short stories and screenplays. "I failed," he confessed to a group of Georgetown University students in 2004. "I couldn't write in a room alone. I fell into television to be with funny people and be forced to write whether I wanted to or not."

Although Hurwitz began his career as a writer in the mid-eighties for *The Golden Girls* (1985–1992), *The John Larroquette Show* (1993–1996), and *Ellen* (2001–2002), he didn't truly hit his stride until *Arrested Development*, in 2003.

Arrested was a perfect forum for his comedic sensibilities and for his desire to tinker with the standard sitcom form. On the surface, it may have seemed like a generic, even stereotypical TV plotline: *Son takes over family business, is forced to deal with crazy family*. But *Arrested Development* was anything but ordinary, and not just because of its gleefully subversive humor—jokes about incest, alcoholism, an attic dweller, physical (and mental) disabilities, and sexually ambiguous thespians don't usually make it onto prime time—but because it was a show that rewarded patience. Hurwitz filled the series with recurring gags that unfolded over several episodes, looping through major plot points and subplots laid out like an elaborate jigsaw puzzle.

Unfortunately, such creative complexity does not often translate into mainstream success. Critics may have loved it, but the majority of TV viewers—who, for better or worse, ultimately control the fate of all TV shows—didn't get it and didn't like it. Hurwitz could have lashed out against the banal state of modern television. He could have insisted that audiences were lemmings jumping off the cliff of mediocrity, or fought harder with the network for his vision. Instead, he reacted with a humility that's uncharacteristic in Hollywood—especially among successful writers.

During his 2004 Emmy acceptance speech, for writing the pilot episode of *Arrested Development*, Hurwitz smiled sheepishly at the crowd and said, "This is such a huge, huge honor, and, I fear, a giant mistake."

Is it true that you were a theology major at Georgetown University when you attended in the early to mid-eighties?

Yes, I earned a theology degree as well as an English degree. I put the English degree to better work. I never pursued theology after college, but

I did learn quite a few answers to some major questions. I wish I could share them with you—I just can't.

Maybe for the next edition.

I know whether God exists or not. That's all I can say.

Do you know what He or She looks like?

That would give away whether God exists or not, so I can't answer that. Sorry.

I was hoping you were going to say Bea Arthur.

No such luck.

Here's a funny thing about Georgetown: At the end of each year the college would create this mathematical formula to figure out the average salary each major would eventually earn. English majors earned, on average, about $30,000 a year. But majors in the fine arts earned more than $1,000,000 a year. And that was because there were only six of them, and one had been [Knicks basketball-team center] Patrick Ewing. So fine arts seemed really good to me. [Laughs] I thought about it, but, in the end, I never went through with it.

Georgetown is not exactly a hotbed of comedy. When I first started, I was thinking about becoming a lawyer. Halfway along I realized, "Um, perhaps I should go the comedy route." I had written a few original plays in high school, in Orange County [California], and I was just always interested in comedy.

Do you remember your high-school plays?

One was called *Wet Paint*, and it was about a kid—believe it or not, exactly my age—who wanted to write sketches. The audience would then see the sketches this character wrote. Most are too embarrassing to even think about now; they were just so hackneyed and amateurish. One was about a disaster movie that took place on an escalator. The escalator stopped suddenly, and all of the riders had to find their way to safety. That was my biting take on automation.

I returned to my high school recently to see the students perform a play they wrote called *Waiting for Hurwitz*, which was about the twenty-fifth anniversary of my original [high school] show. I spoke to some of the performers afterward, and I gave them what I thought was good advice about Hollywood and other such matters. Later, I couldn't help but think that it was very wrong of me to encourage anyone to go into entertainment—let alone these kids.

Why?

It can make a lot of people very, very unhappy. I think exploring creativity, and being a creative person, can be a wonderful joy. But if you do choose a creative career, I think you can do a much better job of making it work than I did. I always took it extremely seriously—even in the early years of my career. I was always very nervous and I never really enjoyed the process. To a certain extent, I'm still nervous. I've always been very hard on myself, and that's taken some of the joy out of all of it.

Don't you need to be a little hard on yourself to become successful?

I don't know. As I've gotten older, I try to figure out how much is necessary to my process and how much is just an old model that I'm still foolishly following. One of my goals as a grown-up is to trust myself a little more—trust my abilities and not second-guess and worry about every little thing.

When I watch *Arrested Development* now, I can really see how hard I was working. Some of the details didn't have to be worked over so much. I see other shows, and they are just fine without being so complex. Everything was so dense and detailed with *Arrested*.

If you were creating the show today, would you do anything differently?

I don't know that I would do anything differently. You only get so many words per script; let each of them really matter. I always wanted *Arrested* to be complex. I like complexity in TV shows. I like shows that challenge me as a viewer—where if I put a little more thought into it, I then get more out of it. This is the way I like to think, even though I don't feel it's necessarily the most audience-pleasing. The presumption going into *Arrested Development* was that there might be an audience who was interested in these details. In retrospect, I was trying to do too many new things, which might have overwhelmed the viewer.

Do you know what a callback is? It's when a writer revisits a past event and then uses it to make a joke. A callback usually gets a laugh because the audience is part of the joke; they've experienced an event along with the characters. But in *Arrested*, I put in "call forwards," which were new for me. I inserted hints of events that hadn't yet happened. And, of course, there's no way you can get laughs out of that.

In a larger sense, *Arrested* paid off with the portion of the audience who wanted to pay close attention. I wanted there to be hidden clues and auguries of things to come. Those viewers who paid attention would be more rewarded than those who didn't.

You just mentioned "complexity." That's not necessarily a word one often hears associated with sitcoms.

Or "auguries," for that matter. Actually, though, complexity really can be a big part of TV comedy. *The Simpsons* was, and is, incredibly complex. I even remember being disappointed with some early episodes when the writers didn't bother to make a store sign in the background funny, or when a joke wouldn't pay off. That's what I enjoyed as a viewer, those details.

In retrospect, perhaps a majority of the audience for *Arrested Development* didn't want to see such a detailed show and didn't want complexity with their humor. And that's understandable. *Arrested* was always a show I wanted people to watch and re-watch over and over again. I wanted to pack the most into those twenty-one minutes per episode.

I thought the length of a sitcom was around twenty-three minutes.

Not for us—and that made a huge difference. *Arrested* was a little over twenty-one minutes, which was a giant obstacle. It made the reality of attempting to do eight story lines that all tied together that much more the folly of a masochist.

The time difference might not sound like much—what is it, less than two minutes? But we're talking close to 10 percent of the show. It became crazy. I would literally edit out single frames between individual words.

I would edit out the second ring of a telephone. I would delete the third step toward the door. I shortened that show literally frame by frame.

And then, of course, the audience who did watch the show started searching for complexity the way I did watching *The Simpsons*—which was great in some ways. The audience was expecting a twist each week, and we felt we had to give them one—maybe even two or three.

When Julia Louis-Dreyfus did the two-parter in the first season ["Altar Egos" and "Justice is Blind"], we made her character blind. But then it turns out that the character really wasn't blind. When she appeared in another episode ["Out on a Limb," Season Two, Episode 11], she was pregnant. And then she was *not* pregnant. Then she was pregnant again. Then she was not pregnant again.

How difficult was it for you as a writer to not only have to create jokes but also to keep track of all the twists and turns for each character?

It was like playing a game of multi-level chess. I had to keep track of a lot of information. Maybe that sounds overly impressive: multilevel tic-tac-toe might be more accurate. What happened in the past? What's going to happen? What does the audience think will happen? What does the audience think has *already* happened?

As a writer, I've always found it hard to deal with anything head-on— what's that phrase? "My appetite is greater than my ability"? "My desire is larger than my ability"? "My eyes are bigger than my penis"?

Yes, the last one.

I work really hard to live up to my own ambition with these shows. But television isn't exactly the ideal medium for that kind of appetite. Television is really about repetition. That's what audiences truly want in a show. They don't necessarily want surprises.

I would think that a lot of what you did with *Arrested Development* is the exact opposite of what screenwriting classes might teach.

[Laughs] Oh, we did a ton of things with *Arrested* that would never be taught in a screenwriting class! Just the fact that we had a narrator who explained the nuances of the story goes against all recommendations. It's always considered "too easy," almost like a crutch. But sometimes you need a crutch. If you twist your ankle, if you try to do a show with eight characters ... these are excellent reasons to use a crutch. Also, the nonlinear structure of the show is something that's not exactly on the curriculum at most first-rate TV schools.

Larry Gelbart once said something very interesting: "Your style is formed by what you *can't* do." I've always loved that quote.

It's one of my favorites, too.

Since I began, I've felt that I've had to attack writing sideways—almost from an unconventional route—mostly because, when I began, I felt I couldn't compete against the brilliant and successful writers of the medium. I couldn't compete with their ability to make any line funny in any situation. So, I started tying things together, trying to make the story the joke—figuring out the last laugh first and then making it the answer to the first joke. I could write half the number of jokes that way and still, hopefully, get the same number of laughs.

Along the way, I did learn the craft of joke writing a little bit—and learned that you could always write a better joke than the one on the page. All of the readings and run-throughs of the show were noted by the executives and rewritten. And then the audience would come in and tell you if it was funny or not, and you had to rewrite it again. Many of the writers for *Arrested Development*—not just me—came from a very solid, traditional sitcom background. So we'd all been through that gauntlet. And we'd learned.

The first television show I ever wrote for was *The Golden Girls*. The producers, Paul Witt and Tony Thomas, were brilliant teachers with creative minds that pushed us all to not only learn the fundamentals of comedy writing but to become better writers. They were the executive producers of *Soap*, and Paul was a producer on *The Partridge Family*. So, a writer for *The Golden Girls* learned all of the sitcom basics. I learned a tremendous amount, which helped me later, when I wanted to create a nontraditional show.

It's like knowing how to play traditional jazz before you learn how to play bop. Or painting: there are a lot of painters who break the rules, but they have to know how to paint figuratively before they learn the abstract approach.

We did it the hard way. For years, we all wrote on very conventional shows—which is not to say that it wasn't a good experience. It was a great experience, but many of us got tired of that particular structure. It just became somewhat predictable. It was like driving a slow car when the only thing we wanted was speed.

That may not hold true for every sitcom writer. I'm sure there are many great comic voices who really don't quite understand what they're doing—who are just true originals. But the rest of us tend to understand what already exists and then try to go further with it.

I saw a television show recently where a cocky male character was about to face off against a young girl, who just so happened to have had a black belt in karate. I thought, There is just *no way* these writers will go for the joke where the little girl beats him up. But they went for the joke where the little girl beats the crap out of the big guy.

How would you have written that scene?

A few years ago I would have written it the same way—presuming I would have thought of it, of course. But now that the twist is a little more expected, I would feel compelled to challenge that and do the opposite: have *him* beat *her* up.

Yes, but you're a professional humor writer. How do you think a viewer at home, not overly familiar with sitcom tropes, would want that scene to play out?

I think that's an excellent point. The twist is certainly nothing particular to me; I think all of us in comedy try to twist whatever is expected. But different audiences expect different things. A sitcom audience would expect one thing, whereas the audience for *Arrested* expected something else. And perhaps that's why *Arrested Development* didn't have a bigger audience. Maybe the writers for *Arrested* were trying too hard to make ourselves laugh. We were all trying to be as funny as we could be, and perhaps we were working on a level that was too removed from what viewers wanted.

How would that karate scene have appeared on *Arrested Development?*

To be different, we'd twist the twist. We might have had the character of Gob [Will Arnett] talk to the family about this little girl who thinks she can beat him up. Michael [Jason Bateman] might have said, "We should get a parking space at the hospital now, just to save time." Everyone would have expected this adorable little girl to beat the shit out of this grown-up.

Or, in the next scene, Gob would enter the house and say something like, "I feel awful. I'm so embarrassed."

"She beat you up?," Michael would ask.

"No, I put her in the hospital. I thought she was gonna flip me. Don't people with black belts always flip you in James Bond movies?"

Whatever I would have done, I would have tried to find a way to point out that the situation was a cliché—and I would then try to get a surprise out of it.

I wonder what sitcom situations will seem cliché to the writers who have grown up with *Arrested Development.*

I think the writers who are coming up now will far exceed what we did. In any creative endeavor, there needs to be progression. If there is no progression—no innovation—you're finished.

But for anyone who wants to try something like this, let me tell you now: It's going to be very exhausting. Perhaps you should use fewer characters? Or try to get more than twenty-one minutes per episode? That could ease a lot of the burden right there.

Exhausting specifically for the writers?

For *everyone. Arrested Development* just depleted everybody on the staff—writers, actors, directors, people who worked on the sets. We would finish one show, and we'd wonder how we were ever going to be able to do another episode. We'd then have this sick feeling in our stomachs: Oh, God! Now we've gotta do it again! We put everything we had into each episode. To do something like that show takes a lot more work than it would for another show.

That's not to say that, deep down, *Arrested* wasn't a traditional show. It was. I really followed the rules that I first learned at *The Golden Girls*. There was never an episode where the characters didn't learn at least one thing. And, as much as the critics praised us for being different, we had a hug in almost every episode.

That policy is the exact opposite of what the writers for *Seinfeld* had: no hugs, no lessons learned.

It was. I was in favor of having emotion—nothing wrong with it in and of itself, but I didn't want to have sentimentality. It's really all in how you pull it off.

With *Arrested*, we had very, very basic sitcom tenets. The difference was that we tried to hide those tenets behind a certain type of cynicism.

Is it different writing for a multicamera show, such as *The Golden Girls* and *The John Larroquette Show*, versus a single-camera show, like *Arrested Development*?

Yes. For a show like *The Golden Girls*, here's the weekly schedule: There's a table read on Monday; you hear the actors read the script out loud, and then you see what does and does not work. You receive notes from the network and from the studio, and you rewrite the script. The next day you have a run-through on the set; the script is basically the same but with new jokes, new lines, a new attitude. Once again, you see what's funny and what's not funny. The joke that didn't work at the table reading might now work with the actors as they perform the lines on the set. You stay up late and fix the current version of the script, and then on Wednesday you have another run-through. This time the network executives watch the episode, and they give you more notes. That night, you rewrite again.

On Thursday, the director begins to block the show with cameras: "Here's where *this* camera is going to be, here's where *that* camera is going to be. We need a close-up *here*, and a close-up *here*." Sometimes a joke is ruined with a close-up. It's strange what will and won't work when cameras become involved.

On Friday evening, an audience arrives. You have a show, which can last for three to four hours, through many reshoots. You watch what jokes get laughs and which don't—and you make more changes accordingly.

And how is that different from shooting a single-camera show?

Once you start shooting the script for a show like *Arrested*, you might make a few changes—but not many. You don't spend days and days tweaking the script after the rehearsals and once the shooting starts.

With *Arrested*, the writers would watch the show on a live feed in the writers' room. If a scene or a joke felt flat, you quickly tried to rewrite it. There was never any external force—like an audience or network executives—telling you what was and wasn't funny.

Did you tailor your jokes to that specific process? For instance, some of the jokes for *Arrested Development* may not have worked with a studio audience.

We did. The audience might have been too nervous to laugh at a certain type of joke for a multicamera show shot before a live audience, or the jokes might have flown by too quickly for them. If we wrote *Arrested* for a multicamera show, it would have been written very differently. I remember one joke in *Arrested* that we never could have gotten away with on a multicamera show. In the "Out on a Limb" episode, we had the one-handed character of Buster Bluth [Tony Hale] sit on a bench that read ARMY SURPLUS OFFICIAL SUPPLY, but all you could see around Buster's body were the words "Arm Off."

A joke like that will never get a laugh in a live setting. With *Arrested*, I could put that sort of joke in because the standard wasn't, *Will this get a studio laugh?* I just didn't care.

Here's another example: In one episode ["Let 'Em Eat Cake"], the whole family was on the Atkins Diet and they were only eating bacon. At one point, George Bluth Sr. [Jeffrey Tambor] pretends that he's had a heart attack. He keeps pushing away the IV, and the doctor says to his family members, "He keeps trying to get this IV out of his arm. I don't understand why. It's just glucose." And Jason Bateman says, lost in thought, "We're all trying to stay away from sugar."

If I had written a similar joke for *The Golden Girls*, it would have been perhaps the same line, but a different phrasing that allowed for punching the joke instead of throwing it away. [Screaming] "Oh, god ... no sugar!" It's the same joke, but it's a different version. It's like two versions of the same song, each performed differently. The *Golden Girls* version would have been loud and brassy; the *Arrested Development* version was acoustic. It was unplugged—because there was an audience that needed to, well, *hear* it.

Do you think performers act differently before a single-camera setup than they do in front of a live audience?

Absolutely. Jason Bateman always used to talk about the difference between acting and performing. He's done both. He would say, "I would perform in front of an audience, but with this show, I'm *acting* without an audience. I'm being a character."

You want to please a live audience. You want to get a laugh. You don't just want to stand up there onstage and bomb. It's no fun to bomb.

How does that affect the comedy?

I think it improves it. It changes the scale. It goes from big to small—unrealistic to real. A character on a multicamera show might have to come out in the second act wearing a chicken suit. On a single-camera show, like *Arrested*, that same character can just come out and act like a normal person. Although, come to think of it, I think we did once have Tobias dress in a chicken suit.

And yet nothing was overplayed on *Arrested Development*.

No—well, not until the payoff. The setup was as real as we could make it. And that was a direct reaction to working on *The Golden Girls* and *The John Larroquette Show*. The actors on those shows always had to sell these jokes really hard. They would sell those jokes to the back row of the audience. Also, there was a very specific rhythm to those shows: bada-da-*dum*, bada-da-*dum*, *bada-da-dum!*

One of the key ingredients with humor is surprise. When you have a rhythm that everyone's familiar with—the rhythm that we've all seen a million times on sitcoms—it takes the surprise out of the equation. We didn't have to worry about that with *Arrested*, which was nice. There's a reason why *bada da dum* works with a traditional show. But we wanted to take a breather.

With *Arrested*, the dry style we used was the only style that would have worked. It was the only style that made me really laugh. Eventually, that style became a rhythm in itself, so instead of [screaming], "I am going to prison!" it became [dryly], "Uh, I'm goin' to prison."

But I must point out that rooting the comedy in reality—or starting in the real world—is nothing new. The first act of any *I Love Lucy* was as real as anything on TV. Lucy would be incredibly centered and reasonable and calm; only later would she earn the right to stuff candy off a conveyer belt into her mouth.

This is a standard question for me, but I'm genuinely puzzled by it: How did a show as unique as *Arrested Development* ever get on the air to begin with?

Mostly because Ron Howard was behind it. Ron is one of the few people who has consistently created art that's also successful with a mass audience. Ron, along with [producers] Brian Grazer and David Nevins, helped articulate and sell the comedy of the premise. I know for a fact that without those guys, the show never would have been made.

The system behind TV development is designed to fail. If you, as a producer, jump through all the hoops that the network asks you to jump through, the show probably won't work. If you look at the success of the best shows, almost all are a result of someone breaking the rules.

Look at shows like *All in the Family* or *Seinfeld*—any great show, really. There are always executives who are going to say, "This isn't going to work. You can't have people not learn a lesson. You can't have unlikable characters." But you have to ignore all that. With that sort of attitude, you're not going to create the best material. Let the creative people do what they feel they have to do. And that's what Ron, Brian, and David have done.

Do you think if writers were given the opportunity to create whatever television shows they wanted, they'd have a better success rate than the executives?

I'd say so, only because their intentions would presumably be "purer." It would presumably be just for what's best for the creative endeavor. I do think it would be more successful creatively. If the question is what will bring in a large audience, it sort of depends on what the network is. There are networks that find audiences by breaking rules and allowing invention. There are others that succeed by keeping the maximum number of people *un*offended, and entertained. Those executives might excel in that regard, but it's kind of a flawed theoretical construct, because there's no material without the writer.

I will say that the most successful TV show in the history of the medium has never received a single note from any executive. It's a shocking fact, but James Brooks apparently disallowed network or studio interference when he agreed to produce *The Simpsons*. They've never been given a note. It's all self-regulated. It's also hugely successful. Perhaps it would have been successful with the noting process as well, but it does seem unlikely. The executives wouldn't have been able to help but to "clarify" and "simplify" it.

But that opportunity can't just be given to everyone. It's a test; it's a gauntlet. You don't tell a soldier, "We want to see if you can climb over that wall, but since you're going to end up on the other side anyway why don't we just put you there to start with?" It doesn't work like that. You have to get over that wall by yourself. Whenever I work with young writers I always tell them that they have to find out for themselves whether they can make it over that wall.

With that said, there are always writers who—even without experience—will be in complete control of their craft. It's like Picasso putting the eye on the wrong side of the head. The real voices out there will always insist that the "eye" goes on the wrong side—and they'll always be right.

All creative types think they're a Picasso, though. Very few consider themselves the next Thomas Kinkade.

Yes, but to succeed you need a vision. And maybe not everyone has a vision.

A lot of writers approach TV work by saying, "Well, I can't write as poorly as most of the shit that's already on the air," and that's not the right way to approach it. I would say that 80 percent of writers come out to Hollywood thinking they just can cash in. You can't approach this job with that type of attitude.

What other advice would you give to young writers wanting to work for sitcoms?

To readers of this book? If you're reading this book in a library or a used-book store, immediately put it down and make your way to a proper bookstore and purchase it at full asking price.

Perhaps the most brilliant advice I've ever heard.

As for specific career advice, I think it's important to work with other writers, in a group setting. Even if you're not a writer yet—even if, at this point, you're just delivering the coffee—it's a great thing to be around like-minded creative people—those who have been in the business for years. One of the great joys of television work is that as a young writer you can find your way and your style and your voice while working with other, similar people. There's a great sense of camaraderie. And that's a good thing. You get to hear a lot of different comedic voices, and you hear things you never would have thought of if you just happened to be writing alone at home.

Also, being around other like-minded people allows you to understand the specific rhythms to comedy. I really consider my years working on *The Golden Girls* to have been a college of sorts. I started off delivering coffee and doing odd jobs, but through that I was fortunate to experience a very strict training. That's difficult to understand when you're only twenty-four or twenty-five years old and attempting to break into a business. You feel that you don't want to be in this type of situation. You just want to be a writer working in the business. You were the funniest guy in college, and you don't deserve to be just delivering coffee.

But you have to learn the basics.

Quick! What are the basics?

Compassion would be one.

Meaning...?

I recently read a spec script by a young writer, and I could just tell that he was very mad at his characters and he had great contempt for his subject matter. But here's the thing: if the writer doesn't like his characters, why should the viewers?

One must assume that David Chase, the creator of *The Sopranos*, had great affection for Tony Soprano. It was just obvious. Yes, Chase explored Tony's flaws as a human being, but that made the show incredibly compelling to watch. When a viewer isn't being preached to, it allows him to gain insight into his own behavior.

At *The Golden Girls*, I was writing for these characters who were fifty years older than me. What did I know about being in my seventies? Absolutely nothing. But even being much younger, I could show compassion for these characters by empathizing with what they were going through. That's all you have to do: show compassion. My grandmother once looked in a mirror and said, "This is not what I really look like." I always thought that was such a sad and beautiful thing to have said. She was old, and she looked old. But inside, she felt young. I later borrowed that moment for *The Golden Girls*. You don't need to live through an experience, necessarily, to write about it with depth and compassion.

But that's not to say that you have to pander. Yes, you can be creative, and you can be different, but it's also essential to have an awareness of what your audience wants—and what it needs.

Do you think people will remember *Arrested Development* as having been influential?

I hope it will be. I can already sort of see the influence it's had on other sitcoms—the *vérité* style, the quick cuts, the more than fifty scenes per episode, and so forth, but perhaps my arrival at that style was the result of influences that other shows are also inspired by.

If young humor writers enjoyed *Arrested Development*, and the show somehow got them interested in comedy, then that's really, really exciting for me.

And if the show happened to have turned them *off* to comedy?

Fuck 'em. [Laughs] But only after they pay full price for this book.

Acquiring an Agent/Manager for Your Script

Advice from David Miner, producer, manager, and partner at 3 Arts Entertainment

1. If you build it, reps will come. Before you start chasing representation, make sure you are ready. Be an artist first; develop your skills and put your best foot forward. Go to where things are happening; immerse yourself in a culture, wherever you see work that's exciting to you. Be a part of it, and let yourself be challenged.

2. The best representative is often the one that finds you, not the other way around. This is because he or she (no matter how high up the food chain) was excited by your work. That is the spark that will drive all of a representative's efforts on your behalf, and it cannot be manufactured.

3. Some representatives accept unsolicited submissions for potential new clients, but it tends to take a while, and you may never hear back. Often, the best way to find a representative is to contact younger agents/managers who are newly promoted and who are hungry to discover new talent.

4. Unsolicited e-mail may as well be spam. Send a letter in an envelope. If it's not worth a first-class stamp to you, it's not worth thirty seconds to me.

5. Your cover letter is more important than you realize, as it may be your only writing that gets read. Generic letters do not work. Know what sort of agent you are submitting to. I can't tell you the number of blind submissions that are addressed to me but that have nothing to do with my specialty. When I see letters about thrillers or action films, I instantly know they're meant for someone else.

6. A writer's first sample is often not their best. One of the common mistakes I see is material being exposed before it's ready to be widely seen. Once material is out of your hands, it's out of your hands. That first writing sample will define who you are, at least until you write something new. However, at that point, you may have cashed in all your favors to get that first piece of material read.

7. Ask a represented writer friend for a reference. References from clients are the ones we take most seriously.

8. Many people ask the difference between an agent and a manager. In the broadest strokes, agents tend to have more clients, seek out work for their clients, and drive negotiation. Managers, on the other hand, have fewer clients and tend to work toward shaping and executing their clients' overall career goals. Managers also make sure all the pieces of a career work well together. Of course, these jobs overlap. The best agents also have brilliant vision, and the best managers have sharp negotiating skills.

9. Last, if you are reading this book and just starting out, go along with the enthusiasm of the representative that is interested in working with you—no matter what his or her title. All that matters is that he or she believes in you.

David Sedaris

David Sedaris describes his suburban upbringing in Raleigh, North Carolina, as something akin to a white-trash gumbo, with a few Greeks thrown in for extra spice. His family includes a father who hoards rotting food, a foulmouthed brother who nicknames himself "the Rooster," a younger sister who tries to lure their father into an extramarital affair with a next-door neighbor, and a chain-smoking mother who welcomes a former prostitute named Dinah into their home on Christmas to share stories. Many critics have tried to sum up the bizarro worldview of Sedaris, but *Publishers Weekly* probably got closest when it called him "Garrison Keillor's evil twin."

While his stories and essays are always irreverent, Sedaris never comes across as mean-spirited, as many humorists tend to do. Whether he's writing about his family or any of the rotating cast of eccentrics and wackos he's met through the years—which have included a breast-obsessed midget jazz guitarist—Sedaris doesn't write as a wry, winking narrator who thinks of his characters as comedy chess pieces. Sedaris, or at least the Sedaris of his essays, is a vain, chain-smoking, morbidly curious, stubbornly naïve outsider who, more than anything, longs to become a part of the craziness.

There's very little Sedaris considers too personally embarrassing to share, from his obsessive-compulsive disorder (which drove him as a child, he writes, to lick doorknobs and light switches) to his amphetamine addiction (which inspired his ill-advised "conceptual art" period). During a particularly memorable moment in his story collection *Naked* (1997), he describes being trapped in a dead-end job washing dishes. But he doesn't feel superior to the other working-class employees. *He's* the deluded one, entertaining himself with fantasies of starring in a TV show with a proboscis monkey named Socrates. The show's working title: *Socrates and Company*.

Becoming one of the most beloved humorists of his generation was not always in the cards for Sedaris. In the late eighties and early nineties, he was just another art-school graduate living in Chicago, trying to figure out what to do with his life. On a lark, he read some entries from his diary—which he'd been writing since 1977—at an underground variety event called Milly's Orchid Show. Ira Glass, host at National Public Radio, happened to be in the audience, and he asked Sedaris if he had any Christmas-themed essays. As it turns out, Sedaris did: the soon-to-be-legendary "SantaLand Diaries."

The essay, which chronicles Sedaris's experience as a Christmas elf at Macy's in New York, was so popular when it first aired in 1992 that it almost single-handedly launched his celebrity status as a humor writer and radio personality. Sedaris became a regular on NPR, a relationship that continued when Glass started *This American Life*, in 1995. Sedaris began contributing to magazines, such as *Harper's* and *Esquire*, and not long thereafter he was signed by publisher Little, Brown, which led to his critically acclaimed and best-selling essay collections *Barrel Fever* (1994), *Naked* (1997), *Holidays on Ice* (1997), *Me Talk Pretty One Day* (2000), *Dress Your Family in Corduroy and Denim* (2004), and *When You Are Engulfed in Flames* (2008).

Sedaris has reached a level of success that few writers, much less comedy writers, ever achieve. Writers are not supposed to headline sold-out Carnegie Hall shows, or get invited by *Late Show* host David Letterman to perform a live reading in front of millions. Has that ever happened before—or since? But Sedaris has consistently broken the rules. When *Time* magazine named him Humorist of the Year in 2001, it was not just pointless back-slapping found with most humor-based awards. Sedaris has a universal appeal that spans a staggering array of ages and sensibilities, cultures and continents. Visit one of his U.S. bookstore appearances and you're likely to encounter a fan base that includes suburban housewives as well as heavily-tattooed young urbanites. Travel overseas, and you're likely to see a similar crowd.

There have been a few attempts to discredit Sedaris—a March 2007 exposé in *The New Republic* asserted that he fabricated or exaggerated many details in his stories—but he remains as popular as ever. The only person who may not buy into the David-Sedaris-as-comedy-superstar hype is Sedaris himself. The author, who now lives in England and France with his partner Hugh Hamrick, had to be talked into quitting his day job as an apartment cleaner in the mid–nineties, apparently unimpressed with his skyrocketing book sales. Even today, he occasionally admits to missing the minimum-wage grunt work.

Which may explain why, after all these years, Sedaris still connects so strongly with his audience.

You began writing somewhat later in life. How old were you?

I started writing in a diary when I was twenty years old, but I didn't write a story until I was twenty-seven. I recently spoke to my first writing teacher about that story, and he said, "I remember that piece! That was such a great parody of Raymond Carver!"

You know, it wasn't meant as a parody. I worked on that first story so hard that I just thought, Well, no one will be able to tell how heavily influenced I am by Raymond Carver. But if there had been a Raymond Carver–parody contest, there's no doubt I could have submitted this story.

Do you remember what it was about?

It was kind of based on my own life at the time. I had taken a road trip across the country with my boyfriend, and we stayed in a motel. That part of the story was true—the other part was made up. I wrote about my boyfriend visiting his parents, which didn't happen.

This first writing teacher had suggested that I go to graduate school. But something inside me thought, No, it's better that I just start writing. That's sort of my job as a writer, isn't it? Just to write?

Maybe it's better that you never did earn an M.F.A.

Any kind of graduate school scared me. I wouldn't have had the nerve to go to an Iowa Writers' Workshop. I wouldn't have had the confidence. Instead I went to art school [at the School of the Art Institute of Chicago], which was kind of perfect. You had to take a certain number of liberal-arts credits, and you had to take some English, and the teachers were very, very good. They had a lot to give. None of the other students wanted what they had to give, but I really wanted it—so it was like I had my own private tutors.

What exactly did you want?

By the time I got to art school, I was much more affected by the things that I read than by what I saw. If I were to go to a museum, I might look at a painting and think, God, I wish I owned that! Where would I put it in my apartment? What if I owned it and then sold it? I could take that money and I could buy that painting over *there*. I wasn't moved by the paintings in the artistic sense.

On the other hand, I also became a reader around this time, which is so important for a writer. If I read a story in *The Atlantic*, I would be in a daze afterward. It just meant so much to me. When I later taught writing at the Art Institute, I could very easily spot the students who never read. Their stories would be shit. I would point to their work and then to a published work. I'd ask, "Do you see a difference between these two things?" A lot of students couldn't see the difference. For them, there was no hope.

Where did this sudden interest in reading and writing come from? It just suddenly appeared when you hit your twenties?

It just came one day. When I was in high school, I would read the assigned books, but it never meant much. I remember having to read Joseph Conrad's *Heart of Darkness*. I hated it. I had to force myself through that book—just awful.

Years later, when I was picking apples in the Northwest, I found myself with time on my hands. There was no entertainment. Absolutely none. I was just living in these fruit camps and I was constantly working—that was it. And it was at this point that I started to read Kurt Vonnegut and other authors. If I liked a book, I'd look at what author blurbed it, and I'd go and read their book. One book led to another, which led to another, which led to another.

I think that it was helpful for me that I dropped out of college at nineteen and took some time off from school. I had gone to Western Carolina for a year, and I then made it through two-thirds of a year at Kent State.

I ultimately left college, and I didn't come back for seven years. So when I finally returned to school, I was a lot older than the other undergraduates. I had had some experience by that point, and I think that helped with the writing.

To be honest, though, I can't read any of my early work now. Actually, I can't even read what I wrote ten years ago, I'm so embarrassed by it.

Ten years ago? Does that include your book *Naked* [Little, Brown]?
Oh, yeah.

What about it bothers you?
Just overwritten, you know. It's too densely written. It's trying too hard. The way that the sentences are put down on paper just bothers me.

I was lazy in certain ways. Years ago I wrote a story about my French teacher ["Me Talk Pretty One Day," from the eponymous 2000 book]. I described how she threw chalk at her students. She used to get up in our faces and mock us. I wrote a story about her, but it never occurred to me that she would actually read it. Someone at the French school read the story when it was published in *Esquire* and showed it to the teacher—and it became my worst nightmare.

I left some details out of the story, because it was easier for me, and less work. I really did like this teacher; all of the students liked her. Even though she threw chalk, she did care about us. But it was much easier to turn her into a monster. She more easily fit into what people's ideas of what a French teacher would be like. To have made her human would have been more complicated for me, and more difficult. It would have just contradicted most readers' ideas about French people. It was easier to make her a cliché—it was less work.

What was her reaction?
She felt betrayed and really hurt. I cringe every time I think about it. If I could take it back, I would. She contacted me, because the school was giving her trouble. So, I had to write a letter to the head of the school and say that she was a really good teacher and I was just kidding and so on.

I don't even go into that neighborhood anymore, I'm so afraid of running into her. And if I did run into her, she'd have every right to spit in my face.

I used to exaggerate a lot more than I needed to. So when I needed readers to believe me, they didn't. Again, it was easier.

Specifically, what do you mean by "exaggerate"?

I guess that's what I meant by "trying too hard." Just this feeling that every character in a book, every little character that I ran across in my life, had to be of equal size and importance to each of the other characters.

Can you give me an example?

I wrote a story called "The Incomplete Quad" [*Naked*]. I did hitchhike from Ohio to North Carolina with a quadriplegic. But did the quadriplegic ask my father for his belt? No. So, just little things like that. And if I had to write that story again, I would not exaggerate so much.

The word "exaggerate" might be the one that bothers certain critics.

In the great scheme of things, the way I exaggerate in a story is the way I exaggerate in life. It's no different. That's just the person I am and always have been.

I'm reading a book now called *Foreskin's Lament* by Shalom Auslander [Riverhead, 2007], who's such a good writer. The book is very funny. There's a scene in which the main character is walking with his family to synagogue on a Saturday afternoon, and the character describes a brown Impala passing them.

After I read this description, I imagined that some readers might ask, "How did the author remember that it was an Impala? And how did he remember it was brown?" There are people to whom that's a big question. Now, me personally, I don't give a fuck. I don't care if the car was brown, I don't care if the car was an Impala, I don't even care if it really happened. It's a good story that I'm caught up in. I just don't tend to think in that way.

If the author were to write, "I think the car passed us, but I don't remember what it looked like ...," well, you can only write that so many times before the reader or listener is going to think, What *is* all this?

It's like telling a story to friends and saying, "God, what's that person's name? I don't remember that person's name ... shit! I just don't remember his name! Anyway, so I introduced him to, *Oh damn it!* She's the one who works at the movie theater...." You can't hold an audience by telling a story like that.

But readers just seem obsessed with that now.

To be fair to readers, your last three books before *When Engulfed in Flames* have been labeled "essays" or "memoir," and not "fiction" or "humor." They also tend to be placed in the memoir section of bookstores.

I want *nothing* to be labeled on the back of my books. But a publisher always wants a label so people will know where to find it in a bookstore. Not that it does any good. My book *Dress Your Family in Corduroy and Denim* [Little, Brown] was found in some stores in the humor section, next to the collections of Cathy cartoons. Or, even worse, in the gay-and-lesbian section, beside the books about sensual massage and arranging your gay wedding.

Whether you want your books to be labeled or not, they still aren't being labeled as "fiction" or even "humor."

Not in America—but elsewhere. In Germany, they're known just as "fiction." In Germany, it's very simple: I wrote a book. That's it. "Did you read the *book*?" It just becomes "a *book*."

When I do interviews in Germany, journalists ask me, "How did you come up with the character of David?" And I say, "It's me." "Well, how did you come up with the character of the brother Paul?" And I say, "I have a brother named Paul, and that's him." "Why did you decide to set the stories in North Carolina?" "Well, that's where I'm from."

In your first book, *Barrel Fever,* there were two sections: "Stories" and "Essays." Why can't your current stories be labeled as such?

It's marketing. I have nothing to do with it. I think if I had to choose any label, and if I had to choose the placement in a bookstore, I would choose "Essays." But I suppose some readers might feel that "essays" are too dry—that they would just be about ideas and not about people.

A reporter [Alex Heard] wrote an article in *The New Republic* [March 19, 2007] about how I supposedly make up things. Now, to research this article, Alex went to North Carolina and talked with my father and some other people I had written about.

There was one story I had written ["Go Carolina," *Me Talk Pretty One Day*] where I described a speech-therapy class in elementary school as hypothetically being labeled FUTURE HOMOSEXUALS OF AMERICA. From what I understand, Alex talked to my former principal and asked, "Did you round up homosexuals and send them to speech class?"

I wrote that as a joke. I don't think it ever occurred to me that someone would take it seriously.

You weren't happy with that article, I take it?

I never read the whole thing. My oldest sister, Lisa, called and read part of it out loud to me.

The reporter made a few accusations: One was that the dialogue in your work seems a little too perfect. He also claimed that you might invent some characters out of whole cloth—or at least their personalities—such as the character Dusty at the upstate New York nudist resort you wrote about in the story "Naked."

Just because someone has Internet doesn't make them a fucking detective. I mean, just because they decided to fact-check my stories doesn't mean they're right.

This reporter asked one of the owners if Dusty was really crabby, which is what I wrote. Well, the owner was one of Dusty's friends. What else is she going to say? It's her friend! If you ask someone, "Is your friend really crabby?" they're probably going to answer, "Our friend's not crabby."

The reporter also asked about this midget guitar teacher I wrote about it in *Me Talk Pretty One Day* ["Giant Dreams, Midget Abilities"]. The specific complaint was that I described the teacher's guitar as being red—but it was really brown.

If I remember correctly, the article was more concerned with your giving this midget guitar teacher a fake name, "Mister Mancini," and then making him out to be a homophobe—where, in reality, he might not have been anti-gay.

Yes, but this reporter didn't talk to this guitar teacher. "Mister Mancini" is dead. The reporter, from what I understand, only talked with a student who also took lessons from "Mister Mancini." I never said he was a bad guitar teacher. He was good. What I implied was that I was a bad student. Most of that story was true. The big things were true. Was every word of it true? I don't have a tape recorder. I don't remember every word that was said to me when I was like eight or even when I was twenty. There are older stories that if you told me to now rewrite, I would rewrite slightly differently. New information is coming into my head that might not have been there ten, twelve years ago. I have to make these stories work, and I have to make them funny. Memoir is the last place you should ever look for the truth.

Would that hold true even for James Frey and his book *A Million Little Pieces?*

I'm sorry, but I can't understand why people would be upset about that. At the beginning of the book, he basically writes, "I'm a fucked-up alcoholic." And now readers say, "That fucked-up alcoholic lied to us!"

Well, that's what fucked-up alcoholics do! He's as much of an asshole at the end of the book as he is at the beginning! It wasn't like, "Oh, I quit drinking and now I'm a wonderful person."

I also think Frey's book was originally labeled as fiction but then labeled "memoir," for marketing purposes. Now, I've been writing fiction lately—these little stories about animals. And what I've found is that audiences listen in a different way when they believe what you're telling them is real. There's just something about reality that makes readers or listeners think, If I had the time, if I just didn't have this job, I could write a book about my life—and that would be *me* up there reading out loud to an audience. But I've got this job, see.

Reality is more effective.

Anyway, it was bound to happen.

What was bound to happen?

Somebody was bound to say, "Okay, we're going to fact-check this story of yours, and we're going to fact-check *this* anecdote and *this* name and *that* detail."

The New Republic also implied that because you're now writing for The New Yorker, and being fact-checked to their notoriously exacting standards, you no longer feel you can get away with some of your crazier details.

I definitely don't insert as many crazy details. And, in a way, that's good. Most of the time, the truth is so unbelievable that adding to it only makes readers think, Wait a minute—okay, I don't believe this anymore. If a reader is stopped by that, well, then you've got a problem.

But I have no problem with fact-checkers. In the case of *The New Yorker*, the fact-checkers work *with* me and not *against* me. They're not sneaking around behind my back and calling my elementary-school principal. It's done in a different spirit.

But to be fact-checked *too* much ... well, sometimes that ruins the humor. I wrote a piece for *The New Yorker* about my family collecting art ["Suitable for Framing," February 27, 2006]. I had a line about a painting costing as much as the average person pays in car insurance. The fact-checker asked, "How much does the painting cost?" I told him, and he called back and said, "That's more than the average person pays." And I said, "Okay. Then insert, 'The average epileptic.'" He called back and said, "You'd have to change that to 'epileptics in Connecticut,' because Connecticut has the highest rate of insurance for epileptics."

Then it becomes a paragraph about car rates. To me, it was just a throwaway line. And there goes the humor.

How do some of the crazier situations you write about happen to you? Are you more attuned to certain situations than others might be?

I wrote a story for *The New Yorker* that was called "Journey Into Night" [December 17, 2007]. I sat in the business-elite section while out on a book tour. This was new to me—sitting there. After we took off, the flight attendant asked, "Do you mind if I move somebody next to you?" The seat was empty. She said something like, "I've got a passenger a few rows up, and people are starting to complain about his crying. He's Polish, and his mother just died; he's on his way to the funeral."

So this guy sat next to me, and it really kind of ruins your good time. If you're watching a funny movie on a plane and the person next to you is crying, it sort of brings the whole thing down. If you're thinking in terms of writing, you ask yourself, Can a crying Polish man sit next to me for six hours? The answer is, Sure. But if you're not a writer, and you're not thinking in those terms, then your reaction will probably be, Fuck this! I don't want a crybaby next to me for that amount of time!

Out of curiosity, what movie was playing?

A remake of *Heaven Can Wait*, with Chris Rock. It was called *Down to Earth*. And, because of the situation, it was the funniest movie I'd ever seen. I mean, I was trying so hard not to laugh that it caused me physical pain. I never included that detail in the story. It almost seemed too perfect. I just left it out.

But to go back to an earlier example, after I wrote about the French teacher throwing chalk, the school sent a representative to talk with me. The representative asked, "If your teacher was throwing chalk at you, and if she was calling you all these names, why didn't you switch to another class?"

But *why* would I have switched? As a writer, this was better than anything I could have prayed for. It was fantastic!

Is that a major worry for you—that when you experience something that will translate beautifully to the page, you might think, No, I can't write this; no one's going to believe it?

It is sometimes. I once read a piece to an audience about this woman who babysat for me and my sisters when my parents were out of town ["The Understudy," *The New Yorker*, April 10, 2006]. Afterward, a lady in the audience said, "I don't believe that your story is really true, because you would have written about this person already." And I said, "Well, no. It's something my sisters and I have talked about for years and years."

My boyfriend Hugh's little nephew just came to Paris. It just amazed me that he remembered me so well. The last time I saw him was years ago, when he was five. When you're a parent, you can try to create these big moments for your kids, like "Okay, we're going to go on vacation, and you are never going to forget it for the rest of your life!" And then, a year later, the kids have forgotten all about it, but what they do remember are some of the details, such as when your father was talking on the phone and putting fingernail polish on one finger. There are things you just don't forget. Sometimes it takes years to be able to process something and then get it down onto the page.

A while back, I wrote about a woman who used to live down the hall from me in New York ["The Old Lady Down the Hall," October 2000]. The piece was published in *Esquire* after she died. But I was never happy with it, so I rewrote it [as "That's Amore," published in *When You Are Engulfed with Flames*]. The story became closer to how I felt about her and the situation. I didn't think, Shit, I wish I'd never written about it the first time. There's no rule that says I can't write about something as many times as I want.

Has your life merely become a precursor for what will eventually end up on the page or the radio? Has your life become a first draft?

Not really. It's odd how you can write about yourself and give the illusion you're exposing so much when you're really not. It doesn't bother me if the world knows I sat in a waiting room in my underpants like I described in *The New Yorker* story "In the Waiting Room" [September 18, 2006].

So the character on the page is different from the real you? Are they two different entities?

There are similarities, but there has to be separation. In real life, you're a person. Once you're on paper, you're a character—and you have to behave like a character.

That's how *you* feel, but how does the rest of your family feel? Even if you consider them "characters," these stories are still about them.

It's not as if the rest of my family doesn't have their own version of past events, but for the most part my family doesn't have a problem with it. My version tends to be very similar to theirs. It's okay for most of them to have me controlling the narrative.

But it has been difficult for them at times. One of my sisters had been having this problem with a neighbor. They weren't getting along at all, and he came over one day and said to her, "Last night, I was reading about you in your brother's book."

It never occurred to me that something like that might happen.

Really? Millions of people read your books and listen to you on the radio and see you perform live.

People often think that my family doesn't know I'm writing about them. They think I've written a certain story just to hurt them. They think the reader and I are in cahoots against a certain person in my family. That's not the case at all. I've never written anything that would hurt anyone in my family.

I always ask a family member if it's okay to write about them. They'll say yes. But then the book comes out and readers say to them, "I can't believe what your brother wrote about you!"

A lot of this is misinterpreted too. There was a story I wrote for *The New Yorker* called "Let It Snow" [December 22, 2003]. I wrote about a snowstorm and how my mother kicked us all out of the house so she could relax by herself and have a drink. This story was then reprinted in a textbook. In the back of the book there was a study guide. One of the entries read, "Explain why David Sedaris's mother was a bad mother." Another read: "Have you had any experience with an alcoholic parent?"

I thought, Wait a minute, I never said she was a bad mother. I also never said she was an alcoholic. It was just me being stupid enough to think I can control how a reader feels. In the end, a reader didn't experience these events like I experienced them.

But with that said, not everyone may realize the power of the page. A family member can easily say, "Sure, write about me," but do they fully understand that this anecdote may soon be read and heard by millions?

I don't think *any* of us did. Even now, it's hard to imagine readers sitting down and reading what I write. There's just something about it that's so abstract. When I go out on tour, people will come to the theater and I'll see them in the audience—I can understand that. But mostly, it's almost as if part of me just doesn't believe that what I write will eventually be read.

I've never written anything that would prevent anyone in my family from getting a job, you know. My brother ["the Rooster"] loves to be written about. On the other hand, my sister Tiffany said to me years ago, "You can't write about me." So I said, "Okay, fine." I didn't, and she said to me, "Everyone thinks you don't like me. Would you write a story about me?"

Didn't Tiffany once tell a newspaper she didn't trust your boundaries?
She wasn't happy with a story I wrote ["Put a Lid on It," *Dress Your Family in Corduroy and Denim*] about her messy apartment. I showed it to her before publication, and I asked, "Is this okay?" She loved it and thought it was funny. I asked, "Do you want me to change anything?" "No, don't change a thing."

Then the story was published, and people came up to her and said, "I can't believe what your brother wrote about you." And she said, "Me neither." Then the local newspaper interviewed her, and the article became all about how I had invaded her privacy.

There are things I'm never going to write about concerning my family. There are stories about my mother I would just never write. I know it would bother her if she were still alive. I don't necessarily want people knowing it.

There's been some criticism that you've made your mother out to be too sarcastic and grating.
I think that's another case of me being too lazy as a writer and too desperate to make a character appear funny. Maybe she wasn't well-rounded enough, and that would be my fault. And yet there were stories that I thought put her in a good light. I wrote a story about my family wanting to buy a beach house on the North Carolina shore, and there was a scene where my mother was coming up with potential names for the house ["The Ship Shape," *Dress Your Family in Corduroy and Denim*]. She said, very excitedly,

"How about something with the word 'sandpiper' in it? Everybody likes sandpipers, right?"

It's such a square and naked and hopeful thing for someone to say. You know, "Everybody likes them! We're going to get a beach house and name it after sandpipers!" It just breaks my heart to think of my mother saying that.

It becomes all the more heartbreaking when it didn't work out in the end—your family never did buy a beach house.

I'm glad I had the confidence to put that line into the story—I might not have if I had written it earlier in my life. I might have thought, Oh, well. Anyone's mom could have said that.

How about your own life? Is anything off-limits? One subject I've noticed you rarely write about is your sex life.

When you're reading out loud to an audience, they're visualizing it. If I wrote about going to the top of the Eiffel Tower, they would picture me getting into an elevator and going to the top. So, if you're reading a story about having sex with someone, well, that's what they're going to picture.

Yes, but many people enjoy imagining others having sex.

True, but I'm in my fifties, so I don't think anybody necessarily wants to picture me as the one doing it.

I recently read a memoir by Edmund White, who's in his late sixties. I went and heard him read from part of this book [*My Lives,* Ecco, 2006]. At one point in the story, he's around sixty-five years old, and he describes himself drinking his boyfriend's urine. Later, Edmund gives his boyfriend a blow job while the guy is defecating.

When I heard this, the only thing I could think of was: My hat is really off to you, Mr. White. I really tip my hat to you for being that honest.

Do you think he went too far?

Not too far for him. I mean, it's too far for me. But maybe he feels the way I do when I write about myself sitting in a waiting room in my underpants. That's the same for him. He must not really care if people know that he once gave a guy a blow job while he was defecating. I, on the other hand, don't really care if people know that I once sat in a hospital waiting room wearing only my underpants. I feel that nothing I've ever written has really exposed me. Perhaps he felt the same way.

If that doesn't expose him, I'd like to read the story that does.

But as a reader, I'm always impressed when authors write stories like that. I enjoy that very much. I admire an author that would be brave enough to do that. It's the same way I would admire someone who could turn somersaults or build a fire with a rock. "Nice job, very impressive!" But I, personally, couldn't do it.

It's going to be difficult to find the appropriate transition from the subject of blow jobs to anything else, so I'll just change the subject without even trying to make a connection. Do you write differently for the page, as opposed to writing for radio or for a live event?

That's one difference between me now and ten or fifteen years ago. I'm just about to go on tour for a month, and I have about fifty new pages to read out loud. After each show, I'll go back to the hotel and rewrite. I'll do this throughout the tour. With *Naked*, or any of the books or stories before that, I wasn't reading out loud—and I paid the price. When the *Naked* book tour happened, I read some of those stories out loud, and I remember thinking, Man! When did I expect myself to breathe? Why did I not listen to my editor? Why did I not cut that part out?

I suppose I was terrified that I wouldn't have enough pages for the book.

You now edit your stories in a live setting?

Sometimes the biggest laugh can come from saying nothing—from just a pause. You can learn a lot by reading your stories to a live audience. When I hear myself reading out loud, I hear things I don't hear when I read to myself.

When I read aloud, I always have a pencil in hand. If I feel I'm trying too hard or I'm being repetitive, I make a mark. An editor can tell you those same things, but you don't necessarily believe the editor. So it's good to just learn those things on your own, and then to fix them as much as you can before you turn in the piece to the editor.

Did you know there's now a version of *The New Yorker* for blind people? The person who reads the magazine isn't an actor. He's not a professional. He just gets a copy of *The New Yorker* and reads it from cover to cover. And that's a great thing. I can hear my piece perfectly when I listen to that. It's as if someone comes to my home and reads it out loud. I can hear the piece again in a fresh way.

You wrote something interesting in your foreword to *Jenny & the Jaws of Life* [St. Martin's, 1987], a collection of stories by one of your favorite fiction writers, Jincy Willett. You said that when you read a story out loud it can easily be made to be funny. But the very same story, when read alone, can be very sad and bleak and more complex.

Right, and that's part of having a good editor like I have with Jeff Frank, at *The New Yorker*. He never hears me read a new story out loud; he just sees the piece on the page. If he can believe the story and if he can understand all of the things I'm trying to communicate on the page, then I feel I have that end covered.

Writing humor for the page is such a solitary activity, usually without any reaction or response from another person. I always wonder if it makes a difference for a humor writer, who—either out of shyness or for other reasons—never reads their work in a live setting. Does that affect the final product?

Most probably. It's like reading a story on the radio. Your only audience is the sound engineer, and you often can't even hear them; you can only see them. If I can see them laughing, I think, Okay, maybe this'll work. But other times, there will be engineers who are talking on the phone, and I don't have a clue as to whether it works or not. I don't know whether to pause and give people a chance to laugh, or to just keep on reading. I never really know for sure.

How long does it generally take for you to write a story?

It can take years. With the first draft, I just write everything. With the second draft, it becomes so depressing for me, because I realize that I was fooled into thinking I'd written the story. I hadn't—I had just typed for a long time. So I then have to carve out a story from the twenty-five or so pages. It's in there somewhere—but I have to find it. I'll then write a third, fourth, and fifth draft, and so on.

Beyond that, I have this file I call "Attempts," which contains bits and pieces of stories that aren't fully formed.

I was stuck a few weeks ago, so I went back to a story I had started six years ago. The problem was that the setup was promising but nothing really dramatic happened. To me, it was a hoodoo story—I had to take this story and either connect it to another story or fashion an ending out of thin air. Sometimes you're in the mood to do that, and sometimes you're not. And when I'm not, that's how things end up in the Attempts file.

Can you give me a specific example of a story that took years to write?

I had a story in *The New Yorker* about going with my brother to buy drugs in a North Carolina trailer ["The Way We Are," February 19, 2007]. I had started the story years ago, but it was just a vignette. A dope dealer and his wife lived in this trailer. So that was all I had. Years later, the water in my house in France had been turned off, and I was forced to make coffee out of the water in the flower vase. I thought, I can connect this story to that other story about buying drugs in the trailer. Those two stories fit nicely—the couple in the trailer and their relationship, and the relationship Hugh and I have.

It's like a jigsaw. When something doesn't work, I hold on to that little piece—maybe I'll find another piece for it in a few years.

What do you attempt to achieve with your endings? When I re-read your work—even going back to *Barrel Fever* [1994]—there seems to be a consistent, almost melancholy tone with the endings. The stories wrap up beautifully.

When you reach the end, you just know. You think, I don't have to write any more. That's how I felt recently with a story. I kind of looked up and thought, Oh my God, that's finished. There's nothing more to be written. It just felt right.

Every now and then when I'm reading a story to an audience, I'll reach the end and the audience will make a little noise. I always want that noise.

What's the noise?

It's as if something was suddenly pulled out from under them—but they landed well. It's like showing someone a puppy, and they say, "Aaaaaaaah." The puppy is cute, but there's also another layer. It's as if to say, "Where the fuck did that puppy come from?"

Is that the type of reaction you want your readers, not just your listeners, to have?

I've received letters from readers who tell me they feel a certain way when a certain story ends. There's one story I wrote about how my family deals with me writing about them; it's called "Repeat After Me" [from *Dress Your Family in Corduroy and Denim*]. Obviously I'm not hearing the reaction of the readers to it, but I'd like to think that everything that needs to be in an ending is in that ending—shame and pride and a big cocktail of uncomfortableness.

My main concern is to not be too corny. I don't want to produce fake emotion; I want real emotion. Whenever it's time to write an ending, I always think of the endings in the stories that I just love—the last two paragraphs of *The Great Gatsby*, or the ending of Tobias Wolff's short story, "Bullet in the Brain" [*The Night in Question*, Knopf, 1996]. Those endings are just perfect—and that's what I want.

Another aspect of your writing I've always admired are your segues. They create a type of flow similar to a movie's. For instance, in "Rooster at the Hitchin' Post" from *Dress Your Family in Corduroy and Denim*, you juxtapose scenes of your brother getting married with scenes of him almost drowning when he was a child. Back and forth, back and forth. It becomes very effective.

I was just going through that process earlier today, actually. I had these two paragraphs that I wanted to connect, but they were redundant.

I thought, Oh, I don't need any of them. But then how does one go from *here* to *there?* It's like when you're a kid and you put the sofa cushions on the floor and you can only walk across the room on the cushions. But all of a sudden you don't have any cushions left, and you have to get to the other side. The next available cushion is twelve feet away, and you're like, This could take all day. So you take off your pants and you stuff your shirt into it and you make a cushion to get from here to there. Hopefully no one will say, "You made that cushion, didn't you? You can't do that!" With a bit of luck and work, it'll all seem natural.

Are you happier now than you were growing up? If so, does that help or hinder your writing?

I don't think my childhood was any more miserable than anyone else's, really. I mean, it didn't help to be gay, but there were people who were gayer than me and who had it worse than I had it. When I was young, I did think, Well, this will pass and I'll get older and things are bound to get better. But my childhood wasn't epic. It wasn't biblical. My parents never did lock me in a dungeon. They never cut off my feet and ate them.

One thing I noticed when I was teaching writing was that my middle-class students were ashamed of their upbringings. It used to be that poor people were ashamed, but that's not the case anymore. Rich people aren't ashamed, either. It's only the middle class who are ashamed. They tend to feel that their lives are inherently worthless, because they grew up in the suburbs.

Many of my students used to write stories about growing up on the streets; it was never believable. For me, it was sad that they were ashamed of something they were not responsible for; it wasn't their fault they had braces on their teeth—or that on the last day of school their parents picked them up in expensive cars.

So when I started writing about my childhood, I thought, "I am *not* going to write about that time of my life with any degree of shame." What does that even mean, feeling that your life is *that* unworthy of attention?

Your breakthrough story was "SantaLand Diaries" [*Barrel Fever*, Little, Brown, 1994], which was about your experiences working as a Christmas elf at Macy's in New York.

Yeah. I read that piece on NPR in December 1992.

It surprised me how well, and how quickly, your humor translated to the NPR crowd. Before you read "SantaLand Diaries," I'm not so sure I had ever heard an NPR anecdote about a 40-year-old retarded man with a dent in his forehead urinating on Santa's lap.

[Laughs] That wasn't me, by the way.

I was surprised, too. The whole piece as I wrote it would have taken about an hour to read. It was Ira [Glass] who edited it down to nine minutes or so. What surprised me more than anything was how many people listened to NPR's *Morning Edition*. I never listened to *Morning Edition* because I was always asleep when it came on, so I didn't really have any notion of what the show meant to people. But the reaction was instantaneous. It was like that moment that everyone dreams about—the before and the after.

After I read that story, my phone immediately began to ring. And it rang and rang and rang and rang. A telephone operator called and said, "I just want you to know I'm late for work, and it's all your fault because I listened to your story on the radio." Then the phone rang again, and it was Alec Baldwin.

What did Alec Baldwin have to say?

"Loved the story on the radio. Do you think you could send me and Kim [Basinger] a tape?"

Did you hear from the rest of the Baldwin brothers? Billy? Adam?

No, but I never expected to hear from anyone. I didn't expect anything like that to happen.

Has there ever been a time when you've wanted to write humor for a different format, such as for television or the movies?

I never seriously wanted to write for television. There was a time when I thought I wanted to write for soap operas. But the type of writing

I always wanted to do is exactly the writing that I'm doing right now. I never really even watch television.

A producer from *Seinfeld* once called and asked if I'd like to write for the show, even though I had never seen it. This must have been an insult to them; here's this number one show, and I've never bothered to ever watch it. So they said, "Why don't you watch the show and then talk to us?"

I watched the show and I wrote them a letter saying, What if *this* happened in an episode? Or what if *that* happened? And that was the end of it. I never heard back—which wasn't too much of a surprise.

What were your suggestions?

I wanted the Elaine character to have a psychiatrist, who would tell her, "You need some companionship. I have this dog I want to give you." Basically, it would be his own dog that he wanted to get rid of.

I had just seen a dog with elephantiasis of the testicles. They were huge and covered with scabs from having been dragged on the ground. So I thought this psychiatrist's dog could also suffer from this, and it would make all of Elaine's friends react in a certain way. A small dog with huge testicles. I didn't think of an ending for it—that was just the premise. I thought it might be entertaining, but obviously it didn't happen.

Actually, I remember that story later appearing on *Full House*. Do you have any humor pet peeves?

I think the biggest danger is always when a writer tries too hard. At readings, people will come up to me and say, "Everyone says that I write just like you, so here's what I've written. Maybe you can help me get it published?" I often think, God, I hope I don't write like this. They just try so damn hard! It's almost as if they think there's a math equation to the whole process: "I need three jokes per page. I need one *here*, and one *here*, and one *here*." Often what makes me laugh is simply word choice—not jokes. In his book *Foreskin's Lament*, Shalom Auslander wrote, "My family and I are like oil and water, if oil made water depressed and angry and want to kill itself." That's perfect.

When you write humor, people think that you just record into a tape recorder and then someone else transcribes your words. It doesn't occur to them that you have to choose *this* word over *that* word—and do so very carefully. I'm often asked in interviews, "How long have you been a storyteller?" To me, that implies some woman in bare feet who comes to the local library and tells stories. I just cringe when people say that. Most people have no concept of writing, or what's involved with the process.

You've talked about your obsessive-compulsive disorder in the past. Does OCD affect your writing?

Yes, and I've always been lucky in that way. I like doing the exact same thing at the exact same time every day—that's what my life is, and that's what I'm all about. So once I started to write for the first time—really, from the very first day—I never had to force myself to write. I don't think I've ever missed a day of writing in more than twenty years. I work seven days a week.

I get up, I go right to work, I take a break, and then I go back to work at night. I don't just sit at a desk for two minutes and then say, "Oh, okay. I tried. Maybe tomorrow." It's the same sort of obsessiveness that makes me want to stay in bed until 10:26 every morning. I'm just wired that way.

You literally wake up at 10:26 every morning?

Sometimes I'll open my eyes at 10:22, and then I'll lie there until 10:26. But I don't ever sleep beyond 10:26.

That's something that obviously can't be—or shouldn't be—taught in writing programs.

No, but you can't teach a lot of things. That's the scam of any kind of art school. There are a lot of people who excel in school, but once they don't have homework anymore, whether it's painting or writing or whatever, they can't function. They need a professor telling them to write a story by such and such a date.

In the real world, the most important part is sitting there and writing. It's not easy to function in that vacuum, but that's what you have to do.

Do you find that writing helps alleviate your O.C.D. symptoms?

If I wasn't writing, I'd be obsessively doing another activity every day at the same time.

How many pages of publishable text do you write in a day?

When I had to turn in *Me Talk Pretty One Day,* I was writing a half-page of text a day—fifteen pages a month.

Your work seems to be both critically and commercially popular among a variety of people: all age groups, straight, gay—across the board. That's rare for a humor writer.

I don't know why my work would be more popular than another writer's. I don't understand why people would respond to something I wrote more than they would to what someone else wrote. Even if I wanted to please a certain segment of the audience, I wouldn't know how. When I first began writing and reading in public, it was for a gay crowd—my audiences were all gay. Soon, the audiences began to look so different to me. If I were to set out to make this or that segment of society happy, I wouldn't even know how to start. I just write what I want to.

When your books do well, there's always a guilt that comes with it. I always think, It's so unfair. What about this *other* person? I feel guilty—as if I'm not a real writer.

I think most successful writers—except for egomaniacs—feel at least partially guilty that they're doing well.

I've known writers who suffer from that guilt so profoundly they can't enjoy any of the spoils. I'm not to that point yet. With that said, it's still no big picnic to be who I am.

There's no one who's harder on me than myself. And that goes for my writing. Nobody's harder on what I write than me.

I suppose if life were a joy, you wouldn't be a writer.

No, I wouldn't.

You're now being published in *The New Yorker* on a consistent basis. Did the magazine mean anything to you growing up?

It didn't come to our house or anything. I wasn't aware of it until I was about twenty.

How did you end up writing for *The New Yorker?*

There was an editor there named Chris Knutson, and after *Barrel Fever* came out, he called me and said he was editing Shouts & Murmurs. He asked if I could write something, and I did, and they ran it. I just couldn't believe it.

But I would never have written anything if they hadn't asked me to. When Chris left, David Remnick called and asked if I had anything available. When he came to France I met with him, and I told him I didn't have anything at the time that was appropriate for *The New Yorker.* He said, "Stop worrying about what you think is a *New Yorker* story, and then everything will be fine."

I stopped worrying about it. And everything was fine.

Do you have to write for space for *The New Yorker?* Are you limited with the number of words you're allowed to publish?

Never. What usually happens is that my editor, Jeff Frank, will give the piece to David Remnick, since David has the last word. If Jeff's not sure, he'll show it around to the other editors, and then he makes some suggestions for me. But, generally, these changes take less than an hour to make. I can write a piece as long as I want—or as short.

To this day, when I have a story in *The New Yorker,* I'm just amazed. When I receive an issue, I always open to the contents page and I think, "Oh, wait a minute—that's my name! That's my name in *The New Yorker!*" I'd love for my twenty-year-old self to see it.

Well, we've been talking on the phone for more than five hours now, you in Paris and me in New York. You must be exhausted, and, more important, my ear is killing me. Do you usually go to bed later than this?

I do, yes.

Where are you now?

In my apartment—upstairs in my office.

Do you have a view of a Paris street?

Yes.

What goes on in Paris at three o'clock on a Monday morning?

Well, tonight there's ... huh, I just stuck my head out the window. There's nobody on the street. It's different on a Friday or Saturday night, when it's so loud you'd think the street is a fairground. But it doesn't bother me. If the people were yelling in English, "Party!" and "Marty!" and "You're a fucking asshole!," then that would get on my nerves. But not when it's in French. It just becomes like the sound of the waves, or an exotic bird.

I thank you for your time ... now get some rest. I realize you have to be up in exactly seven hours and twenty-six minutes.

I do, thank you. Good-night.

Getting a Book of Humor Published

Advice from book editors at HarperCollins, Random House, and Patrick Price at Simon Spotlight Entertainment

1. You can pitch your idea to a publisher on your own, but it helps significantly if you have an agent.

2. It's very hard to place humor that's *just* humor. The humor books I've had better luck with have had some sort of prescriptive "useful" element. In other words, they have a common theme.

3. Keep in mind that the book-publishing business works slowly—it can take three years from the time you pitch an idea to the book's publication. Do not pitch ideas that will become dated too quickly.

4. The selection and evaluation process in this business is highly subjective to begin with, and I can think of no more subjective subject than humor. With that in mind, if your material hasn't been published in a magazine publication, test-market the work among friends to get an accurate read on whether it is—in fact—funny.

5. Do not compare yourself to David Sedaris. Every book editor has heard that so many times that it's seen—at best—as white noise. If you write hysterical, idiosyncratic essays, we'll make the obvious comparison in your future marketing copy.

6. If you're writing a proposal, ask yourself repeatedly if there is, in fact, a book's worth of material in the idea. Many humor proposals I receive can't stay funny and fresh for the length of the proposal—how then will the author be able to squeeze out two hundred to three hundred pages? I would say most of the humor proposals I receive are really magazine pieces in disguise.

7. Do not write in your cover letter, "Perfect for being placed next to the cash register."

8. Do not suggest your book as the first of a series. Things like this—and delivering the proposal with a book cover already designed—make it appear that you're more interested in the *idea* of being published than in actually writing a good book.

9. No wacky packaging or raw materials.

10. Edit yourself. What's clever in ten words can rapidly become tedious in over fifty. Sometimes understated and dry is far better than aiming to impress with literary grandstanding. An editor will happily ask for more, but will usually be turned off if reaching the humor's heart requires an archaeological dig.

11. Only the most brilliant of parodies works—and often even *they* have short shelf lives.

12. It all boils down to "the voice." If you be yourself, it should prove unique. That is half the battle toward being funny and getting published.

George Meyer

George Meyer's "Suicide Note Dos and Don'ts"

1. *Do* curse the living.

2. *Don't* recommend movies or restaurants.

3. *Do* mention a "hidey-hole" of gold coins.

4. *Don't* pin the suicide note to your shirt. It looks desperate.

For two weeks in 2002, TV writer George Meyer gave rare public performances at a West Hollywood theater, co-starring in a play (which he also wrote and directed) called *Up Your Giggy*. Between sketches, Meyer delivered monologues that took aim at many of his favorite targets, including advertising ("an insane, diabolical siren song dragging us all to a horrific *Koyaanisqatsi*"), God ("a ridiculous superstition, invented by frightened cavemen"), and, of course, marriage ("a stagnant cauldron of fermented resentments, scared and judgmental conformity, exaggerated concern for the children, dull weekends in Santa Barbara, and the secret dredging-up of erotic images from past lovers in a desperate and heartbreaking attempt to make spousal sex even possible"). For Meyer's longtime fans, it was further proof that their comedy idol hadn't lost any of his decidedly caustic wit over the years.

Dissecting cherished institutions such as family and religion was nothing new for Meyer. Since 1989, he's been one of the most revered and celebrated writers on *The Simpsons*. Though it was "Life in Hell" cartoonist Matt Groening who first conceived the show (initially as a series of shorts on *The Tracey Ullman Show* from 1987 to 1989), Meyer is largely considered among the writing staff to be its behind-the-scenes genius among geniuses. If you need further proof, just read any newspaper or magazine article about *The Simpsons*. There will most likely be a quote from a *Simpsons* writer, explaining how Meyer is, more often than not, responsible for the best lines and jokes.

To truly understand Meyer's satiric worldview, however, it's necessary to take a closer look at the *Simpsons* episodes attributed solely to him. As pointed out in the 2004 *The Believer* interview with Meyer, his episodes tend to share the following common theme: A character giving up on an "institution or belief system." It could be Homer deciding that he doesn't want to go to church anymore ("Homer the Heretic," 1992, Episode Three), or Bart walking out on a family holiday ("Bart vs. Thanksgiving," 1990, Episode Seven), or even Lisa—the character whom Meyer, a fellow vegetarian and environmentalist, most identifies with—losing faith in the American political system ("Mr. Lisa Goes to Washington," 1991, Episode Three). *The Simpsons* may have originally been based on Matt Groening's family, but their hearts and souls belong to Meyer.

Meyer's distrust of authority (political, religious or parental) began at a young age. Born in Pennsylvania in 1956 and raised mostly in Tucson, Arizona, Meyer was the oldest of eight children in a family of strict Roman Catholics. He's often remarked that his Catholic upbringing was difficult— "It wound my spring almost to the breaking point," he told *The Believer*. He attended Harvard University in the mid-seventies to pursue a degree in biochemistry, but somewhere along the way got wooed by comedy. He became president of *The Harvard Lampoon*, the legendary platform for the careers of countless TV and movie writers, many of whom would go on to write for *The Simpsons*.

After graduating in 1978, two of his Harvard friends (Tom Gammill and Max Pross) recommended him for a staff writing position at *Late Night with David Letterman*, where he stayed for two years (1981–83). After *Late*

Night, Meyer had little difficulty finding writing work, penning scripts for the Lorne Michaels–produced *The New Show* (1984), as well as for *Saturday Night Live* (1985-1987). Then—bored with television—he gave up the lucrative, albeit pressure-filled, lifestyle and fled to Boulder, Colorado.

To some, it might have seemed like career suicide. But Meyer wasn't entirely unproductive while living in seclusion. With the help of some fellow writers, including Jack Handey and Bob Odenkirk, he published a small zine called *Army Man* (billed as "America's Only Magazine"). Although it was little more than a photocopied, self-published newsletter, twelve pages long and filled with absurdist jokes, one-liners, and cartoons, it attracted a cult following. *Army Man* lasted only three issues and had a distribution in the low triple digits, but it was widely read in Los Angeles, eventually finding its way into the hands of a producer named Sam Simon, who just so happened to be looking for writers for a new TV show called *The Simpsons*.

For Meyer, *The Simpsons* was a perfect match: a creative environment in which his ideas and sensibilities were appreciated. As *The New Yorker* observed in a profile of Meyer in 2000 (and quoting the poet Robert Pinsky from an article he wrote for *The New York Times*), the show "belongs to its writers ... to a degree that is almost unheard-of on television." The show was such a comfortable fit that Meyer, who was eventually made one of the executive producers, has remained with it in some capacity long after most of his colleagues have moved on to other writing projects. Not surprisingly, Meyer was picked to co-write *The Simpsons Movie* (2007), and he'll likely have a hand in every subsequent incarnation of the animated family he helped turn into superstars.

Did you always intend to write for television?

When I was young, I wanted to be a priest, then a ballplayer, then a Bond villain. I wanted a lair that was equal parts comfy and death-dealing. I didn't even think about writing for television until long after college. It was like saying, "I'm going to be a professional sweepstakes winner." It just didn't seem like a real career.

I watched a lot of television, but it wasn't that thrilling for me. It was like a piece of gum that you'd been chewing for a while but were too lazy to spit out. For me, television was something to fill the hours, and if I could go back I'd spend more time at the library—or looking for treasure with a metal detector.

Even when I started writing for TV, I knew very little about show business or its history. I was naïve enough to believe that all who came before me were clueless stumblebums whose stale shtick was best swept out of the way. The only shows that made me laugh as a kid were *Batman* and *Get Smart*. I liked their insane premises and lurid showboating. They had bizarre gadgets and secret hideouts and sprawling fight scenes—very appealing to a boy. Then, almost as a bonus, you got this loopy, irreverent humor.

I remember a scene from *Get Smart* where the character of Siegfried, a vice president of KAOS, kept ordering a carrier pigeon to take off—only it was dead. And he repeatedly tossed it in the air and told it to "Flyyyy uupp!" It kept landing with a thump. Other shows, like *My Three Sons*, didn't do jokes about death.

Years later, I got to meet my girlfriend's dad, Lorenzo Semple Jr., who wrote for the *Batman* TV show and created the tone of the series. Lorenzo wrote the first four scripts, which established the campy sensibility of the show. For instance, he insisted that the actors take even the looniest developments seriously and avoid "winking" at the audience. His approach to a superhero show was both ingenious and massively influential. Lorenzo also wrote and co-wrote some classic films, including *The Parallax View*, *Three Days of the Condor*, and one of my favorite cult films, *Pretty Poison*. He's both a serious Yalie intellectual and a high-octane satirist.

You've mentioned that television wasn't too important to you when you were young, but how important was humor?

It kept me alive.

Why do you think it was that important to you?

It showed me an alternative to the grim worldview of thwarted adults.

Would Catholicism fall under this "grim worldview"? In past interviews, you've talked about your dislike for religion in general and Catholicism in particular.

Catholicism was much too frightening for a sensitive kid. A small bloody man presided over each classroom and there was *way* too much talk about mortal sin and eternal damnation. When they weren't scaring you, they were boring you with tiresome doctrine. The word "liturgy" still makes me sick with boredom.

You can see that sensibility in many episodes of *The Simpsons*. As opposed to most shows, *The Simpsons* is never afraid to mock religion and the religious.

I think what we're really satirizing is moral certainty—the myopia of the pious. The religious ferociously defend their own beliefs, but if a Sioux wants to keep a Target store off his sacred land they'll laugh in his face.

Was writing for David Letterman your first professional humor-writing job?

Yes. My friends from *The Harvard Lampoon*, Max Pross and Tom Gammill, told me in late 1981 that Dave and Merrill Markoe were doing a late-night show, and I should submit material. Dave and Merrill took a chance on me, and it radically rerouted my life.

Were you familiar with Letterman's work before you got the *Late Night* job? Had you seen his morning show, or his appearances on *The Tonight Show* in the late seventies and early eighties?

I hadn't seen Dave's morning show at the time, because I was working at a research lab. I didn't really know who he was, in fact.

What were you researching? This was after college?

Right. We were studying glycoproteins, in the hope that they would prove the key to cell-cell recognition—a basic process that goes awry in cancer cells. I learned later that our entire line of inquiry was a dead end.

I graduated with a degree in biochemistry and was accepted into medical school, but ultimately I did not want to be a doctor. The pre-med students I studied with in college were an unimpressive bunch of grinds.

They would sabotage each other's experiments—so lame. And now they don't even make any money, at least not compared to a big-time comedy writer. Enjoy your free notepads, losers!

When you were writing for *Late Night*, did you have any idea of the impact the show was having on pop culture?

We knew the show was making a splash, but the real impact on pop culture took years. It wasn't like a blockbuster movie, when you know how you're doing immediately. Some of our best jokes would air at 1:25 A.M., so it took a while.

Did you find that the show was an easy fit for you as a writer, sensibility-wise?

In retrospect, it was an ideal place for me to hone my skills, but I was a bit of a malcontent back then. I had grandiose aims. I didn't want Dave to repeat things, even if the audience loved them. I wanted to challenge the audience every night, stagger them with brilliance, blast them into a higher plane of existence. In other words, I didn't understand late-night television.

Letterman was notorious for having a very low acceptance rate for jokes. How frustrating was this for you as a writer?

Dave usually took the good stuff, and if he believed in a joke, and it didn't get much of a laugh, he would repeat it for his own amusement—almost like an incantation. I found that endearing.

He would sometimes reject segments that were highly conceptual, or "writerly," and we would get mad. But he knew what he needed out there. If a tightrope walker says, "This guy wire is loose," you don't tell him he's wrong—you fix the guy wire.

What year did you leave *Late Night*, and why?

I left in late 1983, so I could work as a writer on Lorne Michaels's show on NBC, *The New Show*. Whoops!

The New Show was a prime-time sketch show that only lasted a handful of episodes, but it's remembered quite fondly by those who watched it at the time.

The show was a bit disorganized, but the writing staff was remarkable. I shared an office with Jack Handey, who taught me a ton about comedy.

What specifically did he teach you?

He showed me that hilarious runs could be created with simple, unpretentious language. He taught me to can the preamble and just to get to the funny part.

I don't know if it ever aired, but Jack once wrote a *Saturday Night Live* sketch that was later an inspiration for the "Hurricane Neddy" episode of *The Simpsons*, where Homer builds a house for Ned [Season 8, Episode Eight]. The *SNL* sketch was about a shoemaker whose shop was failing. He got a big order for shoes but couldn't fill it in time, so he collapsed in despair. As he slept, elves tiptoed in and made the shoes. When the shoemaker awoke, he was overjoyed, until he realized that the elves' workmanship was incredibly shoddy. Not only were the shoes undeliverable, but all of his materials had been wasted. As I recall, the sketch ended with a gunshot.

It's very difficult to find video for *The New Show,* but I did read some funny sketches online. In one, John Candy plays a food repairman, who literally fixes food that had been broken, such as re-assembling shattered taco shells.

I wrote that sketch, which was lifted by John Candy's gifts. I remember he was utterly exhausted when we taped it, and I thought it would be a disaster, but the camera went on and John just turned on the high beams. I was dancing with delight. The following week John was on a Mardi Gras float, and people were screaming "Food repairman!"

Why didn't *The New Show* last?

The Friday-night time slot wasn't ideal, but the main problem was that it was a variety show. By that time, variety shows had become passé.

And I suppose it didn't help that it ran against *Falcon Crest*.

No, that show was a bulldozer.

From *The New Show* you went to *SNL* in 1985. A lot of writers I've interviewed have expressed frustration with that show. What was your experience like?

It was an exhilarating, frustrating, stressful, and indelible experience.

You've been quoted as saying that your material was too "fringy" for *SNL*. What was so fringy about it?

In retrospect, it was too conceptual. I didn't think enough about creating characters that the actors could play. My good friend Jim Downey, who was the head writer for *SNL* for many years, tried to point this out to me, but I simply couldn't adapt my style. If I could go back, I would emulate Jack Handey, who usually wrote pieces by himself—often for Randy Quaid or Phil Hartman, two gifted and reliable performers.

Most of the sketches I wrote were fatally flawed. I wrote a bit about a chalk factory, which was a twist on coal miners being covered in soot. These guys were covered in chalk dust. For some reason, I thought that would be funny. Maybe it aired; I don't even remember. I just remember fighting with the wardrobe person, because the chalk dust was getting on all the costumes for the other sketches.

Can you remember any sketches you wrote that *did* make it to air?

One that I liked had John Larroquette as a man who had just arrived in heaven. Dana Carvey played the angel who answered all of the nagging questions that John had in life. They went something like: "Was there one true religion that God wanted us to practice?" "Yes, Lutheran." Or, "What ever happened to that $50 I got for graduation?" "Your uncle stole it."

I also wrote a lot of commercial parodies, including "Big Red," about a Viking doll for kids that spun around and sprayed red dye everywhere, and "Handi-Off," about a special over-the-counter acid that burned off any unwanted fingers.

John Swartzwelder, who later went on to write more than fifty episodes of _The Simpsons,_ worked with you at _SNL_. Can you remember any of his sketches?

He and I were on the first season after Lorne returned in 1985. He wrote some crazy stuff. John's sketches stood out because they would always feature something strange, like a frozen cat.

John's an enigma. Of all the writers, he was the only heavy smoker and the only hard-core conservative. He also owns the world's first baseball. Even among comedy weirdos, he stands out. He's irreplaceable.

Where exactly does one buy the world's first baseball?

I think he got it from an auction house for about the price of a car. How good a car, I don't know.

What did he do with it?

I assume it's in a safe-deposit box. The thing is disintegrating.

Before you wrote for _The Simpsons,_ you moved out to Colorado. What were you doing out there?

I was skiing, going to poetry readings, and trying to meet girls from the University of Colorado. For a long time I didn't have a car, and I would try to carry groceries home by hanging a plastic bag from each handlebar of my bike. Not recommended.

And this was where you first created the humor magazine _Army Man?_

Yeah. I was living in a condominium in Boulder. I didn't have many friends, and I needed an outlet.

Army Man is a very interesting publication. There were only three issues produced in the late 1980s, all with a very low circulation, and yet the adoration comedy writers still feel toward it is amazing. Did you have any idea the magazine would become so beloved?

No, and I'm embarrassed when people build it up as this monumental work of comedy. It was just a silly little escapade, never meant to be enshrined.

What even gave you the idea to start *Army Man?* You were reaching millions of viewers through your television writing. So why go from that to putting out a magazine with a circulation of a few hundred?

After all the heavy stakes of network television—especially live network television—a little vanity project with no expectations felt like a cool drink of limeade.

I wonder if the continuing fascination with *Army Man* has to do with the fact that it was produced pre-Internet. It was not widely distributed, and it was (and still is) very underground and mysterious.

The Internet is a wondrous beast, but it has a leveling effect that trivializes and cheapens writing. There's something substantial and even formidable about print. You can't just erase it with a button. A few people have posted *Army Man* excerpts online, which feels intrusive. I guess they think they're doing me a favor, but if I wanted it on there I'd do it myself.

I used to read a lot of zines, and many of them were disappointing, but I was always respectful of the effort and passion required. Blogs seem more disposable to me, like a phone call.

How many original copies do you think exist? How many did you originally send out?

The first printing of *Army Man* No. 1 was two hundred copies—I later printed more. As far as No. 2 and No. 3, maybe a thousand. I still have lots of them in a storage locker. I should send them to a leper colony or something. They're not getting any funnier.

The talent that you amassed for *Army Man* was impressive—Jack Handey, John Swartzwelder, Bob Odenkirk, and Roz Chast. It's almost a Who's Who for the next twenty years of humor writing.

I just asked the people who made me laugh to contribute. I didn't realize they would become illustrious. And I think they sensed that I would not take advantage of their goodwill.

How did these writers even know you were looking for submissions? For instance, how did you even know Roz Chast, whom I'm assuming you'd never worked with?

I used The Riddler's method: skywriting.

Roz is married to Bill Franzen, another contributor. I had to apologize to her, because her cartoons didn't reproduce as well as they did in *The New Yorker*. I knew nothing about printing.

Did you have any editorial rules for the *Army Man* writers?

No, I just had to like what they sent me. And that created problems—I wasn't paying anyone, so I would feel bad if I didn't use their submissions.

Is it true that one of the reasons you were originally hired for *The Simpsons* was because Sam Simon had read the magazine and loved it? When reading the three issues of *Army Man,* it's very easy to see the *Simpsons* sensibility.

Sam's an audacious guy. He'd worked with lots of comedy writers on other shows, but he didn't just hire a bunch of them. He brought in some fresh guns.

Did you ever attempt to take *Army Man* national?

I approached the former Monkee and television producer Michael Nesmith to invest in the magazine. He was very sweet. He said, "Yes, I could invest in *Army Man,* but is that what you really want? Isn't it fine the way it is?"

And I had to admit it was.

Had you seen the animated *Simpsons* shorts when they first appeared on *The Tracey Ullman* Show in the spring of 1987?

No. Sam Simon sent me a compilation reel. I didn't envision a series there, and I unwisely turned down a writing job. In the fall of 1989, Sam gave me a second chance to hop aboard as a "creative consultant," and the minute I arrived from Boulder I could feel the excitement.

What type of excitement?

We'd be laughing uncontrollably, and no dour adults would come running in to quell the party. The funniest stuff would actually get into the script, and onto the air.

And now here you are, four-hundred–plus episodes later...

Somehow, the mix was right. The universe gave us a hug.

It seems that from the very beginning, the writers for *The Simpsons* were left alone to do what they wanted.

That's true. Sam and Matt Groening, who came up with the characters, were in charge. I never saw any network notes the entire time, except for censor and legal notes. If we thought it was funny, we did it.

On a typical sitcom or animated show, every story must be approved by the network. I'm certain they would've shot down many of our best episodes. I'm not saying writers are infallible. I'm just saying that executives who don't understand comedy tend to zero in on the unfamiliar ideas—the freshest and most audacious jokes—and exterminate them. It's what they do. And then they go home.

The show is perhaps the most writer-driven show ever on television. Everything has to be written—even the expressions. I would think that would be exciting for a writer, but also a liability. You're not able to have actors sell a joke that might be considered weak. Everything shows.

We lean on the voice actors a lot, and they often bail us out of uninspired runs with inspired performances.

Then again, I suppose you can pull off many jokes that would be impossible otherwise—such as dream sequences and characters being blown off toilets.

Yes, that's a real luxury. The dispiriting thing in a live-action comedy is how cumbersome it all is. A little three-second gag in which a squirrel gets sucked into a vacuum cleaner could take hours to get right. So there's an unspoken pressure to cut that part and move on.

Also, with live action, you have a limited number of sets—so scenes often take place in the wrong location. For instance, a couple who have just left a bizarre art exhibit would discuss the exhibit on their way home, not lying in bed later that night. But maybe the bedroom set is easier.

Can you can get away with jokes in animation you wouldn't be able to otherwise?

We get away with murder, simply because our roughest material isn't threatening to people. A viewer expects volatile behavior from cartoon characters. From the time viewers are three years old, they see animals lighting dynamite and whacking each other with boards. Some very disturbing material gets a pass.

The Simpsons **is one of the few shows that appeals to both kids and adults. Do you always try to write for both? Who's your intended audience?**

We usually write for ourselves and for our writer friends. But I like to imagine smart, troubled girls in the South Pacific finding solace in our work.

We never actually say that *The Simpsons* is a children's show—much of the humor is too sophisticated for children.

Most people dream about their work. Do you ever dream in animation?

No, and I rarely dream about funny, whimsical things. Most of my dreams are horrifyingly realistic: creeps breaking into my house and stealing my possessions. Strangely, I'm never physically harmed in these home-invasion dreams. I wish someone could tell me what that means.

How often do you watch old episodes of ***The Simpsons?***

Rarely. When I do DVD commentaries, I usually haven't seen the episodes since we finished them.

You mentioned in the commentary to the second-season episode "Bart vs. Thanksgiving" that, like Bart, you would go up on the roof when you got into a fight with your family. Are there other autobiographical elements in the episode?

Sure. Little observational things, like Bart with a can opener, saying in a singsong voice, "Mom, it's broken, Mom, it's broke*nnnn*." Adults abusing their power. And being petty.

Any elements from other episodes that come to mind?

When the Simpsons' car is hit by a train and pushed down the tracks with a horrible screeching noise, and Homer suggests that they all try to get some sleep? That really happened.

Do mistakes, or what you perceive as being mistakes, haunt you as a writer?

Less than they used to. Outside writing, I used to lie awake wincing at some embarrassing things I'd said years before, most of which had to do with drunkenness. Later, my regrets were about opportunities I'd missed—classes I didn't take at Harvard, or girls who had crushes on me in high school and whom I didn't pursue because I was too hung up on some super-hot, unattainable girl with smoky, silver eyes.

You're one of the most successful humor writers in the world, and you're still hung up on the way you treated some girls in high school?

I'm damaged, baby.

Do you think being like this—never forgetting and having memories that haunt you—has affected your writing or humor?

Yeah. You're always trying to get in the last word. That quest for vindication is what makes *Curb Your Enthusiasm* so hysterical.

You've mentioned in the past that some of your best writing is done when you go into sort of a trance. Do you consider writing almost a form of hypnosis, where you lose track of time?

Losing track of time is a sure sign that you're immersed in the joy of the experience. You're in the state that [psychology professor and author] Mihály Csíkszentmihályi calls "flow." Actually, I had to be in that state now, just to get his name right. The work you do in this state has grace and ease and resonance. It's the opposite of what Michael O'Donoghue used to call "sweaty" comedy, when you've laboriously squeezed out something tedious, and the effort shows.

When you're "in the zone," a joke will just land on you like a butterfly, and only if you scrutinize it later do you see how it came together from disparate elements. Maybe it's an amalgam of an old half-idea, or something you saw on your way to work, or a strange symbol on someone's T-shirt. And it happens in an instant. Of course, this state is elusive; it has to be cultivated.

How do you cultivate it?

You have to be prepared. You need basic writing skills, of course, but you also want to have lots of raw ingredients rattling around in your skull: vivid words, strange song lyrics, irritating euphemisms, disastrous experiences that have been bothering you for years. To feed this stockpile, you need to expose yourself to the real world and all its hailstones.

The other essential is humility. You have to be willing to look stupid, to stumble down unproductive paths, and to endure bad afternoons when all your ideas are flat and sterile and derivative. If you don't take yourself too seriously, you'll bounce back from these lulls and be ready for the muse's next visit.

What is it about writing in a group situation that you enjoy? Do you actually prefer this process to writing alone?

Writing solo is lonely and you feel the heat—you want to keep topping yourself. I used to berate myself if I couldn't think of a killer joke for every spot, but I gradually eased up on that. You can't keep bitch-slapping your creativity, or it'll run away and find a new pimp.

Many *Simpsons* writers have acknowledged that you're a master when it comes to rewriting other writers' scripts.

I eventually settled on rewriting as my strong suit. Writing scripts by myself was usually traumatic. On "Brother's Little Helper" [Season 11, Episode Two], the episode where Bart is dosed with a Ritalin-like drug, nothing went right. I couldn't even think of a title. I eventually turned it in with the bad title "Bart A-Go-Go," under the pseudonym Vance Jericho. I was that unhappy with it, but the episode turned out okay.

The fun thing about the rewrite room, when it's working, is that people surprise and challenge you, and the collective mind goes off on unpredictable benders, which can be thrilling. The best times are when everyone tosses in a pinch of spice.

The *Simpsons* writers' room is hallowed ground for other comedy writers. Can you go into the process a little? Do writers shout out jokes and ideas?

There's not a lot of shouting—it's not *Caesar's Hour*—but there is "pitching" of lines or story turns. You wait for a pause, and then toss out your "pitch," often in the voice of the character who'd be saying it. If the room laughs, it usually goes into the script, unless it's too tasteless or raunchy or out of character.

What you're doing is trying to improve on the writer's draft, which usually needs to be "punched up"—made funnier. Slow sections are tightened or cut entirely, and new scenes and characters are invented as required.

Is it true that the only reading material in the writers' room is a dictionary and a thesaurus?

There's not much else. Maybe some garbage from lunch.

Do you have a favorite type of *Simpsons* episode? For instance, a Bart versus Lisa episode? Or an episode that takes place outside of Springfield?

I prefer episodes that are inspired by someone's real-life experience. They're more satisfying, somehow.

Would you say that writing this sort of episode is your strength?

I think my strength is conceptual comedy and creating unlikely juxtapositions that shouldn't work, but do.

Can you give me a specific example?

In "The Parent Rap" [Season 13, Episode Two], which I wrote with Mike Scully, Homer is prowling around Judge Harm's house in a burglar outfit. When she's about to discover him, he prepares to throw a heavy object at her, with the prayer: "O Lord, guide this cinder block ..."

It's an insane thing to say, but you can see the logic, too, so it makes me giggle.

You and the other *Simpsons* writers have written thousands upon thousands of jokes over the years. How do you keep track of previously written ones?

Al Jean, a longtime show runner, has an uncanny memory, so he's the first line of defense. Sometimes we consult books or websites.

On a similar note, there is an incredible number of secondary *Simpsons* characters available for you to use—more than two hundred. How do you keep track of them? Do you mentally catalogue each of them and use them when a specific type of joke is needed?

Ideally, they present themselves as needed. Sometimes we cheat by checking a poster of several hundred *Simpsons* characters.

Characters go in and out of vogue as we explore what we can do with them. For instance, the character of Gil, based on a Jack Lemmon–type schlub, had a good run—he seemed able to fit into anything for awhile. And Fat Tony is a perennial, largely because of Joe Mantegna's mesmerizing staccato delivery—and also because criminals are always useful.

Are some *Simpsons* characters more popular among the writers than others?

Sure. It's always easier to write for a dynamic character with a clear agenda—someone like Monty Burns.

What about for you? Which character do you most enjoy writing for?

Homer, of course, is the big gun. He's impulsive, he's ravenous, and he never looks back. I also like characters who deliver florid speeches, like the bombastic [aliens] Kang and Kodos.

Do you feel that Homer has become too stupid since the show began? In one episode, he literally forgets how to breathe.

It's always a danger with Homer. It actually got to the point where he talked to a framed picture of Lenny, believing it to actually be Lenny ["Homer's Enemy," Season Eight, Episode 23]. This goes beyond mere stupidity into Oliver Sacks–style neurological deficit.

Some fans feel that Homer became more and more coarse over the seasons, while becoming less of the sweet man he used to be. Do you agree with this?

Homer acting crazy is like crystal meth: a little is good; too much can be deadly. [Writers] Bill Oakley and Josh Weinstein used to complain about Homer becoming a "food monster." And we would discuss how nasty he could be. An early episode where he probably crossed the line was "When Flanders Failed" [Season 3, Episode Three]. Homer was relentlessly malicious toward Ned; one of the writers said he was "acting like a mean retard."

If there's no grounding in reality, most people won't be interested. You'll only attract the comedy fanatics.

Fans sometimes talk about a *"Simpsons golden age,"* and they often refer to this time as lasting from 1992 to around 1997. Do you agree that there ever was such a time—when everything seemed to be clicking and coming together?

Those were certainly strong seasons. In general, I prefer the leisurely episodes with simple and involving stories to the frenetic episodes that assault you with disconnected jokes.

What season do you think the show really hit its stride?

By the second season we felt confident, and by the third and fourth seasons we had a real swagger. We were a lean, agile team.

How many rewrites will a typical *Simpsons* script go through before the voice actors even see it?

Some scenes are rewritten five or six times.

Does a script get rewritten even after it is initially animated?

Yes, it's rewritten at every stage of production.

How long is this production process—from first draft to finished cartoon?

About six months.

How draining is the schedule for you? Is it more exhausting to write for a show like this than it would be for a non-animated show?

Most TV shows are exhausting. The network figures out how many shows will literally kill the staff. Then they do one fewer.

Jon Vitti, another *Simpsons* writer, once told *The Harvard Crimson,* "The physical pain [that] lousy comedy costs George is incredible. You don't want to be responsible for that."

It only hurts me if I had a hand in it. I guess I find life so disappointing that I can't bear to be part of the problem.

Are there specific comedic tropes that drive you crazy?

Just material that's lazy and fake. For instance, when a character has to think of a phony name, sees an ashtray, and then calls herself "Susan Ashtray." That's boring. Billy Wilder's first commandment was "Thou shalt not bore."

It's easy to pick up bad habits from watching hackneyed comedy. You'll find yourself resorting to stock situations, straw men, and hokey resolutions. An artful slice of life, even if it isn't totally free of editorial contrivance, will inspire you to build your work on the bedrock of reality.

Do you think that the pace of *The Simpsons* has changed over the years? I've noticed that the early episodes tend to be much more dialogue-heavy than the later ones. Do you think this has to do with the shorter attention spans of viewers?

Probably. The world is speeding up, to no particular benefit. People today are almost proud of their inability to focus; I see it as a crippling handicap. The future belongs to those who can think clearly and don't submit to the jittery rhythms of advertising.

Another change in the show since the beginning is the length of each episode. When *The Simpsons* began in 1989, each episode

was twenty-three minutes. Now each episode runs about twenty-one minutes. Has that affected the writing at all?

Advertising always has a coarsening effect, and its inane monkey chatter makes your story less coherent. As the commercial breaks got longer, we had to start recapping the plot at the top of Acts Two and Three, because you'd forget where you were in the story.

I sense you're not a huge fan of advertising.

It's a conscienceless industry, populated by cowards and idiots, that warps and drains everyone. It eggs on the worst in all of us.

So, let me get this straight: You're not a huge fan of advertising?

If I could eliminate either advertising or nuclear weapons, I would choose advertising.

There are few television shows that have a more ardent fan base than *The Simpsons*. It's shocking to read some of the websites and books—and perhaps even this interview—devoted to it. The knowledge and trivia that these fans possess is incredible.

Ain't it the truth.

From your standpoint, it must be strange to read websites where fans dissect the show to such a point that they know that Marge's pubic hair is blue.

Recently, she started shaving it into a landing strip.

Or that Homer's blood type is B positive, and Bart's is double-O negative.

It is strange, but then I think of myself poring over the Rolling Stones' *Exile on Main St.* cover, or watching Godfrey Reggio's movie *Koyaanisqatsi* [1982] nine times. When you find something that zings you, you just want more, more, *more*.

Some fans criticize the more surreal and flight-of-fancy episodes, such as the two-parter from the sixth and seventh seasons, "Who Shot

Mr. Burns?" Or the episode in the seventh season when President George H.W. Bush moved to Springfield. Do you feel that the show, even temporarily, became untethered to what made it popular to begin with?

It's inevitable that the quality and tone will vary—and maybe this is even desirable. We're not aiming for consistency. We're not making screws; we're trying to innovate and keep a step ahead. And even among *Harvard Lampoon* alums, you'll find wildly divergent views on what's funny.

The season is long and punishing. Sometimes you ring the bell; sometimes it falls on your head.

Is there a common theme that runs through each or most of the episodes? Harry Shearer, who voices quite a few characters, has said he feels that one of the themes is "anti-authority."

Right, and I would add "futility."

Would that be one of the themes in the infamous "Homer's Enemy," written by John Swartzwelder, in which an upstanding, decent and hardworking character named Frank Grimes is driven mad by Homer? It has to be one of the darkest half-hours ever on television, animated or not.

It did have a sadistic tinge. We introduced a character, put him through hell, electrocuted him, then desecrated his funeral service. So in that sense, it was dark.

Ricky Gervais, in particular, has called it one of his favorite episodes, and you can see certain elements of that tone in the British version of *The Office*.

Ricky is a brilliant observer of human suffering. I love his work on *Extras*, particularly the episode in which David Bowie improvises an insulting song about him as he twists uncomfortably. The best comic actors—Steve Martin, Bill Murray, Sacha Baron Cohen—understand that life is basically cruel and random and, by letting their pain show through, the eventual laughter becomes visceral.

Are you happy with the *Simpsons* movie, released in 2007?

There are jokes and runs I find hilarious, but I still mourn the brilliant stuff that got cut out. I have mixed feelings about it. We worked so hard, and people liked it, but it still feels slapdash to me.

What brilliant material was cut out? Can you remember any specific jokes?

When the townspeople are first trying to escape from the dome, Professor Frink finds it's made from a miracle substance: "It seems the harder we pound on it, the stronger it gets." Silly stuff like that.

After the family escapes to the carnival, they get jobs at the water-dunk booth as clown-driers. Hank Azaria, as Scummo the Clown, taunts the rubes, calling them "Skinny Minnie" and "Highpockets." Then he sinks into self-loathing: "Why do I say the things I do?" Most of the writers thought Scummo was a riot, but he got cut out.

In Alaska, Homer gets a job delivering newspapers in a small airplane. He walks into the propeller, gets flung fifty feet, and says "I'm okay." Then he walks away, leaving a little red trail in the snow.

The pressure to create the movie must have been immense. The fans are hard enough on the individual television episodes.

Yes, well, we knew we couldn't please everyone. Just trying to give all the minor characters a line or a piece of business was a major undertaking.

It doesn't sound as if you were very happy with the whole process and outcome of the movie.

It was a tough gig.

Listening to the *Simpsons* DVD commentaries, you hear a lot of "this was a joke about a popular item at the time" or "this used to be popular." How do you think *The Simpsons* will age?

Most of it will still be funny in twenty or thirty years. I always tried to emphasize the timeless and universal, and weed out the topical stuff, unless it was irresistible.

Who has a say on when and how *The Simpsons* will end?

I don't know who controls the rights, but all things must pass.

Have you come to appreciate—if that's even the correct word—the role you played as a contributor to *The Simpsons* and the effect that the show has around the world?

I feel honored to have surfed such a glorious wave. I've gotten to entertain people, spew leftist propaganda, laugh like hell, and meet Keith Richards ["How I Spent My Strummer Vacation," Season 14, Episode Two].

Any advice for the aspiring humor writer? Specific writing tips or otherwise?

Yes. Experience as much as you can and absorb a lot of reality. Otherwise, your writing will have the force of a Wiffle ball.

Famous Last Words (of Advice)

Frank Jacobs, long-time contributor to *Mad*

Do not write down to your audience. Learn how to use the English language. I think the most important courses you can take are courses in English and journalism. Get the basics down. I was lucky enough to have once worked on a newspaper. God! That helped a lot. Deadlines. Deadlines. Create deadlines for yourself. Just get it done, but do it with craft. Care about each scene or care about each paragraph, but do not be self-indulgent.

Al Jaffee

Although writer and illustrator Al Jaffee has created some of *Mad*'s most memorable humor since the magazine's inception, in 1952—from "Snappy Answers to Stupid Questions" to the Vietnam–era, anti-war cartoon "Hawks & Doves"—his legacy will forever be tied to the "fold-in."

Originally intended as a onetime parody of *Playboy*'s foldouts, Jaffee's recurring feature—which has appeared in almost every issue of *Mad* since 1964, numbering more than four hundred total—has become almost as recognized and imitated as Alfred E. Newman's gap-toothed grin. Located on the magazine's inside back cover, it features a drawing that, when folded vertically and inward, reveals a hidden picture and a surprise joke.

What makes the fold-in so brilliant isn't merely the concept. Deceptively simple and seemingly innocuous, the fold-in is a cache of subversive satire. Judging from some of the references over the years, Jaffee has always trusted the intelligence of his audience, even when they were no more than pre- or just-pubescent boys looking for a quick laugh before bedtime or during math class. How else to explain the very adult fold-in punch-lines, such as "Heated Anti-American Sentiments" or "Soaring Prescription Profits" or "Hiding the Homeless Problem"? Or the gag in which an American bald eagle transforms into another, perhaps even more popular cultural icon ... the Big Mac?

One can easily imagine generations of young humor writers, including notorious fans Jon Stewart and Stephen Colbert, reading one of Jaffee's fold-ins for the first time and realizing what could be done with the written word and with the slight tweaking of an image. After all, Colbert celebrated Jaffee's eighty-fifth birthday on his Comedy Central show, *The Colbert Report*, in 2006 by creating a fold-in vanilla birthday cake. It included the message: "AL, YOU HAVE REPEATEDLY SHOWN ARTISTRY & CARE OF GREAT CREDIT TO YOUR FIELD. LOVE, STEPHEN COLBERT." But when the cake's center was removed, it read: "AL, YOU ARE OLD."

Al Jaffee is the eldest surviving *Mad* "usual Gang of Idiots" who still contributes to the magazine—which makes him more than just a senior comedy writer who has stubbornly refused to grow up. It wouldn't be a stretch to call Al Jaffee the elder statesman of adolescent humor.

For someone who's spent more than fifty years contributing to such an American comedic institution, you spent a fair amount of your childhood in a country not necessarily known for its humor.

That's right. I spent six years in Lithuania, from the age of six to twelve. At that time, most of the Lithuanian Jews lived in ghettos. I lived in one, too, in a town called Zarasai.

But you weren't born in Lithuania?

No, I was born in Savannah, Georgia, in 1921. But both of my parents were from Lithuania. My mother was very religious, and she wanted to go back to a place where she felt comfortable. She moved back, and brought me and my three brothers with her. This was in 1927.

How did those six years in Lithuania affect your comic sensibility?

My father remained in America through those six years, and I made him promise to send me American comic strips. Every few months or so, my brothers and I would receive a package of rolled-up Sunday color comics and daily comics. We would just sit there and read them for days and days. My brother Harry, who was also artistic, would take these Sunday comic pages, and we'd cut them up and turn them into little books. A lot of the comic strips were divided into twelve equal panels, so it was very easy to cut these panels into little squares and then place them between two pieces of cardboard and bind them. We loved to make our own comic books. We would provide our own dialogue, maybe with a Lithuanian joke or two.

Most of the comics we received were humorous. Some were adventurous, in the "Little Orphan Annie" mold. You know, there was no TV or radio. So that was pretty much it for us. But I would see humor in everything, even in the religious practices, which didn't quite register with me.

I found religion sort of funny. There was something that just didn't make sense about not being able to play ball or not being able to walk too far on the Sabbath. These very strict religious prohibitions against any kind of enjoyment just struck me as being very old-fashioned and strange. Maybe I was bringing my Savannah influence with me; I don't know. I was sort of straddling these two cultures: the New World and the Old World.

Beyond "Little Orphan Annie," what were some of your other favorite comic strips then?

I loved "Wash Tubbs," by Roy Crane. Oh, God, that was one of my favorites. Crane created these comic strips about a mythical kingdom somewhere in Europe, and I could identify with those things. The mythical kingdom that Crane created was closer to the village I was living in at the time than anything else. That resonated pretty well with me. In addition, Crane was an absolute master cartoonist. His work was realistic, but not super-realistic.

How so?

The characters did not look realistic the way "Superman" characters looked. They looked like cartoon characters, but everything was in perfect proportion. And all of the elements, whether it was a train or an automobile, it all looked very real—but in a sort of animated way.

So these drawings looked authentic within their own world, the world of comics, but not authentic in our world, the real world?

Yes.

Did you adopt this style for yourself later in your career?

I did. I don't consider myself a very good artist. I never have. I really don't know anatomy. I can't draw a specific automobile or a specific train out of my imagination, but I think I can do a pretty good job of imagining an automobile or imagining a train. So I can't compare myself to Roy Crane, because he was head and shoulders above me, but I do have an affinity for the kind of things that he did—when you don't have to go and get a reference book to draw a Chevrolet and reproduce it in perfect detail.

People might be surprised when I refer to myself as not such a great artist, but I only try to meet the needs of the story. Without having a story to tell, my art has no meaning. Rembrandt may have been able to achieve meaning without a story, but I can't.

Then again, if you put a Rembrandt-style artist into *Mad,* the reader would focus so much on the artist's style that it would overwhelm the comedy and the writing.

It's sort of complicated to figure this out, but I really feel that the idea has to precede the artwork, and if the idea says this is a fantasy ... well, then there's no point in going out and getting reference materials. You just draw what's in your head.

How prevalent was anti-Semitism in Lithuania when you lived there?

There was a great deal of anti-Semitism, which was a source of humor for me—dark humor. I'd sit around with my friends in their houses and listen to the grown-ups talk about the latest prohibition against Jewish commerce, or whatever. They would take it seriously, but they would also ridicule and make fun of it.

A lot of the children's jokes that went around at that time had to do with restrictions against the Jews that were set by the government. Between the restrictions coming from our own religious community and those coming from the anti-Semitic government, you were caught in such a ridiculous situation. The only thing you could do was laugh at it, make fun of it.

I suppose there's another response, which would have been to become angry.

Well, I *was* angry at my mother, because she was very strict and she spent a lot of time with her religious activities, leaving both my brothers and me feeling neglected. I just don't believe in fantasies. And it seemed to me that 90 percent of the religious stuff that was being said was fantasy.

It's like Santa Claus. There was no Santa Claus, and there was no magical rabbi, and there was no magical anything. All of it was illusion. But humor was an outlet for me, an escape. It was an escape from what I saw as idiotic behavior by everyone.

I don't think humor is just here to tickle people. Humor has much deeper roots than that.

Why did you eventually return to the States?

My father brought us back when Hitler came to power. This was in 1933. My mother chose to remain behind. She said that she would join us later, but she never did. She died around 1939, although I've never found out how. There are no records. The Red Cross thought it might have been caused by the local partisans eager to help the Nazis after they invaded Lithuania.

Did you speak Yiddish when you returned?

I did, yes.

When you look at the early issues of *Mad* there's a lot of Yiddish used.

Harvey Kurtzman, the founding editor of *Mad*, lived in Brooklyn, and his parents were born in Russia and spoke Yiddish. If you were living in New York, or the Jewish section of the Bronx, which is where we moved after I returned, you heard Yiddish everywhere. All the words that were used to make fun and to insult people were in Yiddish. You know, "Look at that *shmegegge*."

When Harvey started *Mad*, he just got a kick out of that. He brought in a lot of Yiddish, as did some of the other writers.

It's the perfect language for a publication like *Mad*. The words were funny in and of themselves, and they also sounded adult and a little dirty.

When you're doing humor, you use every device you can think of, like funny sounds or words that seem insulting when they're really not. There are elements in humor that have to do with sound and timing, and how the syllables are separated. But a lot of credit has to go to the person who is making it funny. The words themselves can't always do it. For a stand-up comic, it's the inflection and even the buildup, setting the scene. Sometimes you set the scene with just the way your eyes move.

But it's one thing for a stand-up comedian to achieve this and another thing for you, as a comic book writer and illustrator, to pull this off on the page.

I see images. I see the scene, and I see the characters, and I see whether the guy has a big nose or big feet or buckteeth. I see it, and I fashion the dialogue or a caption to it. It's just something that happens automatically for me.

You attended New York's High School of Music & Art with seemingly half of the future *Mad's* original "Gang of Idiots." Who were some of your classmates?

Harvey Kurtzman; Al Feldstein, who took over for Harvey in 1956 and became the editor for about thirty years; John Severin, who was a brilliant illustrator; Will Elder, another brilliant illustrator. And there were others who came afterward, people I only got to know later in the comic business.

Did this school teach fine art or commercial art?

Oh, it was all fine art. In fact, I remember one day in the late thirties, when Will Elder came into school and he had meticulously drawn all of the Seven Dwarfs from the movie *Snow White*. The teacher was not happy. I mean, she really reamed him out, because he was showing these drawings to everybody.

He'd drawn these characters from memory, from having watched the movie just once?

Yes. He had a fantastic eye and memory. He drew them perfectly, without any reference source. There were no books about the movie; it had just come out. And there was no Internet, of course. He saw the movie, and he went home and just drew the characters.

So why was this teacher upset?

Cartooning was not allowed. It was looked down upon. We were there to study painting and sculpture and engraving, and we did all of them. We had very good teachers, but the head of the art department, Miss McDonald, was very strict about not introducing commercial art into the curriculum. Looking back, I think she was right. Getting a good background in fine art is very, *very* helpful when you go on to do even silly cartoons.

What was your first comic-book sale? How old were you?

I was twenty. I went to see Will Eisner, who was the creator of a comic strip called "The Spirit," which was beautifully drawn and very creative. The opening splash pages were all so brilliantly conceived. In the comics field, we all admired this strip tremendously. Will was a genius. He just did beautiful work.

So, I had created a parody of Superman called "Inferior Man," and I wanted to show it to Will. It seems so naïve now, but it seemed like the right thing to do at the time.

Was this the first parody of Superman? This would have been—what? The early forties? Superman had only been around a few years at that point.

At that time, there was another character who was called Stuporman—it was published by DC Comics. I don't know if mine was the first Superman takeoff, but it really doesn't matter. I came up with mine independently. Since then, I've seen a million takeoffs, but, at that time, there weren't many. When I brought this idea to Will, I had no idea whether I was doing something stupid or not. But Will, who was only a few years older than I was, was already very successful. He hired me on the spot to do "Inferior Man" as a filler for his comic books.

It's interesting that it took a Lithuanian, Jerry Siegel, to co-create Superman, and another Lithuanian, you, to parody that character.

The Jewish character of the golem must have influenced Superman. When a people live under extremely oppressive circumstances, humor and fantasy, I think, are necessary for survival. When you're beaten down constantly, what are you going to do? You have to create a fantasy. And either the characters are superheroes, like a golem, who have come down to save the whole community, or they're fools, and they just make fun of their own misery. I suppose Superman and Inferior Man are the two sides of that example.

Has Lithuania ever acknowledged you or Jerry Siegel in any way?

No, and I don't really have a warm spot in my heart for Lithuania.

To have made a major sale at the age of twenty must have been very exciting. Not to mention a real boost to your career.

It was, certainly. But whenever I read news reports or stories about that time, or I hear people talking about it, one element that's usually left out is the realistic atmosphere. Our families had either just come out of the Depression, or were still in the Depression. No one opened the gate and said, "Depression over!" You had a lot of baggage, and some of that was trying to figure out how to become self-sustaining and not have to rely on your parents. So, with the comic-book field the buzz was, "There's work." You can get so much money per page. All you have to do is write and draw cartoons. I was making three times as much as my father was making as a postal worker.

You were working only on your Inferior Man comics?

No, I was also making extra money doing some penciling for a cartoonist who worked for Timely Comics, which later became Marvel Comics. After a while, though, I realized that I was being exploited. I was being paid eight dollars a week. So I became disillusioned and skipped the middleman and went to work directly for Timely Comics.

Stan Lee, later the creator of Spider-Man, had just become the editor at Timely. He was about seventeen years old, maybe eighteen. And I went to see him at his office. He looked at a few of my samples, then handed me a script called *Squat Car Squad* and said, "Let's see what you can do with that. Go illustrate it." When I brought it back, he said, "I don't have any more scripts for you to illustrate, but why don't you keep writing and drawing this one?" So I did a lot of *Squat Car Squad*, which was a simple comic about two policemen. But I had a great time with it.

In doing research for this interview, I read some *Squat Car Squad* comics. You and the other writers and illustrators did a remarkable thing. In a few instances, you wrote yourselves into the plot—a very modern device.

I'm not sure why we did that. I'm assuming illustrators had done that before we came along; I can't imagine we invented something like that. I don't want to sound noble about it, and it's embarrassing to be transparently self-promoting. So I didn't do it for that reason. It just seemed like a funny situation when the story wasn't going anywhere, or these two cops were having some kind of difficulty, and I burst into the panel to berate them and tell them what to do.

It's almost like a Marx Brothers movie, breaking the fourth wall. Or a Warner Bros. cartoon.

That's just part and parcel of thinking funny, of being creative. Don't we all become sick and tired of formulas after a while?

Did you work on any other characters at Timely?

After the war, I wrote and illustrated a teen character named Patsy Walker. I did this for about five years. I didn't create this character—a woman by the name of Ruth Atkinson did—but I worked on it. You know, the American public goes through cycles, and the cycle at that time was teenage humor.

The idealized version of that carefree teen life wasn't the sort of lifestyle you and the other comic artists were leading, I take it?

That's absolutely correct. We were coming out of an economic depression and then war. Many of us were starting to get married and have families. So things were changing. But we were living fantasy lives through our work. We were creating these worlds, in the comics, that we wished our childhoods could have been.

Do you remember any of the gags you created for *Patsy Walker?* In one of the promotional items from that time she was described as a "wonderfully fresh college girl and a bundle of mischief."

I didn't do gags, I wrote stories. I tried to insert humor into those stories, because I think I would have become very bored if things stayed serious. What you had were two women who were fighting over one guy, and that, basically, was the whole thing. But in order to give it some kind of a life, I would have stories in which there'd be a new person in town, a shy or a homely character, and the bad girl—the snooty girl—would make fun of her and not invite her to the party. Then the good girl—Patsy Walker—would convince everybody this was a lousy thing to do, and everything would come out all right. So there was a little moral in there.

I don't think my semi-realistic style of artwork in *Patsy Walker* was anything special, but my writing must have been pretty good. Every time I went to Timely to deliver my work, I'd be handed a shopping bag full of fan mail. I had to spend hours answering it.

Did you ever write yourself into a *Patsy Walker* plot, like you did with *Squat Car Squad?* Perhaps a young illustrator who wanders into town, looking to date a bundle of mischief....

[Laughs] No. I didn't belong in *Patsy Walker.* Not at all.

When did you make the move to *Mad?*

In 1955, three years after the magazine began. Harvey Kurtzman came to me and asked if I'd like to come and work for him. I had freelanced for *Mad* with a couple of pieces, and he liked my work.

Did it help that you were both an illustrator and a writer? Were you considered a double threat?

There was a bit of a special status if you could do both. If anything, it was easier to make a sale. Instead of describing a joke, you could just show an editor the illustration. To describe it is more difficult. How is the editor supposed to know if it's funny or not? It was more effective this way.

Did you realize _Mad_ was something different when you first saw it?

When I saw _Mad_, I loved it. I loved the craziness and the funny draw-ings. I mean, it was just letting go and having a good time. It was much freer than anything else out there. Harvey knew how to cherry-pick the kind of people who would fit in perfectly with the kind of scripts he wanted. _Mad_ had a wonderful crew.

But was it still a big leap for you—leaving the comfort of Timely to go work for _Mad?_

It was. I was making a very nice living at Timely, but it just seemed like the right time. I told Stan Lee I was leaving, and then I called Harvey and said, "I'm coming with you." And he said, "Well, actually, I'm not with _Mad_ anymore. But don't worry. I've got something in the works." He had just left _Mad_ for a new humor magazine published by Hugh Hefner, called _Trump_. This was in the mid- to late 1950s.

Harvey bridled at the fact that he had to pass all editorial decisions through Bill Gaines, who was the publisher of _Mad_, and that bothered him a great deal. So when Hefner came along and offered to produce a slicker version of _Mad_, and it would be in color, no less, it seemed like the right thing for Harvey to do. It wasn't just a money thing for him. What he really wanted was control.

What was _Trump_ like? It was the first of countless _Mad_ knockoffs throughout the years.

There were only two issues produced, but it was a beautiful, sleek product. We took too long to produce it, and it was too expensive. Harvey was just too much of a perfectionist, which is what I loved about him. He made changes in my pieces that nobody else would have made. It really improved the quality of my work. As an editor, he was incredible.

There's a group of _Mad_ aficionados who feel that if Harvey Kurtzman had stayed at _Mad,_ the magazine would not only have been differ-ent, but better.

And then there's a large group who feel that if Harvey had stayed with *Mad*, he would have upgraded it to the point where only fifteen people would buy it.

How did you end up getting hired again by *Mad* after your experience at *Trump?*

In the late 1950s, I went to *Mad* with some scripts, and the new editor, Al Feldstein, bought all of them.

Al was a very hands-on editor. Everything had to go through him. No *Mad* piece was ever bought without his approval. We respected each other's talents. And I think he was a very good editor and a very smart man. He also knew how to delegate, which Harvey never knew how to do. And he was a lot more flexible than Harvey, a lot less rigid in his outlook—at least in my experience.

Al Feldstein brought on board a lot of the writers and artists we now associate with *Mad*.

He did, yes. He brought Don Martin to the magazine, as well as Antonio Prohías, who created "Spy vs. Spy." Also, Dave Berg, who created "The Lighter Side Of ..."

What was Dave Berg like as a person?

Dave had a messianic complex of some sort. He was battling ... he had good and evil inside of him, clashing all the time. It was sad, in a sense, because he wanted to be taken very seriously and, you know, the staffers at *Mad* just didn't take anybody seriously. Most of all, ourselves.

Do you think Dave Berg's inner battle later expressed itself in his strip "The Lighter Side Of ..."?

It came out in a lot of the things he did. He had a very moralistic personality. I mean, he moralized all the time. And his gags were very suburban middle-class America. Plus, he was very religious. He wrote a book called *My Friend God*. And, of course, if you write a book like that, you just know that the *Mad* staff is going to make fun of you. We would ask him questions like, "Dave, when did you and God become such good friends? Did you go to college together, or what?"

I think Dave had a feeling that his contribution to the success of *Mad* wasn't appreciated enough. And I think this bothered him. He once told a staff member that he received so much fan mail that they had to hide it from him. And he really believed this. Naturally, most of us would just roll our eyes, because we didn't expect tons and tons of fan mail; and if there was fan mail, we always received it. I guess Dave felt he was carrying the whole magazine, and he should have been treated royally.

Tell me about the quintessential *Mad* contributor, Don Martin.

Don Martin was the very opposite of what he drew. He was a very nice-looking guy; tall, handsome, extremely soft-spoken. You almost had to bend forward to hear what he was saying. He didn't crack jokes, and he didn't do funny stuff, but he was a great appreciator of the humor of other *Mad* contributors. He was a great listener, and he laughed a lot and had fun, but he was not demonstrative. Not at all. I guess he got it all out in his drawings.

He was a fantastic illustrator. His work for *Mad* was almost like animation. You could visualize his characters moving on the page; you could feel the action. And those sounds he came up with, well, they were not easy to create. With most of the contributors, if we needed sound effects, we tended to stick to the tried and true. For instance, we would use sounds such as "boff" and "zock" and "pow" and "bam." But Don went much further, by creating his own language: "pwang," "splitch," "splawtch." If you read the words, you could hear those sounds. That is just universal and completely unique. And that material hasn't dated at all; it's just as great as it was when it came out. He was really special. *Sui generis.*

Was there a sense of camaraderie in the golden age of *Mad,* from the early sixties through the mid-seventies?

Oh, a great deal. Absolutely! *Mad*'s publisher, Bill Gaines, did something very clever: He would take the whole staff on an annual trip abroad. And we lived together for anywhere from seven to seventeen days. We hung out together. We all went out to restaurants together. And we got to know each other. We became almost like a family. I mean, we weren't in an office environment day-to-day where we got to know each other. A lot of us worked from home. In fact, every artist and writer worked from home—only the editors and art directors worked in the office.

These trips were also an inducement to produce more material; if you didn't hit your cutoff each year, you weren't allowed on the trips. In the beginning, it was twenty pages of published material, and later you had to produce twenty-five every year. The trip was a reward for increased contributions. I was one of a few contributors who was on every single trip. I never missed the cutoff.

Our first vacation was to Haiti in 1960.

Why Haiti?

We went there to pay a visit to the one and only Haitian subscriber to *Mad*. On the entire island, there was only that one subscriber, and he had let his subscription lapse. So when we got there, Bill Gaines took a bunch of writers and illustrators over to this guy's house and knocked on the door. When the guy answered, Bill offered him the gift of a renewal.

Was the subscriber Baby Doc Duvalier? The future ruler of Haiti?

No, I'm pretty sure it wasn't Baby Doc.

In rereading your *Mad* articles, I found that you predicted, or perhaps even invented, quite a few modern-day products.

I did?

I'll give you a few examples. In a piece you did in March 1967, you drew an illustration of a machine, and wrote: "The Idiot-Proof Typewriter will include memory tapes and store millions of words, phrases, and correct grammatical expressions." Sounds very similar to the spell-checker on a word processor.

Wow! I don't remember that.

You pre-dated the re-dial option on telephones and a cell phone's address book when you came up with the "automatic dialer" in 1961. Punch cards were inserted into a phone, which then automatically dialed the saved numbers. And you created "snow surfing," basically, snowboarding, in 1965. "Using a regular surfboard, the Snow Surfer has trees, rocks, and annoyed skiers to lend dangerous excitement."

No kidding.

You don't remember these?

I don't remember, no. I'll have to read your book.

You're being too modest. You also came up with the peel-away, non-lickable stamp in January 1979; the three-blade razor in July 1979; the "vandal-proof building" that repelled graffiti in 1982; and, my personal favorite, from the January 1975 issue, the "acrylic plastic squirt gun" for "doggie doo." When the bulb is squeezed, "two chemicals are forced to mix and squirt from nozzle," covering up excrement. That device has since actually been invented.

Ah, yes. I remember that one.

You should have patented those! You would have made a fortune!

No, no, no. I could imagine those types of things, that was the fun part. But I never had the problem of trying to figure out how to manufacture them.

Did you have any scientific training?

None at all. My father used to manage a department store in Savannah—later, during the Depression, he had to earn a living as a postal worker. Before we all left for Lithuania, my father would take my brothers and me, every Saturday, to the toy department, and we'd just have a ball there. Then we wound up in this little village in Lithuania with no toys whatsoever. We invented toys, out of just scraps of wood lying around the yard. My brother Harry actually made a fire truck that sprayed water. Oh, God, we invented all types of ingenious things! We came up with a device that enabled us to steal fruit from neighbors' yards. It was a pole with a knife attached to the end, and then a basket for the fruit to fall into. So I think all of the inventions came from an interest in seeing what you can make for yourself if you're not able to go to the store and buy it.

Speaking of ingenious invention, tell me about the *Mad* fold-in. How did you first come up with the idea?

At this time—this would have been in April of 1964—every major magazine was publishing some sort of foldout feature. *Playboy*, of course, had made it big by having a centerfold. So did *Life* magazine. They would have one showing, say, the geography of the moon, or something like that. Even *Sports Illustrated* had one at one point. So, naturally, how do you go the other way? You have a fold-*in,* rather than a fold-*out.* I created a mock-up, and wrote on it something like: "All good magazines are doing a foldout, but this lousy magazine is going to do a fold-in." I went to Al Feldstein and showed it to him, but I didn't think the idea had a chance in hell of being used.

Why not?

Because it mutilated the magazine.

There were no advertisements in the magazine at that time. To mutilate an ad might have been a problem, but why would it have been a problem just to bend an article?

Yes, that's a good point. All I know is that when I showed the idea to Al and said, "You're not going to want to do this, but I think you'll get a kick out of it," he looked it over and said, "I like it. Let's do it." I figured it was a one-shot deal, just a gag. Everybody had these beautiful color foldouts. And we had a stinky black-and-white fold-in.

What was the first fold-in? Do you remember?

Liz Taylor and Richard Burton. Rumors were flying around at that time—this was 1964—that Liz was involved with Burton. I drew a crowd scene outside a Hollywood event, with reporters and fans. Burton was on the left and Liz was on the right, and Eddie Fisher was somewhere in the middle. Liz and Richard were looking at each other from a distance. When you folded it in, they wound up kissing. And Eddie Fisher was completely out of the picture. So, you know, it was a very simple thing.

It was so simple at first that it was almost childish. But I kept working on it and honing it through the years. Eventually, the fold-in evolved into what we have now, more than forty years later, which is far more complicated. I've done more than four hundred.

You took on a lot of serious issues with these fold-ins over the years, such as Vietnam, the *Exxon Valdez,* abusive parents, and homeless veterans. Was this an outlet for some of your anger over what was going on in the world?

Not vehemently, but sometimes it became an outlet. But, you know, the fold-in is not supposed to be funny. Who knows what it is? It's a strange duck. One picture turns into another picture. But you have to say something. You can't just have an illustration. It's better to make a comment about the world around us. One of the editors at *Mad*, Nick Meglin, once said to me, "The fold-in is the only editorial cartooning done in *Mad.*" And I guess that's true.

How long does it take to create each fold-in? What's the process?

I'd say about two weeks from start to finish. I no longer look at it as being something formidable, because I've done it for such a long time. I have the feeling now that no matter what it is, I can find a way to do it. But it's still a challenge.

Is it true you never know whether the final version will work or not?

I never see it folded until it's printed.

So how do you know if it's going to work?

I just do. The final illustration is on a flat cardboard piece. But if I have any doubts, I can make a Xerox copy and then cut it and move the two pieces together. But I do make sure that everything connects, and I do that very simply. I have a strip of transparent tracing paper. I lay it down on one side, and I use a pin to hit all the points that are going to touch.

And then I move that over to the right side, and I do the same thing on the left side. And anywhere that it doesn't match, I make the correction.

Have you ever looked at a fold-in you created years ago and actually tricked yourself?

Actually, I have, yes. I've looked at some old issues of *Mad* where I don't remember what the fold-in's answer is. I can't figure it out—which either means I'm a numskull or I'm doing a pretty good job on this thing.

Why do you think the fold-in is so popular with readers?

Because it's a puzzle. It's a participation thing. Whereas with the rest of the magazine, even though a reader may come across pieces that are ten times more interesting or hilarious, they just absorb it. They soak those pieces up, and then they come to my piece and can't absorb it. All they can absorb is half of it. Then they have to do something to get to the other half. I think that creates a little element of interest.

Over the years, how have you managed to keep up with the current pop-culture trends?

To be truthful, I don't. I'm a little too old to be able to keep up with the fashion trends of twenty-year-olds and their music tastes. All you can do is read the newspapers and magazines and try to get a feeling for it. Also, I watch my children and grandchildren and see what they're doing.

Did you feel the same way twenty or thirty years ago?

I think one of my strong suits is I never became infatuated. I've always been on the outside looking in. It goes all the way back to Lithuania, where some of my friends were obsessed with certain leaders of the community—as if they were rock stars. But I'd sit off to the side and say, "What do they see in that guy? He's just an old goat."

How did "Snappy Answers to Stupid Questions" get started in 1965?

The way it got started is how a lot of things get started. You experience something, a little experience, and that leads to an idea. I happened to be standing on the roof outside my house on Long Island trying to fix an antenna, which had been blown over in a storm. And I'm afraid of heights, so I was very nervously tightening the band around the chimney that held the antenna. Suddenly, I heard my son climbing up this ladder. He asked me a question that he asked every time he came home from school: "Where's Mom?" And I answered, "I killed her and I'm stuffing her down this chimney."

He knew I was kidding, obviously, but I thought about this afterward, and it occurred to me that there must be a million times a day we all get asked questions to which you either don't know the answer or it's a pointless question. Up on the roof, how the hell would I know where Mom was?

I think the brilliance of "Snappy Answers" is that the last entry is always left blank for the readers to fill in with their own jokes. I wonder how many professional humor writers got their start writing jokes in those blanks?

Oh, I don't know. Those of us who work in the world of writing and drawing have very little idea of what kind of connection we're making. I mean, some people might come up to you and say, "I loved that thing you wrote," but there are thousands of others who've read it and you never hear anything from them. And that's why I'm always very, very flattered when someone remembers something that I did.

Do you feel that *Mad* has changed over the years? There's been some criticism that the magazine has become too gratuitous.

Certainly I don't have the right to say I'm happy or unhappy with it. I think *Mad* is being produced by very knowledgeable people who are putting out a magazine for the current generation of readers. And I think it's very successful in that regard. There are things in there that, frankly, I'm not too familiar with, because they're for a much younger generation. But I think the editors are doing a wonderful job.

Where do you think *Mad* will be in twenty-five to fifty years?

You know, with technology going the way it is, who knows if there will *be* magazines in the next twenty years—or newspapers for that matter.

What are your thoughts on the future for comic-book illustrators? For a humor writer, one would assume there will always be television or the movies. But illustrating for a comic book like *Mad* seems so specific a talent. Do you think it will survive?

I think there are going to be some drastic changes as far as commercial artists are concerned. Even as you were speaking, I was picturing getting up in the morning and a favorite comic strip is on a panel and it rolls by and it's animated. No longer will it be "Peanuts," with four panels and static little figures. Now it will feature characters walking or kicking a football right in front of you—all on a sheet of something that is no bigger than a page. All of that is bound to come. Truthfully, I don't know what we're going to gain or what we're going to lose. Of course, you both gain and lose from the advance of knowledge and technology.

You've been at *Mad* longer than any other writer or artist. You've been published in more than four hundred issues. And yet you said something recently that I found intriguing: "If I were fired tomorrow from *Mad,* I think the old creative juices, the old inventions, would surge." My question is how much more do they need to surge? You're still going strong.

I'm taking the easy path now. I'm doing things that are available to me, rather than going out and inventing new things and proposing them, because I just don't have the energy to become a salesman for these ideas. I find it really satisfies my creative instincts to do just a fold-in once a month. I think the fold-in is my last hurrah.

Will you be willing to give me a snappy answer to a stupid question? How do you think you'll be remembered?

Is space available on Mount Rushmore?

Maybe I should leave the last line blank so the readers can fill in the answer for themselves?

Sounds good. Do it.

Famous Last Words
(of Advice)

Yoni Brenner, contributor to *The New Yorker, The New York Times, GQ, McSweeney's Internet Tendency.* Screenwriter, *Ice Age 3, Rio,* and *Rio 2.*

#1. Write with an audience in mind. The audience for *The New Yorker* is different from the audience for *GQ* or for *Deadspin* or even *McSweeney's.* This doesn't mean you should pander (pander!), but if your goal is publication, consider tweaking your style to suit what your target publications do.

#2. Hollywood does not think it sucks. Never preface any submission by implying, "What you have made previously is crap but my thing is awesome." Crap their stuff may be, but if you tell them that, the only thing they will remember is that you are an asshole.

#3. Editors have egos. By accepting edits you make your editors feel smart and useful. (Very often your editor is also, in actuality, smart and useful.) That does not mean one should be a pushover, but when it comes to small and inconsequential edits one generally has more to gain by accepting them than resisting them. It's great to be a perfectionist, but it is equally important to be a good collaborator.

#4. Test market. Whenever possible, get feedback on your work from your snobbiest, most pretentious friends before you submit. Sometimes they will be wrong, sometimes they will be insanely wrong; but frequently, a consensus from these friends will help you anticipate how well it will go over with editors/agents/producers.

#5. We all write terrible things from time to time. All of us. If everything you have written has received hosannas and PEN/Faulkner awards then you are either deluded or the King of Belgium. Or both, in the case of King Jacques ("the Sturgeon Whisperer," 1736-1738). Don't dwell on misfires, just keep writing.

#6. When it comes to humor writing, it's easy to mistake a joke for a premise. When you have an idea for a humor piece, really be tough on yourself to identify whether it's a full piece or if it's only a Tweet stretched out over 800 words. In my opinion, a piece should have shape and rhythm and a structure. Otherwise, it's a one-joke pony.

#7. And this is the secret weapon: the most satisfying feeling in creative work is when you make something that you know intuitively that no one else could have done. For our purposes, this means finding the angle no one else could find, or making the joke no one else could imagine. There are a lot of obvious targets in comedy, and a lot of familiar patterns. Avoid them. Push yourself to find the sharper angle and the better joke. Don't settle for mildly-funny, strive for knock-you-off-your-ass funny. If you are consistently able to do that, people will notice.

Allison Silverman

It's difficult to know just how seriously Allison Silverman takes herself and her place in the hierarchy of comedy writing. Having spent time penning jokes for some of the best minds in satire—Jon Stewart, Stephen Colbert, Conan O'Brien—she'd be justified in some self-aggrandizement.

"Over the course of the week [at *Late Night with Conan O'Brien*]," she once said, "[my desk] becomes a dumping ground for scripts, daily schedules, weekly schedules, cast lists, revised cast lists, and beat sheets. A beat sheet lists the comedy bits approved by our head writer. A beat sheet is how the wardrobe department finds out that we need a giant Hasidic ant costume by 2 P.M." For Silverman, comedy is just another way to pay the bills, albeit a means of employment that occasionally involves dressing up actors as Semitic insects.

Long before she became one of the most influential female writers in TV comedy, Silverman was just another lanky Jewish girl growing up among tanned *goyim* in Gainesville, Florida. Though she briefly considered becoming a scientist, she eventually ended up majoring in humanities at Yale University. After graduating in 1994, she moved to Chicago to study with such comedy institutions as ImprovOlympic and The Second City Conservatory, the alma mater of future employer Stephen Colbert. During her graduation show at the Second City in 1996, she performed an original song called "These Are My Gandhi Years," in which she sang about the trials of being poor and underfed as a struggling artist.

A year spent improvising with the Boom Chicago comedy troupe in Amsterdam (1997) was enough to convince her that she preferred the desktop to the stage. She wrote trivia—cooking up amusing minutiae for the ABC quiz show *Who Wants To Be a Millionaire* (1999) and the computer game *You Don't Know Jack!* (2000)—before finally mustering the courage to cold-call *Daily Show* head writer Ben Karlin and ask for a job.

Her perseverance paid off. Her groundbreaking year at *The Daily Show* led to a four-year run writing for *Late Night with Conan O'Brien* (2002–2005), for which she won a Writers Guild award.

Then she did what few comedy writers in her place would have dared: she made a major career gamble, leaving a dependable writing post at *Late Night* to write for *The Colbert Report*, hosted by her onetime *Daily Show* colleague Stephen Colbert. Comedy Central promised only thirty-two episodes, which gave them less than two months to prove their comedic chops and attract a loyal audience.

The Colbert Report was originally envisioned as a spoof of the pomposity and the garishness of *The O'Reilly Factor*. If they had stuck to that premise, the show most likely would have ended the moment the novelty wore off. But Colbert and Silverman transformed a simplistic, one-joke news parody into one of the most subversive shows on TV, even surpassing *The Daily Show* with its satiric verve. Whether he was yammering on about "truthiness," having water playfully thrown in his face by billionaire Richard Branson, or mocking President Bush at the 2006 White House Correspondents' Dinner, Stephen Colbert (the character) was a walking-and-talking indictment of arch-conservative egotism. The right-wing pundit was the fake-news personality that everybody (sometimes even Republicans) loved to hate.

Silverman, who has been *The Colbert Report*'s co–head writer since 2005 and a co-executive producer since September 2007, is largely responsible for much of Colbert's fictional persona—including the idea for Colbert to strut around his desk as guests make their entrance over to the desk.

"That was my idea," Silverman said. "For me, it felt like a strong statement of ego: that Stephen would be jealous of even that tiniest moment when his guests would be in the spotlight. So he diverts all of the attention—to himself."

You're one of only two humor writers I'm interviewing from the South—the other is David Sedaris. My southern friends and teachers aren't going to be too happy.

I grew up in Gainesville, Florida, which is a university town. But, yes, it's very much the Deep South. When I was growing up, I never looked similar to my classmates—or that's how I felt, anyway.

What did the others look like?

It was mostly an environment of blonde cheerleaders, football players, and quintessential Americana. When I was young, I received a lot of questions about where I was from. I remember being told I would eventually be going to hell because I was a Jew. This was mostly in elementary school, before the students realized what they were saying. But by the time I was in high school, fellow students found my Semitism a little exotic.

Do you think your upbringing affected your humor? Did you go inward and become more introspective?

I guess I felt like a bit of an outsider, but I don't think that's too different from how most humor writers feel about their childhoods. I was an introspective person by nature. I was a happy kid, but I did have terrible nightmares. I'd turn on the bedroom lights and spend the rest of the night reading—usually the same few books over and over again. I must have read *A Wrinkle in Time* [by Madeleine L'Engle] fifty times.

Do you remember any of your nightmares?

Dreams about nuclear war, mostly. This was in the early eighties, and I had just learned that Gainesville was high on the list of nuclear targets, because there were a lot of hospitals in town. I also remember a classmate telling me about the nuclear explosions in Hiroshima and Nagasaki, and how the shadows of the victims were forever burned onto the pavement.

I also had many dreams about being poisoned, and my accidentally poisoning others.

[Laughs] What type of kids were you hanging out with?

I can't blame it all on them—I think I had OCD as a kid. I would have recurring thoughts that were mostly uncomfortable to think about.

That's another similarity between you and David Sedaris—and perhaps most of the writers I've interviewed for this book. OCD is a very common theme.

Starting at around the age of nine or ten, I would suddenly feel the urge to stick to a very strict routine. I had to do all these very specific tasks before I felt comfortable enough to do much of anything.

I was obsessed with death and with order. My mother once showed me a biography of Albert Einstein and told me that he didn't wear socks. And she said, "See? This is one of the greatest minds of all time. And he didn't wear socks! He wasn't perfect, so you don't have to be either."

Did that help?

I remember it, so it had some kind of impact.

Do you think this preoccupation with death was a Jewish trait?

I think it might have been, actually. With Judaism, there's very little discussion of the afterlife. I was told that I wouldn't die for a very long time, but then once I did, there would be nothing.

Did this preoccupation ever ease up?

In the late eighties and early nineties, by the time I attended Yale, the nightmares and OCD had improved a bit. Most of my attention was focused on schoolwork, and on an improv group I was involved with called the Exit Players. There were about four improv groups at Yale, but this one was the oldest, and still is.

How did the Exit Players differ from the other groups?

I thought they were the flat-out funniest. There was another group that performed long-form material, but I didn't really understand that method until after I graduated. In retrospect, I prefer long-form. But, at the time, short form was my preference.

What's the difference between short and long form?

Long-form improv was most famously taught by [Second City's] Del Close through his "Harold" method—that's what he called it. Essentially, a group of performers receive one suggestion from the audience and then create a whole piece around that subject. There are three acts, each with three scenes. This method teaches that you shouldn't go for the immediate and easy punch lines. Short form, on the other hand, consists of more gags.

Is this something you'd recommend for humor writers—to start with improv comedy?

Absolutely. I think there are a few reasons why it's a great idea. One is simply that you learn timing—what does and doesn't work with audiences. If you've never experienced an audience in this specific way, it's more difficult to learn later on.

It also helps—if you are going to write for somebody else, like I have for Conan, Jon, and Stephen—to understand the needs of a performer. Sometimes writers become very enamored with their own material—especially those who write for print. But what is very, very funny on the page might not work before an audience. The material might be too difficult for the performer and for the audience to follow. Get rid of all the verbiage, and refine your way to the core of the joke.

Third, I think it's vital that comedy writers don't hole themselves up and work alone. They need to meet and have a community of like-minded people—some of whom might hire you down the line. It is much easier to create this community if you're performing.

Do you get the same high writing that you used to achieve while performing?

It's a different high. I love being backstage and watching one of my jokes really hit. It's the grace of being an anonymous donor, only better. My name is on the credits. It's the best of both worlds.

Did you receive a drama degree from Yale?

I was a humanities major, but it's been mentioned by a few journalists that I was a molecular-biology major—which I definitely was not.

I read that, too. I was very impressed.

I said at some point that I matriculated as a molecular-biology major, but that just means that I started Yale as one. Once I was there, I got much more into the humanities. I do love science, though. I worked in a lab for several summers and got my name on a paper in the journal *Plant Physiology*. The paper is called "Association of 70-Kilodalton Heat-Shock Cognate Proteins with Acclimation to Cold."

I only understood two words: *proteins* and *cold*.

It was about finding the genetic basis for cold tolerance in plants. I performed experiments with the help and direction of people who really knew what they were doing. They were very kind, and they put my name on the paper as a co-author.

Did you approach humor with a scientific eye?

Actually, I did. When I lived in Chicago after college, I would watch the Second City performances, and I would take notes on the performers and on their individual moves.

What sort of moves?

I'd make notes about how each performer responded to his or her onstage partner. Status informs all humor. Specifically, a lot of comedy is about status shifts, and I would mark down whenever a shift would occur.

A "status shift" is about who controls the power in a scene. You see this in real life all the time. You see it with parents and kids; the parents are obviously in control, because they're older and bigger, but when the kid throws a tantrum, the parents try to placate the child by giving them something.

Now the kid is in control. That's a status shift.

So what does that mean within the context of a sketch?

I'll give you an example: John Cleese would often play characters who were in charge but shouldn't have been. A lot of what makes his characters so funny is that they are completely unfit to lead. In the Monty Python

"Kilimanjaro Expedition" sketch, he's leading an expedition to climb Kilimanjaro, but he has double vision and thinks Kilimanjaro has two peaks.

It's not funny to see someone powerless being mocked. I think most people react against that, actually—unless they are a particularly cruel audience. What's *much* more fun is to see someone who does have power, and is in the dominant position, become exposed.

So that's the power structure. When you twist and play with this structure onstage, it hopefully becomes interesting and, in the end, funny.

Can you give me a specific example of how status came into play with any of the television shows you've written for?

I once wrote a sketch on *Late Night with Conan O'Brien* that I liked because it dealt with some issues that were on my mind at the time.

The sketch started with Conan returning from a commercial break and saying something to the effect of, "I've got to tell you, sometimes being a talk-show host makes me feel a little guilty. I could have been a lawyer or a doctor—that would have been *way* more valuable to society."

There was an actor in the audience who piped up, "Excuse me, Conan. I *am* a doctor, and I just wanted to let you know that you couldn't have become a doctor, so just stop worrying about it. You just don't have the skills to be a doctor—or the intellect!" The "doctor" then injures an audience member and demands that Conan prove that he actually could have been a physician. Conan manages to treat this "patient" brilliantly.

It starts with a switch: At first, Conan is in charge and says, "I could have been a doctor." The doctor says, "No, actually, *I* am in charge, and you couldn't have become a doctor even if you'd wanted to." And then it switches once again.

You just mentioned that you liked this sketch because it dealt with some issues on your mind at the time. What in particular?

Certainly anyone who's a comedy writer thinks—at least on some level—that maybe they should be doing something more "real." I still feel that way, truthfully.

Really?

I always think I should be doing something that should more directly affect the lives of others in a more positive way.

You don't think your work on *Late Night, The Daily Show,* and *The Colbert Report* has affected people in positive ways?

I am exceedingly thrilled when people tell me those shows make them happy, but I don't think it's the same as dedicating one's life to bringing more knowledge to the world. Or being a social worker and directly helping people. Or being a teacher.

I'd hate to see where I'd fall: a writer interviewing humor writers.

Clearly, we should both be determining how plants tolerate cold.

One could argue, however, that you *are* bringing knowledge to the world. As you've no doubt heard a million times, many viewers only get their news through *The Daily Show* and *The Colbert Report*.

I appreciate people who might feel that way, but I think they should also be watching other shows and reading the papers.

We were talking earlier about status in regard to humor. The character of Stephen Colbert is very much about status.

Oh, absolutely. Stephen is all about status and the trappings of power. This is a character who looks to be in charge, and he constantly feels threatened by people who have much less than he has. There's a real vulnerability buried deep within that character. His ego is a high-wire act.

One important thing about Stephen's character is that while he's a moron, he's not an asshole. There is an essential innocence to his character. He's well intentioned but poorly informed. And because of this vulnerability, the audience comes to accept him. It also helps that the real Stephen is a genuinely kind person. Even when he plays this character, the audience still detects that Stephen's a good-hearted guy. That's a major factor with our show: if Stephen couldn't pull that off, the show wouldn't be nearly as successful as it is.

Could this have been the problem with other, less successful talk-show hosts? They didn't come across as likeable?

I'd say so, yes. I think it's very important for any host or performer to not battle an audience but, rather, to become partners with them. As soon as you look needy or uncomfortable, the audience becomes worried and stops laughing—which is a big problem. Going out onstage and thinking of the audience as an enemy only makes you look more needy.

He's not the brightest chap, this "Stephen Colbert" character.

That's one of the fun things about him. He is stupid, and yet, every once in a while, he will express some sort of minute knowledge that impresses everyone. He knows exactly how and why car engines work. But the character is a complete moron when it comes to other matters. For instance, he thought *Watership Down*, the book about a society of rabbits, was nonfiction. And it very much bothered him that the rabbits were at war.

The irony, of course, is that Stephen—in real life—is one of the smartest people I've ever met. He's brilliant.

One of the impressive things about *The Colbert Report* is what Stephen manages to do with language—twisting, inverting, and molding it. An example: "This show is not about me. No, this program is dedicated to you, the heroes.... On this show your voice will be heard, in the form of my voice." It reminds me of S. J. Perelman's dense, imploding writing style.

Both Stephen and I really enjoy what can be done with language. Stephen's background allows him to twist words in a very effective way. He is extremely well read and he has a ferocious memory—he can pull it off.

We definitely tread that line between being too verbal and just making the jokes funny. It's like what I was saying before about not becoming too enamored with your own work.

Who coined the word "truthiness"? The word was so popular that it eventually became Merriam-Webster's number one Word of the Year for 2006. Here's the official definition: "Truth that comes from the gut, not books."

Stephen coined that word, and it actually appeared on our very first show [October 17, 2005]. The show has since coined other words, such as "wikiality," which is "reality as decided on by majority rule," and "freem," which was coined by one of our viewers. We used the word visually in our opening, and then someone online decided it meant "freedom" without having to "do" anything—without any responsibility or action.

The show seemed so fully formed right from the beginning; it always had a tremendous amount of confidence. I remember a joke Stephen told the first week about James Brady, who was seriously injured during the Ronald Reagan assassination attempt. That takes a bit of nerve.

That also happened in the very first show. There was legislation in Florida dealing with the issue of being able to shoot another person in self-defense. James Brady was obviously a critic of this legislation, but Stephen just did not understand why Brady would be against guns. It was the character being brazenly and willfully stupid.

The next day we got a handwritten fax from James Brady that read, "You lily-livered Italian-suited four-eyed Jon Stewart–wannabe. You'll be crying in your cravat when I'm through. You want a piece of me? DO YOU WANT A PIECE OF ME?"

Brady really enjoyed the joke, which was fantastic.

How did the audience react to something like that?

Better than I imagined. They're very generous—I think they appreciate the boldness of saying something so wrong as a parody of cable-news blowhards.

The show has a very subversive spirit that I think people enjoy; a lot of viewers wind up participating in the show somehow, whether it's taking Stephen up on a challenge, or creating ideas for the show completely on their own.

Why do you think that is?

I think a lot of times Stephen is asking the audience to play with him. And it's very fun to play with Stephen Colbert.

Also, it's always more fun for the writers when we can interact with the real world. Our first idea for the show was to have a more fictional, sketch-y aspect. But we quickly changed our minds. Stephen's interactions are real—even if his character isn't. It's become almost like a Lazlo Toth–type of situation.

Lazlo Toth was the pseudonym created by *Saturday Night Live* writer, Don Novello. The character of Lazlo would mail—with ridiculous concerns that he took very seriously—real-life executives, celebrities, and other public figures. He would receive hilarious responses back—some of which were later published in book form.

We wanted to create a similar situation with Stephen's character on *The Colbert Report*. It can become confusing, because you're writing on a lot of different levels. Stephen Colbert is a person who plays himself. So, as a writer, you have to consider what you want the character to say. You also have to figure out what the real Stephen is saying. And how the audience will react to it all. And how the guests will respond. It can be overwhelming.

Has it ever felt *too* overwhelming?

Sure, sometimes. But I did feel that I had the right experience for this job, having worked at *Late Night* and at *The Daily Show*. I felt that *The Colbert Report* would be an outgrowth of those two influences: the satirical side of *The Daily Show* combined with the silliness and character-driven aspect of *Late Night*.

You were combining elements from two shows, but by doing so you weren't necessarily making it easier for yourself as a writer.

It wasn't easier, no. It's like a hall-of-mirrors. And it becomes even more complicated on the "Word" portion of the show. You have to write both the argument and counterargument, *and* you have to get jokes out of both.

When the show first started, many humor writers wondered how such a show could sustain itself.

I left *Late Night* to work on *The Colbert Report*, and I only did so because I very much trusted Stephen's abilities. I felt that even if it was a failure, it would have been a smart failure.

David Cross, who plays the Al Franken–type character Russ Leiber on *The Colbert Report*, thought the show was going to be weekly, not nightly. When he found out, he told us we were insane.

Stephen's character, who was inspired by the Bill O'Reillys, Sean Hannitys, and Lou Dobbses of the world, has since come a long way. The show is a function of this character's egomania, and I think the show can go wherever that ego goes.

And it tends to work best when that ego goes into the real world. It's amazing who will play along.

Which leads into my next question: How exactly did you get Henry Kissinger to appear on the "Guitarmageddon" episode in December 2006? Kissinger introduced the challenge between Stephen and the guitarist from the Decemberists by saying, "Stephen, it's time to rock."

A lot of it has to do with the children or grandchildren of these celebrities. In the case of Kissinger, it was a younger member of his family who told him he could have fun on the show—although I'm not so sure he did.

Well, it did look like Kissinger was having fun when he exclaimed, "Crank it up!"

I'm not sure if he was having fun or merely experiencing pure befuddlement.

It surprises me as to who's *not* willing to play along with the joke— they mostly seem to be liberals. One example: Massachusetts congressman Barney Frank.

On a show in 2005, Stephen asked Congressman Frank if his weight was bothering his wife. Barney, being a notorious gay man, did not find this amusing. If I remember correctly, his response afterward was to call the show "sub–Three Stooges." I wish he liked our show more, but not everyone's going to love it. And to be fair to Barney Frank, we interviewed him before the show had even debuted—it must have been extremely confusing for him.

I want to talk about the schedule for a late-night talk-show writer. I was shocked when I heard how little time the writers have to create jokes for each show.

We have a few hours in the morning to work on the bulk of the jokes. We have to work quickly.

Can you run down a typical day at *The Colbert Report?*

A typical day gets pretty hectic—I'm usually there anywhere from eleven to twelve hours.

I arrive around nine thirty. Usually, I've already gotten some news from the papers and from the news shows. I meet with Rich Dahm, a co-executive producer, and Tom Purcell, the head writer. I meet with Stephen, and then with the rest of the writers and producers. We go back and forth with ideas and jokes, and then the writers retreat into their offices to work on their assignments. We then immediately get the production team working on the footage, graphics, music, and props we think we'll be needing.

At one o'clock, the writers' scripts are in, and we begin editing and refining the pieces. There's a second production meeting, to go over new elements we'll need and to stop production on the ones that now seem unlikely to make it to air.

The entire script is hopefully finished by around four. We have a rehearsal at around five thirty, maybe a little earlier, and we're done by around six. We rewrite and edit jokes that need to be fixed until around six forty-five. At around seven, the show is shot in front of an audience. We finish about forty-five minutes later, and we then go over the details for the following night's show.

Is it true that writers work in pairs on *The Colbert Report?* One writer comes up with the lines as the other acts them out?

No, they both write and act them out. There's definitely a need to say Stephen's lines out loud, to hear if they really sound like his character.

You wrote an article for *Slate* magazine in 2001, and you listed the six types of jokes that writers weren't allowed to come up with at

The Daily Show. One of the examples was to avoid "jokes that will get claps instead of laughs."

That's very important, actually. We write so many jokes about the news that sometimes we can move into an area of political statements rather than jokes. Our most important task is to be funny. Everyone who writes for our show wants to be a comedy writer much more than a political commentator. It's easier to get a clap than a laugh.

Were you in attendance at the infamous White House Correspondents' Dinner on April 29, 2006, when Stephen gave a speech and managed to upset not only the president but half the D.C. media?[1]

Yes. A group of writers worked on that speech together. This is the type of material we write every night. It never occurred to me that it would affect the audience so intensely. But what we didn't take into consideration was who the audience was going to be: politicians and press people.

When we had rehearsed that speech a few hours before, in front of hotel staff, we never had any sense that there might be a problem. So when I witnessed the reaction, I was shocked. *Shocked!*

I was actually sitting with Stephen's family. Very close to me were Karl Rove and other insiders. I was in the *thick* of it.

Did Stephen know how badly he was bombing with his immediate audience?

The speech definitely wasn't getting a great response. Stephen is a fearless performer. He just kept committing to it, plowing forward. Having once performed myself, I know how difficult an accomplishment that is. It was inspiring.

---

1 Stephen Colbert: "....Wow, what an honor. The White House Correspondents' dinner. To actually sit here at the same table with my hero George W. Bush—to be *this* close to the man—I feel like I'm dreaming. Somebody pinch me. You know what? I'm a pretty sound sleeper—that may not be enough. Somebody shoot me in the face. Is he really not here tonight? Dammit. The one guy who could have helped...."

Did Stephen have any idea the effect he had on the home audience? It was broadcast on C-Span, and immediately became, as they say, an "Internet sensation."

Not really. Stephen only went up to the dais with the specific purpose of being funny. We had no idea how the speech would be perceived. Even later, when we did find out, we were surprised at the strength of the response. The reaction to that speech was a lesson on how many people wanted a voice of criticism at that moment in time.

Are you tired of being asked what it's like to be one of the few female comedy writers in television?

I am tired of it.

I hesitated to even bring up the question, truthfully.

Most of the time when it's brought up, the question isn't actually about being a woman; it's really about how poorly male comedy writers are perceived. Usually, people want to know how I survive in a writing room with a dozen men, whom they imagine are bullies and misogynists. That hasn't been my experience at all. I've written with great people. And it is important that women hear that being a female comedy writer doesn't mean you're going into battle. Maybe more of them will give it a shot once they know that.

Any more advice?

You have to be patient. You have to give yourself a chance. When you're first pursuing a job in a field like this, there's a strong tendency to panic. When I took classes with Del Close [a Chicago teacher of improv], he would challenge all of us to wait—to not make the cheap, easy joke in a scene but to have faith that something funnier and more organic was on the way. It can be that way with a career too. There are a lot of times when your biggest task is just to stay calm and keep working.

You don't have to write for *Plant Physiology* magazine.

It's a journal, Mike. You just want me to pronounce that article title again, don't you?

Yes, please.

"Association of 70-Kilodalton Heat-Shock Cognate Proteins with Acclimation to Cold."

Got it: "proteins," "cold." Thank you very much.

Thank *you.*

Getting a Job as a Writer for Late-Night Television

Advice from writers at *Late Show with David Letterman*, *The Tonight Show with Conan O'Brien*, *The Daily Show*, *The Colbert Report*, **and** *Saturday Night Live*

1. You don't necessarily need an agent to get hired as a writer on a late-night show, but it helps. When a head writer or producer is readying packets for writing jobs, he or she is going to see instant credibility in the ones who are represented by the large agencies.

2. With that said, late-night shows tend to be idiosyncratic, which is a good thing. These shows are typically open to industry outsiders. They're still more likely to go with a known quantity than a stranger, but they flatter themselves in thinking that that's not always the case.

3. As to how to acquire an agent, there are different ways. Perhaps an original project or film will get you noticed. You could also submit a script or other writing samples. Also, do some research. Find out which agents represent your favorite comedians and writers and then contact

those agents' assistants. In Los Angeles, assistants are typically treated like mules, but they often go on to lucrative, high-level jobs that allow them, in turn, to treat others like mules. Find an assistant, send your packet, and be smart about it. The assistant wants to get in good with the agency as a talent spotter, so if you're talented, the assistant will almost certainly pass along your material.

4. Know the show's voice. As a writer, it's important to have your own voice, of course, but a submission should prove you can adapt to other styles. Keep in mind that your packet should contain material that is meant to be performed and that is not just funny on the page; there's a difference. If you're in doubt, try reading the material aloud. If you stumble or run out of breath, those are red flags. Cut jokes that you think are funny but can't ever imagine the host/character/correspondent delivering. Prove that you watch and understand the show.

5. When submitting to a show, you might be better off addressing your submission and cover letter to the writers' assistant rather than to the head writer or executive producer. You should never address your packet to the host. The show's writers' assistant is usually the first (and often only) judge of whether a submission is passed along. Look for the assistant's name in the credits.

6. Never include with your submission the funny T-shirt you created, or bumper sticker you printed up, or Rupert Pupkin–style tape you made of yourself telling jokes in your bedroom. That sort of thing *will* get passed on to the writers, but only to be mercilessly mocked and eventually chewed to shreds by the office dog.

7. Move to Los Angeles, New York or, maybe, Chicago. Los Angeles has the most opportunity in TV and film. New York and Chicago have more places to develop and form a community of like-minded humor writers.

8. Find your niche. Whether it's a regular comedy club, improv theater, magazine, or website, find a place where you fit in and have a network of people who share a similar sensibility.

9. In general, it's better not to list your comedy accomplishments, especially if they only consist of clips from your college humor magazine.

10. If you have a personal reference, mention him or her in your cover letter—unless that person was fired.

11. Be brutally sparing in the length of your material. You should establish the premise and get out quickly. Sample packets for late-night comedy/variety usually run four to ten pages.

12. The keys to a good packet are variety, concision, and resonance. This usually consists of a few sketches, a page or so of monologue jokes, a handful of free-floating ideas, plus one "bonus," which could be a funny article or story.

13. If you do manage to score an interview with the producer or head writer, do not attempt to be overly funny. This comes across as desperate. It's more important to act intelligent and nice and normal.

Dave Barry

Between 1983 and 2005, Dave Barry wrote a daily column for *The Miami Herald* and, by his own admission, never missed a deadline. He also raised two kids—neither of whom, he delights in telling his readers, thinks he's all that funny.

At its height, Barry's column appeared in five hundred newspapers across the country—about fifty more than George F. Will's—but back in the late seventies, it took a bit of searching to find it. In the beginning, his work was confined to the *Daily Local News* in West Chester, Pennsylvania, and a few other newspapers. This changed in 1982, when *The Miami Herald* offered Barry a permanent position as a humor columnist. Barry left his job—tutoring business executives in the fine art of writing inter-office memos—and relocated to Miami, a city he once called "the weirdest area of the United States." For both Barry and his readers, this was an astute, welcoming move—most business executives were beyond help, anyway.

Like all great writers, Barry isn't brimming with self-confidence. He isn't entirely happy with his decisions in life or the state of the world, which may be a shocking statement coming from a writer who has published thirty books and, in 1988, was awarded a Pulitzer—for having written extensively, and unabashedly, about Neil Diamond songs, the "worldwide epidemic of snakes in toilets," and the Oscar Meyer Weiner Mobile (that he drove for a week).

"Humor," Barry once wrote, "is really closely related to fear and despair." He believes that comedy originates from a mutual understanding among humans that "we live in an extremely dangerous, scary world, run by all kinds of forces over which we have no control. And we're all gonna get sick and die."

Not the lightest quip in the history of humor, and yet not without a heavy dollop of truth.

Is it true that you never missed a deadline in more than thirty years?

That is true. I think one of the advantages I had was that I wrote a weekly column, instead of writing one every other day or three times a week. I had time to do other things, such as write books, which made working on the column never quite as oppressive as it could have been. Sometimes I'd get myself into these situations, like writing about the Super Bowl, where I was committed to produce a column every single day. You're totally in the grip of coming up with another idea, and then another idea, and then another, and I cannot imagine living that way.

I took vacations and trips, but I could still write my column—it wasn't that difficult. But that's not saying I was like Mike Royko. I still don't know how some columnists did it, Royko being Exhibit A.

How many columns did Royko write in a week, first for the *Chicago Daily News* and then later for the *Chicago Sun-Times* and the *Tribune?*

He wrote every day and, you know, if he didn't publish a column, the newspaper sales would drop by $100,000. At least this is the legend. He just felt this immense pressure to be in the paper every day. I don't know what that must be like. I never felt that type of pressure.

Was there ever any frustration that you couldn't spend more time honing and re-writing an article?

No, I had a lot of time. And again, I had the advantage of writing only one column a week. I was always sure when I sent in the column that it was the best I could have done. Now, there were times when having done all that work I would think that that wasn't the greatest topic for me. There were also times when I would look at a column after it was published and think, Man, I could have done that better. But I never had the feeling that I was just getting it in because there was no additional time to work on it. With that said, every now and then, when I would be at a political convention or at a sporting event working on deadline, I might have felt that more time would have been nice.

Does your ability to write quickly come from your background as a reporter?

I definitely think starting out as a journalist is good training for a columnist. You begin to understand the cycle of the paper and the deadlines, and you don't think in terms of writing for the ages and literature and future generations—you just think in terms of getting it in the paper.

Young people who want to become columnists are always talking about how they don't want to be reporters; they just want to be columnists. I'm always telling them they should be a reporter first. Because if you learn to do that, to collect information and write an accurate news story, you'll be much better at making fun of it.

And yet, for a humorist, a week isn't a long time. Many humorists are famous for rewriting a piece endlessly.

Basically, I had a two-or-three-day cycle where all I was doing was dealing with my column, and that's a real luxury to me. After that it would be diminishing returns, or no returns.

When you write humor, it's not funny to you. It's not even really that funny when you first think of the idea. There may be a glimmer of humor because it still seems vaguely original, but after a couple of days it's not funny at all. You're just trusting that it was, at some point, funny, and that your honing and tweaking is really improving it. I would eventually reach a point where I would just think, This feels old, even though nobody's seen it but me.

You once said you were happy that readers didn't know how your humor column was written. That a reader would have been disappointed by learning how the trick is pulled off—you compared it to being a magician.

I've often said that about humor, both spoken and written. It's a lot like a magic trick, in that there's a very mechanical way in which it's done. There are a lot of obvious and basic structural things you do with a sentence and with a joke and how you set it up on the page. And the trick is to do it in such a way that it doesn't look like there was any effort involved—that it's somehow magic.

When a good stand-up comic is performing, he gives you the illusion that he's thinking of these things as he's speaking—every now and then this may be true, but generally it's not. Usually, he has practiced every single joke, every single pause, every inflection, every facial expression, and found the ones that work the best. And when he does this quickly, it's hilarious. To him, it's executing something. And I think that's what writing humor is sort of like. There's a certain amount of inspiration, but there's also a fair amount of work and repetition and practice and mechanics that are involved in making it look like it's just happening magically, right then and there.

Where did your reporting career begin?

I worked for a little newspaper called the *Daily Local News* in West Chester, Pennsylvania, a suburb of Philadelphia. It was boring. I spent a lot of time reporting on sewage. When I was in college, it was nowhere on my radar screen, sewage. I never had any idea as to what happened after you flushed the toilet. But when I got to the paper, as far as I could tell, sewage turned out to be the main thing the local governments dealt with. I spent many, many hours in meetings where people would talk about sewer lines. I never really understood what they were talking about, but I would have to write about it anyway. I'd also write about school-board meetings, and I wrote obituaries. For me, the occasional excitement would be a fire or a shooting—something that felt newspapery.

How did your syndicated humor column begin?

I was writing for the *Daily Local News* for a few years, and then, at the very end of the seventies, the very beginning of the eighties, I started getting a humor column into that and other papers. Sometimes I would even get the column into some of the bigger newspapers, such as the *Philadelphia Daily News* or the *Inquirer.*

Then a teaching opportunity became available. It was totally unplanned and unrelated to [humor] writing, but it was a very fortuitous change for me. It yanked me out of journalism altogether, and it put me into a world where I was traveling a lot and talking to people who worked at big corporations—something I knew nothing about. I was an English major from a small liberal-arts college, Haverford, where we didn't even know what business was. After I graduated, I went into journalism, where I still didn't know what business was about.

And then, suddenly, I was in this new world, dealing with people who participated in the economy and who made paint or who made cars and actually produced things. It was my job to teach these people how to write more clearly. You know, letters and memos and reports. I learned a lot. It was just sort of looking at the world in a different manner. And I had more time to write, because I was in planes and hotels and on the road a lot.

That's really when I concentrated on writing my humor column. I could write about whatever I wanted. It didn't matter to me if it was unlike any other newspaper column, because it was only running in the *Daily Local News*, and it wasn't my full-time job. I thought I was going to be teaching writing for the rest of my life, so, in a way, it gave me this chance to just sort of explore this voice—to become the type of humor writer that I wanted to be, and not have to worry about whether or not some editor sitting at his desk was pleased by it. It didn't matter. I could do whatever I wanted, which was the same thing I had done back in high school and college, writing silly little pieces, similar to Robert Benchley's, who was my idol.

That's quite a leap: from teaching businessmen how to write to having your own nationally syndicated humor column.

It was a slow process. Basically, what really got me going was an essay for *The Philadelphia Inquirer* in 1981. I wrote this long piece about natural childbirth that came to the following conclusion: it hurts. Which was a major insight for me, because the one thing they never mention when you go through all of the childbirth training is that it's quite painful for the woman. I mean, it didn't hurt me, as a man, but it was quite painful to the woman.

So I wrote this essay, and the *Inquirer* played it big, and it was just the right thing at the right time. Every baby boomer was having a baby or two at that point, and every one of them was going to natural-childbirth classes, as far as I could tell. And a lot of them were newspaper people. And that particular column got reprinted, I would say, in two dozen big papers. And it went over really well. A lot of these editors suddenly started calling me and asking, "What else have you written?" I had a year's worth of samples, and it wasn't long before I was regularly being published in a bunch of papers. Not too long after that, in 1983, *The Miami Herald* hired me.

What was Miami like then?

It was very different. In some ways it's still bad, but back then it was much, much more scary, and very unsure of itself. Today, Miami has sort of established itself, I think, as the pre-eminent party city of the United States. This is the natural place for the Super Bowl, because there's nothing but clubs and restaurants here. It's a little bit like Las Vegas in that sense, where people just think of it as a fun place to go. But in the early eighties, a lot of people in Miami were leaving and moving out, and there was quite a lot of fear, especially among the Anglos. There are still people who feel this way, but I think they're mistaken.

So, in 1983, I didn't want to move here. I just didn't. I lived on a shady, wooded road in Pennsylvania. To me, Miami was the weirdest place I'd ever seen in the U.S., but *The Miami Herald* was so determined to have me write for them that they hired me even though I stayed in Pennsylvania—for the next three years. I was the *Miami Herald* humor columnist living in Pennsylvania. Finally, in 1986, I moved here, and I've been here ever since.

Do you think the location has contributed to your humor? That if you had stayed in Pennsylvania, your style or sensibility would have been different?

Not really in the style that I write, no, but certainly the things I wrote about changed. Miami was, and still is, a gold mine for humor. Not long after I arrived, in the fall of 1987, the Pope visited and almost got killed by lightning. That's what I remember most about that time: the Pope was at a gigantic outdoor rally, and just when everything was set up, this huge

Miami thunderstorm rolled in and they had to rush the Pope out of there before he was obliterated into a charred cinder.

I also remember being at a bar on Biscayne Boulevard when the Pope rode past in his Popemobile, and there were maybe eight people on the street. Everyone else had stayed home, because the *Herald* had managed to successfully terrify everybody into not leaving the house and just watching the Pope on television. We heard things like: If you plan to see the Pope, leave now! You should have the following items: flak jacket, raincoat, insulin!

You don't get that sort of thing in Pennsylvania.

When did you win the Pulitzer?

In 1988, for articles I had written in 1987.

Did this come as a surprise?

A huge surprise.

Was there any worry on your part that winning the Pulitzer would affect your humor? That you were now part of the club, and no longer an outsider?

I worried about that a lot. I didn't realize at the time how big a deal it was to win a Pulitzer. I didn't realize that you get bombarded with telegrams, that you get asked to be on all these TV shows, and that everybody you've ever known gets in touch with you. I wasn't ready for that. And I had this feeling like, You know, jeez, does this mean that I'm still allowed to write stupid columns? Because my column won in the distinguished commentary category. No one had ever called my writing "distinguished." So I really wrestled with my first column after winning.

What was that first post-Pulitzer column about?

Even before I won, I had been planning to write about my dog throwing up.

I had a little dog named Zippy, who had this thing about going outside, eating lizards, and then vomiting them up on the rug. And I couldn't understand why that was such an important thing for a dog to do. I could see doing this once, maybe. But pretty much every day? Go out, eat a lizard, then throw it up? What could nature possibly have been thinking when it designed this idiot dog?

So I began my column—and this is very rough paraphrasing—but I said something like: "I was going to write about my dog throwing up lizards on the rug, but then I won the Pulitzer for distinguished commentary. And I don't think I'm allowed to write about that sort of thing anymore. I now need to write about the situation in the Middle East. And the best way to understand the situation in the Middle East is to compare it to a dog who throws up."

I wrote the rest of the column about Zippy. By the following week, it wasn't a big deal anymore.

The Pulitzer will be cited with your name for eternity: "Dave Barry, Pulitzer Prize winner."

More than anything, the reason that it's good to win a Pulitzer is that you then don't have to win a Pulitzer. You've won it, and you'll always be identified that way. It's just another prize, really, but it's a prize that everybody recognizes. Whenever I speak before a group, they introduce me by saying that I won the Pulitzer, and everybody nods, as if that means something.

Were there any topics over the years that were off-limits to you as a syndicated columnist? Newspaper readers are a prudish bunch.

The obvious ones. For humor, you're not going to make jokes about rape, and you don't make jokes about the Holocaust. And, for a while, you didn't make jokes about terrorism, but now it's okay again. Newspaper readers are, in my view, not as prudish as newspaper editors think they are.

When my column first began and it was getting fairly wide distribution, editors often perceived it as being a little bit edgy, pushing the envelope a bit. I would get a reaction like: "I don't know about this. I don't know if we can run this."

There will always be readers who are immediately offended and want to cancel their subscription, but the odds are that if it's funny, there will be way, way, *way* more readers who just laugh and enjoy it. The thing is, though, they don't call or write or anything; they don't let the newspaper know they liked it. So columns or jokes that would actually be amusing to people tend to get killed. This is one of the things that have hurt newspapers—as their circulations have begun to decline, they've become more hamster-like in their fear of everything that might offend anybody.

I'm always amazed when I see something funny in a newspaper.
It's as if it's not allowed.

Especially comic strips.
I know. My god!

Did you ever feel you could get away with less in a newspaper than you might have in a magazine?
Absolutely. In fact, that would probably go for any medium outside of the newspaper. You can say things on television that papers would be reluctant to talk about. The tyranny of the one or two humor-impaired people out there who call ... well, it's just incredible. Editors just don't like being yelled at. They just don't. And they will react to it.

Would you have written differently if you were contributing to *The New Yorker* or *Esquire* or any other magazine?
I don't think those magazines would have published me, because I don't think my humor would have ever been viewed as sophisticated enough for *The New Yorker*. I never had much luck with the city of New York, to be honest. In any way.

Why do you think that is?
I don't know. I mean, I just think my humor is viewed as too sophomoric, and too much as guy humor. It's not what New Yorkers like.

Does this bother you?
No, not at all. I recognize that there are lots of different kinds of humor, and I think there's sort of a New York–editor attitude, like at *The New York Times*. Their humor, for a long time, was written by Russell Baker, who was brilliant, and I don't mean to put it down. It just wasn't

me. It wasn't wacky dog-poop humor, and that's okay. I mean, they know who their audience is. My column did run in New York, in the *Daily News*, but only on Sunday. And as far as I could tell, nobody ever read the *Daily News* on Sunday, including the *Daily News* editors. Maybe that's why my column was in there.

Were there any topics that you were afraid to write about? How about religion?

No, thanks.

Was that off-limits?

No. I wrote a couple of columns about religion, and I didn't really have much of a problem. My dad was a Presbyterian minister, so I grew up with religion all around me. I myself am not religious—never have been, not even when I was young. So I've always found it mildly amusing, but not in the "It's ruining the world and it needs to be viciously mocked" kind of way. I would write columns about attending St. Stephen's Episcopal Church, in Armonk, New York, as a kid, or a column about Christmas. I would write about religion from that angle, but not from the angle of how I wasn't religious.

The things I find fascinating are the types of subject matter that really make people mad and what people really care about. You know, readers are only mildly interested in global situations. Just mildly interested. But then they get really mad about subjects such as cell-phone minutes, or when I criticized Neil Diamond.

What happened with Neil Diamond?

I'm still a little worried. I almost feel as if I should start my car with a remote control, because there still may be a Neil Diamond fan out there somewhere. I can kind of relate to Salman Rushdie. He had his problems, but he never said anything bad about Neil Diamond.

What happened was I once got a call from one of these companies that conduct surveys to find out what songs radio stations should play. This woman played me these seven-second snippets of songs, and I had to say whether or not I liked them. That's all. And I was annoyed, because

I didn't want to talk about those snippets. I just wanted to talk about the songs I didn't want to hear on the radio anymore, such as Neil Diamond's "I Am ... I Said."

So, I wrote a column in which I made fun of that song, but that really wasn't the point of it. The point was this radio's survey. But, man, was there a firestorm! And it lasted forever! Years later, I was watching *The Today Show*, and Katie Couric was interviewing Neil Diamond. She brought up my criticism of his song, and he laughed. His agent or manager then contacted me and said Neil would like me to come to one of his concerts. I never went. I didn't want to be sitting in front of nine-thousand menopausal women singing "Sweet Caroline."

You also made fun of Barry Manilow. You referred to his songs as "weenie music."

I did, yes. But I'm not as worried about his fans. To be honest, I think I can take them.

Reading your columns again, even going back to the beginning of your career, I found a consistent theme: a deep distrust of government and authority figures.

That's true. That's kind of the class-clown thing. When I was a kid, I was the classic class clown, and I would tend to make fun of whoever was telling us what to do. I just didn't respond well to being told what to do. Especially if it's in a kind of nannyish way. I *still* don't. Just ask my wife. I really don't like it, and I'll do things that I know are bad for me.

Is that why you're a Libertarian?

My parents were hard-core, Democrat Adlai Stevenson voters, and I grew up kind of agreeing with them. Then I went to college, during the Vietnam War–protest years, and I was sort of the classic college-student leftist. But then later, when I was working for the *Daily Local News* and got to watch government up close, I realized that everybody who worked for the government—everybody that I met anyway—all meant well, but they were just unbelievably incompetent. And it became clear to me that even though people generally mean well, you don't necessarily want them making decisions for you or having authority over you.

So it's not like I formally joined the Libertarian Party. I'm not a pure Libertarian in the sense that I think there should be no government at all, but that sort of thinking became my fundamental principal. The older you get—when you become the age of everybody running for president and you know more about people, or at least you think you do—you begin to realize that people only run for president to be in charge of everybody. There really isn't any other reason. We're not that stupid.

A lot of people buy into it, though.

Maybe we are that stupid.

A few of your more popular articles have dealt with subject matter with a much more serious bent. You wrote a beautiful article one year after United Flight 93 crashed on the outskirts of Shanksville, Pennsylvania, on 9/11. You compared Shanksville to Gettysburg, and wrote that both towns, just out of chance, became associated not only with terrible events but with heroism.

That was a difficult column to write. *The Miami Herald* really wanted me to write something about that one-year anniversary. In fact, they really wanted me to go to Ground Zero. I thought about that, but I wasn't in New York on 9/11, and I knew that many journalists and writers who had been in New York were going to be attending this event. The sheer volume of material written about Ground Zero was going to be huge and really good. I didn't see what I could add to all that, really. Later, and I can't remember who came up with the idea, the word "Gettysburg" popped up in conversation and everything just clicked for me.

Why?

I've been to Gettysburg a few times. It's one of the most moving places I've ever been. It's not that far from where Flight 93 went down, a few hours away, and there are a lot of parallels there. So that was the genesis of that column, and I was really glad I wrote it. To me, the story of Flight 93 is one of the most amazing of all the things that happened that day.

You returned to writing humor quickly after 9/11. How were you able to gauge that the time was right?

That was a really strange time. I remember talking to almost everybody I knew, including journalists and editors, and asking them, "What do we do now?" There were a couple of days when I didn't want to write *anything*. You know, I was just sitting there, staring at the television and crying. But I also had this feeling that throughout my entire life, all I've ever done, really, is write about silly stuff and make fun of things. There was always the lighter side of everything, and now suddenly, here's this event in which there's absolutely no lighter side that I can see. None. And in that kind of yawning chasm right after 9/11, it was hard to know whether there ever would be a lighter side to anything.

I guess that, intellectually, I must have known better than that, but, emotionally, that's how I felt. It was like, My God, my whole life I've devoted myself to this crap, and here are these brave firemen and others who've suffered, and what is my life about? What am I going to do now? I had all these thoughts in my head. And then God bless *The Onion*. I laughed and laughed when their post-9/11 issue came out. It was great.

Did it seem to you that readers were ready to laugh, even *needed* to laugh again, long before the media decided it was okay to do so?

Exactly right! That is exactly right. I wrote one column after 9/11 that was quite serious. And I got a lot of mail in response, and it was almost all the same, which was, Thank you for that. I agree with you, it was a horrible event, but now please go back to being funny.

I actually went on a book tour pretty soon after 9/11. The media was convinced that the mood of the nation was somber and was going to stay somber for a long time and that everything that everybody said or did on the news had to be somber. But the public very quickly said, All right, these fuckers attacked us. We're gonna get 'em, but we're not gonna stop laughing.

I think, just judging from my own mail and from what I would hear from readers, it was much different from what I was hearing from the media. I kept getting these interview requests from journalists who wanted to talk about what's going to happen to American humor. "Has irony really died?"

I remember thinking, Are you watching television? David Letterman came back on the air, with his show based in New York, and he started making jokes again. The audience and viewers seemed so happy to see this.

I came out of that whole event deeply impressed by ... well, this is kind of corny, but I came away impressed by Americans. They're just an amazingly resilient people.

That's one of the things you dealt with in the Shanksville article. That if you're a student of history, if history tells us anything, it's that humans are very good at moving on and being resilient. And, also, that we need humor in our lives.

Right. And, in fact, there were new topics to write about and to be funny about after 9/11, especially dealing with the Code Purples and Pinks and whatever other codes we had for terrorism.

That whole War on Terror, you know, quickly became its own kind of joke. Obviously, not the part where we're actually accomplishing things with the terrorists but with the ways it actually pissed us off by seeming to not do any good.

How difficult was it for you to write that first humor column after 9/11?

I was very self-conscious. I didn't want there to be anything that would remotely be construed as being in bad taste. But by that time, *The Onion* had returned, and Letterman had returned, and Americans were getting back to speed. I didn't find it too difficult.

My first humor article after 9/11 was generic. It was about a guy who made a jet engine to cool beer. He spent six months working in his garage on this incredibly highly engineered jet engine, and all it did was make a can of beer cold. I just wanted to do something reassuring. You know: People are still out there doing these types of things.

How often, over the years, has a newspaper refused to run a piece of yours?

I would say that with every fourth or fifth column, some paper somewhere would refuse to publish it. I was always amazed by the columns that would, for whatever reason, not run. I got into this one situation—I can't remember the name of the paper—but they kept saying I was on vacation. So, I finally wrote a column directly in response. I wrote: "No, I'm not on vacation and what this paper means is that they don't think you should be reading a column about dog farts." So their editor, who was this prissy little man, started running detailed editor's notes in a separate column, contradicting me and arguing with me.

Is this common? To take a syndicated column that's already been edited and then tamper with it? Or to not run a column at all?

Newspapers can do whatever they want, that's the thing. I used to get so down because of that. People would say, I read your column in this newspaper and then I read it in another newspaper—the same column, and this column seemed a lot funnier than that column. One column would have a huge chunk of it missing, or they would just lop off the last six inches. Sometimes a column would have every punch line scissored out. I didn't want to have a reputation for being a prima donna or anything, but sometimes I'd write letters to these papers and say, Listen, I'd really rather you not run my column at all than do this.

Why would they edit the columns? For length? For censorship reasons?

I'm not sure. It wasn't always clear whether they were shortening it for length or just cutting out what they thought might be offensive.

I always felt bad for Art Buchwald, especially in the last ten or so years of his syndicated column. The size of the column eventually shrank to the size of a postage stamp. How can you be funny with four hundred words or less?

But Art kind of liked that. He used to say to me, "Readers don't want any more than four hundred words! That's all you gotta give 'em!"

How would the lack of space affect you? Did you feel that you had to launch into the humor more quickly than a columnist for a magazine might have?

That's just insecurity. I was always terrified that people would read only halfway through a sentence and not be amused, so I tried to have jokes everywhere. I would worry that it wasn't getting there quickly enough. That's always the advice I give people who send me humor to consider: it needs to be funny from start to finish. I just never had the confidence to take my time, to build slowly. I'm too insecure a writer.

There never seemed to be a distance between you and your readers, which exists between other newspaper columnists and their readership. Like, say, George Will, who is more of a lecturer and teacher.

That's probably because when George Will is writing about something, he's unquestionably done more research and reading and talking and thinking than most of the people reading that column. But when it comes to humor, you can't really act like that. What you're basically saying in a humor column is: I'm funny because you laugh. But that doesn't put you above anybody. Pomposity or authority doesn't work very well with humor.

How often would you use your columns to make a point?

Not often.

I can remember one instance, though, in which you used it to promote bicycle helmets for children.

I did, and that was really the only time I ever wrote a column in which I had a very specific positive goal from the start. I wanted parents to make their kids wear bike helmets because I just went through a pretty awful experience. My son was injured in a bicycle accident in 1996, but he was wearing a helmet. When I was in the hospital with him, I saw parents who had much worse experiences, because their kids weren't wearing helmets.

I was asked many, many times over the years to use my column for one cause or another, and I always said no. I'd say, Listen, what I do is entertain people—that's my job, that's why they're reading this column. If I start using it for other reasons, even if they're good reasons, I am sort of betraying the reason that people have started reading this column in the first place. I'll do what I can for your cause, but I will not use my column for that purpose.

So, for you, the joke always comes before the message?

Readers will say to me, "It's all in good fun, but you do a lot of good." And I've always replied, "Yes, but even if I did bad, I'd still do it, because it's what I do." My goal is to amuse people—that's it.

You've said that you never really thought about why something was funny or not funny until people started asking you about it.

I never realized that I was going to spend so much of my life talking about something that you can't really talk about. I've been asked so many times what's funny, and why is *this* funny whereas that is *not* funny? I've developed a few theories, but I'm not sure they're really my theories or just something I've learned to say in response to the questions about it. I'm still of the belief that A) you can't really know, and B) there is no absolute. My idea of funny is different from another's.

And yet you have the best definition of humor I think I have ever read: "A sense of humor is a measurement of the extent to which we realize that we are trapped in a world almost totally devoid of reason. Laughter is how we express the anxiety we feel at this knowledge."

You know, it actually took me a day to come up with that one. Why do we actually laugh? I don't know that you can explain why we, as a species, laugh. Maybe it's just that there's a disconnect in our brains when we realize that obviously we're going to die but we can laugh anyway. There has to be a release. For me, it's either you laugh or you become religious.

If you were starting your career today, would you go into humor writing for a newspaper? Or would you do it for the movies, or for another medium?

Starting right now, no, I don't think I'd write for newspapers. I think it would be much more likely that I wrote for the Internet. I'm not sure about movies. I sometimes wonder about that medium, truthfully. But the more immediate one, the Internet, is the one I like the most.

So no great desire to start over as a reporter covering the opening of a sewage plant?

No, but there has been a sewage plant named after me in Grand Forks, North Dakota. My career has come full circle. My name is now on the side of a plant that handles human waste. And I'm sure some poor reporter in Grand Forks has to leave the office to go and write about Dave Barry Lift Station No. 16.

Perhaps even as we speak.

Lucky guy.

Selling Your Movie Script to a Studio Executive

Advice from a film executive at Twentieth Century Fox

1. Do not send unsolicited submissions—legally we can't read them no matter *how* funny the title or description. We are liable for *severe* legal repercussions. It has to come from a W.G.A.-agent, manager, or producer.

2. Write your script with a development executive in mind ... we read *tons* of scripts. When a writer has a point of view—a voice and/or a sense of humor in their screen directions—it makes us laugh, and we enjoy the read all that much more.

3. Don't ask for your screenplay back once it's been submitted.

4. If you are pitching your script to an executive, do not offer to act out any of the scenes.

5. Try to be somewhat funny in person, or at least somewhat socialable, likeable, and clean. Never scrimp on personal hygiene. Even though you are a writer, we still need to like the people we want to work with.

6. Do not tell stories about how you refused to take Steven Spielberg's notes on a recent project, or how some "stupid" development executive gave you notes, which you later ignored. We want to know that you will be flexible and responsive when we ask you to make changes.

7. Do not act mean to our assistants, as they tend to get promoted quickly, and you never know who will be working for whom one day. So be extra nice when speaking to assistants—they are *not* there for your every want or need.

Larry Wilmore

Historically, black comics have usually drawn a distinct line in the sand when it comes to racial politics. Richard Pryor and Eddie Murphy and countless others were brilliant at dissecting the absurdity of a racially divided country. But they clearly came from an "Us vs. Them" mentality. Larry Wilmore, the "Senior Black Correspondent" for Comedy Central's *The Daily Show*—a post he's held since August of 2006—examines the ongoing rift between black and white with a slightly more ambiguous perspective.

During his numerous segments for the late-night news satire, Wilmore has mocked racial relations from every conceivable angle. He's argued that white people turned the jazz of Miles Davis and John Coltrane into the style of Kenny G.; that Disney is racist because "even *The Lion King* had no black people and it was set in Africa"; and he announced to "all three black viewers of *The Daily Show* ... that it's now officially okay to tell white people you think [O.J. Simpson] is guilty." One has to wonder: exactly *who* is he making fun of? When he speaks about new terminology like "Blanguage" (how black people, in a "secret language," clandestinely put down white people) and the "Negrometer" (a black scale ranging from Thomas Jefferson to George Jefferson, the lead character in the '70s sitcom *The Jeffersons*), is he poking fun at racism or the culture of oversensitivity that finds racism everywhere?

Like every great comedy writer, Wilmore is fearless. He's never hesitated to push the boundaries of good taste or to potentially offend his audience. One of his most celebrated segments for the *Daily Show* was an investigative piece (along with fellow correspondent John Oliver) on a proposed ban of the "n-word." While interviewing New York City councilman Leroy Comrie, the black politician who championed the ban, Wilmore asked if a voluntary censoring of racist words was similar to "renouncing sweets for Lent," and detailed exactly how this "versatile" word can be used as a noun, a verb, an adjective, and an adverb.

Controversy like this is nothing new for Wilmore. Even before he stepped in front of the camera and became a semi–*Daily Show* celebrity, he was making a lot of people angry, usually because of his racially charged comedy. *The PJs* (1999–2001), a stop-motion animation series that Wilmore co-created with Eddie Murphy, was repeatedly attacked for its supposed racial insensitivity, primarily by critics in the black community, including director Spike Lee and writer Stanley Crouch.

The PJs followed the misadventures of Thurgood Stubbs (voiced by Eddie Murphy), the chief superintendent at the dreary and dilapidated Hilton-Jacobs housing project in an unnamed city. The series took an unblinking look at inner-city poverty, with jokes about firearms, crack dealers, and Asian grocers. Like in an episode of *The Simpsons*, the best social satire was hidden in the background. In the pilot episode, there was a billboard in the distance with the slogan "HUD: Keeping you in the projects since 1965."

Born in 1962 in suburban Los Angeles, Wilmore attended California State Polytechnic University as a theater major, but dropped out early to pursue a career as a stand-up comic. As he told *The New York Times*, he spent his post-college years auditioning for movie and TV roles, often reading for "the part of the fast-talking ex-con."

His big break came in 1990, when he was hired as a writer for the groundbreaking Fox comedy sketch show *In Living Color*. From there, he went on to write for sitcoms such as *Sister, Sister* (1995) and *The Fresh Prince of Bel-Air* (1995). He won an Emmy and a Peabody Award for *The Bernie Mac Show* (2001–2006), a series he helped co-create.

Wilmore was also an occasional producer and writer for the American version of *The Office*, and he appeared in the show's second episode as Mr. Brown, a diversity consultant for the fictional, Scranton, Pennsylvania–based paper company Dunder Mifflin.

The question remains: Whose side is Larry Wilmore on? And more important, does it *matter*? Should a comedy writer pledge loyalty to a political or social agenda, or let his gags speak for themselves? Every time Wilmore smirks at the *Daily Show* audience, revealing nothing more than his delight in confounding everybody who'd fence in his opinions—or worse still, label him as a "black comic"—the answer couldn't be more obvious ... or more perfectly vague.

I once heard you interviewed on the radio, and you described the exact moment you decided to devote your life to comedy. I found this interesting, because exact moments don't happen too frequently in life.

The anecdote sounded like it was made up, but it's not. I was a senior in high school. My parents had already divorced, and I was living with my mother. The situation was difficult and became even more difficult: There was a rainstorm one night, and our roof caved in. I remember turning to one of my two brothers, Marc, and saying, "I don't want to end up in this type of situation. I just can't."

I decided to dedicate myself to comedy. I really had nothing to lose. Comedy made me the happiest. I became a stand-up comedian a few years later, and my brother Marc followed in my footsteps. He also became a stand-up comic and is now a writer for *The Simpsons*.

I didn't voice all of this in that exact moment, but I did want to take control of my life—I definitely didn't want to be a victim of my circumstance. I felt like my mother was very unhappy and her situation was unfortunate, and I knew that I didn't want the same thing to happen to me.

After that roof caved in, I had clarity in terms of not being afraid of going after my dream. I had no fear. I already had nothing—it's not like I could achieve that twice.

What were your career plans before you experienced that humor epiphany?

I was very much into science when I was young, and I wanted to become an astronaut. But when I eventually attended college, I became a theater major. I was always working on a play, either acting or helping produce it. This was at Cal Poly.

Is Cal Poly known for its theater program?

Actually, no. It's a school better known for its agricultural and engineering programs. So it didn't really make sense that I would go there to study acting, but the school was close to Hollywood, and I could sneak onto the movie-studio lots and have lunch and soak in the atmosphere. I never graduated.

A lot of humor writers from the older generation never graduated college, either. Now it seems like a prerequisite—if not for the educational experience, then for the contacts.

I guess I'm old-school in that sense. Most of my contemporaries are Ivy League grads. I'm more of the leave-the-home-and-join-the-circus type of showbiz person.

I taught myself comedy, mostly just writing and then performing stand-up in front of any type of crowd I could find. I learned to write because I needed an act. I didn't graduate from Harvard and immediately snag a writing job for a television show.

I'm amazed when a twenty-one year-old graduates from Harvard and immediately thinks he should be creating a TV show. That just astounds me. The level of hubris that's involved! What do you know about life—let alone about writing?

As a producer, I always try to hire writers who have experience in the real world. There was a young writer on *The PJs* who was very talented. But every time he'd pitch a joke he'd say, "Oh, you know, *The Simpsons* once did a similar joke" on such-and-such an episode.

I came very close to yelling at him. Instead, I said, "Stop pitching me what somebody else has already done. I'm not interested in that. Tell me what your grandfather did for a living. What did he act like?" I told him to write about *behavior*. Stop with the fucking ironic distance. Let David Letterman have that for himself.

Even Letterman had real-world experience.

Absolutely—and there's a lot of humanity in his humor.

I think this self-referential attitude is very limiting, and I think it's one of the reasons why comedy has fallen out of favor—too many writers aren't writing about anything that anyone cares about. It's all pop-culture references.

Television drama is almost Shakespearean compared with the comedies. I'll watch dramas more often than I watch comedies, because nobody's writing about real-world situations in comedy. It's infuriating to me.

A few years ago, I was lucky enough to hang out with Carl Reiner. We talked about *The Dick Van Dyke Show*, especially that first season [1961–1962]. He told me that every Monday morning the writers would ask one another, "What happened to you this weekend? What did your wife tell you this weekend?" That's how the writing session began.

My friend Phil Rosenthal, the creator of *Everybody Loves Raymond*, ran his writing room the exact same way. That's how he'd start his writing sessions: "Tell me what happened to *you*."

And that makes a difference with the writing?

Oh, sure. It's not, "They once did a similar joke on *Friends*." Well, I don't want to know what they once did on *Friends*. Stop telling me that. You're referencing a reference. It's a Xerox of a Xerox.

It took me ten years to learn how to really perform stand-up, but I think I became a better writer because of that experience. When I performed, I worked in every sort of club you can imagine—from biker bars to strip clubs, to comedy clubs to big venues. I was in so many different cities and states. I got a real feel for how to make most people laugh in almost any situation. I learned how to find the joke in something when it didn't seem like a joke could be found.

How would your act differ at a biker bar than at a comedy club?

It wouldn't be my material so much as my attitude. For a more confrontational audience I might start a little more ad-libby or improvisational. There's risk involved with that, because you can fall on your face pretty fast. The audience won't laugh at shit—they just don't care. But if you score in the beginning, you're gold. You can just recite your act in a monotone and it'll still kill. That's the key: the first thirty seconds in front of a tough crowd are very important.

Audiences can smell fear.

[Laughs] Especially bikers. And if they do, you're finished. Dominance is very important. Jerry Seinfeld once said, "To laugh is to be dominated."

Self-deprecation is also important, but you don't want to come across as an asshole. You do, however, want to be in charge of the situation.

Not a bad way to get through life either.

Actually, that's sort of how I do get through it: assert my dominance and then be self-deprecating.

What was your stand-up act like?

It wasn't the type that was going to make me famous. It was a writer's stand-up act.

Meaning what?

The act wasn't purely personality-driven. The audiences really liked it, but it would never get me cast in a movie. I enjoyed writing non-existential jokes that were disconnected—I'd take the audience in one direction and then go down another.

I wrote a bit called "Black Away." I'd talk in a stereotypical black patois, and then I'd put a few drops from a bottle of "Black Away" on my tongue, and I'd begin to speak with clean, WASP intonations. It would take the black right out of my voice.

This type of humor never really fit into the Def Comedy Jam style. For what I was doing with comedy, it was not the right time for me. I wasn't into the "pussy" and "motherfucker" comedians. I was more into the genteel, almost urban-Jewish type of comedy—such as Woody Allen's—in which it was the cleverness and the slyness of what I was saying, rather than the force of my personality. I'm Catholic, so I could completely relate to the neuroses and the guilt.

I'll give you my favorite Woody Allen joke. It goes something like, "Someone broke into my ex-wife's home and she was violated. Knowing my ex-wife, I'm sure it wasn't a moving violation." It's a brilliantly constructed joke. But, beyond that, what type of mind even thinks of a joke that involves your ex-wife being raped?

Anyway, I was never going to get a role in a movie like Eddie Murphy or Martin Lawrence would.

Did you even want to act?

I did want to act, but I also knew that writing and stand-up was my ticket. As an actor, I'd go in for an audition, but I'd change the lines to make them funnier. That just wasn't the correct etiquette.

In the early eighties, I appeared on *The Facts of Life* in a small role [Officer Ziaukus]. I only did a couple of episodes, and I wasn't called back. I would change my lines in rehearsal, and only later did I realize that this was a definite faux pas.

Did you work with George Clooney? He co-starred in a few *Facts of Life* episodes around that time as the hunky construction contractor, George Burnett.[1]

Clooney was on the show around the same time I was, but I never did meet him. We were on different episodes.

What was your first big writing break?

I needed to show people that I was funny by writing my own material, so I applied for a writing job at *In Living Color*—and got it. A lot of that was just timing. My agent heard the show was looking for writers, so I

---

1 *The Facts of Life episode synopsis from sightssounds.net:*

Episode Title: "Into the Frying Pan" – The girls and Mrs. Garret hire a young, surprisingly inexpensive contractor to reconstruct the burnt remains of Edna's Edibles into their new business venture—a trendy gift, card and clothing boutique—but they soon find that his good looks, charm and sociable nature are more appealing than his work habits. George Clooney, 24-year-old son of KNBC and NBC-TV news anchorman Nick Clooney, joins the cast as George Burnett, a Peekskill native recently returned from Kuwait where he worked in construction ... of hot tubs. STARRING: George Clooney (September 21, 1985)

wrote some sketches for a submission packet, and I then met with one of the executive producers, Keenan Wayans. We hit it off, and I was hired.

Did anyone on *In Living Color's* staff think Jim Carrey would become as popular as he eventually did?

We knew—it was obvious. We had no idea that he'd soon be making twenty million dollars a picture, but we knew he was hysterical.

People forget that Jim had already had his big break: a TV show that had failed [*The Duck Factory*, 1984], and a few movies [*Once Bitten, Peggy Sue Got Married, Earth Girls Are Easy*]. So *In Living Color* was sort of his last shot.

Carrey really is one of the nicest guys. I loved working with him; he was astonishing. When we wrote *In Living Color*, we would write enough material to fill a few shows. We'd need a huge packet of sketches at our table reads. Imagine having to read twenty-five sketches. Each of those sketches has a different character, so you're talking about a lot of different characters total for each of the actors. There'd be no chance to read these sketches ahead of time; they were cold readings. But Jim would score every time. He would create these full-blown, three-dimensional characters on the first read. I was just astonished. He was just amazingly talented. To this day, I've never seen anything like that.

When his career took off, was there jealousy from the rest from the cast?

The show was just about over by then; it was pretty much in its last days. But there was no sense of jealousy.

When *In Living Color* premiered, the reviews often included the word "groundbreaking." Do you think it was?

Oh, without a doubt. We felt as if there was nothing else on television similar to that show. It was very exciting and you could feel it in the air.

I remember traveling around as a stand-up comic during that time. People would ask me what I did for a living. I'd tell them I was a comic, and they would nod. I'd then say I also worked as a TV writer. "Oh, what do you write for?" "*In Living Color?*" "What! You write for *In Living Color?*"

That was the reaction back then. The show was huge. There probably hasn't been anything like it since—as far as black TV entertainment goes. It crossed color lines, which was fantastic; it was all-inclusive. It was also one of the first shows to embrace hip-hop culture.

You have to remember that I grew up during a time—the sixties and into the seventies—when very few black performers were seen on television. I'm not even that old—just in my mid-forties. But there were basically three types of black performers when I was growing up. There was the chitlin's-circuit comedian, like Redd Foxx, who was really raunchy and played mainly black clubs. His material was underground and would appear on what were called "party records." It wasn't for the mainstream.

Another type of black comedian was the civil-rights type, such as Dick Gregory. These were comedians who enjoyed taking on current events. They were really loved by the college crowd and the intelligentsia.

And then there was the third type: These weren't really black comics so much as just comedians for the mainstream, such as Flip Wilson and Bill Cosby. Cosby was a storyteller, but Flip was one of the best joke-tellers of all the comics at that time. His show [*The Flip Wilson Show*, NBC, 1970–74] was very influential, at least for people like myself. Flip was very funny—I just couldn't believe how funny he was. He was all personality—all raw. His was a talent that adapted very well to television, unlike some of my other favorite comedians, like Richard Pryor with his show [*The Richard Pryor Show*, NBC, 1977].

Do you think Flip Wilson has received the credit he deserves?

No, not at all. I think he deserves a tremendous amount of credit for influencing a whole generation of black comedians and writers. Flip has definitely been overlooked. When Flip was popular, it was a really turbulent time in this country. He was a clean-cut black comic who wasn't offensive. He didn't scare away sponsors. Nat "King" Cole had a show in the fifties, but it was canceled after a year because it never attracted a national sponsor.

Flip getting his own variety show was pretty much unprecedented. My family gathered together every week to watch the show, and we all felt a kinship with it. Audiences not only had permission to laugh at a black guy but at a whole cast of black performers. The same thing happened later with *In Living Color.*

Did you go straight to *The Fresh Prince of Bel-*Air from *In Living Color?*

No, I first went to a show called *Sister, Sister* [ABC and WB, 1994–1999]. I was there for two years. After that, I wrote for *Fresh Prince* in 1995. Truthfully, *Fresh Prince* was a bit of a frustrating experience for me. I did end up writing a couple of episodes, but I didn't last the season.

The show runner—basically the head writer—was fired just as I arrived, and the show got a new show runner. And then this guy was fired. We got another show runner. This one was not experienced in running a TV show, so I ended up leaving.

I then started working on the *PJs.* Actually, I take that back—I worked on a show for Fox called *The Show,* which was about a white guy who joins the writing staff of a black sitcom. It was a solid idea and fun to work on while it lasted. We had a fantastic actor for the pilot. He was extremely funny and just brilliant, but Fox didn't want him for the series because they thought he wasn't good-looking enough. That man's name? Paul Giamatti.

One of the best character actors of our time, and Fox deemed him not quite attractive enough?

Paul could not have been a nicer guy, and he couldn't have been more hilarious. When the staff heard the news, we were like, "This is insane! Why do they not like this guy?" It was such typical network bullshit.

I learned a big lesson: Never listen to execs. Just do your own thing. Whether it happens or doesn't happen, at least you did what you wanted and you tried. That's what writers have to get into their heads—no matter what you come up with, it won't ever be as bad as the executives' suggestions.

Is this why you decided to work with Eddie Murphy in the late nineties, on *The PJs?* Were you looking for a more liberating experience?

Partly. I was very excited about doing something different. The concept was Eddie's—but it wasn't yet fully formed. He wanted a show that would take place in the projects. He thought all sitcoms were becoming too suburban, and he wanted to do something that was new, that had a different rhythm to it.

For me, it signaled a nice change of pace from what I had been working on.

Do you need different chops to write for animation than for live action?

It is different. You have to write more detail, and you have to get used to a different pace—a faster pace within the show itself. More material is used.

There were a lot of things I had to learn; animation's definitely a different beast. Every detail is storyboarded. You don't have the luxury of having an actor sell a joke or an emotion.

Had you known Eddie previously?

I had never met him, no. I was always a big fan, but I never appreciated how funny he was until I actually met him. Pure force of character. When he's not acting, he's very quiet and polite and soft-spoken—but he's also very, very sharp. Extraordinarily observant. When that light switch is turned on, it's awesome. It's just ridiculous.

I remember that during our first table reading for *The PJs*, Eddie got up and went to the bathroom. He stayed there more than twenty minutes. I was getting scared. I thought, Oh, man, I wonder if he's lost his nerve. He barely worked in television since *Saturday Night Live*, which was fifteen years earlier.

I wouldn't say that he was scared, but he seemed a bit nervous. He finally returned to the reading and just wowed everybody. He exudes raw power.

Eddie Murphy is another example of someone who never attended college and learned everything on his own.

I always respected Eddie because of what you just said. He's a self-made man, and he carved out his own success by sheer force of will. Then again, I think that his youth may have actually hurt him in the early part of his career—he didn't have a chance to really develop his comic voice.

He was very talented as a stand-up, but he didn't have much to say at the time. He never had a chance to be an adult; only a star.

Looking at Eddie Murphy's stand-up films—1983's *Eddie Murphy Delirious* and 1987's *Eddie Murphy Raw*—I'm not so sure he'd be able to get away with half of that material today; particularly, his jokes about homosexuals.

No, it was very adolescent. But here's the thing: The last time Eddie was a private person was when he was an adolescent. So that's where he left off; that's his point of reference.

Before he moved into his New Jersey mansion, Bubble Hill.

Yes, exactly. A lot of people in show business get to an age where they stop growing emotionally.

What age did you stop?

At about fifteen.

Why then?

It's my age of identification. I like doing magic tricks, I like to play and to have fun, and I'm very curious about many different things. I want to learn.

Do you think most comedy writers have stopped at fifteen?

Most comedy writers are still in high school, because in high school you feel like you know more than everybody else. I'd say the majority of comedy writers have stopped at around fifteen or sixteen.

Comedians are even worse. Maybe 7-years-old—at the most eight. And actors are even worse than comedians! Most are stuck at the ages of three or four.

How about an actor/comedian?

An actor/comedian is about eleven or twelve, the period right before their uncomfortable adolescence. They have very low self-esteem, and they're just not sure what the fuck's going on.

Writers are a little more adult than comedians and actors. There's more of a thought process with them; it's not just a knee-jerk reaction. You don't necessarily need to be around others. You can work alone. But they're still not adults. Otherwise, they wouldn't be writers.

What was the advantage of using Claymation on *The PJs,* as opposed to live actors?

The process wasn't quite Claymation, but more stop-motion. Claymation is re-forming the clay. Stop-motion is when you place different pieces onto molded figures to make it appear as if the lips and eyes are moving. You have replacement eyes, replacement mouths. It's a tremendous amount of work. It has all the disadvantages of live action and all the disadvantages of animation. Simple scenes take forever—and are extremely expensive. Each thirty-minute episode cost about a million dollars.

Were you surprised by the controversy that surrounded *The PJs?* A few black TV writers, including Yvette Lee Bowser, the creator of *Living Single,* and Susan Fales-Hill, who wrote for *A Different World,* were highly critical of what they perceived to be the show's negative stereotypes.

I was surprised. We were just making a comedy. We never expected people to get up in arms about the show—especially one featuring clay characters.

I met with the NAACP. They weren't thrilled about a few of the characters drinking beer. I said, "But the father in the *Family Guy* got drunk and fell on his ass in the first episode! And Homer Simpson drinks beer all the time!"

They said, "Well, those characters are cartoons. Yours are real."

We said, "No they're not! They're made out of clay!"

Some of the jokes were very sharp for a show broadcast prime time on Fox. In one episode, a sign is visible on a Housing and Urban Development–controlled building: "HUD: too little, too late."

If we can't make fun of ourselves, who can we make fun of? The NAACP hated everything about the show. They didn't like that we featured a crack addict and a character who ate dog food. But the question was, Who decides what's funny and what's "correct"? The NAACP?

You can't please everyone. You just try to do what you think is funny. If you attempt to appease advocacy groups, good luck. You can do it, I suppose, but it's not going to be funny.

It wasn't just the NAACP criticizing the show. Spike Lee also expressed his displeasure. He called the show "really hateful ... toward black people."

I'm always suspect of people in this business who criticize others' work. Especially someone as controversial as Spike Lee, who is known to paint characters in broad, stereotypical strokes.

Just because you're dealing with certain elements doesn't mean you're condoning them.

Exactly. Bill Cosby gets criticized for saying that black families need to take more charge of their destinies, and that black fathers need to be more responsible. That is not a negative message. That's a positive message, and yet he's routinely criticized. But there are people out there who disagree with this. Even if you say the most obvious things, people will still disagree with you.

In the real world, there are crack addicts and alcoholics. Some of them are black and live in urban areas. We didn't make that up.

Eunetta Boone, a story editor for *The Fresh Prince* and a writer and producer of numerous sitcoms, said that the most difficult thing in Hollywood is to be a black comedy writer.

She also said it was very rewarding, if I remember correctly.

Do you think there are enough black comedy writers on television?

I don't know how to answer that question the way it's phrased, because I don't know what you mean by "enough." I think writing comedy comes from one's particular point of view. I would certainly like more black comedy writers to be able to write on mainstream shows—I think that would be fantastic. But I don't think you necessarily need a certain number from any one group to validate a point.

There's no reason why black writers should write only for black shows, or why white writers should only be allowed to write for a certain type of show; I think that's silly. If a writer has a unique point of view and there's talent behind it, then that's the important point. Race is a bonus to me in some cases, but it's not a necessity.

How did you come up with the idea for *The Bernie Mac Show?*
You were the show's creator and executive producer.

From watching Bernie's stand-up act. In particular, it was his routine about taking care of his sister's kids while she was dealing with a crack addiction—that was based on fact, by the way.

You managed to capture Bernie Mac's act very well. It's not easy for a comedian to make the transition from stand-up to sitcom character.

I was intrigued by the way Bernie would address his audiences. I remember seeing him perform in Charlotte, North Carolina. He said, "Now, Charlotte, you know what I'm talking about. You know Bernie Mac."

I thought it was funny that he would personalize the entire audience as if it were an individual. It occurred to me that this would be a very powerful thing to do with all of America—to treat the country as one single viewer.

The show's tone and format reminded me of a reality show. In particular, the style of camerawork.

I was actually taking my cue from reality shows that had just started around this time. I felt you could transfer some of the unique qualities of this "reality," if you could call it that, to a fictional world. I wanted a sitcom where you felt you were just observing a family— almost as if you were eavesdropping on the action. I didn't want the performances to be thrown in the audience's faces, so they'd be forced to laugh at jokes.

Malcolm in the Middle was a hit the previous year, but it had a kind of hyper-reality, comic-book feel to it. It didn't stay within the bounds of our reality. I wanted to do the opposite. I wanted to create situations that were real within this reality.

Here's an example: There was a scene in the pilot where Bernie is sitting in a chair, talking to the camera about the three kids he's now in charge of watching. You can hear one of the kids, Jordan, crying in the background. Bernie tells Jordan to "Shut up, be quiet," then rolls his eyes and reluctantly leaves the chair to see what the problem is. The camera stays on the empty chair. We—as viewers—had no idea Bernie was going to leave. And because we didn't anticipate this moment, we aren't going to cut away.

This was all about life happening in the moment. As a writer, it was fun to come up with this type of scene. All of those realistic details were written into the scripts. That was the feel I wanted—to break the rhythm of a typical sitcom.

The show definitely had its own unique rhythm that was entirely different from any other sitcom on the air at that time.

I didn't look to television for that rhythm. I looked to the French New Wave movies from the late fifties and early sixties, specifically *The 400 Blows* and *Breathless*. The editing style of those films is so interesting to me; the quick cuts, the back and forth, the camera as the viewers' point of view. It was very unpredictable, and I wanted to go for that type of feel.

To someone who was a fan of those movies, you could see the familiarities right away. But for most people, *The Bernie Mac Show* just seemed naturalistic. It had an effect on them, even if they didn't quite know the references.

Did that New Wave style heighten the show's jokes?

There were many moments you never could have achieved on a three-camera sitcom. You had more at your disposal—more tricks that created truthful moments. Don't forget, the basic premise of this show was that Bernie's sister was on crack cocaine, and Bernie was now in charge of her kids. That's a serious issue. Your heart goes out to these children. I knew if there was an emotional honesty to it—if I treated the subject with pure emotional honesty—I could have Bernie do anything. And, by being honest, I had more leverage when dealing with the darker side of the humor.

There would be no way to write a line like, "When a kid gets one-year-old, you got the right to hit 'em in the throat or stomach," and get away with it if Bernie didn't love those kids—and if that didn't come through for the viewer.

How long did it take for you to notice other sitcoms adopting this approach?

I'd say a couple of years. *Arrested Development* came on after our show, and it used some similar elements, although it had an even more realistic look.

The British version of *The Office* began around the time of our show, and supposedly Stephen [Merchant] and Ricky [Gervais] liked what we had done. The show just blew me away. You believed these characters' emotional lives. You believed these were real people working in a real environment. Hence, the Gervais character [David Brent] could really get away with anything.

Is it more difficult to write jokes for that type of ultra-realistic character, such as David Brent or Bernie Mac? The jokes have to be funny, of course, but also tethered to reality.

I find it easier to write that style of joke, quite frankly. It comes more organically. I find it much more difficult to write the standard style of sitcom joke. It's too artificial. It's much easier to come up with a real response that's genuinely from a character's point of view.

We were criticized by the Fox executives of *The Bernie Mac Show* for that very writing style. Fox wanted a funnier show. They wrote me a memo that said: "No more poignancy." I don't think they liked any episode from that first season. They made me promise to make the show funnier, and I had to beg them to not make the show a gag fest.

We were on at nine o'clock on Wednesdays and we had good, solid ratings for the entire year. But the execs didn't think those numbers were good enough—they felt they should have been much higher. They never understood the show. I think the executives running the Fox network at that time just preferred big, broad fart humor.

Isn't it usually the opposite: that executives want more heart and not as many fart jokes?

They wanted a show like *Welcome Back, Kotter,* where each of the characters would utter the same exact joke every episode. To me, that's not real. Bernie Mac's family wouldn't be cracking jokes each week like Norm did at the bar in *Cheers.*

I was fired in 2003.

From there, you helped develop the American version of *The Office*. The success rate for British comedies remade in America is not very high: *Coupling, Fawlty Towers, Are You Being Served?* These American versions were all disasters.

Greg Daniels [a writer for *SNL, The Simpsons, Seinfeld, King of the Hill*] was the show runner for the American version of *The Office*, and he did a brilliant job of making that show work. I was a consulting producer, which just meant that I was one of the writers for the first two seasons. We knew about those other failures you just mentioned, but we never worked in the negative. We wanted to give the show the authenticity I was talking about earlier—making the characters as real as possible.

How heavily involved were Ricky Gervais and Stephen Merchant in the American version?

Pretty much not. They gave Greg their blessing, and they didn't interfere. They wanted Greg to find his own way of attacking the subject.

The show started out a little shaky; it took time to find its legs.

NBC wanted Greg to shoot the pilot from a script from the British *Office*. I know that Greg did not want to do this, because he wanted to start fresh. It wasn't the best way to break away from the British version. It was only with our second episode, "Diversity Day," when a diversity consultant is brought in for a sensitivity-training workshop, that we had a new script and we really felt we were beginning fresh.

How much does a show such as *The Office* get rewritten? What percentage of your original script ended up on the screen?

The Office gets rewritten a lot. Some sitcoms are rewritten more than others, but Greg is very much into rewriting scripts to make them as good as they can possibly be. It's more work, but it does pay off in the end.

At the very least, the story itself is always broken ahead of time by the writing staff.

What does "broken" mean?

"Breaking the story" means getting the skeleton of it down on paper. Once you have that structure, you can work from it. It's always easier to have that framework ready as soon as possible.

The story comes first, and then the dialogue?

Absolutely.

Does that hold true for all sitcoms?

I can't speak for other sitcoms, but it has certainly held true for every sitcom on which I've been a writer or producer. When I was working on *The PJs,* if the third act didn't work, I'd throw out the entire act. I would do the same thing at *The Bernie Mac Show.* I didn't care about the jokes so much as the story. The jokes are always the easiest to produce.

I would create the bulk of *The Bernie Mac Show* in the editing room. Do you remember the episode in the first season when Bernie takes the kids to church ["Saving Bernie Mac," December 5, 2001]? He's trying to get God into them. But the first act was just too long. We had some good beats in it—meaning those moments that moved the plot along—but that first act just didn't work for me. I gutted pretty much the entire act until there was basically nothing left. It almost immediately went to the second act, but I didn't care. As far as I was concerned, if the first act didn't service the story, it had to be eliminated.

Again, this was in the editing stage, and hopefully you don't have to do that often. It's always much easier to take care of that during the writing stage.

How long do first, second, and third acts typically last in a sitcom?

Not all shows have three acts. But if they do, there's usually what's called a "Teaser" in the very beginning, that will last for about a minute—just a single joke that may or may not be related to the overall plot. The first act is about ten minutes, the second about the same length, and then a third, which might last for one minute.

With *The Office*, Greg overshoots on purpose, to have more to work with. He'll shoot about forty pages of script, which is the equivalent of about forty minutes. That's double what's produced for the typical sitcom.

The first edit will cut the show down to around thirty-five minutes, and then it's edited down further, to twenty-two minutes. That's a lot of material to cut. Keep in mind that it's hard enough to cut down an episode that's five minutes over, let alone twenty. But this allows Greg to have more choices. He can eliminate an entire subplot if it doesn't service his needs for the story.

I'm assuming that a lot of the writers for *The Office* might not be so happy to see their jokes removed.

I would agree with that. But if you want to be successful, you have to learn how to deal with that. These are just jokes. You can always come up with more later. Never become too attached to what you write; otherwise, you'll never survive as a TV comedy writer.

Let's talk about your appearances on *The Daily Show,* as the "Senior Black Correspondent."

When I was first going to appear on the show, Jon [Stewart] wanted me to play a black conservative. I thought that was funny, but I didn't want to be anti- anything; humor runs dry with that attitude. I'd rather speak more in my natural voice. I wanted to sound naturally contrarian, and not as knee-jerk as I could have been. Sometimes I sound more liberal, sometimes more conservative. Who cares, you know? I'd just like to find my particular truth, instead of being pigeonholed. It's less predictable this way. If I'm just a conservative or just a liberal, you know what my stance is going to be on these issues before I even open my mouth.

On one episode in January 2007, you came out against Black History Month. In response to the question, "Don't you feel that Black History Month serves a purpose?" you replied, "Yes—the purpose of making up for centuries of oppression with twenty-eight days of trivia. I'd rather we got casinos."

That came from my own particular grounded reasoning. It wasn't a one-dimensional mockery just for the hell of it. Another black comedian might have said that twenty-eight days is not enough to honor the black experience, but I really think twenty-eight days is *too* much. Maybe there's too much reverence for this sort of thing. I think people would agree with me that it's much better to receive a tax-free casino than an honorary month. I don't think there's much disagreement with that—and the joke becomes richer because of it. There should be no racial loyalty so much as comedy loyalty.

That motto is on my family crest, by the way.

I was going to end this interview by asking if you had any pithy comments, but that was pretty damn pithy.

I like the word "pithy." Pithy's a good word. I'll try to do it justice.

For those young readers looking to get started in a TV-writing career, what advice would you have for them? As a producer, do you look for anything specific with these scripts?

I'm sure other writers and producers would have different opinions on what and what does not work. But for me, in general, I look for a unique voice—maybe something I haven't quite read before in terms of style and imagery. I can point out pretty quickly if this writer has a different point of view. Mediocrity is pretty easy for me to sniff out. Try to write from your experience. Try not to be derivative, like so many writers can be with references to pop culture. Investigate your own life.

Beyond that, only do comedy if you love to do it. I love comedy, and I love to make people laugh. I truly respect the people who came before me and who did it well. It's important to know your history—if only to know what you *shouldn't* be writing.

I never thought I would ever be in the same company with the people I now work with. I recently received an e-mail from David Zucker, a co-writer and co-director of the first *Airplane!* I remember when *Airplane!* came out in 1980. I was like, I could never be this funny as a writer! Now he's sending me an e-mail saying, "Hey, Larry. How's it going?" I thought, Wow. This is just *something*!

I grew up in a middle-class neighborhood, a little down on its heels. For most of my childhood, my father worked as a probation officer. My parents divorced when I was ten. I never graduated college. Things have worked out well.

And they can for you too.

Famous Last Words
(of Advice)

Adam Mansbach, author of five novels and two humor books, including *Go the Fuck to Sleep* [Akashic Books, 2011], and *Seriously, Just Go to Sleep* [Akashic Books, 2012]

When I initially wrote *Go the Fuck to Sleep*, I didn't even intend to publish it. I wrote it as a joke. I sort of wrote it to see if I could tell a story and create a narrative within the given form of a children's book parody. I then sat with the manuscript for awhile and read it to different people, and it went over well. People seemed to like it and they laughed.

Go the Fuck to Sleep was actually not the first book I published. I had been writing novels for ten years, so this was more like my seventh book. My other novels had been published with large publishers—Viking, William Morrow, Random House.

With this new book, I thought, Well, let me show it to Akashic [Books] and to Johnny Temple, its publisher, and see what he thinks—he's a friend, and I know he has kids. I sent it to him; he was the only publisher I sent it to. He thought it was funny and his wife thought it was funny. We had this period of about a month or so when we were sort of on the fence about whether we should publish it. He told me, "This is funny, but I don't know, man, it's not really what we do. And maybe you and I are the only

ones who really think this is funny. Is this going to have a lot of appeal?"
And I said, "I have no fucking idea, Johnny, probably not."

We did a little research, and we took it to a local independent bookstore.
We asked them where they would even stock it—we couldn't even figure
that much out. We said, "Clearly, this doesn't go in the Children's section,
but where *does* it go?" And they looked at it and said, "Oh, we would put
this in the Parenting section." And Johnny and I were like, "Oh, there's
a Parenting section!" It was only at that point that we decided to even go
through with it.

If your primary need is getting an advance that allows you to pay
your rent for the next year, you may be better off trying to sell your book
to a big publisher. If you've got other sources of income, then you might
be better off getting your money on the back end or as profit sharing.
Akashic and other small publishers do this. You sacrifice that upfront
money for possibly a little more money to be rewarded on the back end.
They have to hustle. But that being said, not all small publishers hustle.
Akashic is the best at what they do, they're the best small publisher in the
country, and I've worked with others who don't pay you *and* don't do shit
for you. A small publisher doesn't necessarily mean an invested or smart
publisher, it just means they're small because they're not big. But Akashic
is small to a purpose.

One of the great things that a small publisher can do is move with a
lot more agility than a big one. And when *Go the Fuck to Sleep* did blow up,
we were able to make decisions very quickly and leanly. There wasn't a lot
of bureaucracy. If I was doing it at, say, Random House, I would have said
to an editor, "Hey, I have an idea for a book. So let me tell you about it,
and then let me wait while you run it past your boss, and then let me wait
some more while your boss thinks about it and just puts it in a stack of
things and then runs it by two publicists and a marketing director." With
this book, we were able to move fast, get it accepted, published, and then
keep up with demand, keep up with publicity. We found a way to quickly
publish it by Father's Day [on June 19, 2011]. So that was great.

I have nothing but praise for Akashic, and I can't say that about any
other publisher I've ever worked with. There's literally nothing I wish they
would've done differently with this book. Sticking with a small press really

turned out to be the right move. When it started to gain attention before it was even printed, there were a lot of big publishers who tried to buy it out from under Akashic. They were throwing large numbers at us. They were trying to play "big bank take little bank." The Amazon page had also just gone up, so this enormous viral buzz began, and by the end of that week the book was number one on Amazon—despite no copies even being available yet! These were all only pre-orders. So this led to a lot of media.

There was a sort of moment where I was like, "Shit, should I take one of these offers from the big publishers? Should we get some money here?" We had no way of knowing whether or not the book was going to have any legs. It hadn't been published yet, and we were not sure if it was going to have any life to it, or whether it was a kind of incidental moment that we should cash out on and make the most of. But had we done that, I'd have been kicking myself for the rest of my life. We would have been cutting ourselves off at the legs, taking the short money and not riding it out and not believing in it. So it's a very good thing I stayed with Akashic.

I think the biggest misconception that people have about writing as a profession is that they mystify it and romanticize it, and there's a lot of romance and myth in the culture surrounding writing. Writers have made themselves these eccentric artist figures. And the truth is that every real writer I know, every professional person who makes a living at writing, treats it like a job. We're not waiting for inspiration to strike. We're not bullshitting. We're in the chair writing every day. And we're making business decisions. And some days are more successful than others, but it's about stamina and persistence. And that's assuming that you *have* some talent. You've got to do the work, you've got to read voraciously, you've got to put in hours and build up your ability to sit in that chair and do the work.

Jack Handey

Jack Handey has an unusual problem. His name is so famous that most people don't believe he actually exists. They assume he's a marketing creation, fabricated in order to give an identity to one of comedy's longest running, consistent franchises. "Deep Thoughts by Jack Handey," which became a staple on *Saturday Night Live* during the nineties, sounds like something that was invented by a team of writers, not an actual guy named Jack who, unlike almost every other writer to work at *SNL*, was better than average at self-promotion.

"Deep Thoughts" first appeared in *National Lampoon* in 1982, but it was *Saturday Night Live* that introduced "Deep Thoughts" to a wider audience, transforming Handey, or at least his supposed nom de plume, into the realm of comedy immortality. Each segment would begin with New Age–y music played over shots of soothing and idyllic nature scenes. In a calm, reassuring voice, Handey would read what at first appeared to be a saccharine-sweet aphorism. As the text scrolled across the screen, that aphorism would turn bizarre, and then, more often than not, sinister.

"Deep Thoughts" were essentially one-liners without the corniness of a Borscht Belt routine. It could involve fond memories of a father killed by a clown, or making children cry because they think Disneyland had burned down, or a reminder that laughter won't cure tuberculosis, or the difference between boxing and ballet (hitting), or why it's okay to cut down trees if they scream all the time, for no good reason. At the very least, "Deep Thoughts" proved, beyond a shadow of a doubt, that almost anything is funny if it ends with the chestnut: "And also, you're drunk."

Handey, born and raised in Texas, first attempted to become a professional writer at the *San Antonio Express-News*, but he quickly learned that he lacked the un-ironic sensibilities for serious journalism. He was eventually hired as a writer for *Saturday Night Live*, first in 1975 and then, after leaving the show for a few years, again in 1985. When "Deep Thoughts" became a hit—which led to four best-selling books, including *Deep Thoughts* (1992), *Deeper Thoughts: All New, All Crispy* (1993), *Deepest Thoughts: So Deep They Squeak* (1994) and *The Lost Deep Thoughts: Don't Fight the Deepness* (1998)— Handey expanded his comedy vision to such *SNL* recurring bits as "Fuzzy Memories," which depicted disturbing recollections from a fictional childhood, and "My Big Thick Novel," which were short excerpts from a supposedly thousand-plus page book. He was also responsible for such popular skits as "Unfrozen Caveman Lawyer" (1991–96), "Happy Fun Ball" (1991), and "Toonces the Driving Cat" (introduced in 1989, and named after one of Handey's actual cats).

After leaving *Saturday Night Live,* in 2002, Handey started writing essays for *The New Yorker,* but he never veered far from the comedy terrain of "Deep Thoughts." His pieces—recently published in the Hyperion collection *What I'd Say to the Martians and Other Veiled Threats* (2008)—typically began with a predictable cliché taken into demented, unexpected directions. "Eventually, I believe, everything evens out," he wrote in one of his more popular *New Yorker* pieces. "Long ago, an asteroid hit our planet and killed our dinosaurs. But, in the future, maybe we'll go to another planet and kill their dinosaurs."

Weirdly enough, the world might never have discovered Jack Handey if it weren't for another comedy genius, Steve Martin. During the early seventies, they were neighbors in Santa Fe, New Mexico, long before either had accomplished any discernable success. Martin recognized Handey's unique comedy gifts—"Instead of going one leap forward," Martin told *USA Today*, "[Jack] goes about three leaps forward"—and hired Handey to write jokes for his stand-up act, including his 1980 TV special, *Comedy Is Not Pretty*. Handey penned one of Martin's most memorable routines, called "What I Believe." With mock sincerity, Martin talked about his personal philosophy, which included such inexplicable tenets as never referring to a woman's breasts as "winnebagos" or "golden bozos," and his realization that it was a mistake to buy a "thirty-story, one-bedroom apartment."

How did you first meet Steve Martin?

I was living in a 150-year-old adobe house on Upper Canyon Road in Santa Fe, New Mexico. I think I was twenty-three or twenty-four. This was in the early seventies, when I was working as a reporter for the *New Mexican*. The house had been cut in half. I lived on one side, and Steve Martin lived on the other side. He would come over and play his banjo.

What was Steve Martin doing in Sante Fe? I thought he was raised in California.

I think he was looking to get out of L.A. for a while, and he liked using Santa Fe as a base. He was traveling a lot, performing at Playboy Clubs and other clubs around the country. He wasn't famous yet.

He had already been a television writer for *The Smothers Brothers Comedy Hour* [CBS, 1967–69], but he was now focusing on his stand-up act.

Was his stand-up persona already firmly in place, or was it still evolving?

I told him, "Instead of a spear through the head, Steve, what about an arrow? It's lighter and not as unwieldy." No, I'm guessing his comedy character was pretty much developed by then. A few years after I met him, I moved to San Antonio, Texas, and one night I saw Steve performing on *The Tonight Show*. I said, "Hey, my neighbor!"

I sent Steve some samples of my humor column and asked if I could write for him. He liked my material and said yes. Later, when he got his first NBC television special, *Steve Martin: A Wild and Crazy Guy* [November 22, 1978], he called me out to L.A. to work on it. It was the proverbial "lucky break."

Steve's material was brilliantly funny and a true breakthrough. It was silly and stupid, which a lot of comedy people are afraid of. They'd rather do satire, with a capital *S*. I've never liked that sort of humor.

Did you contribute jokes to any of Steve Martin's albums?

The only album I contributed to was Steve's last, *The Steve Martin Brothers* [Warner Bros., 1981]. One of the jokes I wrote was "I believe that sex is one of the most beautiful, natural, and wholesome things that money can buy."

How would you define Steve Martin's sensibility? It's aged very well and, to this day, seems quite modern. I'm thinking not just of his stand-up act but his first book, 1979's *Cruel Shoes*. One sees the influences from that book on, among other publications, *McSweeney's*.

What's great about Steve's sensibility is that it appeals to smart people and dumb people alike. That, to me, is the best comedy.

I think *Cruel Shoes* is hilarious. Seeing very short, almost cryptic comedy bits like that probably influenced me to write "Deep Thoughts."

How did "Deep Thoughts" get started on *SNL* in 1991?

Originally, it started in print, as a kind of parody of sensitive, diary-type writings. I had several published in the eighties in a college magazine called *Ampersand*, and also in *National Lampoon* and George Meyer's *Army Man* magazine. Later, they began to appear on *Saturday Night Live*.

Did you feel that you had a backlog of jokes that needed an outlet and "Deep Thoughts" could be it?

No, it was always its own thing. And I tried and tried to get them published as a book, with no luck. I have a folder full of rejection slips. I realized that a way to have them seen—and subsequently published—was to put them on TV. I worked on *SNL*, so why not?

How do you know when a Deep Thought works? Do you show it to anyone else? Or does it just ring true?

It's weird, but I'm not a very good judge of "Deep Thoughts." The ones I think are great usually turn out to be not very good. And the ones that I think are okay—or pretty good—are usually the ones that people really enjoy.

What are some of the ones you think work?

One I've always liked is: "Anytime I see something screech across a room and latch onto someone's neck, and the guy screams and tries to get it off, I have to laugh, because what *is* that thing?!" Or: "Consider the daffodil. And while you're doing that, I'll be over here, looking through your stuff."

There are others, but I'm forgetting them. I'll e-mail them to you.[1]

How high is your attrition rate for jokes?

For "Deep Thoughts," the attrition rate is about ten written to one chosen. On a good day, I can write six or seven.

Can you give me some that have failed?

There have been so many clunkers, it's hard to isolate just a few. The main reason they didn't work is they didn't get a laugh. Seriously—for me, sometimes a joke or a piece fails because it's too intentionally dark or weird. Weird doesn't equal funny.

Was there a reluctance at first on Lorne Michaels's part to put "Deep Thoughts" on *SNL?*

Yes. I think there was a feeling that a writer shouldn't have his signature on his work. I wrote some good sketches for the show, bided my time, and eventually was given "Deep Thoughts." It turned out to be pretty popular, and they were eventually published in four book collections.

---

1 Jack Handey's Favorite Deep Thoughts:

> If you define cowardice as running away at the first sign of danger, screaming and tripping and begging for mercy, then yes, Mister Brave Man, I guess I am a coward.

> To me, it's a good idea to always carry two sacks of something when you walk around. That way, if anybody says, "Hey, can you give me a hand?" you can say, "Sorry, got these sacks."

> You know what would make a good story? Something about a clown who makes people happy, but inside he's really sad. Also, he has severe diarrhea.

Most *SNL* viewers don't know which writers are responsible for which specific sketch or joke. But you and Robert Smigel seemed to be the exceptions—both of your names are front and center. Was this one of the advantages to "Deep Thoughts"?

I wasn't trying to get my name out there, so much as to get "Deep Thoughts" on the air. And, ironically, a lot of people think Jack Handey is a made-up name—a character the show created.

How did you get the job at *SNL?*

I first worked for a prime-time version of *Saturday Night Live* called *The New Show*. This was in 1984 on NBC. Steve Martin had recommended me to Lorne Michaels, the producer. I gave up a great house I had been renting in L.A., confident the show was going to be a big hit and I'd be in New York forever. But it was a huge bomb. The show had a great cast, and just an *amazing* writing staff—people like James Downey, Al Franken, Tom Davis, Buck Henry, Max Pross, Tom Gammill, and George Meyer, who later went on to write for *The Simpsons*.

Do you remember any of the sketches George Meyer wrote for *The New Show*?

He wrote one sketch I loved about a guy who realizes he's been drugged: "Been drugged ... must get help ...." Along the way he meets other people who, coincidentally, also sound like they've been drugged, but actually haven't: "You drugged, too?" "No ... from Portugal ... English not so good." Another guy staggers as if he's been drugged, but it's just that his shoes are too tight.

Later, when we were both at *SNL,* George wrote a piece that got huge laughs at read-through. It was a radio version of *The Road Warrior,* in which the characters had to clumsily describe the action, because it was on the radio. That piece never made it to air. A lot of George's material, like mine, was relegated to the last fifteen minutes of the show—or didn't get on at all.

George has a truly astonishing comedy mind. He can magically come up with a great, out-of-the-blue joke. I wrote a piece at *SNL* about salmon migrating upstream. Two salmon were talking about how hard it was to get over a waterfall. George's line was to have one salmon say: "I think the key is you can't be afraid to look stupid." How do you come up with a line like that?

George and I shared an office at *The New Show*. Our office was in the old Brill Building on Broadway, overlooking the Winter Garden Theatre. *Cats* was playing then, and every night a parade of limos would pull up front. One night, George looked out and said, "Look—the pigs are coming to see the cats."

Do you remember any of the *New Show* sketches you wrote?

I wrote one sketch called "No Camera," about a couple who forget their camera, then see all kinds of weird, photographable things: Bigfoot, Jackie Onassis, Hitler swordfighting with an angel. That sketch went to dress rehearsal three times, with three different sets of hosts, before it finally got on. I think the low point was when the sketch was being performed by Paul Simon and his then wife, Carrie Fisher. There was a technical screwup and they were both just standing on the set waiting. Paul Simon turned to the audience and said, "Don't blame me—*I* didn't write this." The piece finally got on another show when Candice Bergen and Buck Henry co-hosted.

The New Show, from what I've read, had some very funny and clever moments. Why didn't it last beyond nine episodes?

Low ratings. At the time, there were only sixty-five or so prime-time network shows on the air, and I think we'd usually come in sixty-fifth. It was a good show, but if there's one thing I've learned about TV comedy, it's that people don't like sketch comedy in prime time. *In Living Color* was the exception that proves the rule. Also, *The Carol Burnett Show*. So I guess what I'm saying is that people love sketch comedy in prime time. No, I'm sticking with my first pompous statement.

That the show even lasted as long as it did was probably due to Lorne's influence with the network. One bad thing about *The New Show* was that it was not live, like *SNL*. So if there was a screwup, you could retape things. Sometimes we'd end up shooting a sketch three or four times, and the audience would get bored, and the actors would try new lines, because the audience had already heard the original jokes. So, eventually, the audience would just get up and leave. I remember one of the writers, Tom Gammill, once yelling after them: "Go on, get out of here, you quitters!" That really made me laugh.

After *The New Show* failed, I moved back to L.A. and worked on some other projects, including Michael Nesmith's very funny show, *Television Parts* [NBC, 1985]—once again, a good sketch show in prime time that didn't get renewed. When Lorne Michaels came back to *SNL* in 1985, he and producers Franken and Davis hired me to join them there.

Was Michael O'Donoghue still writing for *SNL* when you joined? He originally left in 1978, but returned in 1981 to become head writer.

Michael had left again when I joined the show, but Cheryl Hardwick, who was the musical director at *SNL*, was married to Michael. And after read-through, she'd take the scripts home to him. She later told me Michael liked my material—I was thrilled—and they invited me over to their apartment. Michael was an amazingly funny writer, yet he also had this fearsome reputation of cutting people apart with withering remarks. But when I met him, he was very nice.

He and Cheryl once invited me and my wife, Marta, to a Halloween party at his place. Cheryl played the piano, and people recited Poe—it was all very intellectual. Then Michael O'Donoghue stood up and announced that everyone was now going to witness the unveiling of a new, wonderful painting by a young artist, who was then introduced. I thought, Oh, no. He's making fun of this poor guy.

Michael said the name of the painting was *Desi Arnaz as a Young Man*. With a flourish, the painting was unveiled, and there, indeed, was a large oil painting of a young Desi Arnaz, sitting nude on a chair, facing the viewer—only instead of male genitalia he had a big vagina. There was an audible gasp from the entire room. It was a pretty professional-looking painting, actually.

I barely knew Michael, but he was an incredibly gifted comedy writer. Aggressive, dark comedy, when it works, is really the best. And he knew how to do it.

Did you work closely with James Downey, *SNL's* head writer, for many years?

I did. Jim is not only a great comedy writer, but that rarest of things: a great comedy producer and editor. His influence in getting funny material on the air, from the mid-eighties to the mid-nineties, was enormous. He has a very eclectic sense of humor—much more so than mine—and if he thought something was funny he would champion it. It made you so happy if Jim sparked to an idea of yours.

Here's an example of how Jim's mind works: He once went to one of those places in Times Square where you can choose your own headline and have it printed on the front page of a fake newspaper. So Jim had one made up to read something like "CITY COUNCIL TABLES REZONING RESOLUTION."

The guy at the fake-newspaper shop was explaining to him, "No, no, you want it to say something like JACK'S BIRTHDAY CANDLES START FOREST FIRE.

Jim remained unconvinced. He really is a stunningly smart and charming guy, as well as being flat-out funny.

Do you have any favorite sketches you wrote for *SNL*?

One of my favorites is "Unfrozen Caveman Lawyer."

Sometimes you can't tell if a sketch is any good or not. And sometimes you feel as if you're hitting a "sweet spot." That was a sweet-spot piece.

What other *SNL* sketches of yours do you think hit the sweet spot?

Probably "Toonces, the Cat Who Could Drive a Car," "Tarzan, Tonto & Frankenstein," and "Happy Fun Ball."

The "Happy Fun Ball" commercial parody from 1991 was very influential. The format is used by humorists to this day: A short, dry setup ("The toy sensation that's sweeping the nation!") and then a long list of repercussions ("Do not taunt Happy Fun Ball"; "If Happy Fun Ball begins to smoke, get away immediately. Seek shelter and cover head").

Another sweet-spot piece. Unfortunately, it's all too common to *not* hit the sweet spot.

I also loved to write sketches that had anything to do with James Bond. Comedy writers just love James Bond.

Why is that?

I don't really know. Maybe because he's so macho, or because he's such a serious type of character. Abe Lincoln is a very serious character and is also a favorite of comedy writers. Both are bigger than life. And, of course, both drink martinis and drive fast cars.

What was it about "Unfrozen Caveman Lawyer" that you liked so much? Was it Phil Hartman's performance?

Phil Hartman was a writer's dream, because he could play anything. Sometimes certain cast members would be "light" in the show, meaning they didn't have much to do. But Phil was never light—he was so versatile. And he never got flustered. You could go to him in the makeup room a minute or so before the sketch and tell him you had changed certain lines, and he was always cool with that.

Phil was just amazingly talented.

Were there any sketches for *SNL* that you felt didn't come off as you envisioned—where you were unhappy with the result?

Many of them. The obvious fault of most of them was "This idea is not funny" or "These jokes are not funny." Sometimes the set or prop or a sound effect would not be what you had envisioned, or there were technical glitches, like a window that was painted shut that a character was supposed to open. Or you forgot to change something on the cue cards, so the actors were standing there helpless while you were already having a beer backstage, feeling like a moron.

When Andrew Dice Clay hosted [May 12, 1990], I wrote a piece having him explain sex to his young son. The joke was that he used overly graphic terms. At first the censors were okay with it, but when he did a dirtier-than-expected monologue, they decided to cut words out of my piece. The show was on a five-second delay, just for Clay. So they started bleeping out words, manually, as the sketch was going—but that's not easy to do, and one of the "dirty" words slipped by. Jim Downey shouted: "One of our planes got through!"

Some writers, such as Harry Shearer and Bob Odenkirk, have been very critical of the creative process at _SNL_. They've said that _SNL_ isn't a writer's show. But you seem to have a different take. You've said that _SNL_ is a show where writers are never forcibly rewritten.

I don't like to be rewritten, and I don't like to write for characters I didn't create. _SNL_ is probably one of the few shows where a staff writer can achieve that freedom. Maybe it's changed somewhat now, but Lorne was always very good about protecting writers and giving them creative freedom. And it was very smart of him, too, because he knew that writers would really dig deep and work hard if they controlled their own work.

Writers were never made to change pieces, or even cut them down. It might be suggested they do so, but they weren't forced. I once wrote an _SNL_ sketch called "Dad's Sore Big Toe" [February 15, 1986], starring Jerry Hall, Mick Jagger's then girlfriend. The premise was that Randy Quaid had a sore big toe, but he stupidly kept wanting the toe to get hit: "Son, why don't you use that hammer to pound a nail in that loose floorboard, right there by my sore toe." I came up with an absurd ending that wasn't really logical, but it made me laugh. Jerry Hall says, "Your father has gone and hung himself." The ending made absolutely no sense, which is why I laughed so hard backstage, along with some other writers. But Mick Jagger, who's a friend of Lorne's, lobbied hard to get that ending changed. Lorne never did force me to change it. It went on as written.

Another important thing with _SNL_ writers is that they cast their own pieces. You would never see "Fireman #1" in the script. The producers would never cast an actor to play the fireman—the writers did that. The script would read "Mike Myers" or "Phil Hartman." That gave the writers tremendous power. The cast had to be nice to us.

Fred Wolf, a writer friend from _SNL_, was once talking about all the crazy studio notes he now receives as a screenwriter in Hollywood. "_SNL_ was the best job I ever had," he said.

How did you make the jump from writing for television to writing humor for *The New Yorker?*

I have always written print humor. It was my first love. It's the only place where you have control and your name is on it. Before *The New Yorker*, I had done humor pieces for *National Lampoon*, *Playboy*, *Los Angeles* magazine, the *Los Angeles Times*, and lots of other newspapers.

I was editor of my high-school paper, and I received a journalism scholarship. But I was always more interested in writing my humor column than reporting. The column was called "Witty Words to Whittle By." My friend Rob Meek came up with the name. How or why I started writing humor is a mystery to me. Maybe it was to try to be popular. But why humor? How did that come out? Comedy writers and comedians tend to be obsessive-compulsives, which you may have noticed. I also am prone to that. So maybe that's where it comes from—just bad brain wiring that allows one to make weird chemical connections one normally wouldn't make. Hence, jokes. Of course, the downside is it makes you check your alarm clock eight times before falling asleep.

Is OCD a condition you've noticed with many other humor writers? When I spoke with David Sedaris, he mentioned how badly he suffered, and still suffers, from the condition.

I don't know that I'd call it "common" among comedy writers, but I can think of at least four or five others who have it.

How long does it take you to write a typical Shouts & Murmurs piece for *The New Yorker?*

A long time. The hard part is coming up with the ideas, letting the ideas simmer, then going back and seeing if there's anything there.

Specifically, how long are we talking about?

It can take months or even years for an idea to click. I am usually suspicious of any idea of mine that I love right away.

How much rewriting goes into a typical Shouts piece?

Quite a bit. I usually start a piece by writing notes—just a bunch of jokes. I'll spend three or four days doing that. The jokes don't usually change, but *which* jokes are used can change. That's often how I can tell how good a premise it is—how easily the jokes come.

The piece itself usually goes through at least a few drafts. I think it was Ernest Hemingway who said writing is rewriting. And he was a hilarious guy.

Ironically—and this is true of sketches too—the better the idea, the less editing and punching up is usually required. My editor at *The New Yorker*, Susan Morrison, edits with a light hand, which is nice.

How often are you unable to complete a *New Yorker piece* after starting?

Most of them go someplace—sometimes just not to a very amusing place.

And how often is a piece of yours rejected by *The New Yorker?*

Maybe a third. Maybe half. When I first started sending them pieces, back in the eighties, they rejected my first eight or ten submissions. Finally, a very nice editor there, Dan Menaker, sort of took me by the hand and gave me some tips. My next piece got in.

Any last words of advice for those readers looking to break into humor writing?

If you spontaneously come up with funny things—and I mean *writing* funny things, not just saying them—and if other people seem to like them, then consider humor writing. Also, don't kill anyone. When people see "murderer," they automatically think it's probably not funny. That's just the way people are.

Larry Gelbart

Larry Gelbart's Seven Tips to Becoming a Successful Writer

1. Be sure to get to your desk as early as you can and make as many unnecessary phone calls as possible.

2. Check your e-mail and respond at length to anything unimportant.

3. Honor all requests for your autographed photo from anywhere in Poland or India, where you are obviously a star.

4. Thoroughly clean your keyboard and monitor.

5. Go over yesterday's output.

6. Lunch.

7. Nap. (You're not a machine, you know.)

Larry Gelbart became a legend by finding comedic fodder in subjects most people would not consider inherently funny: war, religion, Dustin Hoffman in mascara. Throughout a career that's lasted fifty years—an anniversary that eludes many of even the best of marriages—Gelbart has proven to be one of comedy's rare Renaissance men, responsible for groundbreaking work in every conceivable genre, from TV and radio to Broadway and cinema.

While a teenager in the late 1940s, Gelbart was already writing gags for the likes of such major talents as Bob Hope, Jack Paar and Danny Thomas. Less than ten years later, Gelbart joined the now mythical writing staff of *Caesar's Hour*. Along with Woody Allen, Mel Brooks, Carl Reiner, and Neil (and Danny) Simon, Gelbart was part of a team that many consider to be the finest in the history of television.

The comedy scene soon turned sour for Gelbart, however. In the late fifties he quit Hollywood and moved to England, frustrated over Communist blacklisting. But he returned in the sixties to write a success-ful Broadway play, *A Funny Thing Happened on the Way to the Forum*, and to revolutionize television yet again.

When CBS hired Gelbart in 1972 to create the pilot for a TV adap-tation of Robert Altman's 1970 comedy *M*A*S*H*, he could have easily gotten away with a few warmed-over jokes about the Korean War. Instead, he turned the series into a comedic commentary on the horrors of com-bat—portraying death, surgery, and madness in ways that had mostly been ignored or glossed over by network television. Gelbart continued his creative winning streak into the next decade, writing scripts for *"Oh, God!"* (1977) and *Tootsie* (1982), and, in the process, was nominated for two Academy Awards.

Gelbart continues to write every day, working toward perfecting a skill that many would think he had perfected long ago.

You once said that, as a writer, one's style is formed by what one *can't* do. How did you come to this conclusion? Were there different styles of comedy that you dealt with that were more difficult than others?

I should have said "subject" instead of "style." This would be the subject matter, rather than the style, of a comedy piece. Experience has taught me that what seems like a slam dunk rarely makes the most success-ful finished product. While confidence is always a comfort, risk provides a good deal more adrenaline. The project that requires me to learn about characters I've never met is the kind I enjoy the most. I'm always drawn to those subjects least likely associated with comedy, such as war, or God, or finance—in other words, subjects that I'll have to wrestle with. I want to go to places I've never been before, in a sense. If my interest is piqued, perhaps audiences' will be, too.

Are there any specific examples in which this happened? Where you took on a difficult subject for the challenge?

I was referring to *M*A*S*H* and *"Oh, God!"* And even *A Funny Thing Happened on the Way to the Forum,* which was timeless in its depiction of human frailties but required massive research on ancient Rome—years before HBO discovered it.

A Funny Thing Happened on the Way to the Forum **is such an intricate work. How do you visualize a project like that? The summary of the play, alone, can run more than a full page.**

At the risk of making it all seem somewhat metaphysical, you usually see things in your head, even before you're able to capture it in writing—whether it's a movie or a television show or, in this case, a stage show. You are watching it before anybody else does. You can visualize it. You see the characters; you see the situations, you get it. In my case, I saw it day and night for about five years. The problem, of course, is how to get what you see in your head onto the screen or stage.

Has this become any easier for you throughout the years?

I think so. I mean, after a while it's not so much a question of "Can I do this?" It becomes more a case of, *"When* I do this." You get better at the craft. Your talent for writing may not be sharpened, or your originality. None of that has anything to do with craft.

If practice doesn't make perfect, then it certainly can hone your ability to do the things you want to do. For instance, needing to get the feel of a scene. How do you know when a particular one is finished? You may not need three pages to get across what you need to get across. Half a page will do the same thing. Or even just a single sentence. Or even one word—if it's just *juste* enough.

I keep thinking of what Miles Davis said about his style of jazz. He said, "It's what you *don't* play, you know." However pretentious it might sound, I think of writing as a kind of music. A writer, like a musician, can hit the melody—and at just the right tempo—with precisely the right amount of whatever sense or nonsense is needed.

With comedy, would the jokes be the equivalent of the melody?

The plot is the melody and the jokes are the grace notes. I tend to think in those terms a lot. I think about how much less equipment a writer of dialogue has as compared to what's in a music composer's toolbox. Writers are, by comparison, impoverished. We have to work with what we have.

How old were you when you first started writing professionally?

Sixteen.

That's a very young age to earn a living as a humor writer.

It helped that I was the product of two *shtetls*. I learned jokes from my father, but I learned humor through my mother.

My father was a barber in Chicago for years and years before the family moved to California in the early 1940s. He quickly built up a huge clientele of famous people—and a number of infamous ones as well. Even before we moved out West, he had shampooed and pampered the heads of a good many notable people. The list is extraordinary. Not only was he cutting the hair of people like John F. Kennedy but he had also, strangely enough, been Jack Ruby's barber back in Chicago in the forties. At that time, Ruby was known as "Sparky Rubenstein," his nickname serving as an acknowledgment of his quick temper.

Did the Warren Commission know about all this?

If my father had been working in Texas, I'm sure he would have also been Lee Harvey Oswald's barber. Judging by his photos, Oswald could have used a far better one.

My father knew every joke anybody ever told. That was his currency as a barber—jokes. It was very hard to tell my father a funny story that he didn't already know. And he was great at telling them. He was wonderful at it.

On the other hand, my mother had a really ironic, and sometimes needling, wit. It was from her, I believe, that I inherited whatever talent

I may have for deflating a painful situation by turning something inside out; by making comedy a kind of victory. Where you have, maybe, not the last laugh but the *only* laugh about something. That I got from her.

The first thing my mother did when she arrived in America, from Poland, at the age of fifteen, was to take a job behind a sewing machine in some Chicago sweatshop. I don't think she ever realized her full potential. She was stuck. Her wit was akin to prison or gallows humor; it was always slightly dipped in acid. I just hope she knew what a good audience she had in me.

Can you give me an example of a joke your father would tell versus a joke your mother would tell?

My father would have told a joke like "A bum came up to me and asked for a bite, so I bit him." My mother would probably have just made some smart-ass comment like, "*Anybody* can be a bum today."

What was their first language?

Yiddish. Neither of my parents could write in English, although my father tried to later in life. I actually didn't speak English until I was about five. People who switch to another language tend to treat it with much more curiosity. The second language is fresher to them, and they see more potential for expression in this new tongue.

Wasn't it your father who helped you get your first job?

He did, yes. One of his Hollywood clients was Danny Thomas, who, in the early forties, was appearing on the *Maxwell House Coffee Time* radio show. Danny had about a seven- or eight-minute section on each program, in which he played the role of Jerry Dingle, the Mailman. The character was a Walter Mitty type.

My father would shave Thomas every Sunday afternoon before the program, at the CBS studios. I had written some material in high school: talent shows, sketches, that sort of thing. My father took it upon himself to tell Thomas that he thought his son could be a comedy writer—without ever bothering to tell his son what the hell he was up to. Thomas, being a nice guy, told my father to have me write something so that he might judge for himself. Thomas liked what I came up with and gave it to the show's head writer, Mac Benoff. Mac thought enough about what I wrote to ask, "Why don't you stop by my house after school and work with me?" So, for the next couple of months, I would finish my last class and, still in my R.O.T.C. uniform, stop by to see Mac and learn how to put a radio show together.

What was that first script you showed to Danny Thomas?

Each week, Thomas's character would deliver a package to a dentist, or he would deliver a letter to an architect, and he would invariably be insulted by that person. Very paranoid, Thomas's character would then mutter to himself something like, "Architect, big deal! I could've been an architect!" Harp music would break in and Thomas would become "Jerry Dingle, world-famous architect."

So I wrote a sketch, not too cleverly, but certainly understandably, about Thomas being insulted by a barber. He then dreamt out loud about how he could become "Jerry Dingle, world-famous barber." It was good enough, I guess.

I worked with Mac for two months or so until an agent from the William Morris Agency, a wonderful man named George Gruskin, asked me, "Would you like to do more of this?" Naturally I said yes. George got me onto a radio show called *Duffy's Tavern*, that took place in a bar. I stayed on that show for two years, at a salary of $50 a week.

I'm not familiar with *Duffy's Tavern*.

The show had no running jokes; no relationship jokes. It was very light on story. Really, it was just words, words, words. *Duffy's* relied on a lot of writer tricks: malapropisms and spoonerisms and a few other –isms. Jokes like "This is just a mucus of an idea" or "Let's not jump to seclusion." We'd also write a type of a joke that we'd call a "bull," which would be something like "I don't need any help being stupid." In other words, the character would think he was making a point, but he was really denigrating himself.

I soon got to see what was possible to do with words—how you could bend them, twist them, augment them, play with them endlessly, using words as though each one were a trampoline. I learned that each could be the basis for a wider expression beyond the word's definition.

It was a lesson that was to last a lifetime. If you just listen to an episode of M*A*S*H—not watch it, just listen—it's not a bad radio show at all.

How much material would you and the other writers have to produce for these radio shows over the course of a season?

We had to write a tremendous amount of material. In those days, a radio season was thirty-nine programs a year.

Was this good training for you later in your career—your having to produce a lot of material so quickly?

Invaluable. I notice with some television shows these days that writers do not have to, or are unable to, create a new episode every week. There'll be a repeat, or some other show will be broadcast in its place. Well, nobody ever stood in front of a microphone in the early days of radio and said, "I'm sorry, but we don't have a show this week. So why don't you just listen to this instead?"

But what a great experience! It all seemed so normal then. Now, when I see a sixteen- or a seventeen-year-old kid, I think, My God! At that point in my own life, I was sitting down with grown-ups and writing grown-up material.

I wasn't just some kind of mascot. I was a contributing member of the staff. It must have been a kick for them. It was certainly much more fun for them to have me around than someone they perceived to be a real threat.

How did you start writing for Bob Hope?

I was drafted at eighteen, and when I got out of the army, I teamed up with a writer named Larry Marks, and we went to work for Jack Paar—then starring in his first radio show—and then eventually for Bob Hope. Hope wanted to give us $1,250 each.

So this was $1,250 a year?

No, a week.

A week? What year was this?

This was in 1946. Eighteen and single. Just thinking about it now makes my mouth water. I worked for Hope for four years at that salary, and I never took that job for granted—believe me.

What was it like to write for Bob Hope? He's such a pure joke comedian. You must have been required to come up with thousands upon thousands of jokes.

The most important thing for Hope, always, always, *always,* was the monologue. Whatever else he achieved in his career, he always considered himself primarily a monologist. The writers would look at what was going on in the world—current events, such as Bing Crosby having another son, or maybe it was the World Series, or maybe it was Oscar time. There were also political jokes, but they weren't very barbed. Hope never had any interest in drawing blood. He was very scrupulous at that point in his life about not siding with one political party or the other.

A few teams of writers made up the staff. Each team would write twenty jokes or so on each monologue topic. At a staff meeting, Hope would then read everyone's jokes aloud; hundreds of them. He'd put a check mark next to any joke that he liked. He'd then read them all over again. If he still liked a previously checked-off joke, he'd make a slanting strike through the check mark so that it looked like an "X" with a hook on the left. If he didn't like the joke the second time through, he just drew a line through it, and the joke hit the wastebasket.

Then he would read all the material a third time, and if he *still* liked a joke, he would put a circle around it. Those jokes that survived all three readings were then separated and stapled together and put into some kind of a sequence that would form that week's monologue—which is not to say that he would remain completely satisfied. He might call a writer anytime during the week and say, "Look, I don't like that one joke. Can we get a bigger kid"—he would call his jokes "kids"—"Can we get a bigger kid for that spot?"

Almost as if he thought of them as his own children.

What do you mean "almost"? He saw these kids far more often than he saw his own.

Hope's delivery was so strong. Even if he delivered an unfunny joke, it would become funny just through the sheer force of his personality.

I remember, in the late forties, being backstage at a theater in Blackpool, England. I was with a date, and Bob told a joke with the word *motel* in the punch line. The audience roared, and so did my British date. "Do you even know what a motel is?" I asked her. When she said she didn't, I asked her why she was laughing. Her answer was "I don't know! He's just funny!"

Very often Hope's writers would find ourselves in these remote places—in Alaska or in Okinawa—just weird places. We couldn't travel with a lot of actors on those tours. So, occasionally the writers would be called upon to play characters onstage with Hope. These were roles that would have been assigned to professional actors had we been back in Hollywood. I remember the first time I performed with Hope, each of us standing behind his own live microphone. I delivered my line, and Hope came back with his line, and I felt as though I had been knocked back physically. The power of his delivery was amazing. If Jack Benny was the Fred Astaire of comedy, then Bob Hope was its Jimmy Cagney.

Were you always on call with him?

At any time of the day or night. He'd call you up and casually ask if you had a valid passport ready, because you'd be going to London with him in a day or two—or Alaska or Berlin or Texas. I wrote jokes everywhere, all over the world. I wrote jokes in jeeps, huts, airplanes. It was fantastic training. Just the fact that I had gone to Korea with him during the police action was enormously helpful years later when I got to do *M*A*S*H*.

Were you with Hope when he made the transition from radio to television?

I was. It was a very rough transition. The writers all thought that television was radio with funny hats. We'd send Bob out in front of the cameras with a funny fifty-gallon cowboy hat and a dozen six-shooters hanging from his belt. We weren't taking advantage of the things we could do for that medium. We'd end the sketches like we would for radio. Just some gunshots or another loud noise and then a fade-out to a commercial.

Not long after that, I got a call asking if I'd like to work for Sid Caesar. It was like, "Would you like to come and pitch for the New York Yankees?"

A lot of people might think that you wrote for *Your Show of Shows,* but you actually wrote for *Caesar's Hour,* which was a continuation of that show.

It was the show after *Your Show of Shows,* which had previously been split into three different entities. NBC had said, Wait a minute. We have three very valuable assets here. We have Max Liebman, who was the producer. We've got Imogene Coca. And we've got Sid Caesar. They're all doing the same show. Why doesn't the network get *three* shows out of them? They gave Max his own chunk of prime time [*Max Liebman Presents*], Imogene a sitcom [*The Imogene Coca Show*], and Sid got *Caesar's Hour.* I spent two years at *Caesar's Hour* with Mel Brooks, Mel Tolkin, Neil Simon, Carl Reiner, and Howard Morris.

The writing on *Your Show of Shows* and on *Caesar's Hour* was renowned. Was there a sense at the time that what you were experiencing was special?

We didn't tell ourselves, "Let's be a comedy classic." We just thought, Let's write for ourselves. I didn't hear the word "demographic" until I was fifty. We were the decision-makers. Our sponsors didn't interfere. Affiliates didn't interfere. The network might have interfered, but on a level that we were not conscious of, because Sid was the show's owner/producer. Sid handled all of those affairs at that level. We just had fun. The writers didn't have to worry about anything except doing the best that we could do.

We knew it was special, and we knew it with the kind of brashness that New York inspires and encourages. We knew we were different from anything else on television at that time. We had this powerhouse writing lineup. All kinds of strengths. You put half a dozen funny people in a room, and it's amazing what they'll come up with. We did the show on a Saturday, and we took Sunday off. Monday morning we said, "Okay, what do we do this week?" We had to have it finished Wednesday because the actors started putting the show on its feet and sets had to be built. Costumes had to be sewn. Orchestrations had to be orchestrated. I am older now than the combined experience that was in that room. We were all so young, eager, and fresh. But we pulled it off, week after week after week, for three years.

You've talked in the past about the frustration and the joys involved with the collaborative process. But I assume this show must have been a joy for you?

A joy and a half. Each show seemed like an event. We had this guy to write for, Sid Caesar, who could do anything. I mean, Sid would do these parodies of Japanese movies that he had never even *seen*. We just wrote it, and he performed it. He was a wonder.

He was a real break from the type of comedian who came before him, the stereotypical Borscht Belt comic.

He was much more well-rounded. Sid couldn't do a club date to save his life. The toughest part of every episode of *Caesar's Hour* was Sid saying, "Good evening, ladies and gentlemen." He couldn't play himself. But with characters, he could do anybody and he could be anything.

There's a famous story of Sid punching a horse in the 1950s. Did that really happen?

In the nose. Decked him. It happened in Central Park. It was a rented horse.

Why would he do that?

Because the animal had the temerity to throw Sid's wife, Florence, to the ground, and Sid was not about to take any shit from a horse. Mel Brooks later put a similar scene in *Blazing Saddles*. Sid's massive strength was legendary—and very real. And he had a temper to match. He once threatened to pull a taxi driver through the cab's window. Sid asked him, "Remember how it felt when you were born?"

How was Sid as a boss?

He was very good. He sat in the writers' room with us every second that we worked. How we actually got the script on paper will always be a mystery to me, because there was all this planned anarchy going on. Mike Stewart, who later went on to write the books for *Hello, Dolly!* and *Bye Bye Birdie* and a great many other Broadway hits, sat at the typewriter as the other writers pitched jokes. Mike would look at Sid, and Sid would nod, and Mike would type. If a writer said something really terrible, Sid would suddenly look like a gunner on an aircraft carrier, and he would mime shooting down the joke. So Mike knew not to type that. But as a boss, he was good. I mean, he would have liked to have kept us there every night until midnight, but we were very strict about going home at 6 P.M. Unless it was a real, real emergency.

Sid was a workaholic?

He didn't want to go home.

Even to his wife? The one he so valiantly defended by punching a horse?

A horse is one thing. Marriage is another.

It's strange watching the DVDs of these shows. Sid looks much older than someone who was in his late twenties, early thirties.

That's true. And he peaked so young. He had an unhappy career in a way. It was much too front-loaded.

Why was it front-loaded?

Do you know the competition that finally knocked Sid off the air? *The Lawrence Welk Show.* Sid got into television on the ground floor, when television was new. In the early years, most of the TV sets were owned by affluent people, and affluent people tend to be the most educated people. By the time Lawrence Welk came around, a lot of less affluent and far less-educated people owned sets. And these people would have much rather seen bubbles coming out of Lawrence Welk's ass than Sid Caesar doing a takeoff on *Rashômon*.

The problem with Sid was that he was at the mercy of the decision makers, the network people, who—yes, they respect talent, but they respect numbers a good deal more. If you don't cut it—if your time slot's not paying the rent—it doesn't matter how gifted you are. They would have canceled Michelangelo if no one came to the Sistine Chapel.

Let's switch gears and talk about *M*A*S*H*. You said that you considered the show your favorite piece of work. Is that true?

No, it's not. I don't know. I must have felt that way when I said it, perhaps because that show just keeps reverberating. *M*A*S*H* just hangs on and on. It just won't lie down.

You know what's so interesting about *M*A*S*H*? When Twentieth Century Fox decided to issue it on DVD, they included the option of watching it without the laugh track. If you've ever watched it without a laugh track, well, that's the show as we intended it to be watched. We did not mean for people to be cackling throughout the show; it becomes so much more cynical and heartbreaking without all that cheap, mechanical laughter.

Why did CBS insist on a laugh track?

Because television executives at that time were largely people who had gotten their early training in radio. They were conditioned by that medium, in which there were always three- or four-hundred people sitting in a studio, who actually did laugh as they watched performers doing a live broadcast. These executives, conditioned to believe that was what the American public expected, continued to fulfill that expectation with their television programming.

What was your feeling when CBS demanded it?

Outrage. Anger. On a good day, mere frustration. It was a four-year battle that I lost over and over again. The one concession from the network was to permit us to never have the laugh track in any operating-room scenes.

The canned laughter on *M*A*S*H* seems to arrive almost willy-nilly, appearing at inappropriate times.

There was *no* appropriate time. It was always wrong. We didn't write toward having those laughs in there. We didn't even consider those laughs until we were at the part of the post-production when we had to insert them. And it was painful, and it was wrong every single time we were forced to include it.

When you take the laugh track out of the show, the characters seem different. The doctors don't sound like a bunch of stand-up comics. They don't sound like they're trying to knock each other out with every line; although I must admit that there was still a tendency for the writing to appear that way. It is a little overwritten, which I regret. But I always gave myself the license to write some of those lines; the excuse was that these were educated people. Except for Radar [Gary Burghoff]. And, later, Klinger [Jamie Farr]. But pretty much everyone else in that show was a college graduate and had had medical training, which made their sophisticated comments plausible.

When do you think *M*A*S*H* really hit its stride? At what episode?

Episode number seventeen. It's called "Sometimes You Hear the Bullet," and it's about a friend of Hawkeye's who dies on Hawkeye's table as Hawkeye is trying to save his life. There's a subplot about a young Marine, played by Ronnie Howard, who lies about his age to get into the service to impress a girl. Much to the kid's outrage, after Hawkeye's friend dies of his battle wound, Hawkeye reports that the young Marine is underage and should be discharged. We wanted something a little more hopeful, so we had one death possibly saving another life.

Hawkeye cries at the funeral.

Not at the funeral. He cries in post-op. We had our moments of seriousness up to that point in the first season, but I think that one really opened the door for us. We saw that we could be a bit more dramatic than we had been. We also took pains to let the audience get to know the guy who was to die in combat, rather than just have some extra wheeled out of the operating room with a sheet over his face. This was the same type of attitude we applied years later when we had Colonel Blake die [Season 3, March 1975].

Tell me about that episode, "Abyssinia, Henry" [pronounced "Ah'll be seein' you, Henry"]. No one knew that the character of Colonel Henry Blake, played by actor McLean Stevenson, was going to die?

Only Alan Alda was told. The rest of the cast was shocked. We shot that famous scene in the operating room, when Radar announces Blake's death. Gary Burghoff was brilliant. I was directing that particular episode, and after the scene was done, I turned to our cinematographer and asked him if everything was okay technically. His response was negative. He thought we picked up a shadow that we shouldn't have. Gary then had to enact the scene all over again, and he did it brilliantly. We got it in two takes.

There was another accident with the second take. It was an offstage noise—a medical instrument dropping to the floor. But I loved it, because it was real and it was natural and it broke the silence. So it stayed. It reminded us that we were in an operating room. We panned over to Hawkeye and Trapper, and they're still working on another casualty. They can't stop just because Henry was killed. Life goes on. And so, indeed, does death.

What was McLean Stevenson's reaction when he learned that his character, Colonel Blake, was going to be killed off?

He was on the sidelines of the operating room set, watching the scene being shot. After the first take he went to his dressing room, and we never saw him again. He was supposed to come back for what was going to be the wrap party, because it was the last show of the season. But he couldn't do it.

Was it your intention to kill him off because McLean was leaving for another show? Conceivably he could have returned for a guest spot down the line.

He was leaving for a series of his own on NBC, *The McLean Stevenson Show*. I'm not going to say that there might not have been some anger in our act, but I like to think we were bigger than that. I had the feeling that his departure should mean something. I thought it made a bigger statement than just having an actor leave to get his own series elsewhere.

What were viewer reactions like?

Betrayal. Comments like, "You sucked us in. You made us think you were funny, and then you broke our hearts." Since people took the time to register their reactions, I handwrote a reply to each of them.

The same week the "Abyssinia, Henry" episode aired, a planeload of children taking off from Saigon crashed on a runway, and every one of the Vietnamese youngsters was killed. I responded to some of the letter writers with, "I can only hope that you are as upset by what happened in Saigon to a group of real children as you are by the fictional Henry Blake's passing."

Why did you decide to leave the show?

After four years I felt that I had done my best, I had done my worst, and I had done everything in between. I just wanted to tackle something I knew absolutely nothing about—with subjects and characters I didn't know like the back of my hand. You start out vowing that you're not going to be clichéd, and then you find out that you've invented a few clichés of your own. The pressure to produce that show was tremendous, almost killing at times. It was time to go. Before I did.

What did you make of the show after you left?

I was as critical of the show after I left as I was while I was on it. Some of it I liked. Some of it I didn't. After I left, it was bound to become somebody else's show, and it did.

There was some criticism in the later seasons that the show had lost its satirical bite, that it had become too mawkish. Was this something you felt?

I'd be a cad if I said so.

Did you enjoy the very last episode ["Goodbye, Farewell and Amen," February 28, 1983]?

I'd be a cad if I said anything at all, wouldn't I?

I think you just did. Let's talk about Hollywood. It seems that your experience with film has been—

Spotted. Frustrating. When it comes to movies, in the beginning there was the face. It's not the word. In Hollywood, they hire writers by the six-pack. If you're not willing to do what the executive wants, then another writer can always be paid to be willing. It was very difficult for me with movies. In films, I wasn't a producer, I wasn't a star, and I wasn't the director. I was a writer. But it's not all bad. You meet a nice class of snail at the bottom of the totem pole.

It seems that practically every writer I've talked with has expressed a deep frustration with Hollywood, and yet they still want to write for the movies. What is it about movies that appealed to you?

F. Scott Fitzgerald wanted to write for the movies in a satisfying way, and never got to. It's a great way to tell a story, but writers are not allowed to tell the stories. The stories are just handed over to higher-ranking people. And that's especially problematic when you're talking about comedy. Humor is not an easily shared commodity. It's next to impossible for the writer's vision to end up on the screen.

Was *Tootsie* a happy experience for you? Did your vision end up on the screen?

Tootsie is my vision—despite Dustin Hoffman's lifelong mission to deprive anybody of any credit connected with that movie, except for his close friend, the writer and producer Murray Schisgal. I say that because Dustin appeared with James Lipton on *Inside the Actors Studio* in 2006 and declared that the *Tootsie* idea sprang from Schisgal's intestines. I don't know much about gastroenterology, but I do know that the central theme for *Tootsie* came from me. And the central theme was that Dustin's character, Michael Dorsey, would become a better man for having been a woman.[1] That was the cornerstone of the film. All of the other details are just floating around that idea.

Without that central theme, *Tootsie* would have just been a movie about cross-dressing. It had to have some deeper meaning to it.

When I was asked to work on this picture, I thought, Have I really got the chutzpa to try doing a better drag comedy than the classic Billy Wilder and I.A.L. Diamond did? The answer came back, You may have

---

1 Michael Dorsey (Dustin Hoffman):

"I was a better man with you as a woman than I ever was with a woman as a man."

the chutzpa, but you don't have the balls to do another version of *Some Like It Hot.* So I thought about what this picture had to reflect upon, other than the clumsiness of men in high heels, and that was the contemporary consciousness of gender and the roles each one plays. And *Tootsie* was my take on that.

Are you frustrated with the finished product? Is it painful for you to watch?

Always.

Because of your experience? The script is famous for having gone through many rewrites with different writers, including an uncredited Elaine May and Barry Levinson. Or is it because of how the movie turned out?

There is one sequence that was meant to take place over a one-day period, which, if my clock is right, is around ninety-seven hours long. It just goes on and on and on. Dustin Hoffman's character runs around the city, and then ends up back in his apartment, and then runs around the city again, experiencing scene after scene with character after character. That insane sequence—continuity-wise—just bothers the hell out of me.

There were so many screenwriters and other people involved with that movie that it was almost like a lifeguard giving you artificial respiration in the parking lot. You haven't even put your swimsuit on and you're already being given CPR. It was just way more help than I ever needed, and certainly more than I asked for.

So you feel the movie is stitched together? That it's not as smooth as it could have been?

It is stitched together, yes. And yet it works for the audience, because Dustin is such a brilliant actor—far more brilliant as an actor than he is as a collaborator. I do think he should have won the Academy Award that Ben Kingsley ended up winning in 1983 for *Gandhi.*

Dustin in a dress is just irresistible, and the audience is certainly not sitting there saying to themselves, This couldn't have happened all in one day. The audience *did* like the movie, but there are things I'm still bothered by. *Tootsie* had what Hitchcock called "refrigerator moments." Have you heard this expression?

No. What does it mean?

It means that you see a movie, and everything makes sense, but then, later that night, when you're home and you're hungry and you go to the fridge, you think, Wait a minute … that one scene? The one that took place in the course of a day? The scene that was ninety-seven hours long? It makes no sense!

Has the Hollywood experience gotten any easier for you over the years?

Not really. I recently had the same type of experience with Robert Redford on what was meant to be a sequel to *The Candidate*. He wasted two years of my life trying to scratch an itch he couldn't quite explain. Two years! And it was at a point in my life when that kind of time is no longer petty cash. It was very frustrating. But everybody goes through what I call "star dreck." Paddy Chayefsky's last credit was for *Altered States*, remember? And he refused the credit. If the man who wrote *Network* had to go through the madness of the studio favoring the director's vision of a screenplay over the writer's, what more is there to say?

You know, some people in Hollywood treat me like I'm a monument. They just want to drive around me and take a closer look—maybe even have our picture taken together. But I'd much rather have less of that type of respect and more of the other kind: the kind where they leave your work alone.

Not that I haven't as well, but the business has gotten old. It's also become something I would have to study very hard to be—it's gotten mean. And it's not just movies. Most TV series are now owned by networks. How funny are corporate people? Organization, which is famously known as the death of fun, is now, illogically enough, churning out sitcoms.

I guess the only real original comedy happens in clubs, where you have people of every stripe saying whatever they want to say about anything they choose; people who have yet to get a single note from an executive.

You want to know what I think is missing from comedy today?

What?

Jews.

[Long pause] Are you kidding?

It's too *goyish*, it's too scholarly, it's too ... when we talk about *Caesar's Hour*, when one thinks of that time, all of the material was basically written by first-generation people. They were not that far from Europe. They were children of immigrants, and largely uneducated. There is something else that has crept in now, and it's taken over. More corporate, more smart-ass.

I just think it helps to be hungry. And you don't have to be Jewish to be that. I mean ... I don't think anybody has ever been funnier than Richard Pryor in his early years. You could feel the hunger. There's a smart-alecky aspect to comedy now. I'm not saying you have to be born in a whorehouse or that you have to be born in Poland, but I think there's a disconnect. The money is so huge, all of the hunger seems to come from the corporate side—the hunger to have a huge, revenue-spinning hit.

Are you saying that it's no longer an industry where a sixteen- or seventeen-year-old kid would be invited in and then tutored in the ways of comedy?

I don't think so. Then again, maybe it wasn't the norm then either.

The love of the writing, is that still something that you have?

More than ever. I now think of writing as a privilege—as a gift that's been given to me. Any day that I don't get to write something—anything—is a day I have to spend being someone other than who I am.

Any advice you'd care to give to those writers out there just beginning their careers?

When you're writing and come to a rough spot and the ideas just aren't flowing, put down dummy text and keep on moving—especially if it's at the end of the day and you're going to stop. Your brain will never stop for the day, even if you have stopped working, and there's a very good chance you'll come up with something better. Also, at the very least, you'll have something to come back to the next day, instead of a blank page. That's important.

But in general terms, just sit your ass down in a chair and hope your head gets the message. Isaac Bashevis Singer's advice for the struggling young writer was to stop struggling and write. As for me, I don't have any other advice. If I did, I would have had a far more trouble-free life and a much, much better career.

On September 11, 2009, Larry Gelbart passed away at the age of 81 in Los Angeles.

Canned Laughter: A History Reconstructed

An interview with Ben Glenn II, television historian

How did canned laughter come about?

The concept actually goes back at least five hundred years. History tells us that there were audience "plants" in the crowds at Shakespearean performances in the 16th century. They spurred on audience reactions, including laughter and cheering—as well as jeers.

How about more recently?

Canned laughter was used to a certain degree in radio, but its first TV appearance was in 1950, on a rather obscure NBC situation comedy, *The Hank McCune Show*. Remarkably, there are a couple of clips from the show on YouTube. Shortly after the show's debut, there was an article in *Variety* noting that the show's canned laughter was a new innovation, and that its potential for providing a wide-range of reactions was great. Of course, that eventually came true.

How odd did the laugh track sound to those early TV audiences?

I can only imagine that it seemed odd to viewers, but using a laugh track held many advantages for television producers. The most important was that it made it possible to film exteriors and on location. It gave producers freedom. For example, scenes from *Leave It to Beaver* were shot outdoors on RKO's—and later Universal's—back lot. With the laugh track, a studio audience was no longer absolutely necessary.

Who invented the canned-laughter machine?

Actually, its official name is the Laff Box, and it was invented by a man named Charles Rolland Douglass. He served in World War II, and when he returned to civilian life, he worked as a broadcast engineer at CBS. Douglass was responsible for everything from recording sound levels during production to adjusting them in post-production.

Shows often needed sound correction before broadcast. Sometimes a joke didn't get a big enough laugh, or, in the case of a famous *I Love Lucy* episode, the laugh was too long and had to be cut down. This particular episode was broadcast in March 1957, and it was called "Lucy Does the Tango." The laugh, in response to Lucy dancing the tango with raw eggs stuffed into her shirt, lasted about sixty-five seconds.

There were other reasons, too: For example, I once attended a taping of *Alice* in the seventies, and the actors kept blowing their lines. Of course, by the third or fourth take, the joke was no longer funny. A Douglass laugh was inserted into the final broadcast version to compensate.

How did Douglass originally invent the prototype for the Laff Box?

According to his wife Dorothy, Douglass would bring home tapes of television shows and then pore over them for hours and hours in his living room, finding and isolating the precise audience reactions he wanted. He spliced together tapes into spools—essentially tape loops. There was a keyboard for this machine, and each key was connected to a separate tape loop. At the bottom was a pedal that would either increase the volume or fade it out. So, really, it was like playing a musical instrument. And Charles Douglass was a virtuoso at the keyboard.

It's actual tape we are talking about?

Oh, yes—analog tape, recorded in mono. Incidentally, Douglass ran into a real problem with the advent of stereo television around 1976, when he had to convert his laugh tracks, which were mono, into simulated stereo. The result wasn't entirely successful, as the sound of the re-engineered tapes didn't quite match the sound of the show. It was the beginning of the end of the great Douglass laugh tracks.

Where did the laughs on the Laff Box originate?

Reportedly, the earliest reactions came from a Marcel Marceau performance in Los Angeles in 1955 or 1956, during his world premiere North American tour. This would make sense, because Marceau was, of course, a mime, and therefore, the only sound in the theater was the audience's reaction.

Other reactions are widely thought to have come from *The Red Skelton Show*, especially the show's mime sketches. I can state this with relative certainty, as it has been reported repeatedly by various sound engineers who worked closely with Douglass. It's interesting to note that the Skelton show aired on CBS, where Douglass worked. So, in theory, he would have had access to those tapes. But, in the end, it's also important to note that we may never know his exact sources.

As far as my research shows, there were never any interviews with Douglass or with anyone who worked at his company, Northridge Electronics. The secrecy surrounding his work is Hollywood legend. Only a very few people witnessed him using his machine, and it was always kept padlocked when not in use. Part of this secrecy was to protect his invention, to be sure. But part of it, too, was that, for some, inserting a laugh track may have been the same as admitting that a show wasn't funny—or not "funny enough." There was a real stigma surrounding the use of the laugh track, which continues to this day.

Have you ever seen a Charles Douglass Laff Box?

I have seen photographs of it, but very few people, including myself, have ever seen this machine firsthand.

I've spent a lot of time talking to some of the original "laugh-track men" who worked with Douglass during his heyday. What they have to say is fascinating. What's even more interesting is that they continue

Douglass's tradition of secrecy by speaking only off the record, and with the condition that I not reveal their names. It's still a secret, even fifty years later.

That's astonishing—you can even find C.I.A. and F.B.I. agents who are willing to talk once they're retired.

I know, but this is a very small industry. It's a brotherhood—very insular.

When they spoke with me, they described Douglass's method, which is quite fascinating. Producers would call Douglass into the studio to "laugh" a show. Douglass would show up with his Laff Box, which he carted around on a dolly that he invented. When he was finished, he'd pack up his machine, load it on his dolly, and drive off to the next job.

What made Douglass so good, exactly? Is there an art to canned laughter?

Oh, absolutely. First, Douglass knew his material inside out. He knew his library extremely well, which makes sense, because he had, of course, compiled it himself. He had dozens of reactions, and he knew where to find each one. In addition, he sped-up the reactions just a bit to heighten the effect.

Douglass's work was crisp and clean. It was a real craft. And the range of reactions that he was able to find was incredible. Some of the big belly laughs are great. You just don't hear laughs like that anymore. I also love the "shock" and "surprise" reactions, such as when a big audience says, in unison, "Whoa!" Those were used frequently on *The Munsters* when something extra-outrageous happened.

One more thing—Douglass not only had a terrific "ear," he also had a terrific memory. Over the years he would not just add new tracks, but he would revive old ones that had been retired and then retire the newer tracks. For example, tracks heard in sitcoms of the early 1960s resurface years later in the late 1970s. The ABC series *Delta House,* which was a spin-off of the movie *Animal House,* is a perfect example. However, by this time, Douglass was using his most extreme reactions almost exclusively, and the result was pretty awful. To my ear, it rings of desperation.

How long would it take Douglas to add the proper laughter to each show?

It took him about one day to complete a thirty-minute episode. His daily rate was $100.

And he was the only person doing this? He could have charged a lot more than $100.

I know, which is probably why competitors began to appear, in the mid-seventies. Around that time, Carroll Pratt—who was a sound man trained by Charles Douglass—started his own company, Sound One. One of the company's innovations was a set of new reactions entirely different from Douglass's tracks, which, by then, were so familiar and ubiquitous that they sounded artificial. Sound One's laughs sounded more natural, although they still had some very recognizable reactions. This was quite a departure from Douglass's work.

I'm not a fan of canned laughter per se, but some 1960s sitcoms were so poorly written that I can't help but think that canned laughter only improved them.

No question! In my view, the laugh track only adds to the fun of these shows, whether they are well written or not. I mean, *Mister Ed,* which I think is quite well written, would be so much less fun to watch if it had no laugh track. As far as shows with weak scripts—take *The Flying Nun,* for example—the laugh track *saved* that show.

Do the laughs today differ from the ones in the past?

They most certainly do. Today's sitcoms are based mostly on witty repartée and no longer rely on outlandish situations or sight gags, such as you would see in an episode of *Mister Ed* or *The Munsters* or *Bewitched*—and today's muted laughs reflect that. Generally, laughs are now much less aggressive and more subdued; you no longer hear unbridled belly laughs or guffaws. It's "intelligent" laughter—more genteel, more sophisticated. But definitely not as much fun.

There was an optimism and carefree quality in those old laugh tracks. Today, the reactions are largely "droll."

In what sense?

Just the way in which they sound. In the past, if the audience was really having a good time, it shone through. Audience members seemed less self-conscious and they felt free to laugh as loudly as they wanted. Maybe that's a reflection of contemporary culture.

In the fifties, the laughs were generally buoyant and uproarious, although somewhat generic, because Douglass hadn't yet refined his structured laugh technique. In the sixties, however, you could hear more individual responses—chortles, cackles from both men and women. The reactions were much more orderly and organized.

I can actually tell you the exact year that a show was produced, just by listening to its laugh track.

Have you ever detected an actual, authentic laugh on a live-action sitcom?

Yes, just once. There is one episode of *All in the Family* in which a reaction is real. The next TV season I heard it on a canned-laughter series, and I thought, Hey! That's the same laugh I heard on *All in the Family*! But that's been the only time—so far. I'm always listening.

How about shows that were supposedly "filmed before a live studio audience," such as Cheers?

Cheers and other shows were indeed filmed in front of live audiences, but they were "sweetened" in postproduction by Northridge Electronics. *Cheers* was shot in the eighties and nineties, but you can still hear laughs recorded in the fifties and sixties.

Is there any type of comedy TV show that's not sweetened?

Virtually everything you see on television has been manipulated—except late-night shows where the audiences are pumped. Even *Sunday Night Football* is sweetened. The Academy Awards broadcasts are sweetened—both with applause and laughter. They are sweetened live, right on the spot. In fact, Charles Douglass's son Robert, who now runs Northridge Electronics, has won multiple Emmy Awards for sweetening the Oscar broadcasts.

When Robert accepted his awards, was the applause sweetened?

I'd have to go back and view the tape, but it's quite possible.

Who's in charge of the canned laughter on sitcoms today?

As far as we know, Northridge Electronics still produces the majority of canned laughter on television, and Robert Douglass carries on the family tradition by remaining as tight-lipped as his father. But the business is no longer a monopoly. There are many postproduction houses doing this work. The Laff Box has been replaced by the laptop, and I'm told there are multiple sets of laugh tracks that contain laughs specific to certain countries and cultural groups. Whatever the case, the technique is certainly a lot more sophisticated than in Charles Douglass's day—which, to my mind, is not always a great thing. Nothing will replace those classic, vintage tracks, and I wish they'd bring them back.

And so, love it or hate it, canned laughter carries on into the next generation.

Thank you.

My pleasure.

[Applause]

Acknowledgments

Thanks and love to ...

My parents

Each and every one of the writers—you know who you are (hopefully)

Lauren Mosko, for the complete edit and for her kind ways

S.P. Nix, for his top-notch copy-editing, fact-checking and line-editing skills

Eric Spitznagel, for his tremendous contributions to all of the introductions

Sharon Festinger, Holly Morris, Adam Nadler, and Alana Quirk, for their superior editing skills

Tae Won Yu for his design and illustrations

Louise Zergaeng Pomeroy for her author illustration, page 528

Brandon, Cindy, Kevin, Bonnie, Howard, Reva, Ken, Jamie, Lauren, Carli, Stacey, B.J., Alex, Scott, Jeff, Nancy, Marcy, Bess, Chris, Ellie, R.J., John, Marissa, Stacey, Bob, Phyllis and Fred, Penni, Alan, Sarah, Shimmy, Maer

Ted Travelstead and Julie Wright and Skittles

John Banta and Robert Walsh

Dan Lazar and Julie Trelstad

Sharon Festinger, Darren Springer, Michal Tamar Addady, Bakara Wintner

Katie I.

My friends: Gabe Sanders, Amelia Kahaney, Ezra, Austin Merrill and Gina Rhodes, Chloe and Dylan, Steve Wilson and Erin Mayes, Connell Barrett, Todd Jackson, Jason Eaton and Ian Lendler, John Warner, Jason Cronic, Elaine Trigiani, Scott Jacobson, Eamon Lynch, Kathryn Belgiorno, Laura Griffin, Julian Sancton, Dana Brown, Jason Roeder, Todd Levin, Bruce Handy, David Brody, Brad Engelstein, Corey and Cheryl Spound, Melanie Berliet, Will Tracy, Rob Kutner, Mr. and Mrs. Catfish, Andy Tepper and Shona Shakravartty, Steve Whitesell, Marie Warsh, Steve Bopp, Sohaila Shakib, Sarah Hepburn, Dana Spivak, Mary Flynn, the Ayaldes, Jabari Asim, Leigh Cheng, the other Mike Sacks, Elyse Kroll, Claire Zulkey, Steve Delahoyde, the library at Montgomery Community College in Rockville, and the upstanding citizens of the planned community of New Granada ("Tomorrow's City ... Today").

Lastly ... for Charlie Cocoa, Fritzy the Bumblebee, and The Professor, 143.

mikesacks.com

About the Author

Mike Sacks has written for such publications as *Esquire, GQ, McSweeney's, The New Yorker, Salon, Time, Time Out New York, Vanity Fair,* and *Vice*. He has worked at *The Washington Post,* and is currently on the editorial staff of *Vanity Fair*. He is the author of four books, including 2014's *Poking a Dead Frog,* a sequel to *And Here's the Kicker*.

Printed in Great Britain
by Amazon.co.uk, Ltd.,
Marston Gate.